Memories of Unbelonging

New Southeast Asia

POLITICS, MEANING, AND MEMORY

Justin McDaniel and Nancy J. Smith-Hefner

SERIES EDITORS

Memories of Unbelonging

Ethnic Chinese Identity Politics in Post-Suharto Indonesia

CHARLOTTE SETIJADI

UNIVERSITY OF HAWAI'I PRESS
HONOLULU

Paperback edition 2024

Printed in the United States of America

First printed, 2023

Library of Congress Cataloging-in-Publication Data

Names: Setijadi, Charlotte, author.
Title: Memories of unbelonging : ethnic Chinese identity politics in post-Suharto Indonesia / Charlotte Setijadi.
Other titles: New Southeast Asia.
Description: Honolulu : University of Hawaiʻi Press, [2023] | Series: New Southeast Asia: Politics, meaning, and memory | Includes bibliographical references and index.
Identifiers: LCCN 2023019341 | ISBN 9780824894054 (hardback) | ISBN 9780824896065 (epub) | ISBN 9780824896072 (kindle edition) | ISBN 9780824896058 (pdf)
Subjects: LCSH: Chinese—Indonesia—Ethnic identity. | Chinese—Indonesia—Politics and government. | Identity politics—Indonesia. | Collective memory—Indonesia. | Indonesia—Ethnic relations.
Classification: LCC DS632.C5 S48 2023 | DDC 305.89510598—dc23/eng/20230506
LC record available at https://lccn.loc.gov/2023019341

ISBN 9780824899158 (paperback)

Cover photo: Artist Tintin Wulia painting the *Great Wallpaper No. 470/I/SBKRI/67* mural at Milani Gallery, Brisbane, Australia, 2021. Source: Photo by Carl Warner.

University of Hawaiʻi Press books are printed on acid-free paper and meet the guidelines for permanence and durability of the Council on Library Resources

For my father,
Max Dharmawan Setijadi (Tjie Beng Tjiang)

CONTENTS

Illustrations ix

Preface and Acknowledgments xi

Abbreviations and Acronyms xvii

Note to the Reader xxi

Maps xxiii

Introduction 1

1 The Politics of Remembering 40

2 Enclaves and Narratives of Trauma in Everyday Life 68

3 (Re)learning Chineseness 97

4 Performing Trauma and Indonesian Chineseness 124

5 Chinese Indonesian Organizations and Political Participation 154

6 Chinese Indonesians in the Time of China's Rise 192

Conclusion 217

Glossary of Non-English Terms 231

Notes 235

References 249

Index 277

ILLUSTRATIONS

FIGURES

1.1 A row of shophouses along Jalan Pintu Besar Selatan near Glodok, Jakarta 49
1.2 The May 1998 Monument at Pondok Ranggon Public Cemetery, East Jakarta 57
1.3 The illustrated master plan of the Chinese Indonesian Cultural Park 61
2.1 Security checkpoint to enter a residential cluster within the Kelapa Gading complex 77
2.2 Gates at the end of one of Kelapa Gading's residential streets 85
3.1 Trisakti University and Tarumanagara University 109
3.2 Pahoa School main building 115
3.3 A memorial display wall at Pahoa School 118
4.1 Promotional image for the 2008 film *Sugiharti Halim* 134
4.2 Still image from the 2008 film *Babi Buta Yang Ingin Terbang* 139
4.3 Promotional poster for the 2016 film *Cek Toko Sebelah* 141
4.4 Detail from *Have a Cup of Tea/Meet My Dead Grandfather* 144
4.5 Artist Tintin Wulia painting the *Great Wallpaper No. 470/I/SBKRI/67* mural 145
4.6 Temporary tattoo studio installation as part of Edita Atmaja's *Tato Tolak Bala: Perlindungan Ampuh Warga Setempat* exhibition 148
5.1 Poster advertising the 2021 Koko Cici pageant in Jakarta 163
5.2 Official portrait of Basuki Tjahaja Purnama (Ahok) as governor of Jakarta, 2014–2017 180
5.3 Anti-Ahok protesters descending on Central Jakarta on December 2, 2016 182
6.1 Front cover of the August–September 2015 edition of *Tempo* magazine 215

MAPS

1. Western Indonesian archipelago xxiii
2. Reported sites of the riots and anti-Chinese attacks of May 12–14, 1998, in Jakarta xxiv
3. Location of Kelapa Gading residential estate in the context of the Greater Jakarta metropolitan region xxv

PREFACE AND ACKNOWLEDGMENTS

Writing this book has been a deeply personal and at times difficult intellectual journey. As a Chinese Indonesian woman who left Indonesia for Australia as a teenager in 1997, I was not in Jakarta when the riots and anti-Chinese attacks of May 1998 (and the subsequent fall of the New Order regime) happened. While my family and I were not directly affected by the riots, I remember feeling an immense sense of shock and grief. Like so many ethnic Chinese, I had always felt wholly Indonesian. I did not have a Chinese name, my family did not speak Chinese (coming from *peranakan* backgrounds, my grandparents spoke a mixture of Dutch and Indonesian), and Jakarta was at that point the only home that I had ever known. It was true that every now and again I would be reminded that I was somehow different because of how I looked. Walking down the street near my house as a child, the local *kampung* kids would sometimes yell out "*cina!*" as I walked past, leaving me perplexed as to why I was being called Chinese. However, for the most part, I never felt I was any different from other Indonesians, especially since we lived in a part of South Jakarta where the Chinese and non-Chinese mingled and lived side by side, and my family and I had many non-Chinese friends.

In hindsight, the sense of grief I felt when May 1998 happened was probably a sense of a loss of innocence, when for the first time I came to realize the problematic nature of belonging for the Chinese in Indonesia. This led to many questions that developed throughout my formative years as a young adult. For one, why was it that after so many centuries of being in Indonesia (to my knowledge, both sides of my family had been in Indonesia for at least five generations) the Chinese were still regarded as foreigners? Why was it that despite having to change their names and be assimilated to be more Indonesian the Chinese were still not regarded as being Indonesian enough? Could the Chinese ever be Indonesian enough? Ultimately, if Chinese like me were rejected by the only home that we had ever known, then where could we possibly go? Later, I found that these questions were shared by many other Chinese Indonesians who also felt severely dislocated by the events of May 1998.

And so began my journey to find answers to these questions. Thanks to the wealth of information and scholarly works on Chinese Indonesians in the post-Suharto era, I learned about the long and complex history of race politics in Indonesia and how the "Chinese problem" was tied to issues of class inequality, religion, politics, and ethnonationalism, among others. My eyes were opened to the fact that Chinese Indonesians were paradoxically the victims of the very structures of inequality and exclusion that they were also complicit in maintaining. I became particularly interested in collective memory and trauma, and how contemporary Chinese Indonesians remember and understand their past.

Yet, when it came to determining my own research topic in graduate school, I was initially reluctant to do a research project about Chinese Indonesian identity politics since I feared it would be too close to home, and I was not sure about how my own subjectivities would cloud my analysis. Furthermore, I was also uneasy at the thought of doing research on a topic that was essentially about myself. I was lucky to have had the guidance of my supervisors at La Trobe University, Alberto Gomes and Helen Lee, who taught me to see my personal experiences and subject position as strengths rather than weaknesses. After all, this kind of self-reflective scholarship is not without precedent: major scholars such as Edward Said, Ien Ang, and Stuart Hall have all used their own life experiences as the basis of some of their most pivotal work.

This journey would have been impossible without the many individuals and institutions that have supported me over the past fifteen years. This book began as a PhD project at La Trobe University's School of Social Sciences and Communications (now School of Humanities and Social Sciences) under the auspices of the La Trobe University International Postgraduate Research Scholarship. During fieldwork and archival research, the Centre for Strategic and International Studies in Jakarta and the Royal Netherlands Institute of Southeast Asian and Caribbean Studies at Leiden University generously hosted me as a visiting fellow.

I wish to express my heartfelt gratitude to my PhD supervisors, Albert and Helen. Albert gave his full and enthusiastic support from the start, and without him I would never have embarked on this study. Helen's encouraging words and understanding, especially in times of personal struggle, meant just as much as her careful readings of my work. Nicholas Herriman was instrumental in shaping the core arguments in this book, and a special thank you goes to Dirk Tomsa, who read earlier drafts of the manuscript and gave me much valued feedback.

During the development stages of this book, I was a postdoctoral fellow at Nanyang Technological University's Department of History and then a Visiting Fellow at the ISEAS-Yusof Ishak Institute, both in Singapore, and finally as an assistant professor of humanities (Education) at Singapore Management University's School of Social Sciences. I thank Liu Hong from NTU, Terence Chong and Hui Yew-Foong from the ISEAS-Yusof Ishak Institute, and Dean of SMU SOSS Chandran Kukathas for their support in the form of research and conference grants. In particular, I am grateful to Chandran for generously providing me with school funding for manuscript editing and for the purchase of some images for this book.

The University of Hawai'i Press has been a wonderful partner throughout the different stages of manuscript development. I am grateful to Pamela Kelley, who believed in this book's potential from the beginning and who guided me as I turned my research into a book manuscript. Masako Ikeda showed much care, enthusiasm, and understanding in bringing this book to print. I also thank series editors Justin McDaniel and Nancy J. Smith-Hefner for including this book as part of UHP's New Southeast Asia: Politics, Meaning, and Memory series. Three anonymous reviewers gave the manuscript their careful reading, and I am grateful for their detailed feedback that helped me to improve the manuscript. Malia Collins, Ivo Fravashi, and the production team at UHP have done a marvelous job in producing this book. I am also indebted to Gareth Richards, Helena Dodge-Wan, and Eryn Tan of Impress Creative and Editorial for their meticulous copyediting that brought out the best of this book. I thank Alexandra Jones for producing wonderful maps, and I also thank Rony Zakaria, Joris Aditya, Wulan Dirgantoro, Edwin, Ariani Darmawan, Edita Atmaja, Wahyu Dhyatmika of the Tempo Media Group, and the Indonesian Chinese Clan Social Association (Paguyuban Sosial Marga Tionghoa Indonesia) for supplying me with images to use in this book. Special thanks go to Tintin Wulia for kindly allowing me to use her image and artwork for the book cover.

Parts of this book have appeared elsewhere. Parts of the introduction and chapter 1 previously appeared in two *ISEAS Perspective* papers as "Ethnic Chinese in Contemporary Indonesia: Changing Identity Politics and the Paradox of Sinification" (no. 12, 2016) and "Chinese Indonesians in the Eyes of the *Pribumi* Public" (no. 73, 2017). Parts of chapter 5 previously appeared as "Anti-Chinese Sentiment and the 'Return' of the *Pribumi* Discourse," in *Contentious Belonging: The Place of Minorities in Indonesia,* edited by Greg Fealy and Ronit Ricci, 194–213, Singapore: ISEAS-Yusof Ishak Institute. The quotations and excerpts from these texts that have been used in this book are reproduced here with the kind permission of the publisher, ISEAS-Yusof Ishak Institute. Parts of chapter 6 are a revised and condensed version of my article "'A Beautiful Bridge': Chinese Indonesian Associations, Social Capital and Strategic Identification in a New Era of China–Indonesia Relations," *Journal of Contemporary China* 25 (102): 822–835. I thank Taylor & Francis for their permission to reproduce parts of the article.

I have been extremely fortunate to have had mentors, colleagues, and friends around the world who gave me enormous intellectual and emotional support. I thank Charles Coppel, Wang Gungwu, Gregor Benton, Evelyn Hu-Dehart, Barbara Watson Andaya, Caroline Hau, Adrian Vickers, Marcus Mietzner, Chang-Yau Hoon, Jemma Purdey, Taomo Zhou, Josh Stenberg, Hew Wai Weng, Chong Wu-Ling, Evi Sutrisno, Nobuhiro Aizawa, Jafar Suryomenggolo, Yumi Kitamura, Kung Chien-Wen, Johanes Herlijanto, Wulan Dirgantoro, Monika Winarnita, Eve Warburton, Thomas Barker, Diego Fossati, Ross Tapsell, Nicole Curato, Quinton Temby, Liam Gammon, Malcolm Cook, Ross McLeod, Lis Kramer, Tiffany Tsao, and Wayne Palmer for their advice, feedback, and friendship over the years. In Singapore, I am grateful for camaraderie and encouragement from my colleagues and friends: Ishani Mukherjee, Yasmin Ortiga, Seulki Lee, Ijlal Naqvi, Jacob Ricks, Hiro Saito, Colm Fox, Tan Yoo Guan, Andree Hartanto, Ngoei Wen-Qing, Robin Bush, Ima Abdulrahim, Deepak Nair, Steven Harsono, Paul Lemaistre, Elena Fanjul-Debnam, Ian Storey, Jessica Hinchy, Kate Wakely-Mulroney, and Christopher Holman.

Most importantly, I would like to express my sincere gratitude to the many research informants in Jakarta, Medan, Bandung, Surabaya, and the Riau Islands who assisted me throughout many fieldwork trips. They openhandedly volunteered their time, welcomed me into their homes, and shared their individual and family histories. I thank them for entrusting me with their stories and for opening my eyes to the complexities of Chinese Indonesian lives in the post-Suharto era. In particular, I thank the following: Alex Ferry Widjaya, Christine Susanna Tjhin, Sofyan Tan, Henky Kurniadi, Charles Honoris, Daniel Johan, Haripinto Tanuwidjaja, Tracey Harjatanaya, Finche Kosmanto, Jerry Widjaya, Ivan Wibowo, Wahyu Effendy, Rachman Hakim, Ulung Rusman, Chandra Jap, Teddy Jusuf, Jandi Mukianto, Dede Oetomo, Andreas Harsono, Aimee Dawis, Mely G. Tan, Esther Kuntjara, Setefanus Suprajitno, and the board members of Pahoa School. To filmmakers Edwin, Ariani Darmawan, Lucky Kuswandi, and Steven Facius Winata, artists Tintin Wulia and Edita Atmaja, poet Awi Chin, and journalist Randy Mulyanto, I am continuously inspired by your creativity, and I sincerely thank you for allowing me to include some of your work in this book.

Finally, I would like to thank my family and loved ones for their unending support and love, even at times when I lost faith in myself. To James Mythen, I will always be grateful for all the support that you gave me. My sister Adeline, brother-in-law Eddie Huynh, nieces Reina and Kirana, and aunt Dian Poerwito, you bring so much joy to my life. To Sebastian Dettman, thank you for reminding me to take moments to breathe, for being patient and kind, for listening to me read drafts of the manuscript out loud, and for always displaying an infectious sense of calm, even in the most challenging of situations. You make me want to be the best version of myself. To my mother Naniek Setijadi, thank you for inspiring me with your passion for lifelong learning. Lastly, to my father Max Setijadi, I am grateful that you have shared with me your love of history from a young age. Thank you for not letting me forget our family's stories, and it is to you that I dedicate this book.

Charlotte Setijadi
Singapore

ABBREVIATIONS AND ACRONYMS

Baperki	Badan Permusjawaratan Kewarganegaraan Indonesia (Consultative Council for Indonesian Citizenship)
BKPM	Badan Koordinasi Penanaman Modal (Indonesian Investment Coordinating Board)
BRI	Belt and Road Initiative
COEA	Chinese Overseas Exchange Association
CWFHHA	Conference of the World Federation of Huaqiao Huaren Associations
DKI Jakarta III	Daerah Khusus Ibukota Jakarta III (Special Capital Region of Jakarta III)
DPR	Dewan Perwakilan Rakyat Republik Indonesia (People's Representative Council of Indonesia)
DPRD	Dewan Perwakilan Rakyat Daerah (Regional Legislative Council)
FPI	Front Pembela Islam (Islamic Defenders' Front)
G30S/PKI	Gerakan 30 September/Partai Komunis Indonesia (September 30 Movement/Indonesian Communist Party)
GANDI	Gerakan Perjuangan Anti-Diskriminasi (Anti-Discrimination Movement)
GEMA INTI	Generasi Muda INTI (Young Generation INTI)
GEMAKU	Generasi Muda Konghucu (Young Generation Confucians)
Gerindra	Partai Gerakan Indonesia Raya (Great Indonesia Movement Party)
Golkar	Partai Golongan Karya (Party of Functional Groups)
Hanura	Partai Hati Nurani Rakyat (People's Conscience Party)
ICBC	Indonesia-China Business Council
INTI	Perhimpunan Indonesia Tionghoa (Chinese Indonesian Association)

IT	information technology
JTM	Jaringan Tionghoa Muda (Chinese Youth Network)
Komnas Perempuan	Komisi Nasional Anti Kekerasan Terhadap Perempuan (National Commission on Violence against Women)
K-pop	Korean pop music
KPU	Komisi Pemilihan Umum (General Electoral Commission)
LGBTQIA+	lesbian, gay, bisexual, transgender, queer, intersex, asexual
LPKB	Lembaga Pembinaan Kesatuan Bangsa (Institute for the Cultivation of National Unity)
MATAKIN	Majelis Tinggi Agama Khonghucu Indonesia (Supreme Council for the Confucian Religion in Indonesia)
MP	member of parliament
NGO	nongovernmental organization
NU	Nahdlatul Ulama (literally "Revival of the Ulama")
OCAO	Overseas Chinese Affairs Office (Qiaoban)
PARTI	Partai Reformasi Tionghoa Indonesia (Chinese Indonesian Reform Party)
PDI-P	Partai Demokrasi Indonesia-Perjuangan (Indonesian Democratic Party of Struggle)
PERPIT	Perkumpulan Pengusaha Indonesia Tionghoa (Indonesian Chinese Entrepreneur Association)
PKI	Partai Komunis Indonesia (Indonesian Communist Party)
PP10	Peraturan Presiden No. 10 tahun 1959 (Presidential Regulation No. 10 in 1959)
PPP	Partai Persatuan Pembangunan (United Development Party)
PR	permanent resident
PRC	People's Republic of China
PSI	Partai Solidaritas Indonesia (Indonesian Solidarity Party)
PSMTI	Paguyuban Sosial Marga Tionghoa Indonesia (Indonesian Chinese Clan Social Association)
RGE	Royal Golden Eagle

SARA	*suku, agama, ras, dan antar-golongan* (tribalism, religion, race, and interclass relations)
SBKRI	Surat Bukti Kewarganegaraan Republik Indonesia (Republic of Indonesia Certificate of Citizenship)
SD	*sekolah dasar* (primary school)
SMAN 2 Jakarta	Sekolah Menengah Atas Negeri 2 Jakarta (Jakarta State Upper High School 2)
SNB	Solidaritas Nusa Bangsa (Solidarity for the Motherland and Nation)
THHK	Tiong Hoa Hwee Koan (Chinese Association)
TMII	Taman Mini Indonesia Indah (Beautiful Indonesia Miniature Park)
UI	Universitas Indonesia (University of Indonesia)
WCEC	World Chinese Entrepreneurs Convention

NOTE TO THE READER

Throughout this book, I have used the reformed Indonesian spelling system, Ejaan yang Disempurnakan in use since 1972, when several changes were made; for example, *oe* became *u*, *dj* became *j*, and *j* became *y*. For instance, "Suharto" and "Sukarno" are spelled with the new spelling instead of the old "Soeharto" and "Soekarno." Exceptions are for those personal names for which individuals have opted to continue using the old spelling.

Chinese names are written with the family name before the first name, except in instances where someone has chosen to write their first name followed by their surname in the Western style. The romanized Chinese pronunciation (*hanyu pinyin*) has been used for Chinese names, places, and terms. Whenever known, I provide the Chinese characters for Chinese names and terms on first appearance.

Following Indonesian naming conventions, most of the public figures in the book are identified by their full name on first mention, and then identified by their given name rather than surname in subsequent mentions (for example, Megawati Sukarnoputri to Megawati, Anies Baswedan to Anies, and so on). It is also common in Indonesia to refer to public figures by their popular nicknames. For such cases, these individuals are identified by their full name on first mention and then their nickname in subsequent mentions (for example, Joko Widodo to Jokowi, Basuki Tjahaja Purnama to Ahok, and so on).

Names of individual informants have been changed to pseudonyms, apart from those who are known public figures, such as politicians or artists, or those who have requested to have their full names and affiliations revealed. To protect the integrity of the anonymization process, I provide details only of when and where the interviews took place for interviewees who have been identified by name.

Most of the interviews in this book were conducted in Indonesian, and I transcribed and translated them into English myself. In translating the interviews, my main objective was to communicate the meaning of the original message and interactions as accurately as possible. Because of this, I often had to use English words that are not a direct translation of the Indonesian words used by the participants and to change some grammatical structures.

Throughout the book, the term *pribumi* is used to refer to native or indigenous non-Chinese Indonesians. This was a matter of great ethical concern to me during the writing process. I am aware that the 1998 Presidential Instruction officially abolished the use of *pribumi* in government documents and official capacities. I am also very much aware of the possibility that, in using the term, I risk reproducing the very category of nativist othering (itself a form of state-sponsored violence) that I seek to criticize. The same goes for the use of other terms considered to be derogatory, such as *cina* to describe the Chinese. I was also concerned that revealing my informants' use of the term *pribumi* would portray them (and by extension all Chinese Indonesians) in a negative light. If misunderstood, misquoted, or taken outside of the analytical context of the book, I worried that anecdotes from the book could be used to justify inflammatory anti-Chinese rhetoric, discrimination, or, worse, violence.

After much deliberation and in consultation with scholars I respect, I decided to be as true as possible to the data that I collected and use the term *pribumi* whenever it appeared in interviews or other communications. I understand that doing so carries risks, and so I ask the readers to be sensitive in understanding the historical contexts within which the term was used. I use the term *pribumi* to reflect the fact that both my Chinese and non-Chinese research participants still use the term widely in their daily lives as well as in their interviews with me. The term *pribumi* has also made a comeback in recent years in mainstream political discourse, particularly in the wake of recent waves of ethnonationalist sentiments in Indonesia. In using the term, I acknowledge that it is itself an arbitrary monolithic ideological construct, and that it covers a wide range of peoples and communities from the country's multitude of diverse ethnicities and linguistic groups. Whenever possible, I note my *pribumi* respondents' ethnic or tribal (*suku*) affiliations (for example, West Javanese, Batak, Menadonese, and so on). I use the terms *pribumi* and "non-Chinese" interchangeably, whereby *pribumi* is used whenever my informants used it or when I engaged in discussions about specific instances of nativist/exclusionary politics.

It goes without saying that I am solely responsible for the contents of this book. I made the decisions about what to include, how to represent my informants and observations, and how to frame the analyses. While it is impossible to please everyone, my sincere hope is that I have done justice to the stories that my informants entrusted me with.

MAPS

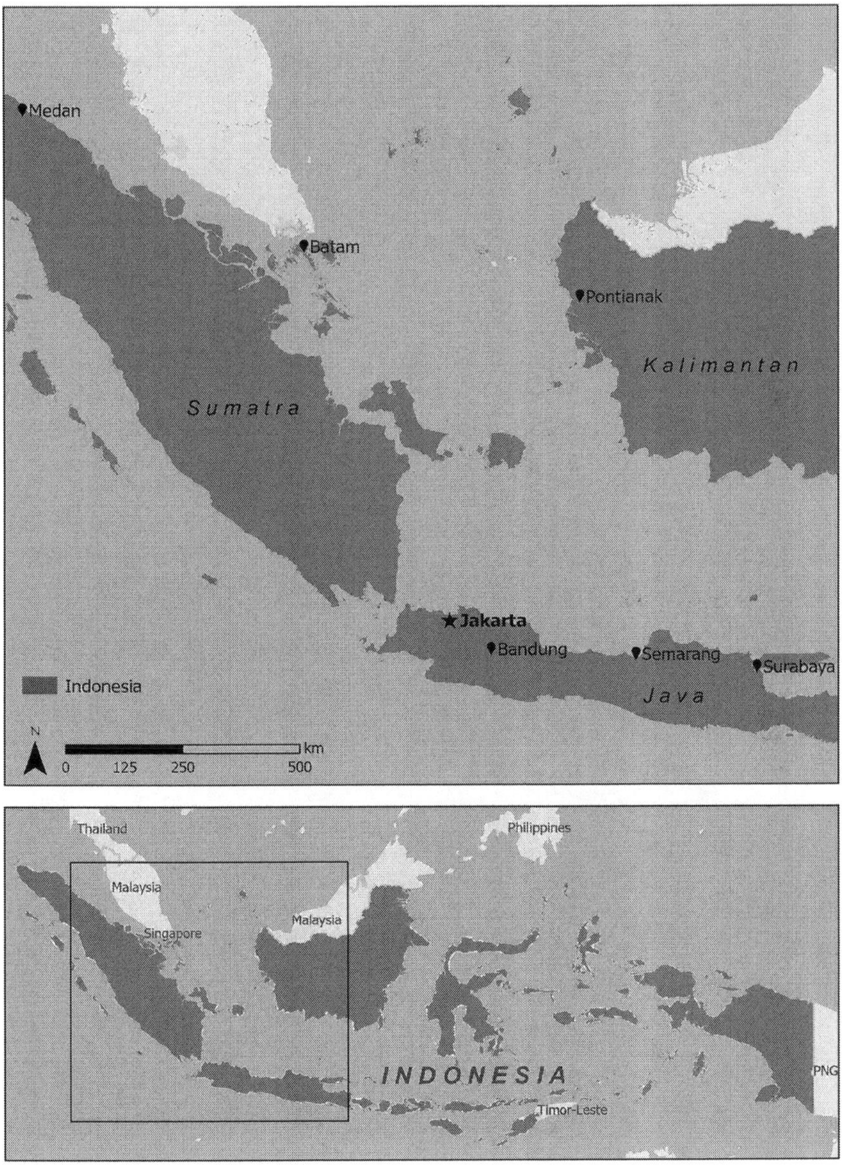

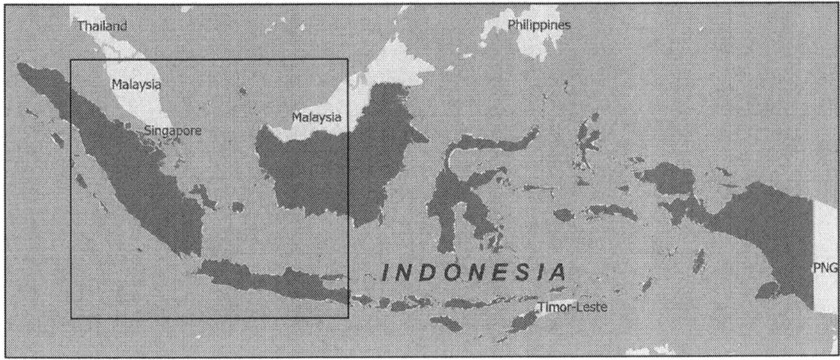

MAP 1. Map of western Indonesian archipelago indicating the location of Jakarta as the capital city and main fieldwork site, along with other major cities where the author also conducted fieldwork.

Map by Alexandra Jones.

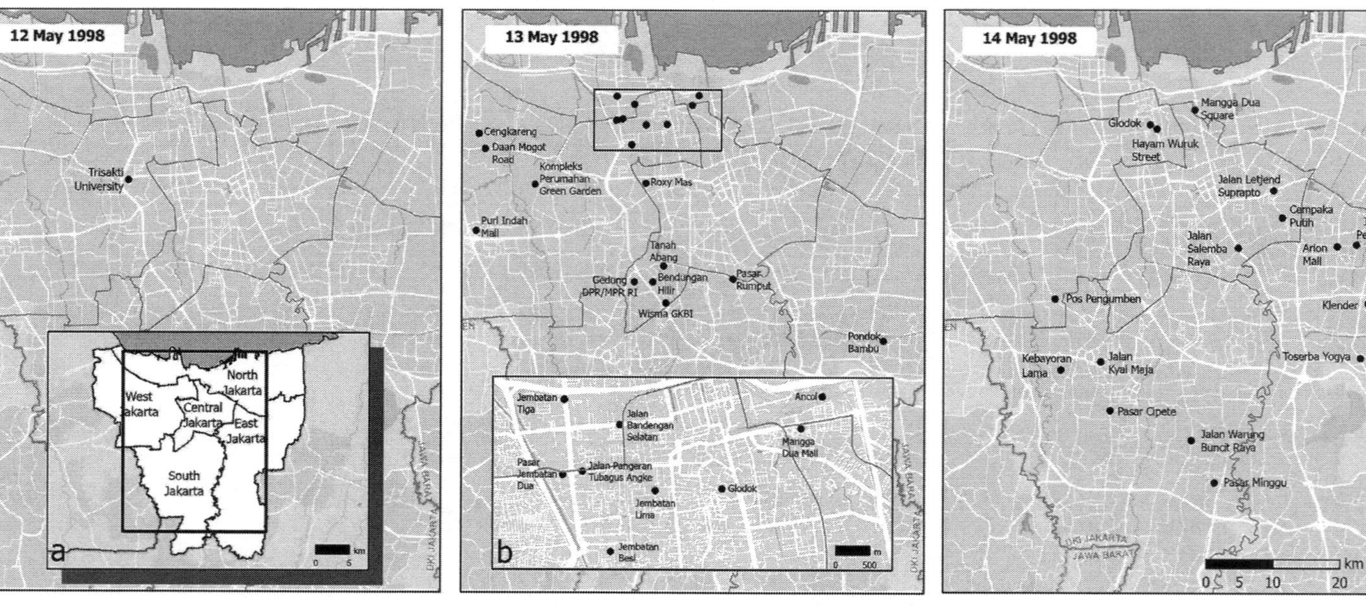

MAP 2. Reported sites of the riots and anti-Chinese attacks that took place on May 12–14, 1998, in Jakarta. Attacks in Jakarta's Kota Tua "Chinatown" area are highlighted in inset b. Locations compiled from various media and eyewitness reports.

Map by Alexandra Jones.

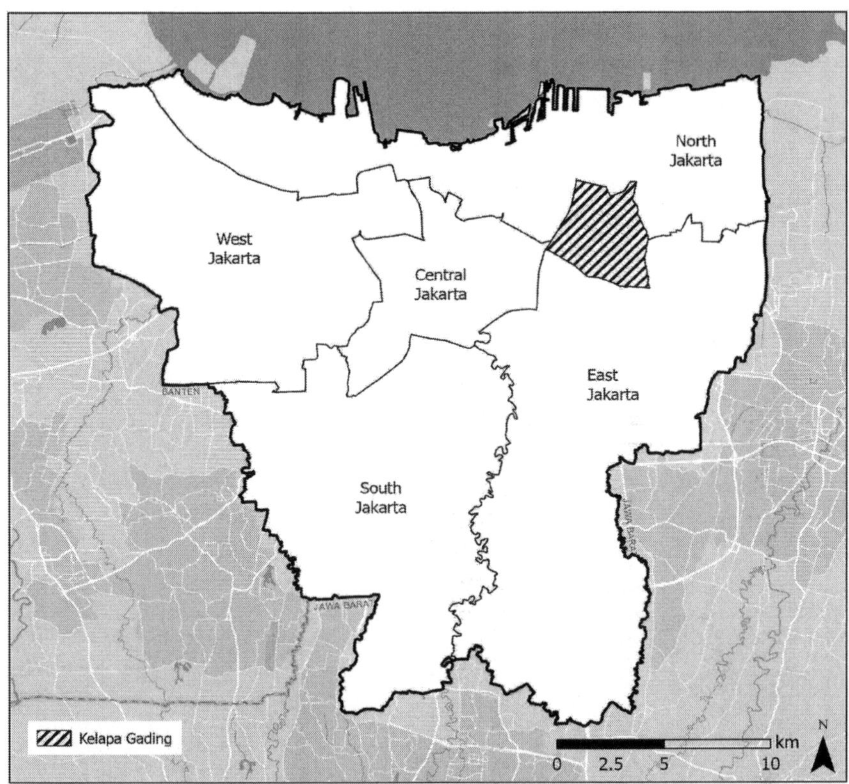

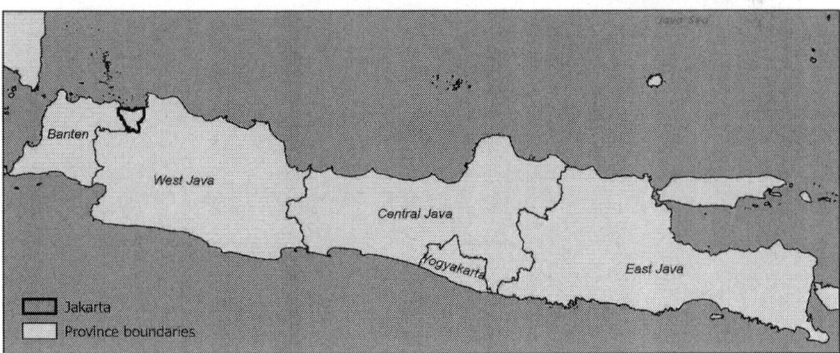

MAP 3. Location of Kelapa Gading residential estate in the context of the Greater Jakarta metropolitan region.

Map by Alexandra Jones.

Introduction

Early on during my fieldwork research in 2007, I visited one of my research respondents, Alin, at her fabric shop located in Tanah Abang Market (Pasar Tanah Abang) in Central Jakarta. She was a twenty-three-year-old ethnic Chinese woman and had been running her business for several years. On the day I had come to interview her the market was bustling. Alin's shop was small and located among many other shops owned by both Chinese and non-Chinese (mostly Javanese) merchants. After showing me around and introducing me to other shop owners, we sat down at the front of her shop to talk. I learned that Alin's parents were originally from Pontianak in West Kalimantan, and that her family spoke both Teochew and Mandarin at home. Alin was born in Jakarta, had been educated in private schools, and briefly went to university until she decided to quit and started her own business instead.

The interview was going smoothly until I asked whether she had ever felt discriminated against because of her Chinese ethnicity.[1] In hindsight, I was quite naive not to have been more aware of the sensitive nature of my questions, especially in such a public space. I noticed that Alin seemed restless and anxious, and she kept looking around to see whether other shop owners and customers nearby were listening in on our conversation. Although she initially answered my questions about racism in a hushed tone, she finally said, "Let's go somewhere else so I can talk more freely." She closed up her shop and we went to a quiet restaurant in another part of the market.

After settling in our new location, Alin explained the reason for her nervous behavior: "Sorry, it's not that I didn't want to answer your questions, I was just afraid that the *pribumi* in the other shops could hear us." Alin then asked me to repeat some of my earlier questions, and I again asked her about whether she had had experienced anti-Chinese discrimination in the past. Alin answered:

> Yes, of course! I am Chinese, so of course I've experienced discrimination. It [discrimination] is everywhere! Since I was little, people would call me *cina* when I walked down the street. . . . As a business owner now, I get discriminated by local government officials, market officials, the market security, suppliers, everyone. I must pay more for official documents and security money, all because I'm Chinese. It is very annoying but that's just how it is.

I was a little taken aback by her answer, especially considering that from our previous interactions it seemed like Alin had a good relationship with the non-Chinese store owners and market staff whom she had introduced me to. To this Alin said:

> I have a good relationship with the *pribumi* in the market, but it doesn't mean that I trust them fully. I had a *pribumi* shop assistant a few times, and almost every one of them had stolen money from me at some point. You really must keep an eye on them [*pribumi*], they are very opportunistic. . . . My parents have always told me that as a Chinese businesswoman, I must be able to rely on myself, and that is what I am doing now. . . . When the May 1998 riots happened, shops like mine were looted, and if I had been there, I would have been raped! I don't know what I would do if something like that happens here. I don't think that my *pribumi* friends in the market would protect me.

I asked Alin why she still held sentiments against the non-Chinese in the post-Suharto reform (*reformasi*) era when the sociopolitical environment for the ethnic Chinese was supposedly better following the abolition of the New Order's assimilation policies. Did she not think that things had improved for Chinese like her over the last ten years or so? Alin laughed and replied:

> No, most things have remained the same for the Chinese, everyone knows that. It's great that now the Chinese can celebrate Imlek [Chinese New Year] and all that, but in everyday life, the Chinese are still discriminated against, and there's still a division between the Chinese and *pribumi*.

This interview left a lasting impression on me. It was 2007 and almost a decade after the beginning of the *reformasi* era that saw a greater recognition of Chinese Indonesian rights in the public domain, and I had hoped to find evidence of improved relations between Chinese and non-Chinese. To hear someone so young expressing such strong prejudices against non-Chinese was quite shocking. Alin was born in 1984, so she was only thirteen or fourteen years old when the violent riots and anti-Chinese attacks of May 12–14, 1998, took place in Jakarta. Though Alin and her family had not been directly affected by the riots, the collective memory of the tragedy still remained vivid for her to the extent that it continued to affect the way she perceived her security as a member of an ethnic minority and to influence her everyday interactions with the non-Chinese around her. I was also surprised that Alin had so casually used the term *pribumi*—a term historically used to describe native or indigenous Indonesians—to refer to non-Chinese in our conversations. In the post-Suharto era, divisive terms such as *pribumi* and *cina* (meaning Chinese, though the term is considered by many Chinese to be derogatory) were not supposed to be used anymore, at least not in government and official capacities, yet I very quickly learned that both Chinese and non-Chinese still regularly used them in everyday speech, especially for the purpose of demarcating the Chinese as non-*pribumi,* as non-native.

Throughout the course of fieldwork research conducted mostly in Jakarta (I also conducted shorter fieldwork trips in other cities, including Medan, Surabaya, Bandung, Semarang, and Pontianak) at different periods from 2007 to 2019, I found that for many Chinese like Alin the post-Suharto reforms meant little apart from the fact that various forms of Chinese cultural and religious expression could now be performed in public. Time and time again, Chinese research participants from different backgrounds told me that, despite celebrations of Chineseness in the period shortly after Suharto's demise, things for them were largely the same at the everyday level, their daily lives and rituals remained unchanged, and they still experienced the same systemic discriminations they had endured during the New Order (1966–1998). The Chinese were still frequently treated with suspicion, mutually negative stereotypes persisted between the Chinese and non-Chinese, and many Chinese continued to live in separate social enclaves.

Looking back, I realized that my initial surprise at the persistence of what was known as the "Chinese problem" (*masalah cina*) in the post-Suharto era was reflective of my own subject position as a Chinese Indonesian who had left the country at a young age and did not fully comprehend the contemporary realities of everyday race relations. Having left Indonesia for Australia in 1997, and thus not having had firsthand experience of early post-Suharto reforms, I had returned as an anthropologist in 2007 quite naively expecting that policy changes at the national level would have automatically resulted in significant societal changes. It seemed to me that, while there were indeed some improvements in public recognition and acceptance of the Chinese following the abolition of assimilation policies, old prejudices about race, class, and national belonging still persisted.

In the early years of *reformasi,* for a while it did look as though the situation was rapidly improving for the Chinese and that perhaps what the New Order government had for over three decades called the "Chinese problem" would at long last be solved. A creation of the state, the "Chinese problem" was an official term used to remind the Indonesian public that the supposed economic dominance and what was perceived as suspicious politics of the Chinese were problems that needed to be fixed.[2] Still reveling in collective victories such as the abolition of New Order assimilationist regulations like Presidential Instruction No. 14 of 1967 (Inpres No. 14/1967) on Chinese religion, beliefs, and traditions in 2000, and the recognition of Imlek as an official national holiday in 2002, many Chinese activists and elders optimistically told me at the beginning of my fieldwork that soon the Chinese would no longer be seen as a problem, and the sociopolitical gap between the Chinese and non-Chinese would be narrowed. This optimism began to wane in the mid-2010s, most notably with the rise—and later the fall—of the Christian and ethnic Chinese politician Basuki Tjahaja Purnama (widely known by his Hakka nickname Ahok).

As discussed at different points in this book, perhaps more than anything else that has occurred in mainstream Indonesian politics in the past decade, Ahok's meteoric rise as a politician prompted controversy and heated debates about the roles that Chinese could (and should) play in nation-building in the post-Suharto era. Rising rapidly from his first political office as the regent of East Belitung to becoming a member of the People's Representative Council (Dewan Perwakilan Rakyat Republik Indonesia, DPR) and then eventually as the running mate of the future president, Joko Widodo (Jokowi), in the 2012 Jakarta gubernatorial election, Ahok cultivated an image of a competent, straight-shooting, and honest public administrator. When Jokowi became president in 2014, Ahok was left to assume the Jakarta governorship and suddenly the prospects of a non-Muslim ethnic Chinese becoming a key player in national politics—or, as some predicted, even running for president—became very real.

However, things took a turn for the worse for Ahok when he made a comment during a speech that allegedly insulted verse 51 of the Al-Ma'idah chapter of the Qur'an. Within weeks, a series of mass protests organized by hard-line Islamist groups such as the Islamic Defenders' Front (Front

Pembela Islam, FPI), involving hundreds of thousands of Muslims from all over Indonesia, took place in Central Jakarta (Setijadi 2019). Protesters called for Ahok to be jailed for blasphemy against Islam, with many even calling for the death penalty. What started as a religious issue soon also developed into an issue of race and class. Very quickly, the angry chants on the streets took on a hateful and racist tone against both Ahok and the Chinese as a whole (Fealy 2016; Setijadi 2017). Following the first mass demonstration on November 4, 2016, groups of protesters then went to the exclusive Pantai Mutiara residential estate in North Jakarta where Ahok and his family lived in order to continue their protest. The majority of the residents in this estate were affluent Chinese, and the protesters' threats to riot and torch houses in anger echoed the horrors of the May 1998 riots. The protesters eventually left without much drama, but anti-Chinese rhetoric intensified in the months that followed, particularly on social media.

The implications of the blasphemy allegations against Ahok for both Chinese identity politics and Indonesian politics more broadly are discussed in greater detail in chapter 5. In short, Ahok lost the Jakarta gubernatorial election in April 2017, and the following month he was found guilty of blasphemy and sentenced to two years in prison. Scholars and casual observers alike were taken aback by Ahok's dramatic downfall. However, from the perspective of Chinese identity politics, the rise of anti-Chinese narratives seen throughout the run-up to the Jakarta gubernatorial election and Ahok blasphemy case suggests that old stereotypes and negative prejudices against the Chinese have persisted in spite of the post-Suharto reforms.

MEMORIES OF UNBELONGING

This book is an examination of the state and dynamics of ethnic Chinese identity politics in the post-Suharto era. The basic questions that underlie this examination are simple. Firstly, does the "Chinese problem" still exist in Indonesia despite years of continuous institutional efforts to restore Chinese civil rights and bridge interethnic differences? What old and new narratives about the ethnic Chinese persist in contemporary Indonesia, and how are these narratives used by different social actors? How do the Chinese themselves make sense of and take advantage of their newfound sociocultural and political freedoms in a democratizing Indonesia? These questions are important and timely because even after more than two decades of reforms relatively little is known about whether policy changes at the macro level have led to fundamental shifts in how ordinary Chinese and non-Chinese perceive and interact with each other at the everyday level.

I argue that the collective memory of the long history of anti-Chinese discrimination is at the very core of Chinese identity politics in post-Suharto Indonesia. Based on extensive ethnographic data, I demonstrate how intergenerational trauma and narratives shape the ways in which the Chinese remember their collective past, negotiate their identities, establish boundaries, and inform their political participation. Far from being passive subjects, I also illustrate how ordinary Chinese try to push or even dismantle the boundaries of identities and spaces that have been made available to them. In domains such as education, the creative arts, literature, and politics, younger Chinese in particular employ unique and imaginative strategies to continually define and redefine what it means to be ethnically Chinese in Indonesia today. These negotiation strategies demonstrate how Chinese as social actors understand their place and exercise agency and autonomy within the structures of belonging that have historically both oppressed and enabled them.

This book builds on the existing body of literature on Chinese Indonesians and expands the discussion by focusing on how collective memory and trauma narratives shape ethnic identity formation. In my analyses, I draw on social theories that seek to explain the relationship between collective memory and group identity formation, notably the work of Maurice Halbwachs and Jeffrey C. Alexander. I also utilize Pierre Bourdieu's concept of the *habitus* in discussions of how historical memory shapes present-day social environments for the Chinese and how groups and individuals learn to operate within these specific milieus. As this book examines ethnic Chinese identity politics in the post-Suharto era, it also contributes in a comparative sense to the growing scholarly discourse on ethnic minority politics in post-authoritarian states like Indonesia.

CHINESE INDONESIANS AS NON-*PRIBUMI*

While the Chinese are a relatively small minority group in Indonesia, their story is an important one because their notoriously problematic existence is deeply entwined with the sociohistorical and political processes that underlie the very creation of the Indonesian nation.[3] The social construction of Chinese as non-*pribumi* has a long historical precedent that dates back to Article 109 of the Netherlands East Indies Constitution

(Regeringsreglement voor Nederlands Indië) of 1854, which distinguished Europeans from the "native" population, and then the revision of the constitution in 1906 that categorized the inhabitants into three groups according to "race": Europeans (*Europeanen*), natives or indigenous populations (*Inlander*), and "foreign Orientals" (*vreemde Oosterlingen*), the latter comprising Chinese, Arabs, Indians, and other non-European foreigners (V. Chang 2020, 230). The fact that many Chinese acted as middlemen for the Dutch in trade dealings with the *pribumi* contributed to the perpetuation of a negative stereotype of them as economically opportunistic and willing to profit from the suffering of the indigenous populations. Loathed for their perceived economic dominance while being politically weak, the Chinese thus became an easy target of racialized violence and riots that would flare up during episodes of political or economic instability in both the colonial and postindependence eras. As Anthony Reid (1997, 55) argues, during the struggle for independence and the early days of the Indonesian Republic, the position of the ethnic Chinese as foreigners within made them "one of the most important 'others' against which the new national identities defined themselves."

Scholars have repeatedly pointed out the constructed and arbitrary nature of the *pribumi*–Chinese distinction in the Indonesian national imagination (Suryadinata 1978; Heryanto 2008; Tan 2008). For one, Indonesia's supposedly unified and monolithic *pribumi* population is actually made up of diverse peoples from the many ethnicities and linguistic groups that exist across the vast archipelago. Prior to the national awakening of the early twentieth century, struggles against Dutch colonial occupation were localized within smaller polities such as kingdoms and regions. It was not until the nationalist independence movement started to gain serious traction in the early 1900s that tribal, local, and regional leaders began to organize and conceptualize themselves as part of a unified national project, or what Benedict Anderson (1983) famously calls an "imagined community."

The ideological concept of the *pribumi* as the original peoples of the Indonesian archipelago with easily identifiable homelands (for example, Sundanese from West Java and Banten and Balinese from Bali, and so on) became an important one, particularly within the context of the then imminent need for a unified anticolonial struggle and nation-building. Ethnic and local identities have continued to be important to this day, but—while not unproblematic—the *pribumi* construct as a central marker of nativeness became a shared common ground among those who could claim that they authentically belonged to a native homeland.

This racial division persisted even after independence, with the term *pribumi* by this time having acquired connotations of anticolonial and anti-foreign native empowerment. While the term "non-*pribumi*" by definition theoretically describes anyone who does not belong to a community considered indigenous to the country, in practice it is almost always used to refer to the ethnic Chinese, frequently in a derogatory manner (Hoon 2006a; Setijadi 2016a). Indonesians of Indian or Arab/Hadhrami (Yemeni) descent are almost never referred to as "non-*pribumi*." In other words, *pribumi* has become a politically charged term, laden with the historical baggage of decades and more of state-sanctioned discrimination against the Chinese.

The categorization of the Chinese as a monolithic non-native category also undermines and diminishes their significant internal diversity. Scholarship on Chinese Indonesians in the twentieth century generally differentiates them into two broad groups—*peranakan* Chinese and *totok* Chinese (Suryadinata 1976). The term *peranakan* refers to the acculturated Chinese who came to Indonesia in the very first waves of migration and have lived in the country for centuries, and intermingled with local cultures to create a hybridized mixed ancestry. *Totok* are generally understood to be Chinese who came to the Indonesian archipelago in later waves of migration in the late nineteenth and early twentieth centuries, and are thus less assimilated with the local cultures and still very much culturally oriented toward China, and are seen as "pure" or unacculturated. Such distinctions should be seen only as a common yet somewhat outdated way to differentiate between different groups of Chinese, as there are further diversities within them, for example, between speakers of various Chinese languages, such as Hakka, Teochew, and Hokkien; ancestral village affiliations; generations; and class. However, while scholars now generally regard the *peranakan–totok* distinction to be outmoded, the terms are still frequently used by Chinese when referring to the degrees to which their families adhere to Chinese cultural traditions (Hoon 2006b; Tsai 2008). As I show later, the meanings of these terms and distinctions continue to evolve.

In the course of Indonesia's nation-building, modern ethnonationalism has never managed to successfully accommodate the Chinese and their internal diversity. This situation has benefited successive governments who have manipulated the vulnerability of the Chinese as a minority group by using them as scapegoats in times of crisis. It is important to note that the beginning and the end of Suharto's New Order regime were marked by major episodes of anti-Chinese violence, which analysts argue were at least partly encouraged by military-backed factions keen to exert and expand their power by controlling crisis situations through the use of force and military interventions (Suryadinata 2004; Tan 2004; Purdey 2006). The fact that enforcing assimilation policies purportedly intended to erase all traces of Chineseness was one of the New Order's first major acts as a government illustrates how the ethnic Chinese—and by extension, Chineseness—were widely seen as a problem that sowed discord and therefore needed to be fixed. This predicament experienced by the Chinese was perfectly encapsulated in the words of the celebrated writer and political prisoner Pramoedya Ananta Toer, who in 1960 wrote, "They [the Chinese] have been here since the time of our ancestors. In fact, they are real Indonesians who live and die in Indonesia. However . . . they suddenly become foreigners who are not foreign at all" (Toer 1960, 54).

Over the three decades of assimilation under the New Order, Chinese culture and identity were in many ways erased or at least hidden and suppressed from public view. The use of Chinese languages was banned, Chinese schools were closed, Chinese-language media and political organizations were disbanded, and public expressions of Chinese culture were forbidden. In a law passed in 1966 (Cabinet Presidium Decision No. 127), Suharto's first cabinet suggested that Chinese families should consider taking up new, more Indonesian-sounding names: for example, the Chinese surname Tan would be replaced with Tanuwijaya or Tanumihardja; Lim would be replaced with Salim; and so on. It was not legally mandatory for Chinese to change their names, and many, such as the student activist Soe Hok Gie and human rights lawyer Yap Thiam Hien, refused. However, the Chinese came under immense social and institutional pressure to do so to prove their loyalty to Indonesia and their commitment to becoming what was seen as real Indonesians. The implication was clear: Chineseness was ideologically suspect, and those who did not voluntarily erase their Chinese identities risked being accused of disloyalty or—worse—political subversion.

Yet even with the oppressive and humiliating pressure to change one's name, there were ingenious strategies employed by Chinese who complied with name changing while still resisting—or at least subtly protesting—the state's efforts to erase their ancestral heritage. Some changed their names to sound more Indonesian by combining the three (or two) words of their Chinese names into a one-word name (which is common for Javanese names, for instance, Suharto) while retaining the same spelling as their original Chinese name. An example of this was the historian and writer Ong Hok Ham, who famously Indonesianized his name by simply changing it to Onghokham. Others changed their names into Indonesian-sounding names that still somewhat sounded like their original Chinese names; my grandfather did so by changing his Hokkien name from Poey Wie Tiong to Poerwito. This clever act of noncompliance through compliance is but one of the many negotiation strategies employed by Chinese to assert their agency within the structure of forced assimilation.

The New Order's assimilation policies were deeply problematic and paradoxical. The whole justification for these policies was to solve the "Chinese problem" by absorbing the Chinese minority into majority *pribumi* society. Yet the very fact that the Chinese were deemed to be the main group requiring assimilation singled them out as *the* problematic ethnic minority. Moreover, since careers in politics, the military, and the civil service were effectively off-limits for ethnic Chinese, one of the few domains left available for them to operate in was the world of business. Their high visibility in commerce, combined with the corrupt system of patronage and cronyism linking Suharto's family members, friends, and associates with prominent Chinese business tycoons such as Liem Sioe Liong (Sudono Salim, 林紹良), Ciputra (Tjie Tjin Hoan, 徐振煥), and Bob Hasan, only served to reinforce the public image of Chinese as what Amy Chua (2004, 6) famously termed "market-dominant minorities" and Ruth McVey (1992, 9) called "pariah capitalists."

Another example of the New Order's contradictory assimilation policies was the requirement that all Chinese acquire a Republic of Indonesia Certificate of Citizenship (Surat Bukti Kewarganegaraan Republik Indonesia, SBKRI). According to Presidential Decision No. 52 of 1977, all Chinese Indonesians had to have an SBKRI in order to prove they did not possess dual nationality with the People's Republic of China, despite the fact that most were born in Indonesia and were already Indonesian citizens. Only ethnic Chinese were required to have this citizenship document. As such, while the SBKRI system was installed under the guise of supposedly aiding the assimilation process, in reality it had the paradoxical effect of further differentiating the Chinese and thus exposing them to increased bureaucratic and societal discrimination.

During this period, language had much to do with the othering of the Chinese at the everyday level. The importance of semantics was clearly something that the New Order government understood well. One of its first acts in 1967 was to issue Ampera Cabinet Presidium Circular 6 of 1967 (Surat Edaran Presidium Kabinet Ampera Nomor SE-06/Pres.Kab/6/1967) instructing that the term *cina* rather than "Tionghoa" be used to refer to the Chinese in official documents. This move was widely considered a deliberate insult since the term was (and still is) regarded as derogatory by many Chinese Indonesians. In addition, *cina* implied an ideological closeness to Communist China, thus carrying sinister overtones at a time when Indonesia–China relations were still at a standstill following accusations that China had been involved in the abortive Indonesian Communist Party (Partai Komunis Indonesia, PKI) coup of September 30, 1965 (known in Indonesia during the New Order as G30S/PKI). At the same time, throughout the New Order period, the Chinese continued to be called "non-*pribumi*" ("non-*pri*" for short) in both official state discourse and everyday speech.

Despite the scale of the New Order's oppression and suppression of Chinese identities and cultures, it needs to be emphasized that the enforcement of its assimilation policies was not uniform across the vast archipelago, and that—just like the examples of name-changing strategies—various Chinese communities employed different tactics to mitigate the local effects of forced assimilation. In most of the scholarship, it is generally agreed that, while major policies such as the closure of Chinese schools and media outlets were enforced nationally, other aspects of assimilation, such as the ban on the public use of Chinese languages, were more strictly implemented in Java than in other areas as it is the center of political power and national culture. Particularly in non-Javanese towns and regions with high concentrations of Chinese, such as Medan in North Sumatra, Bagansiapiapi in Riau, Pontianak and Singkawang in West Kalimantan, the Bangka-Belitung Islands, and the Riau Islands, some communities were able to continue to openly speak Chinese languages and practice their cultural traditions (Somers Heidhues 2003; Hui 2011; Lyons and Ford 2013; Tsai 2013; Stenberg 2019; Setijadi 2023). Even in Java, Chinese from different backgrounds adopted various tactics to assert themselves and make the most out of their situation within the confines of assimilation. For instance, in his study of Chinese Muslims, Hew Wai Weng (2018) argues that even those Chinese who converted to Islam as an assimilation strategy still asserted their Chineseness through the incorporation of Chinese symbols in their Islamic religious practices.

The reality is that not only did the government's assimilation policies fail to erase Chineseness, the diversity of Chinese identities and cultures still thrived in the in-between spaces that the New Order regime had sought to undermine. While this book focuses on collective memories and group identity politics at the national level, it also acknowledges that the collective past—which includes the New Order's assimilation policies and other instances of anti-Chinese discrimination—was experienced and thus remembered in different ways by different ethnic Chinese communities across the country. In fact, as I show later, a major point of contestation in post-Suharto Chinese identity politics is which community's narrative(s) should be the one(s) to represent Chinese Indonesians as a whole.

REFORMASI: A NEW BEGINNING FOR THE CHINESE?

As has been extensively documented, the political situation dramatically changed when, after months of economic crisis, instability, and student protests demanding Suharto's resignation, the chaos culminated in large-scale rioting, the looting and destruction of property (many owned by the Chinese), and the rape and sexual assault of ethnic Chinese women. The violence took place on May 12–14, 1998, in Jakarta, Solo, and other major cities (Purdey 2006). Soon after, Suharto resigned the presidency, the New Order collapsed, and a new era of reform began with promises of greater democracy, civil liberties, a more open civil society, and justice for those who had been wronged by the regime.

For the Chinese, the end of the New Order marked the beginning of a new era of identity politics that started with demands for the abolition of assimilationist laws and justice for the victims of the May 1998 violence (Turner 2003; Budiman 2005; Purdey 2006; Jusuf et al. 2007). Indeed, post-Suharto governments were only too eager to prove their commitment to human rights and distance themselves from the harmful legacies of the New Order and the May 1998 violence by implementing new laws that recognized Chinese rights. The government of Bacharuddin Jusuf Habibie (1998–1999) began these reforms through Presidential Instruction No. 26 of 1998 that abolished the use of the terms *pribumi* and "non-*pribumi*" in official government documents. In 2000, the newly elected Abdurrahman Wahid (Gus Dur, 1999–2001) revoked Presidential Instruction No. 14 of 1967, allowing Chinese languages and cultures to be practiced openly in public again. Megawati Sukarnoputri (2001–2004) designated Imlek as a national holiday in 2002 as an official gesture of recognition for the Chinese, and in 2006, Confucianism (Konghucu) was recognized as one of Indonesia's six official religions. Furthermore, in addition to Habibie's initial directive on the cessation of the use of the term *pribumi,* in 2006, Citizenship Law No. 12 was enacted, which recognizes all individuals born in Indonesia as *asli* (indigenous), thus giving Chinese unprecedented rights, including the right to run for president. The stark contrast between New Order and post-Suharto policies led many to see the *reformasi* era as a time for the revival of Chinese culture.

It is easy to understand why many Chinese were enthusiastic about the potential for change in the post-Suharto era. For the first time in over three decades, expressions of Chinese culture, identities, and religions that were previously hidden could now be celebrated and performed openly. Mandarin and other Chinese languages could be publicly spoken and taught in schools, and the Chinese-language press and other media reopened. In the public domain, there is now a much more visible Chinese presence, particularly during the annual Imlek celebrations, when shopping malls and commercial spaces around Jakarta and other major cities are decorated with red lanterns and red money envelopes (*angpao*).

The number of Chinese organizations increased rapidly so that by 2007 there were an estimated 176 Chinese voluntary and social associations across the country, the majority being clan associations that had been dormant throughout the New Order (Dawis 2010b, 61–62). Many of the larger umbrella organizations, such as the Chinese Indonesian Association (Perhimpunan Indonesia Tionghoa, INTI) and Indonesian Chinese Clan Social Association (Paguyuban Sosial Marga Tionghoa Indonesia, PSMTI), were new and were created as part of a concerted effort by leaders and activists to ensure greater sociopolitical representation for ethnic Chinese.

A number of these associations have had some success advocating for more recognition of Chinese rights. For example, INTI, the now defunct Chinese Indonesian Reform Party (Partai Reformasi Tionghoa Indonesia, PARTI) and the Anti-Discrimination Movement (Gerakan Perjuangan Anti-Diskriminasi, GANDI) were instrumental in the passing of Citizenship Law No. 12/2006 that recognizes all Indonesia-born ethnic Chinese as citizens, thus solving the problem of statelessness for many Chinese who still lacked proper documentation. Furthermore, partly due to long-term lobbying by INTI, President Susilo Bambang Yudhoyono (2004–2014) repealed Ampera Cabinet Presidium Circular 6 of 1967 in 2014 to officially enforce the adoption of the much more widely accepted term "Tionghoa" in official government use instead of the term *cina*. On the cultural front, PSMTI successfully lobbied for and then built the Chinese Indonesian Cultural Park (Taman Budaya Tionghoa Indonesia) at the Beautiful Indonesia Miniature Park (Taman Mini Indonesia Indah, TMII), while the Supreme Council for the Confucian Religion in Indonesia (Majelis Tinggi Agama Khonghucu Indonesia, MATAKIN) was successful in pushing for the recognition of Imlek as a Confucian national holiday.

It is important to acknowledge at this point that, right from the beginning, there were a few forms of recognition toward Chinese that were considered to be problematic and controversial, even among the Chinese themselves. One example of this is the recognition of Confucianism as an official religion in 2006 (Long 2019). For over two millennia, Confucianism has existed as a moral, social, and political philosophy, or as a nontheistic set of cultural ideals that had merged with popular folk religion in China, other parts of East Asia, and among the Chinese diaspora. Nowhere else in the world is Confucianism institutionalized as a religion. Here, the institutionalization of Confucianism in Indonesia needs to be viewed as part of Chinese efforts to fit their belief system and culture within the state's framework. In her research on adherents of Confucianism, Evi Sutrisno (2018) shows how, throughout the New Order, Indonesian Confucians consistently negotiated to have their religious and cultural rights recognized by (re)framing Confucian beliefs as a religion that could be institutionalized as one of the state's official religions. Even in the post-Suharto era, Confucianism had to first meet some rigid criteria (for example, having a holy book, a monotheistic deity or prophet, a hierarchy of priests, and official rituals) before it could be instituted as a religion. As such, while the successful recognition of Confucianism has mostly been celebrated as a triumph, it also needs to be problematized as yet another example of the Indonesian state's taming and suppression of the diversity and dynamics of Chinese cultural practices.[4]

Regardless of some of the inherent contradictions in post-Suharto Chinese identity politics, the return of Chinese to the public domain continues to be celebrated, particularly in the field of mainstream politics in which a growing number of Chinese have participated in local and national elections. Based on data from the General Electoral Commission (Komisi Pemilihan Umum, KPU) (KPU 2004, 2014), I estimate that there were at least 100 ethnic Chinese candidates in the 2004 elections, 213 in the 2009 elections, and 315 candidates in the 2014 elections. From 2014 to 2019, I estimate that there were sixteen elected ethnic Chinese members in Indonesia's two national legislative chambers from various political parties, representing roughly 2.8 percent of the Indonesian population, proportionally slightly higher than the estimated percentage of the country's ethnic Chinese population (Harun et al. 2004; DPR-RI 2010; Bustami 2014). In my estimation, this number went down slightly to fifteen in the 2019 elections, but it is still quite high considering that these elections took place in the aftermath of the Ahok case (see chapter 5).

Post-Suharto optimism can also be seen in much of the scholarly literature on the Chinese. While pre-1998 literature on the Chinese largely focuses on colonial history, *peranakan–totok* politics, and critiques of the New Order's assimilation policy (Somers 1965; Coppel 1983), the literature after 1998 tends to concentrate on the new landscape of Chinese identity politics in the *reformasi* era.[5] For instance, scholars have documented how post-Suharto policy changes have affected institutions, identity politics, and civil society more generally. Among many others, there are studies that focus on the revival of Chinese-language media (Hoon 2006a, 2006b; Prasetyo 2010), the recognition of Confucianism as an official religion (Suryadinata 2005, 2010), and the increasing visibility of Mandarin in public spaces as well as its integration in school and university curricula (Giblin 2003; Kaboel and Sulanti 2010). However, some scholars are more critical of the current situation than others. In his concluding remarks in a study of post-Suharto Chinese identity, Arief Budiman (2005, 101) notes that as "Chinese Indonesians are still trying to find their place in Indonesia . . . within a still unstable society undergoing a slow transition toward democracy, this is not a simple process and its outcome cannot be predicted."

Indeed, reforms at the policy level do not necessarily guarantee their thorough implementation. For instance, in an analysis of the state of Chinese citizenship status, Thung Ju Lan (2012) writes about how local government bureaucrats still demanded to see SBKRI documents from Chinese for verification purposes even though it is no longer necessary to produce such documents (see also Effendi and Prasetyadji 2008). Furthermore, as discussed earlier, government instructions to end the use of the discriminatory terms "non-*pribumi*" and *cina* in official and public discourses also do not mean that these terms automatically fall into disuse. More importantly, mutually prejudicial beliefs and behaviors between Chinese and non-Chinese are still widespread (C. Chua 2008; Hoon 2006b; Tsai 2008).

Of course, there are also many examples of improving interethnic relations. However, considering the numerous changes that have occurred at the policy level, there seems to be relatively little change at the societal level as a whole. If anything, paradoxically, post-Suharto Chinese identity politics appears to have differentiated the Chinese even further, arguably widening the gap between them and the non-Chinese.

The reality is that growing up for young Chinese in the post-Suharto era is in many ways not so different from how their parents experienced the New Order. While the sociopolitical and cultural landscapes have changed, much of the everyday lived realities of the younger generation remain the same.

Many middle- and upper-class Chinese families still live in urban enclaves for safety reasons, and the younger generation has grown up with the knowledge of their vulnerability as members of a problematic minority ethnic group. Here, the collective memories of the May 1998 riots serve as a reminder that the next anti-Chinese attack could happen at any time. Combined with their parents' memories of forced assimilation and their grandparents' memories of the 1965–1966 anti-Communist purges, the Chinese must deal with a collective intergenerational trauma that ultimately emphasizes the need to be alert and cautious of the non-Chinese at all times.

RIDING THE WAVE OF CHINA'S RISE

At the same time, the rise of the People's Republic of China (PRC) as a regional and global power has been and remains a major external factor in changing Chinese Indonesian identity politics since 1998. In terms of affect, after decades of forced assimilation and feeling like they do not belong in Indonesia, many Chinese now find comfort and belonging in once again expressing themselves as Chinese. This is especially the case with older *totok* (the pre-1965 generation), most of whom had a Chinese education and felt deeply embittered by the forced erasure of Chinese identity and cultural expression during the New Order (Sai 2010). For these Chinese, the rise of China as a global power has roused a sense of ethnic pride and legitimation.

Many young Chinese Indonesians have embraced this newfound freedom to reconnect with Chineseness, most notably through learning Mandarin. In the last fifteen years, the increased demand for Mandarin-language learning, particularly among students, has led to more language courses being offered in many private and public schools, often as part of National Plus schools in which classes are delivered in a combination of Indonesian (Bahasa Indonesia), English, and Mandarin. The number of providers of private Mandarin-language courses has also mushroomed in the last decade, especially in urban residential neighborhoods that are home to large concentrations of middle- and upper-class Chinese families (Kaboel and Sulanti 2010; Hoon and Kuntjara 2019).

Today, Chinese Indonesians also have many channels by which to access pan-Chinese culture—through the Internet and the flow of transnational Chinese popular music, films, and television dramas into Indonesia. While the older post-1965 generation mostly gathered and consumed images of Chineseness through their consumption of kung fu films and television series imported from Hong Kong and Taiwan, today's generation now has a greater abundance of images of Chineseness to choose from (Dawis 2009; Kusno 2012, 2016; Suprajitno 2020). The relative popularity of Mandarin pop music and television dramas (mostly from Taiwan) in Indonesia means that contemporary images of modern and cool Chinese culture are now more available for Chinese Indonesian youth than ever before. Combined with the phenomenal popularity of Korean television dramas and pop music (K-pop), young Chinese can now also relate to and identify with images of East Asian modernity that allow them to be proud of their "Oriental" characteristics (see Chua and Iwabuchi 2008). Nowadays, the visibility of ethnic Chinese faces in popular Indonesian media is greater than ever before, with celebrities and public figures acknowledging their Chinese heritage, whereas in the past most celebrities were quick to disown it. This trend has particular significance for young people, who, for the first time, can see ethnic Chinese celebrities being publicly proud of their Chineseness.

From a more practical perspective, the rise of China presents an unprecedented opportunity for Chinese Indonesians to act as intermediaries in (mainly commercial) dealings between Indonesia and China. A central assumption here is that a shared ethnicity, along with the ability to speak Mandarin, will give Chinese Indonesians an advantage in forging kin- and network-based preferential personal connections (*guanxi*) with business counterparts in China or other Chinese communities worldwide. For younger Chinese Indonesians, the desire to keep up and ride on the wave of China's rise is the main motivation for learning Mandarin and maintaining an active interest in developments in China.

An increasing number of Chinese Indonesian youth from affluent families go to China not only to study Mandarin but also for their tertiary education degrees. Data from the Indonesian embassy in Beijing suggests that in 1998 only around 1,000 Indonesian students studied at Chinese universities; in 2012 the number had risen to over 9,000; and by 2018 it was over 15,000, making Indonesians the tenth-largest cohort of foreign students in China (Priyambodo 2012; Jegho 2021; Han and Tong 2021). This is a growing trend away from the preference for Australia and other Western countries, such as the United States and Britain, as traditional destinations for Indonesian students pursuing an overseas education. While non-Chinese Indonesian students are included in this trend, a large majority are Chinese who hope to create a future employment niche for themselves not only with an overseas university degree but also knowledge of modern Chinese language and society.

Bilateral diplomatic relationships between China and Indonesia have blossomed over the last fifteen years. This is evident in the establishment of a Sino-Indonesian strategic partnership in 2005, and the signing of a memorandum of understanding between the two countries for further Chinese foreign direct investment in Indonesia as part of the Belt and Road Initiative (BRI) and the Twenty-First Century Maritime Silk Road Economic Belt (popularly known as the New Maritime Silk Road) visions announced as part of Chinese president Xi Jinping's ambitious expansion plans (Silaen and Sentana 2013). The fact that Xi announced this New Maritime Silk Road plan during a state visit to Jakarta in October 2013 is a reflection of how important Indonesia is to China's long-term strategy in the Asian region.

From Indonesia's point of view, Chinese investment is very important, particularly for the building of infrastructure projects and to increase bilateral trade (Amin 2015; Tiezzi 2015; Rakhmat 2021). This is a quite remarkable development, especially in the context of the diplomatic freeze between China and Indonesia from 1967 to 1990 following allegations of China's involvement in the abortive Communist coup of September 30, 1965, which sparked strong anti-Communist and anti-China discourses in Indonesia. Today, the potential for Chinese Indonesians to act as trade, cultural, and linguistic intermediaries is well understood, not just by Chinese Indonesians themselves but also by the Chinese and Indonesian governments.

Historically, appealing to, and garnering support from, ethnic Chinese communities and the diaspora abroad has been an important part of China's foreign policy. This has continued to the present, when the narratives projected by Beijing reveal the role it envisions for ethnic Chinese communities worldwide. In speeches given to various Chinese communities around the world over the last few years, Xi has repeatedly stressed the importance of overseas Chinese as a bridge strengthening the relationship between China and their host countries of these overseas Chinese (MFA PRC 2013; Suryadinata 2017a, 2017b). The same official line has been echoed by Chinese officials, for instance, in a speech to INTI made in September 2014, Overseas Chinese Affairs Office (OCAO or Qiaoban) chairman Qiu Yuanping said, "The ancestral land [of the Chinese] will never forget the major contribution of the *huaqiao huaren* [Chinese citizens and ethnic Chinese outside China] overseas. China will always be the strong backer of the people of Chinese descent overseas" (cited in Suryadinata 2015).

As discussed in chapter 6, thus far, Chinese Indonesian organizations and prominent individuals have actively played a bridging role in trade and cultural exchanges between Indonesia and China. Sociocultural Chinese organizations such as INTI and PSMTI as well as smaller clan and religious organizations hold regular cultural and philanthropic events (particularly around the time of Imlek) that are often done in cooperation with the Chinese embassy in Jakarta or at least attended by embassy officials.

Amid all these developments, however, many within the Chinese Indonesian community have become increasingly worried about a potential backlash to overt public displays of Chinese culture, the widespread use of Mandarin, and the growing confidence of the *totok* business elite in displaying their close ties with China. The fact that such worries exist indicates that there are still negative ideological connotations in post-Suharto Indonesia about China and the loyalty of Chinese Indonesians. Even now there are frequent attacks in the media from various right-wing and Islamist groups accusing Chinese businesspeople and politicians of being China's puppets in Indonesia.

While anti-China discourses do not necessarily cause or go hand in hand with negative perceptions of Chinese Indonesians, history has shown that—for better or worse—perceptions of China in Indonesia have inevitably affected them. In the meantime, for Chinese who are worried that any overt displays of Chineseness might perpetuate negative stereotypes of foreignness and disloyalty, the fear of a backlash is real.

COLLECTIVE MEMORY, TRAUMA, AND IDENTITY

Of central interest in this study is the intersection between memory, identity, race, and ethnicity, a nexus that has been pinpointed as a central theme in social theory (Halbwachs 1992; Nagel 1994; Olick and Robbins 1998; Bell 2003; Low 2015). Memory making, analyzed as a sociopolitical and cultural process, sheds light on local, national, and transnational instrumentalization of the past for present-day motivations in relation to a range of memory actors, sites, and texts. Through the perspective of collective and personal histories of the Chinese Indonesian past, of Chineseness, and of China, this study interrogates the appropriation of memories for the purposes of performative ethnic identity politics.

I argue that the common thread that connects the variety of contemporary Chinese Indonesian experiences is a collective memory of anti-Chinese discrimination. While keeping in mind their heterogeneity, at some stage all Chinese Indonesians had to learn about their position as Chinese within their immediate social environments and the country at large. Even if a Chinese individual refuses to identify or be associated with Chinese cultural practices, their physical features mean that they are likely to be automatically racialized as Chinese by other Chinese and non-Chinese Indonesians alike.[6] While most contemporary scholarship now generally understands race as an ideological and not biological construct, the reality is that the assumption of essential difference based on race "still wields monumental power as a social category" (Cornell and Hartmann 2006, 23). In Indonesia, this automatic racial categorization signifies the inability of the Chinese to escape the connotations of unbelonging and the inherent foreignness that their Chineseness implies. Collective memory plays an important part in the maintenance of Chinese group consciousness because contemporary notions of belonging (and unbelonging) are shaped by recollections and residual feelings of past trauma.

The vast majority of Chinese today have had no firsthand experience of anti-Chinese violence such as the anti-Communist purges of 1965–1966, and those under the age of twenty-five are too young to have their own memories of the May 1998 riots. However, the lack of firsthand memory or experience does not mean that this generation is not affected by the trauma that has resulted from centuries of discrimination. At the family level, parents, grandparents, and extended family members pass on their memories of past discrimination and anti-Chinese violence as cautionary tales to warn young people to behave appropriately and remain on their guard. Among Chinese social networks and communities, stereotypes, rumors, hearsay, and stories circulate, perpetuating and maintaining existing discourses about both the Chinese and the *pribumi,* even though the younger generation lives in quite different social circumstances than their parents or grandparents did. These younger Chinese must digest all this information to decide for themselves which aspects of this collective memory are still applicable to their lives.

Memory, as Kevin Yelvington (2002, 236) notes, is too frequently conceptualized "as an unproblematic, possessable, recollection of an authentic past." However, far from being stable and uncontested, memory functions within social circumstances "that bear the friction of cross-cutting structured processes" (Davidson and Kuah-Pearce 2008, 7). These structured processes are not only culturally charged but also subject to political interference that can create biased representations of the past. For instance, war memories constitute an important element of a collective memory experienced by an entire community, and it is thus not surprising that representations of these memories are highly dependent on the political climate at the time at community, regional, and national levels. The act of remembering, at least at the group level, is never simply about retrieving memories but is a conscious and politicized act of choosing which aspects of the past should be illuminated to transform the present.

Reflecting on the importance of collective memory in individual and group identity formation, the philosopher Maurice Halbwachs (1985, 1992) argues that human memory can function only within a collective context. While human beings can remember their individual histories, they cannot freely choose the circumstances and conditions of their remembering because social environments influence and shape an individual's capacity to remember and to recall. According to Halbwachs, collective memory is therefore "the complete stock of memories a society of each epoch can reconstruct within its present frame of reference" (cited in Schreiner 2005, 269). He adds that collective memory is always selective; different groups of people have different collective memories, which in turn give rise to different modes of behavior. Given the selectiveness of remembering, it is important that narratives and memories be understood in terms of the local conditions in which they are recollected. Nostalgia, for example, is frequently activated by changes in physical landscapes, migrations and other forms of mobility, or sociopolitical movements, and is therefore tied up with feelings such as belonging, dislocation, and security (or lack thereof) (Sully 2004; Savage 2008; Duyvendak 2011).

The fragmented nature of memory making highlights the notion that memory is socially constructed and that, like identity, memory should be recognized as an ongoing process (Olick and Robbins 1998, 122). Errors and contradictions are part of this process and remind us of the "subjective meanings of historical experience" (Thomson 1999, 33). People routinely add to, erase from, recall, and reconstruct events, and in this study at least focus is placed on what is remembered, by whom, and why different social actors recall the past in particular ways. These acts of selective remembering are crucial for the construction of group identity as they give the members of the group a sense of solidarity and pride in their uniqueness of character as a marker of difference against those perceived as outsiders or others. Particularly among minorities, socioeconomic and political marginalization routinely causes the marginalized group to idealize positive aspects of their past while at the same time collectively mourning and commemorating dark and traumatic moments in history that are deemed to be attacks on the group's existence or culture (Smelser 2004; Sztompka 2004).

The same can be said about the act of forgetting. As much as discussions center on remembering, forgetting also plays a crucial role in the study of memory. Both deliberate and unconscious historical amnesia throws light on how the omitting of select memories ties in with present-day situations and future goals. The politics of remembering thus also requires taking a closer look at the politics of forgetting to examine which narratives are forgotten or appropriated, as well as who is telling what stories to whom, and under what circumstances. In group situations, this often results in factions who contest the writing and rewriting of the memories of their community, in order to claim political control and "gain ascendancy on cultural and mnemonic interpretation" (Davidson and Kuah-Pearce 2008, 7).

Collective memory is disputed territory in this case, and one that is inevitably reshaped and appropriated by individuals from different generations, genders, classes, and beliefs. The selection of what to remember and how is both a personal choice on the part of individuals and a collective choice for the community as a whole, depending on what cultural elements are viewed as key to the survival of their individual and group identities. Individuals and communities consciously choose what they want to remember and pass down to the younger generations, and here "identities appear as sites of transit between layers of historical experiences" (Mageo 2001, 2).

Furthermore, as Barry Schwartz (2015) reminds us, while individual memories are the fundamental units of collective memory, it would be a mistake to conclude that collective memory is merely the larger framework for the interpretation of what a group of individuals remember. Schwartz argues that, because collective memory refers to a *distribution* throughout society of what individuals as a collective know, believe, and feel about the past, collective memory denies the possibility of fully shared conceptions of the past. In other words, use of the term "collective" here should not be seen as unproblematically consensual and free from power relations. Rather, collective memory is more often shaped by the dominant memories of influential individual members with the economic, social, and cultural capital to influence the group's collective memory as a whole.

Memories are also embodied in everyday landscapes and experiences and, as such, they are central to the processes of individual and group place making. In his seminal work on collective memory, Pierre Nora (1989, 7) conceptualizes "sites of memory" (*lieux de mémoire*) as spaces "where memory crystalizes and secretes itself." Nora argues that in fast-paced, "hopelessly forgetful" modern societies, collective memories are constantly reworked, reappropriated, and detached from historical specificities, and the reproduction of memories becomes rooted "in the concrete, in spaces, gestures, images, and objects" (8). Public commemorations play an important role here, through which acts of commemoration and memorialization—especially public ones—distinguish particular events and figures as more deserving of remembrance as compared to those that are remembered only at the individual level. As such, the terrain of collective memory is far from equal, as is the case for Chinese Indonesian collective memories and trauma.

For the Chinese as a group, the most significant memory in recent history is arguably the long trauma of anti-Chinese discrimination experienced during the New Order regime that culminated in the May 1998 riots. Alongside this most recent and highly commemorated incident in Chinese Indonesian history are other episodes of anti-Chinese violence, such as the Batavia Chinese massacre (*Chineezenmoord*) of 1740 and the killings committed during the anti-Communist purges of 1965–1966, that are archived within the Chinese collective memory as evidence of injustices endured throughout their long existence in the country.

In his reflections in the immediate aftermath of the riots of May 1998, anthropologist James T. Siegel (1998a, 96) writes that the word used time and time again to describe how the Chinese felt about the violence, and in particular the rapes of Chinese women, was "trauma." Directly adapted from English, since the word does not have an Indonesian equivalent, Siegel argues that the word "trauma" describes how, unlike past instances of anti-Chinese violence that would quickly evaporate into everyday business as usual, the "stain" (*aib*) of the May 1998 violence and rapes would not go away. In the months and years after, Siegel (96) and other scholars identify reports of "disease, suicide, pregnancy, depression, and broken family lives" that resulted from this unresolved trauma (see also Lochore 2000; Sutrisno 2002; Sai 2006; Winarnita 2012). In the decades that followed, these traumatic memories would from time to time be brought to the surface, recalled, and appropriated, utilized to justify or lend weight to particular viewpoints and decisions. Sadly, the direct victims of the violence mostly get forgotten amid the commemorations, their names lost to history.

For some Chinese, the trauma of past anti-Chinese violence motivates them to strive to become model Indonesian citizens and assimilate to an even greater degree in order to prove their loyalty to the country and fight negative stereotypes about the Chinese. For others, the same trauma justifies their own xenophobic and racist attitudes toward *pribumi*. For others still, the history of anti-Chinese discrimination, combined with the recent rise of China and the increased confidence of Chinese in the post-Suharto era, inspire feelings of ethnic pride toward their resilience and the success they have attained in the face of great adversity.

Analyzing the relationship between what he calls traumatic events, memory, and collective identity, Jeffrey C. Alexander uses the concept of cultural trauma to explain how certain harrowing moments in history can forever shape the way particular groups view both themselves and others. According to Alexander (2004, 1), "Cultural trauma occurs when members of a collectivity feel they have been subjected to a horrendous event that leaves indelible marks upon their group consciousness, marking their memories forever and changing their future identity in fundamental and irrevocable ways." Alexander stresses the constructed nature of trauma and memory in that, like identity, both trauma and memory exist in narration and are embedded in everyday life. When traumatic events occur, a community can bind together in solidarity or be irreversibly damaged, even destroyed, as a consequence. Constructing cultural trauma is an essential part of any imagined community and, as such, understanding how groups remember traumatic events is central to understanding how they "retain a sense of the past, and . . . how a sense of the past can inform a group's politics, religion, art, and social life in general" (Roth and Salas 2001, 1).

In most cases, the instinctive response to instances of collective trauma is for the victims (and other concerned parties) to demand justice and eliminate the cause(s) of suffering to achieve a measure of closure. The assumption here is that trauma needs to be dealt with so that the process of healing can begin. This can be seen in relatively recent atrocities such as the Holocaust in Europe, the Rwandan genocide, and the Khmer Rouge's killing fields in Cambodia, after which outrage from local and international communities resulted in demands for justice. A problem arises when justice cannot be achieved due to a lack of clarity about the facts. In countless cases of state-sanctioned violence and human rights violations, a lack of state transparency as well as reluctance among witnesses and victims to come forward have hampered efforts to bring the perpetrators of these crimes to justice. When the causes of collective trauma are unresolved, the victims may feel a sense of grave injustice that in the long run can result in widespread distrust of the judicial system, the state, and others outside their group more generally. In many cases, prolonged acts of discrimination against a community can give rise to a strong discourse of victimization and long-term social problems within the marginalized groups (Kleinman et al. 1997; Young 1997; Sztompka 2000).

In Indonesia, the public's trust in the national judicial system is generally very low, and for good reason. Time and time again, perpetrators of major crimes have either been freed or let off lightly because of corrupt police, prosecutors, judges, and government officials. Corruption and nepotism are so rampant and so much a part of the country's public culture that honest judicial officials are considered rarities (and often have powerful enemies). More recently, despite public demands for national inquiries into the many unresolved historical atrocities and violations of human rights that occurred during the New Order, post-Suharto governments have been either unable or unwilling to open up real investigations into these cases. High on the list of mass crimes to be investigated are the 1965–1966 anti-Communist killings, the disappearances of political activists and dissidents during the New Order regime, the 1984 Tanjung Priok massacre, and the May 1998 riots (Zurbuchen 2002; Schreiner 2005; Heryanto 2006). This is not to mention the allegations of state-sponsored terrorism in areas such as Aceh, Papua, and East Timor (now Timor-Leste) by the New Order military.

In the aftermath of the May 1998 tragedy, although the Habibie government quickly condemned the attacks and announced the formation of a fact-finding team to investigate, the full extent of the violence and the identity of those responsible remain largely unknown. As will be discussed in chapter 1, despite their efforts, the team failed to bring any perpetrators to justice (Purdey 2006; Himawan et al. 2022). The May 1998 tragedy has thus become yet another issue reaffirming the Indonesian public's lack of trust and confidence in the judicial system. For the many individuals whose lives continue to be affected by Indonesia's unresolved crimes against humanity, the lack of closure and reparations means that the past haunts the present, both figuratively and literally.

In a study of the social and cultural problems surrounding the bodies of victims of the 1965–1966 killings, Adrian Vickers (2010) writes that in Bali—where it is estimated that at least 80,000 people were killed during the anti-Communist purges—sites where killings occurred and where bodies were dumped are considered by the local communities to be haunted (see also Cribb 1990; Robinson 1995; Parker 2003). In Bali, as in many other parts of Indonesia, where the spiritual world is believed to be intrinsically linked to the living world, angry or unsatisfied spirits can bring grave imbalance to the natural order. They cause recurring problems for the living—as manifested in spirit possessions, ghost sightings, sickness and madness among local residents, and episodes of misfortune—that will continue until the spirits are appeased through offerings and ritual purification. It is for this reason that, particularly in the post-Suharto years, when it was permissible to talk about state-sanctioned historical atrocities, many families of the disappeared in Bali decided to purify and appease the souls of the deceased, themselves, and their local communities by performing cremations in the absence of corpses in order to placate the lost spirits of the dead. Whether or not one shares the spiritual beliefs of the Balinese, the point is that, like wandering spirits, memories of unresolved traumatic events will continue to haunt the living unless some form of purification or closure is performed. And in the absence of justice from the state, it is extremely challenging to achieve purification, and trauma will most likely remain in the collective consciousness, shaping present-day identities and social landscapes.

Since memory making is an inherently subjective process, there are many dimensions to post-Suharto memory work among the Chinese. Among the points of analysis explored are how collective memories of ethnic discrimination, trauma, and unbelonging are interpreted and shaped by various social agents at play in post-Suharto Chinese identity politics, including the state, Chinese organizations, institutions, families, and the individuals themselves. Just as important are questions about why some memories are regarded as more significant than others in the processes of constructing identities and boundaries. For instance, how do traumatic memories such as the May 1998 riots shape the daily lives of contemporary Chinese from different backgrounds? How do they perceive their sense of security in the post-Suharto era in light of the country's long history of anti-Chinese discrimination and violence? What strategies have post-Suharto Chinese employed and continue to apply in order to safeguard themselves against the kinds of discrimination experienced in the past?

More particularly, what about the younger generation of Chinese, especially those born in the post-Suharto era? As noted earlier, since this generation has no firsthand memory of the New Order's assimilation policies or the May 1998 riots, their collective memories of anti-Chinese violence rely almost exclusively on stories passed down from previous generations. Do we now have a postmemory generation? According to Marianne Hirsch (1997, 2008), the term "postmemory" describes the relationship that the generation after bears to the personal, collective, and cultural trauma of those who came before. This postmemory generation remembers its collective past only by means of the stories, images, and behaviors that are shared in the communities in which they grew up. How do these postmemory Chinese make sense of their inherited collective memories, and how do they incorporate, reject, or appropriate these memories in their own processes of identity construction?

By focusing on how collective memory and ethnonationalist politics intersect, this book offers a different approach to understanding the lived experiences of Chinese Indonesians. It also contributes to the study of minority identity politics more broadly, as the interrelationship between collective memory and identity construction that is explored here sheds light on some fundamental aspects of everyday racial politics that can be found the world over. The case studies of post-Suharto Chinese provide insights into postassimilation ethnic identity politics. Earlier studies of forced assimilation of minority groups—such as the Armenians in Turkey (Cagaptay 2004); the Ainu in Japan (Howell 2004); Aboriginal and Indigenous peoples in Australia, New Zealand, and Canada (Armitage 1995); and indeed the Chinese in Indonesia (Coppel 1983; Aizawa 2011)—have provided valuable critical analyses of the processes and results of the systematic implementation of these policies. However, less is known about what happens to these affected communities in postassimilation scenarios. How do minority groups adjust after assimilation policies are abolished and they are subsequently allowed to conduct their cultural, religious, and linguistic practices once more? What identities do they assume once they are no longer forced to assimilate? How does the majority national body react when a previously assimilated minority returns to the traditions, cultures, and rituals that in the past were deemed to be politically and socially unwanted or even illegal?

The case studies of post-Suharto Chinese that I discuss in this book show that the answers to these questions are complex. What will become evident is that, despite top-down policy changes implemented from the beginning of the reform era in 1998, Chinese–*pribumi* relations at the everyday level continue to be problematic. Likewise, exclusionary behavior from both Chinese and *pribumi* continues to exist, thus perpetuating long-held beliefs about the supposed essential differences between them. To understand why policy changes have not altered patterns of interethnic interactions at the everyday level, we must examine the ways in which collective memories and intergenerational trauma affect the various group mentalities and boundary-making practices of the Chinese. This could lead to further critical examination about the potential roles of the state and civil society in acknowledging past historical injustices toward ethnic minorities such as Chinese Indonesians and help communities to come to terms with their respective collective traumas and begin (or aid) the process of healing and reconciliation.

MEMORY AND AGENCY IN THE *HABITUS*

Emphasizing the historical and interactional processes that produce ethnoracial social boundaries, my analysis is informed by works of anthropology and social theory that deal with the formation of collective worldviews.

I have found Pierre Bourdieu's concept of the *habitus* to be particularly useful in explaining why and how contemporary Chinese Indonesians engage in exclusionary boundary-making practices. Bourdieu (1990, 53) defines the *habitus* as "systems of durable, transposable dispositions, structured structures predisposed to function as structuring structures, that is, as principles which generate and organize practices and representations that can be objectively adapted to their outcomes without presupposing a conscious aiming at ends or an express mastery of the operations necessary in order to attain them." Simply put, the *habitus* is a framework for explaining the relationship between what social actors do in a given field, and the multiple limits that shape and constrain their actions within that field. Concerned with the diverse and subtle ways in which power and social order are maintained within and across generations, Bourdieu argues that the subjectivity of individuals are products of in-group collective histories. Here, the *habitus,* itself "the product of history, produces individual and collective practices, and hence history, in accordance with the schemes engendered by history" (Bourdieu 1977, 82). Within this structure, individuals learn behaviors as an acquired system of generative schemes that "makes possible the free production of all the thoughts, perceptions and actions inherent in the particular conditions of its production" (Bourdieu 1990, 55).

In much of his writing, Bourdieu describes the *habitus* in terms of inherited dispositions, which manifest as feelings, thoughts, and tastes, among others. Through his concept of dispositions, he essentially seeks to show that these dispositions are socially produced, yet so embedded in human consciousness that they are internalized, unconscious, and largely determine the actions social agents take (see Reed-Danahay 2005). In other words, it is through this system of acquired dispositions that individuals make sense of and deal with the social world. For instance, individual lifestyles, tastes, opinions, and emotions do not occur naturally but are cultivated through inculcation in the family and within social classes, and then reinforced via institutions such as the educational system and the media. Likewise, feelings and prejudices about race, class, and politics, as well as knowledge of one's place in society, are cultivated through interactions within the *habitus.* From birth, individuals are embedded in social relations with other individuals in their *habitus,* and it is from these relationships with others in their *habitus* that they learn the repertoire of permitted actions that is circumscribed by a particular group objective. The *habitus* maintains itself not through mechanical determination but through the subtle mediation of learned orientations and limits.

Bourdieu argues that a person's *habitus* is structured by their position within a social space, which in turn is determined by their sociological characteristics in the form of the amount and the types of economic, cultural, and social capital possessed (Bourdieu 1984, 114; 1998, 6–8). According to Bourdieu (1986), economic capital refers to material resources that can be turned into money, financial assets, or property rights. Meanwhile, cultural capital refers to both nonmaterial goods (such as knowledge types, skills and expertise, educational credentials, and aesthetic preferences acquired through upbringing) as well as material goods, all of which can be converted into forms of economic capital. Social capital refers to networks of contacts that can be used to one's social advantage. Bourdieu argues that in order to safeguard their capital, social actors tend to defend the status quo of the milieu they are in. This helps explain the siege mentality that can be seen among many Chinese Indonesians who prioritize the accumulation and utilization of capital—through practices such as paying security money for their businesses and living in safe gated enclaves—to secure their individual and group safety.

However, there are limits to the *habitus*'s utility in explaining the behavior of individuals within groups. Critics of the concept have long argued that the *habitus* is too deterministic a concept, and that Bourdieu fails to properly account for individual agency and group capacity for social change (DiMaggio 1979; Jenkins 1982; Brubaker 1985; Farnell 2000; Croce 2015). In his critique, Anthony King (2000) argues that, while Bourdieu attempts to account for individual agency by highlighting the ability of individuals to engage in the mutual negotiation of social relations (especially in Bourdieu's theory of practice), at the end of the day, the *habitus*'s emphasis on the internalization of objective social structures means that an individual's capacity or willingness to innovate is limited. Indeed, as King points out, Bourdieu himself argues that individuals demonstrate a love of destiny (*amor fati*), which leads them to live out what they perceive to be an objective social destiny learned and adopted within the *habitus* (Bourdieu 1984, 244). The implication here is that there are inescapable boundaries constraining the choices and reflective attitudes of individual agents, and that all the seemingly conscious decisions that these agents may make have already and always will be in accordance with the *habitus* in what Mariano Croce (2015, 328) calls "a close feedback loop."

In response to his critics, Bourdieu attempts to construct a theory of social change for the *habitus* by developing the notion of the hysteresis effect (Bourdieu 1984, 1990). The hysteresis effect happens when the *habitus* lags behind changes in the objective material conditions that gave rise to it. In other words, the *habitus* can fall behind new trends and modes of thinking, and when this happens, discontent can occur within the *habitus,* causing progressive individuals—Bourdieu calls them virtuosos—within the group to push for change. Here, Bourdieu argues that individuals within groups also have agency in shaping the conditions and extending the boundaries of their *habitus.* Furthermore, Bourdieu discusses the existence of multiple *habitus* among members of the same social and cultural groups and argues that "just as no two individual histories are identical, so no two individual *habitus* are identical, although there are classes of experiences and therefore classes of *habitus*" (Bourdieu 1993, 46).

Yet, even when taking into account the hysteresis effect and the possibility that individuals can inhabit multiple *habitus,* there is still a limit to how much social change progressive individuals can enact within each *habitus.* The hysteresis effect assumes that the *habitus* will eventually catch up with changes to its objective conditions, the hysteresis effect will be resolved, and the *habitus* will continue to reproduce its objective structures. This means that, while the *habitus*'s orientation and shape can alter over time, the *habitus* itself can never truly be changed or even dismantled completely. This framework is monolithic and stifling, and it undermines the struggles and creativities of individual actors who try to unpack the structures and boundaries of their respective *habitus.* Bourdieu's *habitus* does not account either for individuals who act against the supposed objective interests of their group or for common experiences and collaborations that exist between individuals from opposing groups. Bourdieu's *habitus* also overlooks the in-between liminal spaces where individuals engage in what Brenda Farnell (2000, 397) calls "dialogic, signifying acts" to negotiate new forms of identity and rules for social engagement. Given the concept's limitations, while I utilize Bourdieu's *habitus* in explaining why and how post-Suharto Chinese engage in a variety of boundary-making practices, I am also critical of the fact that it is not an adequate model to fully explain the agency and creativity of individuals trying to break free from the constraints of the social structures imposed by society and the state.

This book is not the first to use Bourdieu's concept of the *habitus* to examine various aspects of Chinese Indonesian identity politics. In his studies of Chinese Christian churches (Hoon 2016) and multicultural education in an Indonesian school with a Chinese-majority student body (Hoon 2013), Chang-Yau Hoon uses the *habitus* to explain how institutions such as churches and schools reproduce culture and class. In her study of how ethnic

Chinese politicians and businesspeople in Medan and Surabaya navigate the democratizing political landscape of the post-Suharto era, Chong Wu-Ling (2018) deploys the *habitus* and field as frameworks to examine how the Chinese utilize their capital strategically to protect their businesses and personal interests. In Chong's application of the *habitus,* she also finds the concept to be rigid and thus supplements it with Anthony Giddens's structure-agency theory to make sense of how individuals exercise agency within social structures.

My application of Bourdieu's *habitus* throughout this book serves the purpose of highlighting the importance of collective memories and trauma narratives in the maintenance and reproduction of Chinese Indonesian social environments. However, in my discussions, I also show how, while it is true that Chinese are constrained by various conditions that are both internal and external to their group dynamics, individuals also play a role in carving out spaces for themselves for activism and empowerment.

Indeed, the case studies presented in this book illustrate how Chinese from different walks of life are dynamically pushing the boundaries of sociopolitical activism, cultural production, and self-reflection. I argue that not all of this is done in the interest of self-protection or to maintain the Chinese status quo. In fact, many Chinese engage in activities and life choices that challenge and subvert the status quo of previous generations, such as by engaging in nontraditional career pathways like politics or by choosing to reject the social norms of their in-group social milieu. In addition, I also show examples of the many instances when Chinese and non-Chinese actors collaborate with one another to challenge long-standing hegemonic narratives about ethnicity and belonging in Indonesia. In doing so, they create a new, in-between *habitus* where fresh meanings, practices, and modes of identification may be generated. Throughout the book, I try to do justice to the remarkable agency displayed by some of the Chinese I encountered who try to uncover and expose the ambiguities and contradictions of their respective *habitus.*

STUDYING POST-SUHARTO CHINESE INDONESIANS

This study utilizes an anthropological ethnographic approach to locate the everyday experiences and encounters of post-Suharto Chinese Indonesians. The primary methods used are both structured and semistructured interviews, supported by participant observation (among consenting key informants), events-based analyses, and a number of critiques of social texts comprising media reports, artworks, films, music, archival material, and anecdotal sources. A multiperspective stance is adopted in connection with grounded theory building, in order to present and analyze the different ways in which Chinese conceptualize, express, and perform their ethnic identities.

Since the main focus of this research is on collective memory, much of the data collected from interviews are in the form of individual, family, or community oral narratives about ethnic Chinese history that have been passed from one generation to the next, and intergenerational trauma. Much importance is placed on these oral narratives, even though they are not necessarily historically accurate or corroborated by other evidence. These stories feature quite heavily because they reveal much about how Chinese youth view their personal and family histories and how they perceive their own position in their immediate environment. Indeed, Bourdieu (1999, 511) highlights the importance of personal narratives as data: "Narratives about the most 'personal' difficulties, the apparently most strictly subjective tensions and contradictions, frequently articulate the deepest structures of the social world and their contradictions." While these personal narratives feature prominently, they are always analyzed in the context of other forms of data collected through the mixed methodologies employed in this study.

Most of the fieldwork for this book was conducted in Jakarta over the course of two years, from January 2007 to December 2008, and again for a period of six months, from March to September 2009. I also conducted shorter fieldwork trips in other cities and regions, including Medan, Bandung, Surabaya, Semarang, Pontianak, and towns in the Riau Islands, but as most of the data for this book was collected in Jakarta, data from these other localities is treated as supplementary. In the decade from 2009 to 2019, I repeatedly traveled back to Jakarta to collect updated data and to keep up with new events and processes in both ethnic Chinese and Indonesian politics more generally that I deemed to be relevant, such as documenting the rising anti-Chinese sentiments seen surrounding the political fall of Ahok in 2017. As such, this book offers a long-term perspective of ethnic Chinese politics in the second decade of the post-Suharto *reformasi* era.

Jakarta was chosen as the main site of research because, as Indonesia's capital and main city, it is the center of national-level sociopolitical activities, and the social trendsetter for the rest of country. The city is home to several major Chinese organizations and prominent Chinese figures, including politicians, intellectuals, businesspeople, community leaders, and artists, and is the main site where Chinese identity politics is played out at the national level. Jakarta has the largest population of ethnic Chinese in Indonesia, some 5.53 percent of 10.8 million residents according to the 2020 national census (Badan Pusat Statistik 2021), and since many Chinese living in Jakarta have migrated from various rural areas in Indonesia and different parts of China, Jakarta's Chinese population was deemed the most diverse and representative sample for this study. Importantly, Jakarta was the main site of the May 1998 riots (and the subsequent fall of the New Order) as the last major traumatic anti-Chinese event in recent collective memory.[7] As will be discussed in chapters 1 and 2, the physical and emotional scars from the May 1998 riots and other anti-Chinese events are still found embedded in buildings and spaces all over the city, so I spent a considerable amount of time during fieldwork analyzing how the Chinese inhabit and appropriate these specific spaces of trauma.

Throughout the course of fieldwork, I conducted participant observation and interviews in both private and public domains within which Jakarta-based Chinese perform and express their ethnic and cultural identities. I visited homes and workplaces, attended community meetings and events, followed politicians on campaign trails, and participated in various cultural traditions, such as those performed during Imlek and other Chinese festivals. Since the younger generation is a major focus in this study, I also spent time in the typical institutions and places where these young people pass most of their time, such as schools, universities, sporting facilities, church youth groups, shopping malls, and cafés. I also paid particular attention to sites of interaction between the older and younger generations (for example, the home, schools, and organizational and institutional settings) to gain a broader perspective on how narratives, behaviors, and ways of being Chinese are articulated, maintained, and passed down from one generation to the next within various *habitus*.

During the participant recruitment process, the snowball effect was applied by recruiting participants through a number of key contacts that were made in different communities. In the end, 120 participants were recruited for interviews, comprising mostly Chinese under the age of thirty-five (at the time) as well as their parents, elders, and leaders within the wider community. Non-Chinese participants from different socioeconomic backgrounds were also interviewed in order to obtain different viewpoints of Chinese–*pribumi* dynamics from the other side, so to speak. The opinions and observed behavior of the non-Chinese respondents provided valuable comparative data about how Chinese self-perceptions differ from how non-Chinese view them.

Of the interviewees, only thirty became key informants whose stories ended up being major case studies. While other participants were only interviewed once, these key informants were interviewed at least twice; they were chosen because their lives were thought to be representative of the different Chinese communities in Jakarta. In the end, despite my efforts to maintain a gender balance when selecting participants, there were more male participants than female (around 60 percent being male), particularly from the activist community. This is due to several reasons, mainly to do with the fact that men dominate the field of organized Chinese identity politics. This is true for both the older and the younger generations; the women who are involved in these forms of activism are few and far between. Much of this can be attributed to a common perception in Indonesia that politics and social activism are largely male domains. Despite this imbalance, I am confident that female participants' viewpoints are well represented in the book.

Because of the themes I explore, and particularly because of my interests in politics and the arts, the research gravitated toward middle- and upper-class Chinese. The reality is that in Indonesia, individuals who are involved in political activism, the creative arts, or have the ability to engage in public forms of self-reflection are often well educated and belong to that social class. This demographic is more likely to have both the financial and social capital and access to elite circles in both government and civil society. As such, middle- and upper-class Chinese are visible actors in the publicly performative aspects of post-Suharto identity politics, and influential players and opinion leaders in the shaping of public discourse on Chineseness.

The focus and scope of the book mean that there are some inherent weaknesses that need to be acknowledged. While I had initially intended to include Chinese from less privileged socioeconomic backgrounds as part of my fieldwork sample, I quickly realized that addressing the issue of class differences within Chinese communities would require a level of inquiry beyond the scope of this study. For one, the experiences and perspectives of the Chinese from lower socioeconomic classes are not extensively covered in my discussions of how collective memories influence contemporary life and lifestyle choices. In Jakarta, Chinese from the lower socioeconomic classes for the most part cannot afford to live in the kinds of exclusive residential enclaves or send their children to the expensive private schools that are discussed here. Instead, they tend to live either in the high-density lower-class older areas of North, Central, and West Jakarta, such as in the Kota Tua area of northwestern Jakarta that is locally known as Chinatown (Pecinan) (discussed in chapter 1), or in the inner suburbs of East or West Jakarta, such as Cipinang or

Meruya, where they live alongside non-Chinese neighbors from similar socioeconomic classes. There are also Chinese in Jakarta who live in poverty, such as the well-known community of *cina benteng* (fortress Chinese) in Tangerang who have been subsistence farmers for many generations and who have faced both ethnic and class-based forms of oppression over many centuries, such as land dispossession (Lohanda 1996; Purwanto et al. 2017).[8]

Lacking the level of economic and political capital possessed by wealthier Chinese, these lower-class Chinese were unable to flee Indonesia or pay for protection in times of political turmoil, so their memories and experiences of events like the May 1998 riots are different. There are many accounts of the riots from ethnic Chinese who escaped the attacks only because they were helped by their non-Chinese neighbors. Some of the poorer Chinese that I encountered during my fieldwork expressed anger that the conduct and public image of wealthy Chinese had reflected badly on all ethnic Chinese, including those who were too poor to escape major episodes of violence. They complained that, in times of trouble, wealthy Chinese would think only of themselves, disregarding the plight of the poor. These anecdotes show how class shapes interethnic relations in Indonesia, and how there are also vast class differences among Chinese from various socioeconomic backgrounds. However, while this book does not delve into class diversity among ethnic Chinese, the issue of class is addressed in those sections where I discuss interclass relations as part of boundary-making practices between the Chinese and non-Chinese, and between Chinese from different class *habitus*.

The focus on Chinese in Jakarta also means that the book does not thoroughly examine the broad diversity of local Chinese identities and cultures across the archipelago. I am conscious of the Java-centric nature of many studies of Chinese Indonesians, and it is important to acknowledge here the regional heterogeneity of the different communities. As briefly mentioned earlier, there are Chinese communities (particularly those outside of Java) that were less severely affected by the New Order assimilation policies than others. Because of this, these communities were able to retain their cultural traditions and use of Chinese languages to a greater extent, and they therefore have different collective memories of their local experiences of assimilation. However, I maintain that the centrality of Jakarta in Indonesia's national politics means that the Chinese political agenda that is negotiated and played out in the capital also has impacts on the lives of the Chinese in many other parts of the country. Some of these aspects of regional differences are addressed in the book, particularly in chapter 5, where I examine electoral politics and Chinese political participation.

There are a few themes that could not be exhaustively addressed in this book, primarily gender and religion. Gender in particular has been a very important part of post-Suharto Chinese identity politics, especially considering that activism in the reform era began in no small part as a reaction to the May 1998 riots that included the rape and sexual assault of many Chinese women. In this regard, ethnic violence and trauma for the Chinese have been highly gendered. As such, it is virtually impossible to ignore the gender dimension when speaking about the atrocities of May 1998 (for more on this topic, see Wandita 1998; Purdey 2004; Strassler 2004). Gender has also continued to be a significant divide within Chinese communities, as men and women have different societal expectations, cultural norms, perceived gender roles, and means of organization. While gender and female perspectives are not the focus of the book, they both underlie and inform much of the analysis and discussion in later chapters on urban social spaces, political participation, and the means of creative expression.

Likewise, religion has been and continues to be an important part of Chinese lives and identity politics. For instance, one of the major forms of public recognition of the ethnic Chinese in the post-Suharto era was the problematic recognition of Confucianism as one of the state's six official religions, and the declaration of Imlek as a Confucian religious national holiday. Religion is also an aspect of Chinese lives that has been studied most rigorously in recent scholarship. Of particular note are Juliette Koning and Heidi Dahles's (2009) critical analysis of the rise of Pentecostal-Charismatic Christianity among Chinese; Chang-Yau Hoon's (2011) study of the interrelationships between ethnicity, class, and religion in Chinese Christian schools; and Hew Wai Weng's (2018) book on Chinese Muslim communities. While my own research does not focus on religion, its importance in how identity politics is articulated at the everyday level means that discussions on religion and religiosity are present throughout. For instance, as discussed in chapter 5, one of the main reasons for the perception of essential differences between Chinese and non-Chinese is because the vast majority of the former are not Muslims, making them a minority from both ethnic and religious standpoints.

ORGANIZATION OF THE BOOK

Chapter 1 begins with an examination of the politics of commemoration that surrounds how the May 1998 riots and its Chinese victims are remembered. From annual public memorial events coordinated by Chinese organizations to monuments dedicated to the victims and the abandoned torched buildings around the Glodok area (also known as Pecinan, meaning Chinatown) that serve as silent witnesses of the riots, I argue that reminders of past anti-Chinese violence embedded in these physical structures are central to post-Suharto Chinese identity politics. In the second part of the chapter, I look at new buildings and physical spaces that have been designed to represent Chinese history and culture in the post-Suharto era. Most notable among these is the Chinese Indonesian Cultural Park at the TMII, a Suharto-era extensive national cultural park designed to showcase Indonesia's many ethnic groups and supposed multicultural harmony. I demonstrate how the design of these structures reflects the desire of the Chinese to continue to reinvent their identities, traditions, and public image.

As the first key ethnographic discussion, in chapter 2, I continue to explore the link between collective memory and the construction of ethnic boundaries by examining in more detail how narratives of Chinese victimization are perpetuated in everyday life. I present a case study of Kelapa Gading, an exclusive residential suburb known in Jakarta for its large middle- and upper-class Chinese population. I examine Kelapa Gading closely as an example of a Chinese residential enclave. I follow the lives of one particular family—the Tanumihardjas (a pseudonym)—as an archetypal *totok* family who live sheltered lives, assured of their safety from potential anti-Chinese discrimination or attacks. I closely examine their relationships and interactions with the non-Chinese individuals who they have within their private and semiprivate domains: the domestic servants, drivers, and security guards they employ. I argue that the levels of trust and comfort that middle- and upper-class Chinese attach to the different categories of non-Chinese involved in their lives reflect the intricate politics of racial inclusion and exclusion that exist at the everyday level.

Chapter 3 addresses how Chinese Indonesian identities are shaped through the processes of schooling, language learning, and other educational experiences. In the first part of the chapter, I examine local educational institutions (high schools and universities) as sites where young Chinese learn about Chineseness and become exposed to the ways in which racial segregation between Chinese and non-Chinese occur. In the second half of the chapter, I discuss the case study of Pahoa Integrated School (Sekolah Terpadu Pahoa) as an example of the growing number of Mandarin-medium private schools that have been established in the last ten years. As a school that was relaunched by the alumni of the former Chinese Pahoa School (Sekolah Pahoa) that was shut down by the government in the 1960s, the school represents a new model of post-Suharto Chinese linguistic and cultural education.

Chapter 4 focuses on how a new generation of Chinese filmmakers and contemporary artists portray the topic of collective memory and trauma through their work. I first look at the stories of young filmmakers who, since 1998, have made films about their own personal struggles of growing up as Chinese in Indonesia. I then examine the works of the female contemporary artists Tintin Wulia and Edita Atmaja. By conducting a textual analysis of a selection of their works, I show how their art portrays painful memories of political stigmatization and anti-Chinese racism. I argue that, by drawing on their own personal and collective memories, these artists have shaped a creative space within which they could ask important questions about their own individual identities and place within the Chinese *habitus,* within the Indonesian nation-state, and also in the world more broadly.

In chapter 5, I chart Chinese political participation in the forms of sociocultural organizations (for example, voluntary associations and clan/hometown associations), grassroots political networks, and electoral politics. I discuss the various political and cultural ideologies that motivate different groups and generations of Chinese to participate in sociopolitical activism. In the last part of the chapter, I discuss Chinese politicians who, in the past decade, have risen to the ranks of members of parliament (MPs), regents, governors, and ministers to analyze how their political rhetoric reflects the internal dynamics of both Chinese identity politics and racial politics more generally. In particular, I examine the political career of Ahok, whose meteoric rise and eventual downfall reflect the challenges faced by all aspiring Chinese politicians. I also argue that the use of strong anti-Chinese rhetoric by Ahok's political opponents played a major part in his fall from power, and that this case provides evidence that anti-Chinese sentiments are still alive and well despite more than two decades of reform and Chinese identity politics.

As the final ethnographic chapter in the book, chapter 6 critically examines how the Chinese envision and then strategically place themselves in relation to China. Here, I focus on the Chinese business elites and various organizations that play a bridging role in bilateral relations between China and Indonesia. I discuss how the momentum of post-Suharto identity politics, the rise of China, and the blossoming of Sino-Indonesian diplomatic relations have resulted in Chinese Indonesians placing an increasing importance on building and facilitating trade links both with China and the transnational overseas Chinese *guanxi* network. Given the complex history of the "Chinese problem" in Indonesia, I also examine the inherent suspicions that still persist surrounding the perceived closeness between Chinese Indonesians and China, and what they reveal about the present discourse of Chineseness in Indonesia.

The conclusion summarizes the findings of this study and rearticulates the key arguments put forward in the book. Collective memory and trauma are central to post-Suharto Chinese identity politics, and they will continue to shape Chinese identities and Chinese–*pribumi* relations for the foreseeable future. Nevertheless, I argue that rather than lamenting the persistence of ethnonationalist racial and religious prejudice, scholarly focus should shift toward understanding how ethnic Chinese individuals and groups self-reflect, navigate, and negotiate their identities amid their present-day realities and hopes for the future. To many Chinese Indonesians, this future constitutes a closer relationship with China and the worldwide network of overseas Chinese, especially with China's rise as a regional and global superpower. Yet little is known about the effects and implications of this re-Sinification process, particularly in terms of how closer affiliation with China influences local racial politics. I end the book by advocating for more critical inquiry into the phenomenon of (re-)Sinification and its potential effects in Indonesia and other Chinese communities around the world.

1 The Politics of Remembering

From annual public memorial events prepared by Chinese organizations to monuments specifically dedicated to the May 1998 victims to abandoned torched buildings around the Glodok area that serve as silent witnesses of the violence, reminders of historic anti-Chinese violence are central to post-Suharto Chinese identity politics. Memories of violence and injustice embodied in these public commemorations and physical structures fuel the momentum of Chinese ethnic politics, and the absence of any national apology or due judicial processes for the May 1998 victims only adds a greater significance to these sites of memory.

My exploration of Jakarta's Chinese spaces begins with an examination of how contemporary middle- and upper-class Chinese remember past traumatic incidents. I focus on areas around Glodok and the Kota Tua area (known locally as Jakarta's Chinatown district) in North Jakarta where the majority of the anti-Chinese attacks on individuals, houses, and businesses occurred in May 1998 (see map 2 for the reported sites of the riots). While many of the ransacked buildings have been demolished, renovated, or rebuilt over the past two decades, Chinese Jakartans still associate certain buildings and specific localities with traumatic memories. As a result, these buildings act as unofficial monuments or "sites of memory" (*lieux de mémoire*) that represent the lack of justice and closure for Chinese as collective victims (Nora 1989).

In the second half of the chapter, I look at public structures designed to represent Chinese Indonesian history and culture that have been erected in the post-Suharto era to analyze how these structures reflect a quest on the part of the Chinese to reinvent their identities, traditions, and public image. Most notable among these is the Chinese Indonesian Cultural Park at the TMII, an extensive cultural park built during the Suharto era to showcase Indonesia's many ethnic groups and supposed multicultural harmony.

REMEMBERING, FORGETTING, RECONSTRUCTING

In the aftermath of the May 1998 tragedy and the fall of the New Order the same year, activists, victims' groups, academics, and the media immediately called for the uncovering of events and histories that had been previously suppressed by the regime. Expectations mounted that post-Suharto governments would use their powers—through judicial channels, new legislation, or fact-finding commissions—to expose and examine different parts of the nation's past under public scrutiny as part of a new commitment to transparent democratic practices in the *reformasi* era. And there is indeed a great deal of dark history that needed and still needs to be addressed. At the top of the list are the anti-Communist purges of 1965–1966, the killings and kidnappings of student activists under the New Order, and, of course, the May 1998 riots and the associated anti-Chinese violence. This is not to mention the comprehensive catalogue of extrajudicial killings, illegal detentions, disappearances, political imprisonments, forced removals, suppression of protests, gender violence, censorship, and other injustices that various sections of Indonesian society would still like to see addressed.

The New Order nurtured fear, silence, and self-censorship, and the military-backed monopoly over the production and interpretation of the nation's history and memory clearly served as a key tool in legitimizing the state's control (van Klinken 2005; Zurbuchen 2005a). Normative and ideological spheres were shaped through strict control over textbooks, the media, arts institutes, museums, monuments, public ceremonies, and national symbols. After Suharto was ousted, the pressure to examine what needed to be recalled and revised was intense. Among activists and urban intellectuals, the grassroots drive to fighting forgetfulness or fight forgetting (*melawan lupa*) has been one that continues to this day, both despite and due to the lack of action taken by post-Suharto governments to correct past historical wrongs and injustices.

For the Chinese, the quest for historical truth in the immediate post-Suharto period very much centers on the May 1998 riots. Other instances of anti-Chinese riots, both in living and distant memory, also form part of the discourse on Chinese victimhood and identity politics. However, the May 1998 events are pivotal to post-Suharto Chinese trauma narratives, not only because it is the most recent major episode of violence, but also because the tragedy brought the stark realization that "the assimilation project had indeed failed," as well as a renewed awareness among the Chinese of the inevitability of "their ethnicity and particularly of their vulnerability in Indonesia" (Purdey 2003, 23).

Early in the post-Suharto era, efforts were made by the Habibie government (under local and international pressure) to investigate the truth of what happened during the May 1998 riots and other associated incidents. However, as scholars such as Jemma Purdey (2006) and Eunike Mutiara Himawan et al. (2022) have documented, a government-assigned fact-finding team found it difficult to uncover the truth, due in no small part to the lack of cooperation from state apparatuses such as the police and military.

In an interview, Sandyawan Sumardi, a former Jesuit priest who was a member of the May 1998 fact-finding team, expressed great dismay over the impossible conditions that the team were up against in their investigations:

> Nobody really knows exactly what happened on May 13–15, 1998. . . . What we know is that the riots had to be engineered systematically and that the scale of the events is so massive. . . . The nature of the crimes, particularly those against ethnic Chinese women, made it very difficult for the victims to come forward because they felt immense shame and trauma. . . . What is more is that we [the May 1998 fact-finding team] had a very short period of time to conduct our investigation and we found governmental and military structures to be extremely reluctant to divulge information. . . . So much secrecy by people who of course only want to protect themselves. . . . We did our best to present the facts and catalogue the victims, but the truth remains elusive. (interview, January 10, 2007)

The challenges faced by Sumardi and other members of the fact-finding team reflect how, even in the post-Suharto era, the reform agenda has not translated into greater transparency from the military and the government. The team also encountered significant difficulties in convincing rape victims to come forward to give their testimonies due to a well-founded fear of societal condemnation and retribution. Consequently, the truth of what happened during May 1998 remains largely unknown to this day. Those events have suffered from the same fate shared by so many of Indonesia's violent and traumatic historical episodes, where a lack of closure or justice means the past remains a haunting presence.

Trauma and narratives of victimization are always produced after the event and reproduced in (and through) the processes of representation and commemoration. In the aftermath of the May 1998 riots, the lack of clarity regarding the truth meant that a myriad of interpretations and speculations were rampant in both local and international media. Siew-Min Sai (2006) suggests that the representation, annual commemoration, and general "eventing" of the tragedy in the media and other public domains have cemented its subsequent centrality in post-Suharto Chinese identity politics (see also Lochore 2000). Indeed, immediately after the news of the May 1998 riots and rapes first broke, rumors about what had taken place, alleged eyewitness accounts, gruesome photographs of supposed rape and murder victims, cries for help, and even tips on how to defend oneself in the event of an anti-Chinese attack began circulating on Internet mailing lists and online bulletins boards,[1] in particular among the international ethnic Chinese outside China (*huaren*) network and the World Huaren Federation's website (Heryanto 1999; Lochore 2000; Ang 2001a). These reports and images were quickly picked up by local newspapers and international news outlets, and the ensuing panic that followed did little to calm the nerves of the already confused and anxious Chinese living in and outside the country.

In the absence of verifiable facts, it was these rumors and gruesome images that the Chinese have repeatedly resorted to as proof of their collective suffering, even now, more than two decades after the event. In this regard, it almost does not matter whether rumors are verifiable or not because in a situation where victimhood can be a tool for political and social leverage, rumors can be even more useful than facts. To this end, Sai (2006, 53–54) observes: "Rumour and gossip do not answer questions of 'truth' and 'evidence,' but they do offer satisfying ways of dealing collectively with the May rapes. . . . Rumor and gossip about the May violence are not fundamentally concerned with the search for truth, yet they have influenced the way truth claims are narrated and interpreted." In the post-Suharto era, the ways in which the May 1998 violence, as well as the ambivalence surrounding it, have been interpreted are certainly complex and multifaceted. Nevertheless, they all essentially point toward the reaffirmation and restrengthening of an already existing notion of victimhood that is intrinsically linked to Chinese identities. Sai also argues that how the May 1998 rapes of Chinese women have been "evented" significantly contributes to how Chinese Indonesianness is imagined in the post-Suharto era.

Similarly, in her study of how Chinese Indonesians were represented as victims following the May 1998 riots, Gloria Arlini (2010) aptly argues that public representations of the attacks are also influential in the shaping of trauma narratives. Here, Arlini suggests: "On the contrary, acts of violence alone do not inherently give rise to victimization or cultural trauma. It is what comes *after* the event—the representations, imagination and interpretation of the violence—which give rise to socially constructed meanings that transcend the actual particularities of the act" (5, emphasis in original). Indeed, especially amid the murkiness of known facts, public representations play an important role in how the May 1998 riots have subsequently been remembered. The fact that the events of May 1998 have often been portrayed in the media as anti-Chinese riots, even though the riots were tied to broader political power plays and most of the victims were lower-class *pribumi,* shows how public representations of violent acts could oversimplify what in actuality were deeply complex events (see also Purdey 2002; Jusuf et al. 2007). As such, trauma narratives surrounding the May 1998 riots and other past instances of anti-Chinese violence must be understood as part of broader structures of post-Suharto politics of representation.

Publicly acknowledging the existence of collective trauma is certainly an important part of a group's healing process, and narratives of survival from experiences of victimization can also be potent tools of empowerment for former victims. However, speaking about the use of narratives of victimhood as part of post-Suharto Chinese Indonesian identity politics, Ien Ang (2001b, 22) cautions: "The problem with an unchecked cultivation of victim status, however, is practical: in their binary simplification of the world between good and bad, and in their historical positioning of the subject as a true 'goodie,' they generally fail to grasp the moral, as well as factual, *complexity* of history. Identifying ourselves exclusively as historical victims not only inhibits critical self-reflexivity . . . but also constrains the creation of the conditions of possibility for reaching out, reconciliation, and coexistence, especially with those we feel rightly or wrongly victimized by" (italics in original). Furthermore, discourses of victimhood could easily be manipulated by those in positions of power to further particular political goals. At the everyday level, a sense of perpetual victimhood may also result in an atmosphere of fear in a group's *habitus.* As Ang (23) contends, the danger for the Chinese is that they could be perpetually "trapped in ambivalence" where their subjectivities and meaning making could be articulated only through the discourse of victimhood itself.[2]

Throughout my fieldwork, almost every Chinese family I encountered had at least one story about a past anti-Chinese attack that a member of the close or extended family had reportedly experienced personally. The details and time frames of the stories varied, from accounts of family members who had to evacuate their shops and homes during the May 1998 riots to hushed rumors about the disappearances of politically rogue neighbors and acquaintances during the 1965–1966 anti-Communist purges. In the majority of these stories, the facts provided were murky and unverifiable. However, the truth is almost irrelevant for the processes of remembering.

As I have noted elsewhere (Setijadi 2016b, 825), as of now the exact number of victims of the 1965–1966 anti-Communist purges is still unknown, and the issue of whether the Chinese were deliberately targeted during the acts of violence is still widely debated. Robert Cribb and Charles Coppel (2009) estimate that around half a million people were killed in this period, and that most of the victims were non-Chinese members and associates of the PKI. Furthermore, Cribb and Coppel argue that some of the studies that have been done on the 1965–1966 purges incorrectly identify them as anti-Chinese killings (see, for example, Harff and Gurr 1988; Wang 2000). Other research, such as Jess Melvin's (2013) study of anti-Chinese violence in Aceh in 1965–1966, argues against Cribb and Coppel's assessment, contending instead that while a large proportion of the victims were non-Chinese, a significant amount of the localized violence that happened *did* have an ethnic angle that specifically targeted the Chinese.

While it is very difficult to discern fact from fiction when it comes to these events—and indeed such instances of violence are very often motivated by a combination of different factors—I agree with Cribb and Coppel (2009, 447) in their suggestion that the narrative of the 1965–1966 violence as being anti-Chinese in nature has survived partly because it "inspires a sense of urgency in combating discrimination against the Chinese themselves." Nevertheless, despite what the truth may be, for those who feel affected by the events, the factual correctness of the myths often matters little in the greater scheme of memory making (see also Vickers 2010).

Among my Chinese informants, I found that family and group narratives of the May 1998 riots mostly focus on the Chinese victims of the violence, either ignoring or omitting the fact that many of the victims of the riots were non-Chinese who died while trapped in burning buildings.[3] I do not believe this emphasis on Chinese victims is deliberately intended to forget or belittle non-Chinese victims. In fact, when reminded that a large number of non-Chinese were also casualties of the 1998 riots, the research participants often immediately agreed and corrected themselves. What this reveals to me is that the act of remembering is both selective and strategic. For my informants, emphasizing the victim status of ethnic Chinese in past traumatic events was an important component of their worldview and self-perception.

Particularly in situations where exact historical facts cannot be established, individuals and communities often fill in the gaps themselves or emphasize certain elements to create acceptable (although often contested) narratives that fit their own agendas. After all, history and memory are two very different things. In most cases, there is only one official history while there are many versions of collective and individual memories because memories are not bound by defined narrative boundaries and are continually molded by present experiences. As Pierre Nora (1989, 8) argues, "Memory is life, borne by living societies founded in its name. . . . History, on the other hand, is the reconstruction, always problematic and incomplete, of what is no longer." While it is not always easy to separate personal memories from official histories, in cases such as for the post-Suharto Chinese, when the marginalized or victimized group finally has a chance to contest oppressive official histories, previously suppressed personal memories become very important in the construction of new historical narratives. Here, the processes of recollection are contingent on memories and oral history, particularly in grassroots and unofficial efforts to produce what Nora calls "sites of memory" in the form of texts, events, and sites of commemoration as "there are no longer *milieux de mémoire,* real environments of memory" (7).

However, considering the malleable and fluid nature of memory making, critical questions need to be asked regarding who gets to shape a community's collective memory, which stakeholders stand to benefit from particular constructions of the past, and in what ways they may gain. By focusing on the negotiations involved in the creation of texts and sites of memory, it is possible to begin to decipher how and why certain memories are produced, represented, and disseminated through various channels of remembrance.

LANDSCAPES OF MEMORY

While incidents of anti-Chinese violence and discrimination have not been publicly commemorated or acknowledged via public monuments, it does not mean that such traumatic memories have been forgotten or erased from the everyday lives of ordinary Chinese. On the contrary, both individual and collective memories of trauma are evident in almost all aspects of Chinese lives and are embedded within the built environment, particularly for those who live and work around the areas that were affected by the May 1998 riots.

Walking around the bustling inner-city streets of Jakarta's Mangga Dua shopping and business district one afternoon in May 2008 with Angga, a twenty-eight-year-old IT business owner, and his fiancée, Lia, a twenty-five-year-old owner of a clothes shop, it was easy to forget that the riots had happened on these very same streets just ten years earlier. Angga and Lia took me to the area because Angga wanted to show me his new business space in one of Mangga Dua's shophouses (*rumah toko* or *ruko* for short) just off Jalan Mangga Dua Raya. He was particularly proud of his new office because he had bought it with his own money, without financial help from his parents. Parts of the new office were still under construction, but it looked nice and spacious, and I could see why Angga and Lia were both happy with the purchase. The office was centrally located, and the business would benefit from proximity to other small businesses in the area. Angga showed me around the place excitedly, explaining what he planned for each room and where everything would go. Leading me out the door and into the dusty, hot Jakartan air, Angga showed me the car park, and then he pointed toward the security post just outside the office, saying, "The security guard [*satpam*] post is really near, so I don't have to worry too much about burglars or looters if there are riots [*huru-hara*] like in 1998."

I was struck by the casual matter-of-fact tone of Angga's remark, so I asked him whether the possibility of another riot was a genuine concern for him. Puzzled, Angga looked at me and said, "Of course, it is always a concern for us [Chinese], isn't it? We never know when a riot will happen again, but we all know that it *will* happen." Lia nodded in agreement, adding that among her own community of shop owners inside Mangga Dua mall, the vast majority of whom were Chinese, there was the constant worry of when the next anti-Chinese riot will occur. In hushed tones, she added: "There are those who are jealous of us Chinese who have successful businesses, so they loot and attack us whenever they get the opportunity to do so. It's hard not to be scared of that, especially for a female business owner like me. If my building is attacked by a mob, how will I escape?" Listening to Angga's and Lia's comments as we gazed out on the perpetually busy Mangga Dua commercial strip clogged with traffic, I realized that, even amid this sense of normalcy, the Chinese who live, work, and pass through this area will never forget the 1998 riots. In fact, it is virtually impossible to forget.

On May 13, 1998, the commercial districts of Roxy—located less than two kilometers from the Trisakti University (Universitas Trisakti) campus where the student protests and subsequent shooting by the army had taken place the previous day—and Glodok were two of the first areas targeted by looters and rioters (see map 2). Shopping centers like Roxy Mas (now ITC Roxy Mas) in West Jakarta were known to house many Chinese-owned electronics stores, and Plaza Orion, Harco Glodok (now TM Harco Glodok), and Glodok Plaza were all located within a few hundred meters of each other in the Kota district in northwestern Jakarta, making them obvious targets for those who intended to specifically attack Chinese-owned businesses. On the way from Roxy to Glodok on Jalan K. H. Hasyim Ashari, Jalan Gajah Mada, and Jalan Hayam Wuruk, abandoned shops had the words "*milik pribumi*" (*pribumi*-owned) hastily painted on their shutters in a vain attempt to convince would-be looters that the shops did not belong to Chinese. Glodok was looted and burned within hours, and both Chinese and non-Chinese eyewitnesses all said the same thing—that the police and the military did nothing to stop the violence (for more recent eyewitness reflections of the May 1998 riots in Glodok, see Lamb 2016; Lestari 2018; Wargadiredja 2018).

While Glodok was burning, the nearby shopping district of Mangga Dua was looted but not burned. According to the Chinese shop owners I met, what made the difference was that, seeing how Glodok was burning, Mangga Dua shop owners paid extra security money to the police and security forces to prevent rioters from setting the buildings alight. The shop owners I spoke to were sketchy on the details of how much money was paid, who did the paying, to whom the money was paid, or even whether such payments ever happened at all. However, the lesson to be had was clear: in anti-Chinese attacks, the state's security apparatus could not be relied upon to protect the Chinese unless they were bribed. It must be noted that the areas around Glodok and Mangga Dua were and are still home to middle- and lower-class Chinese merchants, many of whom live above their shops. Unlike their wealthier counterparts, who lived in secure residential enclaves such as Pantai Indah Kapuk or Kelapa Gading (see chapter 2), these Chinese could neither afford the high payments of security money, nor did they have the military connections to ensure protection, and they also could not escape overseas when the violence happened. Many had no choice but to return to the sites of trauma that were their homes and businesses immediately after the violence ended. To protect themselves against future attacks, many lower-income families did the only thing they could afford to do at the time, which was to install metal bars on all doors, windows, and balconies, literally imprisoning themselves inside their own homes and businesses. The optics are jarring and serve as a constant reminder of the need to protect the ethnic Chinese body, even if it means erecting physical barriers that disconnect and separate them from the neighborhood they have lived in all their lives (figure 1.1).

FIGURE 1.1 A row of shophouses (*ruko*) with metal bars on the windows, entrances, and balconies along Jalan Pintu Besar Selatan near Glodok, Jakarta, 2016.

Source: Photograph by Rony Zakaria. Reproduced with permission.

While it is true that there are no monuments or buildings in any of these sites that were specifically constructed to commemorate and acknowledge the anti-Chinese violence, the lack of official commemoration does not mean that past atrocities are forgotten. On the contrary, the absence of monuments may in fact strengthen the community's resolve not to forget one of its most painful memories. As Abidin Kusno (2010) suggests, much of the existing historical and cultural studies scholarship on commemorations emphasizes how events are officially remembered and represented. Not enough attention, however, is paid to how alternative and unofficial sites of commemoration may be just as powerful in invoking collective memory. Here, Kusno (104; emphasis in original) argues, "By focusing on the fact of commemoration, the studies in question rarely look at objects that were *not* built for a commemorative purpose but which are equally significant in registering, as well as forgetting, memories of past events. The everyday built environment, like moments constructed for commemoration, enacts the dynamics of memory and forgetting, but operates often without demanding a state of spectatorial concentration to gain effect." In the absence of official monuments, seemingly ordinary aspects of the built environment, such as buildings and landmarks located where the riots took place, have become unofficial sites of remembrance for the Chinese, no matter where in Jakarta they live. These sites stand as everyday reminders of the violence, injustice, and lack of meaningful acknowledgment endured by the Chinese, and their ever-insecure position in Indonesian society.

Within weeks of the May 1998 riots, President Habibie and his administration began plans to rebuild the ransacked Glodok district to restore it to its former commercial glory. Rebuilding began relatively quickly, most significantly with the construction of the new Glodok Plaza mall in early 2000, built on the ruins of the burned and looted mall. As Kusno (106) points out, the building of the new Glodok Plaza, along with other reconstructed buildings around the area, was done in "a manner that intimates the dynamics of remembering and forgetting after the May riots." The former buildings were quickly razed, and the new architectural designs incorporated features that were meant to symbolize the transition from a dark and sad past into a bright and hopeful future. For instance, Kusno (108) observes that the concept behind the new Glodok Plaza is one in which "the electronic and computer age of the new millennium" is celebrated and the focus is on the future and not the past.

There is no mention of the plaza's dark past or the reason for rebuilding, and no acknowledgment of what the building used to look like. This is in contrast with examples from around the world where commemoration plaques and memorials have been erected—by governments, developers, or nongovernmental organizations (NGOs)—at sites that have been rebuilt following destruction caused by war, genocide, or terror attacks. Perhaps the most famous example of this is the World Trade Center site (often referred to as Ground Zero) that is now the location of the new One World Trade Center and the National September 11 Memorial and Museum commemorating the victims of the 9/11 attacks. An example from Southeast Asia is the rebuilt MacDonald House in Singapore that was the site of an Indonesian bombing attack in 1965, at the height of the Indonesia-Malaysia confrontation (Konfrontasi). On the fiftieth anniversary of the attack a memorial was dedicated to the civilian and military victims of the bombing and Konfrontasi. MacDonald House was also gazetted as a national monument.

Obviously, the designers and management of the new Glodok Plaza wanted to project a welcoming aura, emphasized by large glass doors, windows, spacious design, bright lights, flat-screen television displays, and the new tenants themselves. In what Kusno (108) terms "imagery of the present and the future," traces of the old are hidden under all the new developments and products, although literally and symbolically the foundations of the old building still support the new one. However, to this day, ordinary Chinese like Angga and Lia who live and work in the area still remember what Glodok Plaza signifies. The same can be said of other buildings and locales of similar history that are scattered around Jakarta.

Throughout the city, rebuilt, abandoned, and demolished buildings serve as constant reminders of past traumatic events. Glodok Bazaar (Pasar Glodok) near Glodok Plaza; Supermal Lippo Karawaci in Karawaci, an outer western suburb just outside Jakarta (administratively part of Banten); Yogya Plaza (also known as Mal Klender) in East Jakarta; and Apartemen Mitra Bahari in Pluit in North Jakarta (where many of the rapes and sexual assaults of Chinese women are alleged to have happened) are some of the other ransacked buildings that were rebuilt and reopened without any acknowledgment of the hundreds of lives that were lost and affected at these sites (see also Kusno 2003). Perhaps most bizarrely, the Jakarta provincial government has since designated Glodok and Mangga Dua as a Chinatown area for tourism purposes, complete with newly built Chinese gates, welcome signs (in Chinese and Indonesian), and new buildings with architectural styles that celebrate both Mainland Chinese and colonial *peranakan* styles. This simultaneous act of celebration and depoliticization of Indonesian Chinese history seems contradictory, although it does represent some of the more superficial efforts implemented by post-Suharto governments to recognize Chinese identities.

There are a few obvious winners in efforts to rebuild the Glodok area, chiefly the national and Jakarta provincial governments who benefited from the public relations exercise of encouraging pluralism, rebuilding an area of significant national trauma, and absolving themselves from responsibility for the May 1998 riots. From an economic standpoint, property developers benefited from the new building constructions, and local business owners could potentially profit from the influx of tourism from Glodok's new official exoticization as a Chinatown tourist district. However, for the many Chinese who still live inside shophouses with barred windows in Glodok, having never received any compensation for their material losses and emotional scars, the rebuilding and rebranding of their area did very little to soothe their pain. These minor acts of recognition from the government are seen as opportunistic and insincere.

Nevertheless, whether officially acknowledged or not, the histories represented in landmarks around Glodok have become constant physical reminders of the ever-present possibility of anti-Chinese violence. Most young Chinese who have grown up in the post-Suharto era have never directly experienced acts of anti-Chinese violence. But, as Angga and Lia mentioned, physical reminders of past violence justify a heightened sense of alertness and constant vigilance. For Melly, a twenty-six-year-old interior designer from Pluit, the fear of another anti-Chinese attack meant she stuck to Chinese areas that she considered safe and avoided certain other areas, particularly at night:

> Our family lives in Pluit, so we're quite close to the sites where the rapes of Chinese girls happened in 1998. Sometimes when we go out, my mother will point out the apartment buildings and shophouses where it is said that the girls were raped and killed. . . . It is scary to think that horrible things like that could happen to people just like me. . . . I think that especially [Chinese] girls need to be smart about where they go, especially at night and definitely not on their own. I usually either go with friends or with my driver, and I tend to stick to areas that I know, around Central and near here in North Jakarta.

Ironically, the areas in Central and North Jakarta that Melly identified as being safe and familiar are some of the very spaces where the May 1998 riots took place. Yet these are the spaces that Melly and those in her *habitus* understood best, and to them knowing the terrain and potential risks of an area meant that they felt they knew what to expect and how to defend themselves within it.

Narratives about safety and caution expressed by young people such as Angga, Lia, and Melly highlight two important points about the dynamics of memory work among the Chinese: first, that trauma narratives are maintained through oral histories that are passed down and circulate within families and social milieus; and second, that self-preservation discourses lead to the perception that enclaves can safeguard the ethnic Chinese from future anti-Chinese attacks and other forms of criminality. This kind of intergenerational siege mentality is born out of long-standing trauma, and throughout the book we will see examples of how this conservatism manifests itself both in everyday behavior and decision making, and in contestations about narratives of Chinese identity politics at the national level.

COMMEMORATIONS AND (LACK OF) MONUMENTS

In the post-Suharto era, public commemorations of anti-Chinese violence are almost nonexistent. In the few years immediately after the May

1998 riots, efforts were made by various NGOs, Chinese organizations, and victims' groups, most notably by Solidarity for the Motherland and Nation (Solidaritas Nusa Bangsa, SNB), to erect various monuments to commemorate and honor both the Chinese and non-Chinese victims of the May 1998 riots. However, in the absence of justice and any official state acknowledgment of the incidents, these attempts have largely been small-scale, underfunded, and little known to the general public. One notable exception is the Tragedy of 12 May Monument (Monumen Tragedi 12 Mei) at Trisakti University in West Jakarta, at the site where four Trisakti students (one of whom was an ethnic Chinese named Hendriawan Sie) were shot and killed by the military during the student protest widely acknowledged as the beginning of the May 1998 riots and the large-scale protests that signaled the end of the New Order. Every year on May 12, Trisakti University holds a public ceremony to commemorate the shootings at the monument.

Other victims' groups have not had as much success in their efforts. For instance, mainly due to a lack of resources and support, SNB has failed in its attempts to secure its three desired outcomes for the victims of the May 1998 riots: first, due judicial processes for the lower-class (mainly non-Chinese) victims; second, an official acknowledgment from the government of the atrocities committed during the riots; and third, the construction of a house of commemoration for the victims. As part of their efforts to educate the public about the events of May 1998 and other cases of human rights violations in the country, SNB also supported other victims' groups and held multicultural and humanitarian educational workshops for youths. The founder and chairperson of SNB, lawyer Ester Indahyani Jusuf (an ethnic Chinese), who was just twenty-seven years old at the time of the May 1998 riots, cowrote a book titled *Kerusuhan Mei 1998: Fakta, Data, dan Analisa: Mengungkap Kerusuhan Mei 1998 Sebagai Kejahatan Terhadap Kemanusiaan* (May 1998 Riots: Facts, Data, and Analysis: Exposing the May 1998 Riots as Crimes against Humanity) to try to expose the truths behind May 1998 (Jusuf et al. 2007). While the organization now appears to be defunct, SNB was a good example of a multiethnic organization that tried to bridge the gap between Chinese and *pribumi,* and treated the riots (and the associated violence) as state-sponsored human rights violations that mostly affected the poor from different ethnic communities. Although Jusuf is ethnic Chinese, she openly challenged the narrative that the May 1998 riots affected only Chinese, and she urged both Chinese and non-Chinese to look beyond the ethnic divide to examine more closely various state agencies' roles in inciting and escalating the violence.[4]

Chinese organizations have not fared much better. In the aftermath of the riots, a number of proposals for a commemorative monument were put forward to the Habibie, Abdurrahman Wahid, and Megawati Sukarnoputri governments, predominantly from Chinese sociopolitical organizations and lobby groups. Of these proposals, the one monument that was eventually agreed upon was the Brotherhood Monument (Monumen Persaudaraan) that would feature a "statue of two men (one ethnic Chinese) holding aloft the national symbol of the Garuda eagle" (Zurbuchen 2005b, 30). The design was championed by the now defunct PARTI, and the statue was to be designed and sculpted by the Balinese artist Nyoman Nuarta, famous for his Garuda Wisnu Kencana statue in Jimbaran, Bali. After negotiations on where the monument should be erected (the initial proposed site of the gardens in front of Jakarta Kota station in North Jakarta was rejected by the city council, citing spatial issues), it was finally agreed that it should be built on a garden strip in front of the protected Candra Naya heritage building (once home to the colonial-era Chinese *Majoor* Khouw Kim An) in Glodok, North Jakarta, near buildings that were burned down during the May 1998 riots.

On May 13, 2004, Megawati attended the half-built monument's dedication ceremony (Unidjaja and Aurora 2004). However, despite the initial public interest in the project, by the time I conducted my first fieldwork trip in 2007, I could no longer find the monument at the site where it was supposed to be located. After asking around, I discovered that the project had stalled (perhaps along with the breakup of PARTI, who had lobbied for it) and the monument seemed to have been forgotten. This is a sad end for a monument project that was intended to prevent the public from forgetting past anti-Chinese atrocities. Perhaps this ending is also symbolic of post-Suharto governments' and the general public's commitments to civil society and political reform, where, after an initial period of feel-good enthusiasm, interest in these projects waned before they were eventually abandoned and forgotten.

Writing about plans to erect monuments to commemorate and honor the victims of violence such as the May 1998 riots, Mary Zurbuchen (2005b, 30) notes that such building attempts are a "'sad detachment' from the reality that no one has yet been held accountable" and none of the victims have ever received justice (see also Hoon 2006b). Thus any resulting monument may serve only to remind the public of the gross injustices that happened. But for a country like Indonesia, with a long history of injustice, impunity, state-sponsored terrorism, and historical amnesia, the erection of any monument for victims would already be a big step forward. It needs to be remembered that, with the exception of the New Order's Sacred Pancasila (Pancasila Sakti) monument commemorating the six military generals and personnel murdered by alleged Communist radicals during the G30S/PKI coup, no other large-scale national monument has been dedicated to the victims of any form of mass violence. The victims of the anti-Communist purges of 1965–1966 remain unacknowledged, just like those who were victims of the Malari demonstrations and riots in 1974, the Tanjung Priok massacre in 1984, or the many disappearances that happened throughout the New Order. Within this historical context, a monument for the May 1998 victims would be a significant form of acknowledgment and public remembrance, regardless of the brute fact of continuing injustices.

This situation is comparable with many other cases around the world in which dark historical events that shook both state and society to the core have remained (officially) unacknowledged. In Asia alone, one need think only of the 1989 Tiananmen Square protests and massacres (known in China as the June Fourth incident), or the May 13, 1969 Chinese–Malay race riots in Kuala Lumpur, Malaysia. While both incidents resulted in political action in the forms of arrests, leadership changes, and sweeping policy reforms (for example, the New Economic Policy affirmative action policy in Malaysia), the politically sensitive nature of the incidents has meant that no monuments or other significant forms of public acknowledgment have ever been erected at the sites to commemorate either the incidents themselves or the victims. Grassroots efforts by lobby groups or victims' associations to memorialize the events have been repeatedly quashed by the respective states out of fear that public commemorations may draw (more) unwanted attention to the events, or that community-led commemorations may contradict the states' official narratives. For the sake of national unity, the avoidance of national shame, or for the protection of political elites implicated in the events, these incidents have been relegated to mere footnotes in these nations' histories, with the victims often unable to get closure for their grief.

The closest thing to a monument of remembrance for the victims (both Chinese and non-Chinese) of the May 1998 riots is the May 1998 Monument (Monumen Mei 1998) at Pondok Ranggon Public Cemetery (Taman Pemakaman Umum Pondok Ranggon) in East Jakarta where many of the unnamed victims of the tragedy are buried (figure 1.2). Designed by ethnic Batak sculptor Awan Simatupang, and unveiled in 2015 after a long campaign by the National Commission on Violence Against Women (Komisi Nasional Anti Kekerasan Terhadap Perempuan, Komnas Perempuan) and other victims' groups for its establishment, the imposing, dark concrete structure depicts a large hand with an open palm covered by an overhanging shroud. On the shroud is a long needle with red thread stitching a rip in the fabric. At the monument's base is a black marble slab with a short explanation of the May 1998 riots etched in gold. The inscription (written in Indonesian) reads:

> MAY 1998 MONUMENT
> The May 1998 tragedy is a dark moment in the history of the Indonesian nation, where, because of violence, thousands of lives were lost, and sexual violence occurred toward female victims. This tragedy culminated from social, economic, and political upheavals that gave birth to the era of Reform. The May 1998 monument, with the symbolism of a thread and needle that stitches the wound and hope, is a memorialization of our nation's history, a sign of respect toward the victims, and a lesson so that an incident like this may never happen again.

Standing on a two-hundred-square-meter site, the monument towers above the 113 graves of the unidentified victims of the May 1998 riots located opposite it (see Dirgantoro 2021 for a detailed analysis of the monument's designs and symbolisms). The inscription at the base reflects how the monument was intended to be a gesture of public recognition toward the victims.

At the ceremony of laying the monument's foundation stone on May 18, 2014, then Jakarta vice-governor Ahok said that the building of the monument needed to continue not "out of a sense of revenge toward the perpetrators, but as a mark so something like this does not happen again" (cited in Romadoni 2014). In his speech, Ahok also emphasized that he and other politicians owed a debt of gratitude to the victims and their families, arguing that had the riots not happened, there would not have been the *reformasi* era nor would he as a Chinese have been able to be elected vice-governor. It needs to be remembered, however, that while the monument was cosponsored by the Jakarta provincial government, it is far from an official state acknowledgment of the tragedy at the national level. But it is at least a sign that the May 1998 tragedy has not been forgotten by the general public, and that its commemoration is supported by some levels of government, especially by reform-minded politicians.

Every year on the anniversary of the May 1998 riots, small-scale remembrance ceremonies are still held at the May 1998 Monument, at university campuses where student activists died, and at various NGOs, usually organized by victims' groups. Some Chinese organizations still hold small

FIGURE 1.2 The May 1998 Monument (Monumen Mei 1998) at Pondok Ranggon Public Cemetery, East Jakarta, with a description at its base, 2018.

Source: Photograph by Dr. Wulan Dirgantoro, University of Melbourne. Reproduced with permission.

remembrance ceremonies, but the majority—including INTI and PSMTI—have moved on and concentrated their efforts on other forms of public recognition for the ethnic Chinese. Some of these other forms of recognition that were being proposed at the time of writing include museums, cultural centers, and cultural parks. I view this decision by Chinese organizations to move away from demands for May 1998 commemorations and due judicial process to be motivated by a conservatism that is born out of a fear of provoking the state and the non-Chinese public. As one elder of a Chinese organization told me, large organizations like INTI and PSMTI must be diplomatic, and the Chinese in general must avoid being seen as if they are demanding too much. Instead, in the absence of official sites of acknowledgment and remembrance for past violence, Chinese organizations have had to settle for other forms of government and public recognition, some of which have generated their own controversy among Chinese communities and the general public.

THE CHINESE INDONESIAN CULTURAL PARK: A CONTESTED MUSEUM

An example of the controversy that surrounds how Chinese Indonesian history and culture should be represented can be seen in the Chinese Indonesian Cultural Park, an open-air museum located inside the TMII. Conceptualized by members of PSMTI very soon after the organization's establishment in 1998, the Cultural Park was envisioned as a center showcasing various elements of Chinese culture and heritage. While the idea of a museum or cultural park dedicated to a particular ethnic group is certainly not a novel one (think of the China Ethnic Museum in Beijing or various ethnology museums around the world), the Cultural Park is unique and significant not only because of the political circumstances behind its development but also because of its inclusion in the TMII.

As scholars have noted, the TMII was an important part of the New Order's cultural policy and ideology (Pemberton 1994; Hitchcock 1998; Schlehe 2011). The idea was initially put forward by Suharto's wife Siti Hartinah (Ibu Tien Soeharto) in 1971 allegedly after a visit to Disneyland (Pemberton 1994, 241). The TMII was intended to be an all-in-one cultural park, open-air museum, and entertainment complex that showcased all of Indonesia's major ethnic groups. Indonesia's postindependence cultural policy was, and still is, based on the motto "Unity in diversity" (*Bhinneka tunggal ika*), and the park perfectly illustrates the New Order's hegemonic cultural ideology and national narrative and is a microcosm of the New Order's vision of the orderly management of the country's ethnic, cultural, and religious diversity. State, culture, and society were viewed as inseparable, and society was envisioned as a collective organic unity bound by an ethnonationalist belonging to the idealized space of the Nusantara (a mythical united Indonesian archipelago). Aimed at strengthening national unity while also providing recreation, education, and information, the park primarily targets domestic visitors, as it is an affordable spot for the majority of people; it is still popular among domestic tourists (particularly those from lower socioeconomic classes), as well as a common destination for compulsory school field trips.

The TMII was not meant to be a profit-making venture. Built on 150 hectares in East Jakarta, its design featured miniatures of Indonesia's ancient monuments such as Borobudur in Central Java, representative religious buildings of Indonesia's then five state-approved religions (now six), recreational attractions such as a train system and amusement rides, museums (one of them dedicated to the country's oil and gas industry), an IMAX movie theater in the shape of a golden snail shell (a later addition built in 1984, the design inspired by a popular Hindu Javanese folktale), and a big outdoor performance arena, among other facilities. As John Pemberton (1994) notes, the park's centerpiece is an 8.4-hectare man-made lake with little islands representing the Indonesian archipelago that visitors can survey from the air in a cable car. Furthermore, "of particular importance are the twenty-six display houses representing the 'genuine customary architectural styles' of each of Indonesia's provinces" (241). In keeping with the creation of new provinces that resulted from decentralization in the post-Suharto era, seven more pavilions have been built to represent Indonesia's now thirty-four provinces (at the time of writing, the province of North Kalimantan did not yet have a pavilion). While the government controls the general concept and management of the park, the provinces are responsible for the design and curation of their individual pavilions (*anjungan*). Guides are available at the pavilions to provide explanations to visitors on the culture, traditions, and resources of each of the provinces. Ethnic culture (*kebudayaan*) in this context refers to houses, clothing, ornamentation, folklore, music, songs, dances, and theater performances.

This practice of staging culture and ethnicity as appearance can of course be traced back further than the New Order regime, as it was also part of the colonial legacy and classificatory system: the mapping and standardization of communities following traditional or customary law (*adat*), with each community supposedly rooted to discrete territories and each with its own defined cultural norms. By the same logic, ethnic groups and cultures represented in such official classifications are thus acknowledged as possessing legitimate claims of belonging to the land and the Indonesian nation.

From the time the TMII was built until the end of the New Order, the Chinese were never included as one of the ethnic groups represented at the pavilions. While other non-*pribumi* ethnic groups such as Arabs and Indians were also not provided with an exhibition space, not being included in the park was a sore point for many Chinese, as they saw themselves as having made important contributions to different aspects of Indonesian history and society. My informants from Chinese organizations such as PSMTI also argued that the Chinese were a large enough ethnic group to warrant a pavilion at the TMII, especially compared to ethnic groups with smaller numbers, such as the Makassarese of South Sulawesi and the Sasak people of West Nusa Tenggara, both of whom are represented at their respective provincial pavilions. It is no wonder then that one of the first demands made by PSMTI was the inclusion of Chinese at the park. Teddy Jusuf (Deyi Xiong, 熊德怡), then chairman of PSMTI and a retired brigadier general of the National Armed Forces (Tentara Nasional Indonesia), explained the motivation behind the organization's efforts to develop an exhibition space: "Having a Chinese Indonesian exhibition space at the TMII is an important recognition for Chinese Indonesians. We were denied a place in Indonesian society throughout the New Order and faced discrimination, and our absence from the TMII was a symbol of that. . . . Now we have our own space at the TMII, so people can see that we are a legitimate part of Indonesia. We want people to understand that we are also a native tribe of Indonesia" (interview, August 15, 2008). Following a 4.5-hectare land donation in 2004 from Our Hope Foundation (Yayasan Harapan Kita), set up by Ibu Tien Soeharto to administer the TMII, building of the Chinese Indonesian Cultural Park began in earnest using money collected from private Chinese donors.[5] From the beginning, the design and construction of the Cultural Park was a controversial and continuous process of negotiation. For one thing, the land donation was seen by some as overt preferential treatment toward the Chinese as the government's way to appease them after the May 1998 violence, in particular via institutions connected to the Suharto regime (*Kompas* 2010). The land for this project is also much larger than the usual one hectare that was given to each of the provincial pavilions. It should be noted that none of the other victims' groups that suffered under the Suharto regime received any compensation, let alone public spaces for commemoration.

The Cultural Park was also criticized by Chinese and non-Chinese alike for being built within the TMII, essentially conforming and adhering to the New Order's system of ethnic and racial classification. Many Chinese are of the opinion that PSMTI's push to have the Chinese recognized as a native tribe is a step in the wrong direction, precisely because it conforms to the very assimilationist discourse Chinese should be fighting. On this, Yumi Kitamura (2007) writes, "If we take into consideration the significance of Taman Mini in the national cultural policy and its impact to the Indonesian public, it is clear that the selection of Taman Mini as a venue for the Chinese Indonesian Cultural Park is for Chinese Indonesians to be recognized as one ethnicity by the state and accepted by the Indonesian people. . . . PSMTI believes that creating a museum within Taman Mini ensures a place for Chinese Indonesian ethnicity in the Indonesian nation." Clearly the push for the TMII as the location of the Cultural Park was a symbolic choice, and one that the elders of PSMTI and the project donors hoped would give the

Chinese the space and belonging they deserved in the state-sanctioned exhibition space for "nativeness." Even Suharto himself visited the park in 2005 for a thanksgiving (*syukuran*) ceremony to mark the start of the building process in an event that was widely publicized by PSMTI (ibid.). Ironically, the Chinese were now finally "assimilated" into the New Order's idea of nativism.

More than anything else, the biggest controversy regarding the Cultural Park has been about its design. At the time of writing, not all of the buildings planned for the Cultural Park have been constructed, but after looking at the plans, drawings, and the few buildings that have been built, its design seems to be very much inspired by Mainland China (figure 1.3). From these plans, the proposed completed park includes a seven-story octagonal pagoda, a replica of Beijing's Forbidden City, an enormous gate made from materials imported from China and inscribed with Chinese calligraphy, a Chinese junk (modeled on one of Admiral Zheng He's ships from the Ming dynasty armada), a replica of the Candra Naya building, an imitation of a typical Jakarta Chinatown house and market, and a replica of a Fujian Hakka

FIGURE 1.3 The illustrated master plan of the completed Chinese Indonesian Cultural Park at Taman Mini Indonesia Indah.

Source: Image courtesy of PSMTI. Reproduced with permission.

earthen-walled village (*tulou*). As Kitamura (2007) points out, the park's nod toward China is evident even from the entrance gates, which were "modeled after the gates of the Western Qin Tomb and Eastern Qing Tomb which represent the Qing dynasty."

Considering Indonesia's history of anti-China sentiments and accusations of Chinese Indonesians as being China's fifth column, the inclusion of a replica of the Forbidden City in particular has predictably caused outrage among Chinese Indonesians who see such blatant association between Beijing and them as politically dangerous. The connection with China is made more obvious in the design of the gate that was based on the gates of the Western and Eastern Qing tombs, and the replica of Zheng He's ship. Carvings, ornaments, and Chinese calligraphy that adorn the pillars and walls of the buildings also add to the Mainland Chinese feel of the Cultural Park; notably missing (at least at the time of writing) from representation are *peranakan* buildings, paraphernalia, and any general *peranakan* cultural presence as well as any reference to Indonesia's history of anti-Chinese violence.

The original blueprint of the Cultural Park was designed by a team from the Department of Architecture at Parahyangan Catholic University (Universitas Katolik Parahyangan) on commission from PSMTI and based on design suggestions from their members and the general public. Ultimately, PSMTI elders and the project's main donors decided to reject the initial designs and instead commissioned the Xiamen-based company Xiamen City Planning Group to revamp the original plans in December 2005 (Kitamura 2007). News reports suggest that the decision to go with a PRC design agency (apparently with direct input from the mayor of Xiamen) rather than a renowned local university had to do with differences in aesthetic preferences and complaints from the TMII management that the original design plan from the Parahyangan Catholic University team was too old-fashioned or outdated (Putri 2015).[6] It is still unclear exactly which elements of the design were deemed to be old-fashioned, or why the TMII management was so influential in determining the final design.[7] However, the symbolism and irony of commissioning an agency from China to design the first large public display of Chinese Indonesian culture in the post-Suharto era were not lost on both Chinese and non-Chinese critics. Among the Chinese I spoke to about the matter, there was even speculation that the Xiamen-based design agency was ultimately chosen because the project had received funding from China and the Fujian provincial government. While this speculation was strongly denied by the PSMTI elders I spoke to, the existence of such rumors revealed a sense of discontent and wariness over the park's cultural (and ostensibly political) orientation toward China.

Defending their final design and aesthetic choices, PSMTI elders gave various justifications to explain that the park was not intended to showcase a cultural orientation toward China. Rather, the designs were supposed to be symbolic of Chinese Indonesians' ancestral connections with China, while at the same time also symbolizing their rootedness in Indonesia. For instance, the decision to have a replica of the Forbidden City at the center of the Cultural Park was because PSMTI leaders thought that the Forbidden City was an instantly recognizable symbol of global Chineseness. In the same way, the replica of the Forbidden City was meant to represent the heart of the Cultural Park (Kitamura 2007). Likewise, as Kitamura (2007) also notes, the PSMTI elders told me that the five roofs of the gate actually symbolize the five ideological state principles of Pancasila.

Regardless of the PSMTI elders' justification for the park's design, many Chinese criticize it strongly for being unrepresentative of the heterogeneity of Chinese Indonesians. Of particular concern is the lack of *peranakan* culture or architecture on display in the Cultural Park. Sugi, a *peranakan* who is active in INTI and other charitable organizations, complained that the Cultural Park is a representation of only one version of Indonesian Chineseness: "If you look at the plans for the park, you'll think to yourself, 'This is a replica of Beijing!' Very little of the park represents the average Chinese [Indonesian], particularly the *peranakan*. There is almost nothing in the park that represents *peranakan* culture, which is odd, because our *peranakan* culture is unique to Chinese in Indonesia and should be something to be proud of.... *Peranakan* Chinese Indonesians like me would look at this park and would not be able to relate to anything of it." I found that Sugi's concern was shared by other Chinese (both activists and the general public) who felt that the Cultural Park represented the vision of only a handful of China-oriented, elderly PSMTI leaders who possessed the economic, social, and political capital to determine how Chinese Indonesian culture was to be represented publicly. This discontent reflects the kinds of ruptures that can happen in the Chinese Indonesian political *habitus,* where groups with differing opinions (and levels of capital) engage in contestations about the agenda, orientations, and boundaries of the *habitus.*

As Eric Hobsbawm (1983) argues, in the field of ethnic identity politics, what often happens is that although all group identities are highly contested and diverse, certain power holders within the community (usually prominent members/elders) can represent a reduced and essentialized identity by appropriating or reinventing specific cultural aspects and traditions. Consequently, only a select few cultural expressions are displayed as representative of all within a heterogenous group. The processes behind the public commemoration seen in the park reflect Barry Schwartz's (2015) argument about the uneven terrain of collective memory, where those with more capital within the group have greater control over how the group's collective memories are constructed and represented.

While it is easy to dismiss or fault the Cultural Park as unrepresentative, essentialist, or too China-oriented, it should also be remembered that all museums and other forms of public representation are the products of compromise and continuous negotiation. For one, the PSMTI elders were mostly of the pre-1965, Chinese-educated generation and told me that they felt that it was part of their duty to remind contemporary Chinese of their Chineseness. As the building of the Cultural Park was entirely reliant on private donations, these donors played a major role in making design decisions. For instance, as Claudine Salmon and Myra Sidharta (2018, 10) note, the Indonesian Hakka Museum building modeled after a Hakka earthen-walled village within the park was funded by the Prosperous Indonesia Hakka Association (Perhimpunan Hakka Indonesia Sejahtera), which means that, although Hakka Chinese comprise only a relatively small percentage of all ethnic Chinese in Indonesia (and an even smaller number of those whose ancestors probably actually lived in an earthen-walled village), their financial patronage ensured they have a greater visible presence in the park.

The problems and controversies to do with the building and design of the Cultural Park illustrate the complex politics of commemoration and representation of Chinese Indonesian identity in the post-Suharto era. In the postassimilation period, when there was a sudden desire for self-representation and belonging (in terms of both ethnicity and national identity), what resulted was a scramble to secure recognition and to carve out public space for representation, no matter how artificial or superficial the representation might seem. Representing a culturally and linguistically diverse people such as Chinese Indonesians is no easy feat, particularly when the majority are the products of centuries of acculturation and decades of assimilation laws that have left most unsure about their cultural heritage. A further complexity arises when attempts are made to fit the full Chinese heterogeneity into the rigid and monolithic ethnonationalist category of a unified Indonesian Chineseness, in accordance with the state's version of ethnic/racial taxonomy. The reality is that, regardless of how outdated this categorization is, it is one that still prevails. Hence one of the few ways for Chinese to be recognized as belonging to the nation is by asserting themselves as a single and unified "tribe" with defined cultural characteristics and history.

Without a clear consensus of what Chineseness should look like, elders—such as those from PSMTI—with the necessary financial, social, and political capital become key players and cultural gatekeepers in public representations of Chinese Indonesian culture. They rely on a popular and romanticized collective memory of what constitutes acceptable Chineseness. For the PSMTI elders, the aesthetics of the Forbidden City, tiered pagodas, Zheng He's ship, and other pan-Chinese paraphernalia symbolize a mode of Chineseness they had previously been denied. As such, the design of the park, as controversial and essentialized as it is, satisfies three important objectives for its creators: first, as an elaborate showcase of the resilience of Chinese Indonesian cultural uniqueness despite decades of assimilation; second, to try to claim a physical space (if not an ideological one) within Indonesia's ethnonationalist imaginings; and third, as a show of power for PSMTI's elders who demonstrated their capital and ability to negotiate with both the Indonesian and Chinese states in securing land for the park and its design.

After all the effort that has been put into lobbying for and then building the Chinese Indonesian Cultural Park at the TMII, it must be said that the park is (at least at the time of writing) still not categorized as part of the thirty-three existing pavilions that represent Indonesia's provinces and major ethnic groups. For one, in terms of location, while all the pavilions are located next to each other around the main lake, the Chinese Park is located on its own plot toward the back of the complex. On the TMII website, the Chinese Park is also not listed as one of the official provincial pavilions.[8] I cannot help but see this subtle exclusion as symbolic of the well-intentioned but ultimately failed attempt by PSMTI elders and the park's other sponsors to have Chinese ethnicity and culture acknowledged as "native" to Indonesia.

There is no doubt that the Cultural Park is a problematic form of recognition and representation for the Chinese, especially in light of the lack of significant action from the state for justice or recognition for victims of past anti-Chinese violence. Further, the concerns at the start of construction that the park's inclusion in the TMII would serve only to legitimize the New Order's brand of nativism have now evolved into worries that the park's China-inspired design may only further confirm long-standing stereotypes of Chinese Indonesians as China-centric foreigners with loyalties divided between the two countries. These concerns have intensified in recent years, when many Chinese in Indonesia appear to be establishing closer ties with China in terms of trade and investment, education, language learning, and other forms of cultural affiliation (see chapter 6). As I demonstrate later, these efforts have drawn heavy criticism from other Chinese Indonesians who fear that overt displays of closeness or cultural orientation toward the PRC will eventually result in a backlash. These kinds of fear only illustrate how the collective trauma of anti-Chinese discrimination and violence continues to lurk beneath the surface despite decades of postassimilation reforms.

The issue of commemoration is contentious and sensitive for Chinese Indonesians, not only for the May 1998 riots but also for other instances of anti-Chinese discrimination and violence in the past, such as the attacks that occurred during the 1965–1966 anti-Communist purges. The question of how to represent such a diverse group of people with different expectations and vested interests is difficult to answer. After all, as the case studies in this chapter illustrate, commemorative activities are both social and political, because they involve the coordination of individual and group memories. While these commemorative activities may appear to be organic and unified representations of the community, they are in fact the products of continuous negotiations or even struggles. While some want commemorative monuments and dedicated sites of remembrance as acknowledgment of the plight of the Chinese, others argue that such monuments draw too much attention and that the best course of action is to simply move on.

At the beginning of this chapter, I discussed how traumatic memories of anti-Chinese violence play out in the everyday lives of Chinese Jakartans in the post-Suharto era. For the Chinese who live near sites where the May 1998 riots happened, memories of the tragedy are embodied in the new buildings that have been constructed on the remains of properties ransacked during the riots. Far from erasing painful memories, these new buildings serve as a reminder of Chinese vulnerability in Indonesian society and as their potential to be victims of future attacks. It is this sense of latent trauma and victimization that underpins the choice of many Chinese families to live in the safety of Chinese-dominated spaces. However, from the case studies presented in this chapter, it is also evident that there are various individual and community stakeholders with different agendas involved in the shaping of Chinese victim narratives.

The problem with portraying all Chinese as victims is that it both robs them of their agency and masks their own contribution to exclusionary race politics throughout Indonesian history. Furthermore, as Ang (2001b, 23) argues, representing the Chinese as victims and the non-Chinese as perpetrators might render the Chinese unable to break free from "the discourse of victimhood" in the long run. Indeed, a generalized victim subject positioning grossly oversimplifies the complexities of Chinese history, Chinese–*pribumi* dynamics, and the cycle of mutual marginalization that exists between the two groups.

2 Enclaves and Narratives of Trauma in Everyday Life

For Jakartans, the walls, gates, security posts, and other structural barriers that guard middle- and upper-class Chinese residential enclaves are the physical embodiment of the perceived differences between Chinese and non-Chinese. To the mostly lower-class non-Chinese who often live in nearby villages (*kampung*), the grand houses and air-conditioned spaces of gated communities are unreachable and segregated places that serve to confirm stereotypes about Chinese wealth and aloofness. However, for the Chinese who live within these enclaves, gates and walls offer a sense of security from the lingering fear of jealousy and resentment from the non-Chinese that their enclaves paradoxically perpetuate. While it is easy to assume the simplicity of the situation, the psychological rationale for the maintenance of ethnic exclusivity through the erection of walls and other physical boundaries is much more complex than it appears on the surface.

Kelapa Gading is an example of an exclusive residential estate or suburb known in Jakarta for its large middle- and upper-class Chinese population (see map 2 for the location of Kelapa Gading in the context of the Greater Jakarta metropolitan region). Unlike other Chinese-majority areas of Jakarta (such as Glodok and Pluit, discussed in chapter 1), Kelapa Gading was never directly affected by the May 1998 violence. As such, my analysis focuses on how the Chinese residents of this enclave remember the collective past and construct appropriate trauma narratives that support their long-standing desire for safety, even though their enclave has never been directly affected by anti-Chinese violence.

I tell the story of one family—the Tanumihardjas (alias)—as an archetypal middle- to upper-class *totok* family who have largely lived sheltered lives within Kelapa Gading to ensure their safety from potential anti-Chinese discrimination or attacks. The case study shows how inside inherited safe spaces trauma narratives are passed down from one generation to the next, and how younger Chinese maintain the boundaries and collective memories of their *habitus*. Furthermore, a close examination of the Tanumihardjas' relationships with the non-Chinese individuals who also live within their private and semiprivate domains (namely the domestic servants, drivers, and security guards they employ) reveals the existence of different levels of trust extended toward different categories of non-Chinese. This complicated relationship in turn reflects the intricate politics of racial inclusion and exclusion that exist at the everyday level.

The examination of how Chinese engage in self-imposed physical and social separation reveals much about the dynamics of racial politics in post-Suharto Jakarta, where, fueled by long-standing prejudices and trauma narratives, the unspoken lines between the Chinese and non-Chinese still run deep. However, there is also strong evidence of intergenerational shifts, where there are those among the younger generation who reject the rules of the *habitus* they grew up in and have opted to forge their own paths. The case study of Kelapa Gading illustrates how the politics of inclusion and exclusion in ethnic enclaves is complex and shaped by a combination of intergenerational trauma and changing perceptions of safety amid evolving sociopolitical circumstances.

WALLS AND GATES IN EVERYDAY LIFE

As with other big Indonesian cities such as Surabaya and Medan, there is a common perception in Jakarta that exclusive residential estates are where the Chinese live. When I first arrived in the city and began recruiting Chinese research participants during my fieldwork, my non-Chinese informants and friends would tell me to go straight to one of Jakarta's many gated residential estates, especially those located in the northern and western parts of the city. "If you want to find the Chinese," a friend told me, "then you must go to an estate like Kelapa Gading or Green Garden; they all live there." As an ethnic Chinese whose family did not live in one of these residential enclaves, I used to resent this characterization when I was growing up in Jakarta in the 1990s. However, it cannot be denied that many urban Chinese families do live in these estates, and the popular image of wealthy Chinese living segregated lives inside gated communities has persisted, reinforcing long-standing stereotypes of Chinese aloofness.

Throughout the turbulent history of the Chinese in Indonesia, walls and gates have come to represent safety, and living in close proximity to one another in secure communities to ensure that there is strength in numbers being part of a survival strategy that can be traced back to the Dutch colonial period. This tendency to opt for physical segregation has drawn sharp criticism from non-Chinese, who accuse the Chinese of exclusivity, and many of the calls for interethnic reconciliation in the post-Suharto era have to do with appealing to ethnic Chinese elites to emerge from behind their gates and walls. As Yen-ling Tsai (2008, 41) argues, "walls and fences have been powerful local idioms through which socialities between the Chinese and the *pribumi* are framed and articulated in Indonesia."

For the middle- and upper-class Chinese who can afford to live within these enclaves, these secure gates and walls are a normal and accepted part of everyday life, deemed necessary for their safety. Every day, they pass through multiple gates and checkpoints at the entrances and exits of their streets, to enter their private residences, and to gain entry to shopping malls, schools, and offices. They are so used to the numerous security measures in multiple domains in their lives that they do not even notice their presence anymore. Yet, at an underlying level, such security measures are crucial to their sense of well-being and even empowerment. Having secure spaces and gated communities (through economic success) is a way for the Chinese to take some immediate control over their own destinies in a country where they mostly feel politically disenfranchised and physically vulnerable. Indeed, as in Angga's and Lia's story in chapter 1, to many Chinese, security considerations are just as important as those about location, facilities, and the design quality of buildings when making a real estate purchase.

From a class perspective, walls and gates also separate the middle- and upper-class Chinese from the much-feared poor masses who occupy the nearby *kampung* and shantytowns (Peters 2013). In this regard, they share a similar culture of class segregation with middle- and upper-class urban non-Chinese, who are also increasingly moving toward lifestyles contained within gated communities. That being said, however, I argue that the specificities of racial politics that motivate the desire for safety in Chinese enclaves distinguish them from the non-Chinese who also live in exclusive residential spaces. The growing culture of gated communities in contemporary urban Indonesia can certainly also be seen as part of a trend in different localities around the world where the practices of walling satisfy the need to control the circulation and movement of differently classified bodies. This phenomenon is the subject of a growing literature on "fortress cities" and gated communities from different continents (Blakely and Snyder 1999; Caldeira 2000; Leisch 2002; Low 2015; Chen and Shin 2019). While scholars differ in their ways of grounding global movements in local histories, their views converge in seeing gated communities in places like South Africa and Brazil as instances of a new urban social order that corresponds to globally produced inequalities and neoliberal spatial governmentality (see Merry 2001; Bagaeen and Uduku 2015).

While I agree with the view that the act of walling facilitates class and ethnic avoidance, I suggest that the dynamics of segregation in Chinese enclaves are not as simple as they may seem, at least in Jakarta. As well as acting as sites of segregation and surveillance, I contend that walled and gated spaces are also important sites of complex interethnic and interclass encounters. Although these Chinese enclaves are generally designed to exclude unwanted threats from the non-Chinese lower class, the Chinese who live in these enclaves also desperately need the services of the many non-Chinese who are specifically employed to work and live among them as domestic servants, drivers, gardeners, and security guards. Many middle- and upper-class ethnic Chinese children are practically raised by a small army of nannies who look after them from a young age, maids who attend to their every need at home, drivers who convey them to school, and the men who guard their homes and school complexes. For many Chinese families, these non-Chinese employees are often regarded as part of their family. These seemingly contradictory acts of inclusion and exclusion highlight the intricacy of interethnic interactions that occur inside and outside private homes, and around gates and walls. It is also important to note that for Chinese youths who grow up sheltered in these enclaves, the complex interactions with the non-Chinese that occur within gated communities also comprise a large part of their understanding of how the dynamics of racialized relationships work.

In the following section, I divide the case study of the Kelapa Gading residential estate into two domains—the home and the gated neighborhood—in order to discuss in greater detail the acts of inclusion and exclusion that occur within these environments.

KELAPA GADING: A CHINESE CITY WITHIN A CITY

Sitting in a taxi as we drove from Central Jakarta into Kelapa Gading through the residential estate's main access road, I was amazed at the change of urban landscape that was immediately visible. After having endured almost ninety minutes of Jakarta's notorious gridlocked traffic on Jalan Tol Lingkar Dalam Jakarta from Central Jakarta, the wide, leafy boulevards with tall trees and relatively smooth traffic made me feel like I was entering a different world. It was the height of the dry season in the middle of July, and outside of Kelapa Gading the chaotic streets of North and East Jakarta were hot, dry, dusty, and perpetually busy. On the drive there, the taxi passed through several large intersections where, at every red traffic light, scores of beggars, buskers, and peddlers (many of them small children) would descend on the stationary cars to either offer the goods they had for sale or to beg for money. This is a common sight in Jakarta, and the taxi driver politely reminded me not to open the windows, give any money to the beggars, or even use my mobile phone while the car was stationary for fear of theft, as children posing as beggars have been known to smash car windows and run away with snatched mobile phones. None of this chaos existed in Kelapa Gading, and the troubles of the outside world seemed like a distant reality as soon as we entered the estate's gates.

As we entered Kelapa Gading's main commercial strip, my middle-aged taxi driver informed me that we were lucky that there were not so many cars on the road that day because it was the school holidays. At peak hours during the school term, the estate's main boulevard is usually jammed with chauffeured cars taking children to and from school. I asked the taxi driver whether many motorcycles contribute to the traffic problem during peak hours (as is the case with the rest of Jakarta), and he replied that there were not too many motorcycles in the area because rich people drive cars instead. I was quite taken aback by his answer, but then I realized he was merely confirming what I and most Jakartans already knew, that Kelapa Gading is a middle- and upper-class gated community where the wealthy live and where the predominance of Chinese families on the estate since the 1980s has resulted in it gaining a reputation as a Chinese enclave. In fact, I was in Kelapa Gading that day to meet Handy and Jessica Tanumihardja, siblings in their early twenties whose family had been living in Kelapa Gading since the late 1980s. The Tanumihardjas had kindly invited me to stay with them for a week, and on the phone Handy and Jess sounded eager to show me around the neighborhood where they had grown up.

As a residential estate, Kelapa Gading was a product of Jakarta's rapid urban development and expansion from the 1970s onward. However, the popularity of suburban enclaves such as Kelapa Gading among middle- and upper-class Chinese families was also shaped by the socioeconomic and political changes that marked Jakarta's urban history. The first Chinese settlements in what was then the Dutch colonial city of Batavia were concentrated near the port in the northern part of the city. Historians such as

Leonard Blussé (1981), Jean Gelman Taylor (1983), and Mona Lohanda (1996) generally agree that there was no distinct Chinese area in Batavia before 1740, since the Chinese were the dominant population and could therefore be found almost everywhere inside the port city. However, historians such as Anthony Reid (1980), Johannes Widodo (2004), and Robert Cowherd (2021) also point out that, as part of the Dutch system of social organization and control based on race and occupation, enclaves existed to segregate Batavia's populations according to different levels of the colonial societal hierarchy. As Dutch power structures solidified, so did the system of social segregation, but as a whole, the Chinese worked well within this system, and, as Cowherd (2021) suggests, many of the highest-ranking Chinese officers were on good terms with the Dutch administrators and lived side by side with them in prominent parts of town (see also Lohanda 1996). This changed with the Chinese massacre (*Chineezenmoord*) of 1740.

After years of brewing disenfranchisement over the treatment of Chinese laborers, among other factors, a rebellion of Chinese plantation workers approached Batavia from the south. The rebellion was ultimately crushed, and in retaliation, on October 8–10, 1740, and in the days that followed, Dutch soldiers and indigenous populations attacked, plundered, and burned an estimated six to seven thousand Chinese homes inside the city walls (Vermeulen 1938; Blussé 1981; Somers Heidhues 2009). Estimates vary on how many Chinese were killed both inside and outside the city walls during the massacre, but citing contemporary sources, most historians put the number at well above ten thousand (see van Hoëvell 1840; Vermeulen 1938; and Kemasang 1982, among others).[1] After the Batavia massacre, most Chinese subjects were no longer permitted to live within the city walls (only the most trusted Chinese elites were allowed to remain) and were instead allocated a special quarter just south of the walls in the area now known as Glodok. Over time, the Chinese were gradually allowed back into the city and their population flourished, particularly in the market areas of Glodok and Weltevreden (including the areas now known as Pasar Baru, Gunung Sahari, Pintu Besi, and Mangga Besar) in the early nineteenth century (see Setiono 2008 and Lohanda 1996 for more detailed accounts of the Chinese repopulation of Batavia after 1740). Since then, areas like Glodok and Petak Sembilan have become firmly established in the minds of generations of Jakartans as Chinese areas.

By 1930, the population of the city of Batavia had grown to around 435,000 (Cribb and Kahin 2004, 50). Of this number, it was estimated that up to 72,000 were Chinese, comprising around 16 percent of the total population (see Abeyasekere 1987). Things remained relatively stable until the Japanese occupation began in 1942, when many Chinese businesses in the city were forcibly closed or seized and Chinese citizens were treated with suspicion and discriminated against by Japanese forces. The situation worsened for many during and shortly after the independence struggle in 1945–1949, when aggressive local militia groups began attacking those considered enemies of the independence cause, which included Europeans, Japanese, and Chinese residents. Attacks (even some alleged massacres) by these militia groups, such as the one led by Haji Akhmad Khaerun in 1945 in the western outskirts of Jakarta, forced thousands of Chinese to flee into the city (Cribb 2009, 53–54). Throughout these turbulent periods, it became a common belief among the Chinese that they needed to live in enclaves where they had strength in numbers in times of trouble.[2]

By the 1970s, the majority of Chinese lived clustered near each other in traditionally Chinese inner-city areas like Tanah Abang. This demographic pattern was different from non-Chinese ethnic groups, who instead were dispersed throughout the city. However, as Susan Abeyasekere (1987) observes, as living standards declined in inner-city areas like Glodok due to overcrowding and poor sanitation, an increasing number of well-off Chinese families moved to newer residential suburbs, such as Tomang in the west and Kebayoran Lama in the south. This exodus was amplified by the opening of new housing estates catering to the emerging middle and upper classes in the 1970s and 1980s, when suburbs like Kelapa Gading (developed by the PT Summarecon Agung Tbk company chaired by the ethnic Chinese businessman Soetjipto Nagaria), Green Garden, Bintaro Jaya, and Pondok Indah (built by the Ciputra Group, a Chinese-owned real estate developer) became popular among young Chinese families desiring cheap and ample land away from the crowded inner city, but not too far from the city center.

These newer suburbs offered young families relatively affordable access to private facilities such as hospitals, schools, and sports centers, along with proximity to new, climate-controlled public spaces in modern malls and shopping complexes. These families certainly would not be able to afford such luxuries in Central Jakarta. Most importantly, these new residential estates marketed themselves as exclusive gated communities that came fully equipped with their own private security measures. As Abidin Kusno (2006, 110) points out, "By the late 1980s . . . security became a major component in the selling" and promotion of Jakarta's new real estate developments. Kusno also rightly argues that this discourse of security tapped into the New Order regime's emphasis on militaristic power and order. For instance, advertisements for some of these new estates from the late 1970s and 1980s show young families (with two children, as per the government's family planning program at the time) exercising outdoors and walking on paved sidewalks in front of big houses with sprawling lawns (see also van Leeuwen 2011). This image was a far cry from the crowded, dirty, and crime-ridden inner-city areas of Jakarta, and the middle and upper classes could buy their way into this idyllic and crime-free world by purchasing homes in gated estates.

Although these new residential complexes were not specifically designed or marketed to the Chinese alone, many of these neighborhoods (particularly those in the western and northeastern suburbs of Jakarta) became popular among the Chinese because of their relative proximity to the traditional Chinese areas such as Glodok and Tanah Abang. The residential areas of Green Garden, Kebon Jeruk, and Kedoya Selatan in the west, and Kelapa Gading and Sunter in the northwest, are now predominantly populated by Chinese. Although there are middle- and upper-class non-Chinese residents in these estates as well, they are a minority.

Until the mid-1970s, the inner-city area now known as the estate of Kelapa Gading "consisted of undeveloped swamplands and rice fields" with few immediate sources of fresh water (iGADING 2009). By 2009, Kelapa Gading occupied an area of around 1,633 hectares, or a little over 2 percent of Jakarta's total area (and less than 0.2 percent of its total greater metropolitan area) (ibid.). Along with the general economic boom and urban expansion of the 1970s, the Jakarta provincial government gave the authorization for PT Summarecon Agung Tbk to develop the land into a residential and commercial complex designed to be a self-sustaining city within a city (*kota mandiri*). Since then, Kelapa Gading has expanded and is now divided into three categories of development: the main residential zones catering to the middle class; more exclusive and affluent zones catering to the upper class, such as Bukit Gading Villa, Villa Artha Gading, and Kuta Residence; and a commercial zone for malls, businesses, hotels, hospitals, and other public services. In 2020, the suburb's population was recorded as 144,219 residents, around 1.3 percent of Jakarta's total population and 7.8 percent of North Jakarta district's population (Badan Pusat Statistik Kota Jakarta Utara 2021).

While it is very difficult to get an accurate number or percentage of Chinese residents in Kelapa Gading (the Jakarta provincial and municipal governments do not release data on the ethnic composition of different districts), an official from the North Jakarta municipal government told me in

2010 that the unofficial estimate was that over 65 percent of Kelapa Gading's residents were ethnic Chinese. This rough estimate was also echoed by the Kelapa Gading administrators and residents I spoke to and in an online article about Kelapa Gading on a community news portal (iGADING 2009). Although this number seemed high to me, even if the actual percentage was only half of the estimate, Kelapa Gading still has a very high concentration of Chinese residents compared to the total percentage of Chinese in Jakarta, which was estimated to be 6.62 percent of the total population according to the 2010 census (Ananta et al. 2015, 217).

Typical of other urban residential developments of the 1980s, Kelapa Gading's developers intended to maximize profits by bundling a range of facilities into interconnected clusters. As such, services such as office towers, restaurants, and shops that are normally located outside of residential areas became self-contained. This was reflected in advertisements, such as one I found from 1989 that boasted how the building of the Kelapa Gading Plaza (now Kelapa Gading Mall) along with new schools, petrol stations, and banks meant that the estate's elite residents would not need to venture out of its confines or leave the comforts of their bubble.[3] While advertisements like these did not mention the issue of safety, the exclusivity and lifestyle that Kelapa Gading provided implied that its residents would be kept safe from the potential criminality of Jakarta's lower-class non-Chinese from *kampung* areas and shantytowns. As discussed below, the focus of Kelapa Gading's developers and residents on safety greatly intensified almost overnight after the May 1998 riots, as the rioters and looters came very close to breaching the estate. After this traumatic experience, barbed wire fences, gates, and security checkpoints were installed, changing the estate's landscape to what it is today.

Looking out the window of my taxi in 2009, I saw clear evidence of Kelapa Gading's self-sufficiency. The main street, Jalan Boulevard Raya Kelapa Gading, was lined with shophouses with all sorts of businesses, from restaurants offering cuisines from all over the world and regions of Indonesia (although most offer some regional variety of Chinese cuisine) to real estate agents, bookstores, clothing shops, banks, property display suites, private health clinics, karaoke centers, and other entertainment venues. There were also three shopping malls located right next to each other, creating one big commercial complex with department stores and supermarkets, as well as many local and international brands (some of them global luxury brands). Driving further along the boulevard, I could also see fast-food chains (including drive-throughs), a hospital, gyms, a golf course with other sporting facilities, gated private schools, churches, mosques, and car dealerships. The range of amenities on display at Kelapa Gading's commercial area was impressive, and I realized that the estate was not just an ordinary residential suburb but that it was indeed a city within a city. I began to understand how Kelapa Gading's residents could spend almost their whole lives there if they wanted to, especially considering how relatively ordered and well equipped the estate was compared to the disorder of the streets outside the estate and throughout Jakarta.

It was obvious that my taxi driver was familiar with Kelapa Gading's backstreets as we turned off from the main commercial boulevard into one of the residential areas. To me, all the small streets looked identical: clean and tree-lined with gated houses on both sides. This scene is typical of Jakarta's many middle- and upper-class residential estates, and every few hundred meters or so, we passed a security post or guardhouse (*gardu*), each manned by a security guard employed by the estate management. After several confusing turns, we arrived at the entrance to the street where Handy and Jessica lived.

We stopped at a manual boom gate where we were greeted by a security guard who gave my taxi driver a military-style salute. The driver rolled down the window and the security guard asked, "Which house are you going to?"

FIGURE 2.1 Security checkpoint (*gardu*) to enter one of the main residential clusters within the Kelapa Gading complex, 2021.

Source: Photo by Shabach Creative. Reproduced with permission.

(*Mau ke rumah yang mana?*) as he looked inside the car and nodded to me when he spotted me in the back seat. The driver gave him the address and I added from the back seat, "I want to go to Mr. Andreas's house, sir" (*Saya mau ke rumah Bapak Andreas Pak*). Obviously satisfied by my answer and my appearance as an ethnic Chinese woman who looked middle class and who was unlikely to be a security threat, the security guard replied, "Oh, Mr. Andreas's house, it's at the end of the street there, please pass through" (*Oh, rumah Pak Andreas, di ujung jalan situ ya, silahkan*) as he raised the boom gate and waved us in. Upon entering, I noticed that the houses on this street were bigger than the ones we had passed earlier that were closer to the main boulevard, and I realized that Handy and Jessica's parents must be some of the wealthier people in Kelapa Gading. I got out of the taxi, paid my knowledgeable driver, and looked up at the big, two-story house with its imposing gate that would be my home for the next week.

HOME

After ringing the doorbell at the house gate, I was greeted by a middle-aged Javanese woman who was quite small in stature. She wore a clean but old cotton dress, had her long black hair in a tight bun, and gave me a kind, weary smile as she walked toward the gate. I found out later that her name was Mbak Karti,[4] a housekeeper from the city of Magelang in Central Java who had been working for the family for twenty-three years, since Handy was born. Mbak Karti opened the gate for me, took my travel bag despite my protests, and asked me to go straight in the house, as Handy, Jessica, and their parents were expecting me. I walked the few meters past the small front garden to the main entrance of the house (while Mbak Karti took my bag into the house via a side door in the garage), entered through the big open teak and brass-handled doors, and met my hosts sitting in the front room.

I had never met Handy and Jessica's parents before, and the only thing they had heard about me was that I was a researcher who wanted to know more about what life was like for Chinese families living in Kelapa Gading. Pak Andreas Tanumihardja, the head of the family, was a sixty-one-year-old commercial lawyer who owned his own practice in the nearby suburb of Sunter, and his wife, Ibu Lanny, was a fifty-seven-year-old stay-at-home mother who filled her days with charitable activities at the local Catholic church that the family attended. Handy, a twenty-three-year-old engineering graduate, had just returned home after spending five years in Melbourne as an undergraduate student, and Jessica was a twenty-one-year-old medical student at Atma Jaya Catholic University of Indonesia (Universitas Katolik Indonesia Atma Jaya). The siblings had an older brother, Michael, who was living in Singapore after getting a job there as a banker. The family descended from a *totok* lineage, although according to Pak Andreas they were "not too *totok*," because none of them could speak Chinese, but they did try to observe Chinese traditions during big annual celebrations.

After a quick welcome and introductions, we sat down on the big couches in the sitting room. As if on cue, Mbak Karti emerged from the nearby kitchen with glasses of a cold, red, syrupy drink, and then just as quickly she disappeared again into the kitchen. Ibu Lanny asked me what my research was all about, and I gave a simplified explanation about my interest in the relationship between the memories of trauma and everyday life among middle- and upper-class Kelapa Gading Chinese just like them. Pak Andreas, obviously keen to fill me in on some information about life in Kelapa Gading, proceeded to tell me about what motivated Chinese like him to purchase homes there: "When Kelapa Gading first opened in the early 1980s, the marketers were smart because they didn't just advertise the place as a residential area, they marketed it as a place where everything is nearby, convenient, and safe. The Chinese liked it because within Kelapa Gading, there are shopping centers, food courts, everything is nearby, and you don't need to leave the neighborhood. This is just like in Tanah Abang where I grew up, where everything is close." Pak Andreas's story is typical of many young middle- and upper-class Chinese families who moved to Kelapa Gading in the early 1980s from traditional Chinese neighborhoods like Glodok, Tanah Abang, Pluit, and Muara Karang. For many of the early Chinese residents of Kelapa Gading of Pak Andreas's generation, the new suburb's proximity to other Chinese areas made maintaining familial and community ties easier. At the same time, a fully equipped, self-sustaining gated community also offered convenience and protection from the unpredictable world outside, making Kelapa Gading an attractive place to start a family somewhere new while still retaining the comforting lifestyle of living near other Chinese.

I asked Pak Andreas whether it was true that not many non-Chinese live in Kelapa Gading; he replied that there were a few *pribumi* families that he knew in the neighborhood. Handy added that the nearby Al-Azhar Kelapa Gading Islamic School was a private school that catered to the children of the mainly Muslim families who lived in Kelapa Gading, although he admitted that the Chinese made up the vast majority of the area's residents. Indeed, while non-Chinese families also moved into the area in the 1980s and 1990s, their numbers were nowhere near those of the Chinese residents. Perhaps because Kelapa Gading was regarded as too expensive, or perhaps because it was perceived to be a Chinese area very early on, the number of non-Chinese residents has remained low from the start. Ibu Lanny carefully commented that it was a good thing that the non-Chinese families who lived in Kelapa Gading were "proper families" (*keluarga baik-baik*), adding that these families were also middle class (although in reality they were more upper class) and educated, so they were not people from *kampung* areas. Pak Andreas's and Ibu Lanny's initial comments and assessments of the Kelapa Gading neighborhood revealed a class-based differentiation between those who were regarded as acceptable *pribumi* (those from the same socioeconomic class as them) and those who were not. They made no mention of poorer Chinese, although it was clear from their comments that their Kelapa Gading milieu consisted of middle- and upper-class Chinese.

After our introductory chat, I was told to make myself at home and then shown to my room by Jessica, who was very excited about having a big sister figure in the house (she insisted on calling me *cici,* which is Hokkien for "older sister") after having grown up with two older brothers. I was assigned the second-floor guest bedroom that had its own en suite bathroom, a queen-size bed, teak furnishings, and a view of the street from the large (but metal-barred) windows. Jessica also gave me a house tour, at which I learned that the house had five bedrooms, four bathrooms, and a garage large enough for the family's three cars. The house was of a neoclassical design that is quite common for middle- and upper-class houses in Jakarta's suburban enclaves, whose owners aspire to project their wealth and status through grand, European aristocratic-style homes. There were two large pillars at the exterior of the house with a second-story balcony adorned with a wrought-iron vine leaf railing, and inside the house there was a large spiral staircase with a matching vine leaf railing that connected the lower and upper floors. Also typical of Jakartan middle- and upper-class homes were the maids' quarters, a small area at the back section of the second floor of the house where the maids were free to socialize among themselves or watch television in their separate living area when they were not working; at night, Pak Andreas closed and locked the main door separating this area from the rest of the house.

Later during my stay at Pak Andreas and Ibu Lanny's house, I came to know the other domestic staff who worked there. Along with Mbak Karti, the most senior domestic servant, there were two younger women who looked to be in their early twenties. Mbak Karti did the cooking and maintained the household's general order, while the other two did the more mundane physical tasks, such as laundry and cleaning the floors. The family employed two drivers; one of them, Pak Dadang, a middle-aged Betawi man who lived in a village in nearby Cakung, had worked for the family for over twenty years. In fact, Pak Dadang was the one who drove Ibu Lanny to the hospital when she was in labor with Jessica. Ibu Lanny later confessed to me that she felt very lucky to have had such loyal and dedicated domestic staff. She commented that some of her (Chinese) friends had horror stories of bad domestic servants who stole and brought young men to the house, including one who even conspired with thieves and cleaned out the house of one of her friends while they were away. She said that this was why she and Pak Andreas treated Mbak Karti and Pak Dadang well by giving them above-average wages and generous holiday bonuses during Ramadan, putting their children through school, and paying their families' medical bills. Ibu Lanny added, "If we treat them well, then they will treat us well too and not get up to any trouble" (*Kalau kita baik sama mereka, mereka juga akan baik dan nggak macam-macam*). I was not quite sure what Ibu Lanny had meant by "*macam-macam*" (causing or making trouble), but I gathered that she felt that Chinese employers like her needed to make sure that they treated their domestic staff well (in no small part through financial incentives) in order to minimize the potential for unwanted—or even criminal—behavior.

Of all the daily interactions in the Tanumihardja household, I was most interested in the interaction between the family and their non-Chinese helpers. Jessica was obviously very close to Mbak Karti, who had practically raised her since she was a baby. As a child, whenever she needed someone to braid her hair or mend a loose button, it was not her mother she went to but Mbak Karti. Mbak Karti also knew intimate details about the household, such as each family member's favorite foods and where the smallest items were stored around the house. Likewise, Pak Dadang had driven Jessica to school and then to university every day since she was young, and Handy told me that it was Pak Dadang (and not his parents) who first taught him how to ride a bicycle. Despite these domestic intimacies, both the employers and the employees in this situation knew that the non-Chinese helpers could never be regarded as equals. There were racial and class barriers here that could not be transgressed, and any attempt to cross these boundaries would just make all the parties involved feel uncomfortable. For instance, when I asked Mbak Karti to stop addressing me as "Non" (Miss) and to just call me by my name instead, both Mbak Karti and Jessica (who was sitting nearby) stopped and looked at each other awkwardly before going back to what they were doing before. I realized that I had crossed unspoken ethnic and class lines, and Mbak Karti ignored my request and continued calling me "Non" for the remainder of my stay.

In the literature on the sociology of labor, domestic service is most often characterized as "work in homes" where the relationship between domestic workers and family members is regarded as a work relationship, not a familial one (see Colen and Sanjek 1990; Elmhirst 1999). While this may be true to a certain extent, viewing the relationship between domestic workers and their employers as strictly professional simplifies the complex class, ethnic, and kin interactions that occur in situations like that of Mbak Karti's valued presence within the Tanumihardja household. In her study of Javanese domestic servants working in middle-class homes, G. G. Weix (2000, 137) argues that the kinds of relationships that occur between Javanese *pembantu* and their employers can only be interpreted as those in which the domestic servants are "in the home and outside the family." Here, Weix suggests that despite allusions that domestic servants are considered part of the family (for example, children of employers calling female servants "*mbak*" or male servants and drivers "*abang,*" which is West Javanese for "older brother"), they are actually permanently located outside of the employing family's kin and class structures (see Stoler 2002 for more on the history and dynamics of domestic servitude during the colonial period of the Dutch East Indies). With the addition of the ethnic and class dimensions in Chinese families, Tsai (2008) argues that what transpires are situations where the *pribumi* domestic servants are essentially "intimate strangers" who are simultaneously integrated into a Chinese family's domestic routines yet also fully aware of the boundaries that separate them from their Chinese masters.

The seemingly contradictory behavior toward the non-Chinese that I saw in the Tanumihardja household got me thinking about the dynamics of racialized inclusion and exclusion in Chinese enclaves like Kelapa Gading, and what roles exist for the "acceptable" non-Chinese who inhabit the Chinese milieu. For example, Jessica never traveled by public transport or even taxis because she was both forbidden by her parents and because she was scared to do so. Ibu Lanny and her husband insisted that she be driven everywhere by Pak Dadang, because they were afraid of the dangers that awaited their daughter if she traveled by herself, with Ibu Lanny remarking, "I don't let Jessica go anywhere by public transport, especially when she's by herself.... She is a pretty girl, has fair skin, and looks well-off.... She would be a sitting duck for robbers, thieves, rapists, and bad people in general who would immediately target her if they saw her on a public bus!" There was also a clear gender dimension in the family's discourse of safety, as Pak Andreas and Ibu Lanny worried about their daughter's safety and her ability to protect herself much more than that of their son. As seen in Ibu Lanny's remarks, this is tied to fears of rape and other forms of sexual violence considered to be far more likely to befall Jessica than Handy. With the collective memory of the rapes of Chinese women during the May 1998 riots still very much in their minds, middle- and upper-class young Chinese women like Jessica are seen to be prime targets of sexual violence by lower-class non-Chinese men. Yet it was fine, even preferable, for her to go out while in the care of their driver Pak Dadang. The family's attitude toward Pak Dadang was another example of contradictory behavior toward non-Chinese, where those who are deemed to be trustworthy were afforded a degree of intimacy.

Clearly, the Tanumihardjas did not regard their domestic staff as potential looters and rioters or as taking part in any potential anti-Chinese violence. The family evidently had a lot of trust in them, at least partly because they had shown their loyalty and dedication when Kelapa Gading was threatened by the May 1998 riots. Both Pak Dadang and Mbak Karti were already working for the family when the riots happened. Pak Dadang remembered hurriedly driving Pak Andreas home when the looting and burning of shops in the Sunter area began. He recounted how they could see the smoke from burning buildings and had heard rumors that the rioters were heading toward Kelapa Gading. Pak Dadang also kept watch over the house and the neighborhood during the days and nights of the riots, returning to his own house only once in three days so that he could stay with the Tanumihardjas instead. When I asked Pak Dadang whether he had been worried for his own family in Cakung (especially considering that the Klender area near his home was one of the areas that was looted), he said that he knew that they would be safe (ostensibly because they were not Chinese), and that his son was looking after his family. Mbak Karti told me that during the riots she was scared too, but her main priority was to calm the children and Ibu Lanny (who at that point was nearly hysterical with fear). The incredible loyalty displayed by Pak Dadang and Mbak Karti evidently went beyond that of an employee-employer relationship. The presence of non-Chinese staff within ethnic Chinese households and domestic milieus raises questions about their roles as intimate outsiders in the ethnic Chinese *habitus*, and the possibility of cross-*habitus* collaboration and solidarity between Chinese and non-Chinese.

Yet, as discussed earlier, this trust and closeness with the lower-class non-Chinese who inhabit their domestic sphere only went so far. In addition to these relationships with those from lower socioeconomic classes, their interactions with non-Chinese of the same religion and similar socioeconomic classes also seemed to have a limit. Throughout my stay with the Tanumihardjas, Pak Andreas mentioned several non-Chinese friends and colleagues, some of whom he regarded as close friends (*teman dekat*), and Ibu Lanny also knew some non-Chinese Catholic women with whom she volunteered at their church. However, while they had a number of non-Chinese friends and acquaintances, there were still interethnic boundaries that could not be crossed. Similarly, Handy and Jessica both had non-Chinese friends from school and church but noted that their parents would "absolutely object" (*pasti melarang*) if they brought a non-Chinese boyfriend or girlfriend home. When I asked why, Handy said, "I think my parents have a distrust toward them [*pribumi*] in general, even if they are Christians too. I think that this is because my parents are afraid of things that they don't know, and they have their prejudices too." Jessica agreed: "Yeah, Mama and Papa have stereotypes about different tribes [*suku*] of *pribumi,* like they think that the Menadonese are big spenders, the Sundanese are lazy, the Batak people are confrontational. . . . I know this sounds a little bit racist, but I guess they [the parents] have had bad experiences with *pribumi* in the past and they're trying to protect us. . . . I don't think they have anything against them [*pribumi*] personally." Handy added that he knew Chinese friends who had dated non-Chinese, and these relationships almost always ended badly, even when they were of the same religion and class. In most of these cases, the couples broke up due to family pressures.

Like many other young Chinese in Indonesia with similar backgrounds, Handy and Jessica had grown up with these paradoxical attitudes toward the non-Chinese. Growing up in an enclave where non-Chinese are simultaneously feared and needed, they have learned the intricate negotiation and boundary management skills that are necessary to maintain both their safety and ethnic/class identities in their home and other everyday domains.

GATED NEIGHBORHOOD

During my stay, Handy took me on afternoon walks around the neighborhood to show me where he used to play as a child. There was a small park near the Tanumihardjas' house, with a basketball court and several benches where Handy and his neighborhood friends played after school during their primary and high school years. Handy told me that when they were young boys, he and his elder brother used to ride their bicycles while supervised by Pak Dadang along the very same streets we were walking on. The boys knew almost everyone who lived on their street and were friendly with the security guards who would tell them not to ride their bicycles so fast around the corners and to be careful of cars. Clearly, Handy had a happy childhood in Kelapa Gading which he recalled fondly: "I had quite an idyllic childhood growing up here because in a [residential] complex like this, all the kids can play on the streets, and I had all my friends living nearby. My school was five minutes away by car and all the extracurricular activities I did as a child were all located within the neighborhood." Handy said he felt safe in Kelapa Gading and also felt lucky because he realized that there were not many places in Jakarta where children, especially Chinese children, could play freely on the streets. I found what Handy said to be very interesting, precisely because the only reason that he could play freely on the streets as a child was because his family had employed household staff (Pak Dadang) and security personnel who watched over him the whole time. There were also security posts and manual boom gates at the entrance to almost every

FIGURE 2.2 The double protection of manual boom gate (*portal*) and high steel gates at the end of one of Kelapa Gading's residential streets, 2021.

Source: Photo by Shabach Creative. Reproduced with permission.

street, making sure that the movements of visitors like me were always known to the security guards. Handy said that he did not even notice the gates and security posts anymore since they were such a fundamental part of daily life for him and those in the neighborhood.

Recalling my own experience of dealing with the neighborhood security on my way to the Tanumihardjas' house, I asked Handy whether there had always been so many security measures in place. Handy replied that there had always been security guards around even when he was little, but he remembered security being tightened after the May 1998 riots. According to him, almost immediately after the riots, higher and stronger metal gates were erected at the main entrance points to Kelapa Gading, and additional security checkpoints with boom gates were installed at major access roads. In addition, extra security personnel were added to make sure that every street was regularly patrolled. While he could not remember much about May 1998, Handy remembered feeling confused and scared:

> I was only twelve when the riots happened so I can't remember much. All I remember was that I was at school in my SD [*sekolah dasar,* primary school] and suddenly the teacher told us that we were going to go home early. Pak Dadang picked me up and took me straight home, and my mother was panicking at home, watching the news on TV about all these buildings being looted, while on the phone to my dad telling him to hurry home. . . . The next two nights were really tense, my dad joined the neighborhood watch with the security guards and other men from the complex, and we did not leave the house at all because there were rumors that the rioters had already burned Sunter Mall.

At the time, Handy did not fully grasp the weight of a situation in which Chinese like him were being targeted, but was gradually made aware of the fact by his parents: "Dad explained to me later on that we were actually in real danger during the riots because we are Chinese. . . . I didn't really comprehend what that meant at the time, but I understood more as I grew up. I can imagine what it must have been like for my parents, barricaded at home with young children while a riot was at your doorstep." When I asked him how this realization made him feel, Handy shrugged and said, "It's sad, but what can you do? It's just a fact of life here in Indonesia, we just do what we can to mind our own business and keep ourselves safe."

Later Pak Andreas told me that when the May 1998 riots broke out, the Kelapa Gading residents realized that their neighborhood was an obvious target for the rioters, especially since the area was known to be where the rich Chinese lived and was located not too far from the affected areas of Pluit, Glodok, and Sunter. Indeed, the rioters came to Kelapa Gading's doorstep. Pak Andreas recounted how police and military personnel were nowhere to be seen at the beginning of the riots, despite there being a police station right in the middle of Kelapa Gading's commercial district; this contributed to the popular belief that spread after the riots that the Indonesian National Armed Forces and other security forces were partly behind the chaos and that they deliberately withdrew their personnel. In response, both Chinese and non-Chinese residents, along with male domestic staff such as Pak Dadang, manned the security posts themselves and barricaded the neighborhood's streets with whatever large furniture and household items they had at their disposal. They armed themselves with metal rods and homemade sharpened sticks, and were prepared to defend themselves, as it was deemed too late to try to escape because the rioters were blocking the main roads in and out of the area from both the Sunter (north and west) and Pulo Gadung (south) sides.[5] According to my informants, help did not come until late at night on May 14, when the military finally arrived to guard the estate and repel the mob.

Pak Andreas suspected that Kelapa Gading's administrators (or perhaps powerful residents with military connections) must have paid a lot of money to have the local military garrison barricade and guard the estate to prevent rioters from getting in. In retrospect, while he cannot prove it, Pak Andreas believed that this security payoff was their saving grace, as the military would not have mobilized (or at least not as quickly) without the payments. This belief that the state's security apparatuses cannot be relied upon to protect the Chinese unless they are sufficiently paid echoes the experiences of the Glodok and Mangga Dua Chinese residents discussed in chapter 1. After May 1998, Kelapa Gading residents' associations (*rukun tetangga*) decided that more security measures were needed in case of other anti-Chinese attacks. Almost overnight, the number of security posts and checkpoints multiplied, as did the number of boom gates and fortified fences at the end of each street. Nighttime curfews were imposed, and both residents and visitors who wanted to enter and exit a street had to register with a round-the-clock security guard. The years of instability and criminality that followed the May 1998 riots and the fall of the New Order further justified these reinforced security measures among an already terrified community.[6] The walls and gates of private homes also became taller, and suddenly the physical landscape of Kelapa Gading no longer resembled the carefree, safe neighborhood that was advertised in the 1980s.

At the time of my fieldwork in Kelapa Gading, it had been over ten years since the May 1998 riots, with no recent anti-Chinese attacks in the area; however, the metal gates and security checkpoints were still in place. I was surprised to hear Handy say that he still saw them as necessary, as protection not just from the threat of future riots and potential *pribumi* violence, but also from Jakarta's rising criminality: "In the news, you hear a lot about burglaries and even murders committed in residential complexes like Kelapa Gading. . . . Sometimes burglaries are even committed in broad daylight! Because of things like this, you need security checkpoints to make sure that no shady characters lurk around the neighborhood. . . . There was a case recently near here where some thieves posed as delivery drivers, were let in at the security gate, and ended up robbing a house and killing the domestic servant. . . . I guess these days you can't be too safe." Handy's opinion was shared by his good friend Yohannes, a twenty-four-year-old photographer who went to school with Handy and also grew up in Kelapa Gading: "I think the security [presence] is necessary, although it is kind of annoying coming across so many of them. You have to stop and roll down your car window to get into your own street, and you have to go through bag checks and metal detectors these days to get into malls and offices. . . . But I understand that these things are necessary, especially now with terrorist bomb threats and all that."[7] Handy's and Yohannes's views of the importance of security are common among the young Chinese who live in Kelapa Gading. While most agree that having to go through so many security checks on a daily basis is annoying and time-consuming, they also regard it as a necessary and normal part of everyday life in Jakarta. To these young Chinese, the need for multiple security measures arises from a combination of fears of anti-Chinese riots, crime, and terrorist attacks.[8]

In recent decades, the presence of private security has become so ubiquitous in exclusive Indonesian residential enclaves that they have also become a symbol of prestige (Leisch 2002; Bunnell and Miller 2011; Hellman et al. 2018). However, more than just serving as status symbols, Abidin Kusno (2006, 148) emphasizes that the presence of private security (guardhouses in particular) has "complex roots" in local history. He argues that the reliance on private security is the product of cross-cultural Chinese–*pribumi* encounters and conflicts whose origins are intimately tied to the racial and spatial politics of Dutch colonialism, the Japanese military administration, and the Chinese historical experience of self-defense. Viewed in this way, neighborhood security structures such as the guardhouse "play a crucial role in . . . regulating public memory, and defining territory and collective identity"

(98). In Chinese urban spaces, the "mundane *gardu*" (98) and the private security personnel that man them, as well as high fences and metal gates, are everyday necessities that embody protection and safety.

The reliance of Chinese on private security services also highlights their historical trauma, and distrust toward and lack of faith in the military and state security apparatuses. In his study of the politics of protection rackets in Indonesia, Ian Wilson (2015, 1) points out that "in a variety of regional variations and manifestations," civilian paramilitary groups have been an important part of "both [Indonesia's] recent and more distant history." In the absence of a cohesive and centralized military, local armies and protection gangs played an important part throughout Indonesia's wars for independence; these forms of paramilitary civilian security continued to be important during the New Order, often as criminal gangs operating protection rackets (known locally as *preman*), the largest and most influential of which is Pancasila Youth (Pemuda Pancasila), which had close links to the Suharto-era military. Wilson notes that "in lieu of a functioning official police force," these *preman* gangs (Wilson calls them "*jago* networks") "also operated as an informal form of security for which they extracted payment from local businesses, especially ethnic Chinese" (14; see also Lindsey 2001). The form of protection offered here is coercive, and "implicit in the relationship is the threat of violence" (Wilson 2015, 6) and intimidation if money is not paid. Their political and social vulnerability, along with their economic abilities, make the Chinese of all social classes the ideal targets of these protection rackets.

While the security guards employed in residential enclaves like Kelapa Gading are not protection rackets, and their work is far from being coercive, the principle of the Chinese expending a significant portion of their economic capital for the purpose of private protection is still the same. While they are certainly not the only Indonesians to employ private security (wealthy non-Chinese almost always employ private security as well), their reasons for doing so have to do with the specificities of their collective trauma as an ethnic minority group. The lack of reliable police and military protection (that they did not have to pay for) during crises such as the May 1998 riots only serves to reaffirm this long-held belief that private protection is a necessity. It is also ironic that the vast majority of those employed to do private security work are younger non-Chinese males from lower socioeconomic classes, the very same group of people the Chinese are most afraid of and consider to be the perpetrators of anti-Chinese violence, thus indicating an underlying historical pattern of protection rackets.

These kinds of private protection come at a high price, not only in the form of salaries for the security guards but also for the maintenance of the security infrastructure, the periodic neighborhood security fee (*uang keamanan lingkungan*) that residents must pay to the residents' consortium, and, perhaps more importantly, the unofficial expenses of maintaining good relations with those employed to guard their safety. Reflecting the long tradition of Chinese–*pribumi* patronage, residents like Ibu Lanny and Pak Andreas are often relied upon to lend or give money to the many domestic servants, security guards, and other lower-class non-Chinese individuals in their lives who require assistance to pay for medical treatment, weddings, circumcision ceremonies, religious festivities, school fees, and other needs. While these everyday acts of financial patronage are often portrayed as the goodwill (*itikad baik*) of the Chinese patrons, there is significant social pressure on Chinese families to meet these financial requests in order to avoid being seen as stingy (*pelit*). As Ibu Lanny noted, these kinds of micropatronage are important to keep the non-Chinese who live and work in the households of middle- and upper-class Chinese from "making trouble."

MEMORY WORK INSIDE AN ETHNIC ENCLAVE

On my last night in Kelapa Gading, Pak Andreas and his family took me to one of its most famous seafood restaurants for a farewell dinner. They also invited along their good family friends Pak Bing, his wife Ibu Mira, and their teenage son, Andi, whom I had previously met at the Catholic church the family attended. During dinner, Pak Bing pointed out how crowded the big restaurant was and how Kelapa Gading was known all around Jakarta as the best place to go to dine out. Because Kelapa Gading's Chinese residents are heterogenous and are from different parts of Jakarta and throughout the Indonesian archipelago,[9] the variety of regional Chinese cuisines (for example, Hokkien, Hakka, and Teochew) on offer was impressive. Pak Andreas added that it was not just the food; Kelapa Gading had all the modern conveniences one could want, making it "like Singapore" (*seperti Singapur*). Pak Andreas's comparison between Kelapa Gading and Singapore was one I had encountered a few times during my stay, among both older and younger residents.[10] At first I did not understand the comparison but after spending time living among Kelapa Gading's Chinese residents, I understood the feeling of pride that stemmed from the estate's survival as a secure island amid Jakarta's (and more broadly, Indonesia's) sea of uncertainty. Just as Singapore went from being expelled from a Malay-dominated Malaysia to rapid development as a modern-day economic powerhouse dominated by the Chinese, Kelapa Gading has thrived as a self-sufficient, affluent, and prosperous Chinese community in the face of adversity and anti-Chinese opposition. Further, much like how the Singapore state has developed a siege mentality following decades of self-reliance, Chinese Indonesians have also developed a similar mentality of defensiveness and exclusivity.

Before I visited Kelapa Gading, I had thought that at least some of its Chinese residents must feel trapped by their isolated and segregated existence in an ethnic enclave. However, none of the Chinese residents I encountered seemed to feel that way. To young middle- and upper-class Chinese like Handy and Jessica, living in a self-sufficient Chinese-majority enclave with numerous security measures is an everyday reality and a normal part of life they have grown up with. Their fortified homes, private schools, and air-conditioned shopping malls, among other climate-controlled, predictable, and highly secure spaces, provided them with safe havens from the uncertainties and potential dangers of the chaotic, *pribumi*-dominated world outside (see van Leeuwen 2011 for a comprehensive analysis of the centrality of malls and air-conditioned spaces for middle-class Jakartans). Nina, Jessica's Chinese university friend and a fellow Kelapa Gading resident, said that while sheltered spaces (such as malls) could get boring, they were nevertheless safe and clean: "On the weekends, I usually head down to the mall and hang out with my friends. Where else can I go outside the house? Everywhere, the traffic is jammed [*macet*], and plus I can't just walk around the streets. Malls are safe, even if it does get boring sometimes. . . . In here, there is a much lower risk of being pickpocketed or mugged. It's nice having that peace of mind." Born, raised, and now living their own adult lives in Kelapa Gading, Handy and Jessica were used to an existence segregated from the rest of Jakarta; thus their understandings of fundamental matters (such as the boundaries between Chinese and non-Chinese and the former's collective position in Indonesian society) and views on other socioeconomic classes were shaped by their existence in their Kelapa Gading Chinese *habitus*.

At first, it seemed strange to me that the residents of Kelapa Gading felt and embodied so much trauma from the events of May 1998 when their estate had not been directly attacked by the rioters. Unlike areas such as Glodok and Mangga Dua, Kelapa Gading never experienced the lootings, property destruction, killings, or rapes and sexual assaults of Chinese women during the May 1998 riots. So why did the Chinese residents of Kelapa Gading develop such a strong siege mentality when they had never personally suffered from the traumatic event that has served as such a singular reference point? I realized that, for the most part, the answer lay in the fact that the rioting mob had come very close to Kelapa Gading. Throughout my interactions with the Chinese residents, they kept repeating the narrative of how the May 1998 rioters were "at their doorstep" (*sudah didepan pintu*), and that they survived only because they were vigilant in employing self-preservation tactics such as paying off the military and initiating a community neighborhood watch. These residents considered themselves to be lucky (*beruntung*) compared to their Glodok compatriots, either forgetting or omitting that they were generally wealthier and therefore had more capital to use for various forms of self-protection. Combined with the long history of anti-Chinese violence in Jakarta and the push for self-sufficiency behind the initial move to Kelapa Gading in the 1970s and 1980s, the memory of May 1998 as a close call continues to motivate the Chinese residents to be ever vigilant in protecting the safety and interests of their exclusive *habitus*.

There are of course obvious gaps in the memory work that takes place in ethnic enclaves like Kelapa Gading. For one, the narrative of Chinese self-sufficiency largely does not include stories about the solidarity, sacrifices, and help of their non-Chinese friends and staff. Their own class privilege is often forgotten and the narrative of Chinese suffering becomes monolithic, glossing over the fact that there were many more vulnerable lower-class Chinese who were potential victims during the May 1998 riots, such as those in places like Glodok.

Kelapa Gading is only one of many Chinese residential enclaves in Jakarta and in other big cities of Indonesia, such as Surabaya and Medan. Over the years, newer gated estates such as Pantai Indah Kapuk in northwestern Jakarta also became more prestigious places for middle- and upper-class Chinese to live. While each of these enclaves has its own local history and has experienced anti-Chinese events (such as the May 1998 riots) in different ways, there are many similarities in how they have responded to the lessons learned from the riots, primarily by increasing the number of private security personnel and the erecting of more protective barriers. In the post-Suharto era, as Jakarta's urban sprawl expands and the city's inner-city dwellers move further out to escape overcrowding, poor urban infrastructure, flooding, and traffic jams, more and more of these exclusive residential exclaves have been developed in outer suburban areas—for example, Bumi Serpong Damai developed by the Widjaja family's Sinar Mas Group, and Lippo Karawaci, developed by the Riady family's Lippo Group, both of which are major Chinese Indonesian conglomerates. In much the same way that developers marketed new residential estates in the 1970s and 1980s, these newer residential estates also advertise spacious land and modern infrastructure that enable lives of comfort and self-sufficiency. However, there is an additional marketing feature to these new estates: safety.[11] While these assurances of safety are not necessarily direct references to the May 1998 riots (estate developers also promise safety from Jakarta's annual flooding and from lower-class criminality), the discourse of safety is alive and well. For the Chinese, it is also a trope that is tied to the memory of targeted violence.

CHINESE SELF-SUFFICIENCY AND ITS CRITICS

Unsurprisingly, the self-sufficiency and segregated lives of the Chinese in sheltered upper-class communities like Kelapa Gading are not without their critics. For many ordinary working-class non-Chinese, the stereotypical image of Chinese as wealthy, unsympathetic, distant, and aloof is reinforced every time a Chinese family gets out of their luxury car and walks into an exclusive mall while their non-Chinese driver parks the car, or when the upper-class Chinese socialize at trendy air-conditioned venues inaccessible to the poor. This kind of negative image is commonly held, even among the non-Chinese who claim to be open-minded and not racist. For instance, Boy, a thirty-year-old music teacher of Timorese heritage, remarked, "I have many Chinese friends and students, but I do understand why many *pribumi* hate the Chinese so much. Can you imagine what it feels like to go to a mall and see all these Chinese spending so much money? Some of the things that they buy cost more than what I make in one month! It hurts to see something like that, and this is coming from me, someone who is not a racist. No wonder they [the Chinese] are the ones targeted when there's a riot." Bondan, a twenty-four-year-old university student of Sundanese heritage, was less sympathetic in his observations: "The Chinese who live in places like Kelapa Gading and Pluit are different . . . they don't want to be friends with guys like me, and in malls and other places, they look at me with suspicion, especially if I'm in their territory. . . . Maybe because they think I'm poor. . . . This is why the *pribumi* often think that the Chinese are snobby [*sombong*]. . . . They have their own Chinese areas, employing *pribumi* as housemaids and security guards. . . . How do they think other people will think of them?" Boy and Bondan came from middle-class families themselves and claimed that they did not harbor discriminatory feelings toward the Chinese. However, both agreed that Chinese exclusivity as embodied in gated communities is alienating and confronting.

There are also many Chinese who agree with criticisms of Chinese enclaves like Kelapa Gading, often with much harsher negative sentiments. Marcus, a thirty-two-year-old Chinese freelance writer from East Jakarta, even went as far as labeling Kelapa Gading and its Chinese residents as a form of apartheid: "Kelapa Gading is a Chinese ghetto. The whole thing is quite scary. After May 1998, we [Chinese] went around complaining that we were marginalized and discriminated against. We demanded to have the respect we deserve. But in reality, the Chinese also erect barriers to keep the *pribumi* out. What we see in Kelapa Gading, it is just like apartheid. . . . How can the Chinese ever fully integrate if those rich enough to buy protection continue to live separately and refuse to engage with the *pribumi?*" Although Marcus's opinion is strong, the essence of his sentiment is certainly shared by other Chinese who are concerned about how the exclusive lifestyles of a small portion of well-off and privileged Chinese may affect how all Chinese are perceived.

There are also a number of Chinese who outright reject the self-sufficiency narrative of the middle- and upper-class Chinese *habitus,* even leaving the *habitus* they grew up in as protest. For instance, Eli, a thirty-year-old female NGO worker, grew up in a residential estate in West Jakarta but then went out of her way to live among some of Jakarta's poorest residents and participated in civil society and political activities:

> I came from a very comfortable, middle-class family. However, I was always really bothered by the fact that our residential complex was located right next to a slum area. We had a family driver from that slum area and every night he would leave work at our big house [to go] back to his own ramshackle house. I hated this difference, and I could only imagine what poorer *pribumi* may feel about this gap. . . . After the shock of May 1998, I wanted to do something to bridge this gap and break the Chinese stereotype, because there are poor Chinese too in Indonesia and not all Chinese live segregated lives. So I joined an NGO that helps the poor and lived in the slums on the banks of the Ciliwung River for a while so that people could see what an ethnic Chinese woman like myself can do. . . . I'm not trying to be altruistic [*sok baik*], but I really think that something needs to be done to break the stereotype. Ultimately, I believe that this is how we Chinese can have a more peaceful future here in Indonesia.

Individuals like Eli and Marcus represent a rupture in the ethnic Chinese *habitus* from which they came. Dissatisfied and discontented with the rules, boundaries, and what they saw to be the negative effects of their *habitus,* these individuals are determined not to repeat the mistakes of the older generation, and in the process they have created a new, in-between *habitus* that attempts to bridge the gap between the Chinese and non-Chinese.

Through an account of the time I spent with the Tanumihardjas as a typical middle-to-upper-class Chinese family in Kelapa Gading, I analyzed the different domains of ordinary life inside an ethnic residential enclave. I came to understand the complex dynamics of racialized inclusion and exclusion that occurred within their home and the gated neighborhood, where the Chinese simultaneously fear and need the non-Chinese with whom they live in close proximity. Here, Bourdieu's concept of *habitus* is useful in helping us understand why some Chinese engage in exclusionary boundary-making practices. As a system of embodied social learning, the *habitus* subtly shapes the identities and dispositions of individuals living within a specific social milieu. At the same time, by adhering to the borders of this milieu, individuals also play an active role in maintaining the boundaries of the *habitus.* Within this process of boundary maintenance, the "*habitus* thus implies a 'sense of one's place'" and instills within individuals a "sense of the place of others" (Bourdieu 1989, 17).

The dual processes of embodied social learning and discourse reproduction are evident in families such as the Tanumihardjas, in which Handy and Jessica, as members of the younger generation, have learned how to behave and conduct themselves in various spaces and social situations through interactions within their families and the larger Chinese social milieu. Growing up in a milieu in which the importance of being safe (*aman*) is heavily emphasized, young people like Handy and Jessica learned to stay within their own safe spaces, socialized almost exclusively within their established social networks of other middle- and upper-class Chinese, and made life decisions that did not veer far from the well-beaten track (such as the choice of life partner, career, and place of residence). Handy and Jessica also internalized a sense of distrust toward non-Chinese as the essentialized others and learned appropriate ways in which to interact with them within well-maintained boundaries. At a broader level, they also continued to cultivate a distrust toward the ability (and willingness) of the state to protect the Chinese in times of crisis. Feeling comfort and safety in their own secure neighborhoods guarded by private security personnel, Chinese families like the Tanumihardjas believe they need to utilize their resources strategically to protect themselves in the absence of protection from the state.

The stories presented in this chapter illustrate how ethnic and class marginalization is a two-way process in which it can be unclear exactly who is marginalizing whom. The fact that such a segregated lifestyle is still deemed necessary in the present time indicates how little has changed in the Chinese victim narrative. Having said that, I also demonstrated how the exclusive lives of middle- and upper-class ethnic Chinese have reinforced their negative stereotypes as wealthy and aloof. There is a clear paradox here where these Chinese believe that their exclusivity serves the best interest of their group but actually has the opposite effect of only strengthening the narratives that have motivated targeted violence against them in the past. In this regard, what can be understood as the objective interest of the group is subjective. Many younger Chinese, such as those discussed at the end of this chapter, have realized this contradiction and are making concrete efforts to either challenge the victim narratives embedded in their *habitus* or to break away altogether.

3

(Re)learning Chineseness

For any family, choosing which primary school, secondary school, or higher education institution to send their children to is rarely a simple or straightforward decision, and is one that usually combines pragmatic, ideological, and sentimental considerations. After all, planning a child's educational path is a key step in the quest to achieve not only the child's individual goals but also their family's (and broader community's) collective aspirations, whatever they may be. For Chinese Indonesians, these choices are further complicated by a desire for safety and cultural preservation. In this chapter, I discuss how the perceived need to maintain ethnic, class, and religious boundaries has continued to motivate Chinese families to send their children to Chinese-majority schools. This was the case even during the New Order, when Chinese schools were not officially allowed to exist. Consequently, the segregation between the Chinese and non-Chinese has been normalized from a young age.

Similar to the justification provided for the formation of ethnic enclaves, as discussed previously, many Chinese families have felt like they had little choice but to engage in self-segregating practices when it came to choosing schools for their children. Following the gradual tightening of restrictions and then eventually forced closure of Chinese schools from the late 1950s to the late 1960s, and within the context of institutionalized racism and discrimination under the New Order, private Christian schools were viewed as the only options available for Chinese families who did not want their children to attend state-run or Islamic schools. For these young Chinese, attending Chinese-majority schools and universities provided a sense of security and belonging with spaces they could claim as their own. Over time, particular Christian private schools (especially those located near Chinese residential areas and enclaves) have become known as unofficial Chinese schools, with this pattern of segregation continuing to the present. This segregation has also had the effect of perpetuating mutually negative stereotypes between the Chinese and non-Chinese, where the non-Chinese view private-schooled Chinese youth as wealthy, snobby (*sombong*), and spoiled (*manja*), while the Chinese view state-schooled non-Chinese youth as lower class and rough (*kasar*).

In the post-Suharto era, the education landscape for Chinese youth has become more complex, with the reemergence of private schools offering Mandarin as a primary language of instruction. These schools have mostly opened in middle- and upper-class residential areas with large Chinese populations, and they usually offer a National Plus curriculum that delivers the standard national curriculum in a combination of Mandarin, English, and Indonesian as the three languages of instruction.[1] In an era when the idea of learning Mandarin and rediscovering a "lost" Chinese identity appeals to many, these trilingual schools are gaining popularity. At a more pragmatic level, the rising prominence of Mandarin as an international language of trade and commerce has also motivated many young Chinese to pursue overseas language learning or higher education in the PRC and Taiwan, with these trilingual schools being an ideal stepping-stone to achieving these goals. These new trends have changed the educational field for Chinese youth, who are now exposed to more varied ways of being Chinese and (re)learning Chineseness via means their parents and grandparents were once denied.

MAINTENANCE OF CULTURAL AND LINGUISTIC ROOTS IN COLONIAL CHINESE SCHOOLS

As has long been noted, schools are one of the main sites where social order and structures such as class and racial politics are maintained and reproduced across generations, normalizing inequalities that exist between individuals and groups (Bourdieu and Passeron 1990; Nash 1990; Levinson and Holland 1996). In his theorization of the *habitus,* Bourdieu (1974, 1996) views the school as one of the main institutions where systems of thought and dispositions are reproduced. Reflecting the role of schools as an agent in the shaping of consciousness beyond the family, Bourdieu contends that "it may be assumed that every individual owes to the type of schooling he has received a set of basic, deeply interiorised master patterns" (cited in Nash 1990, 435). Schools have also historically functioned as one of the arms of modern nation-states, disseminating state ideologies through compulsory subjects and mandatory nation-building activities. For instance, during the New Order, school students were required to complete the state's compulsory ideological education courses, such as the Guidelines for the Appreciation and the Practice of Pancasila (*Pedoman Penghayatan dan Pengamalan Pancasila*), as part of their curriculum requirements and to attend flag-raising ceremonies every Monday morning, something Indonesian students still do today. As Lyn Parker (2003, 206) argues, during the New Order, schools were "overwhelmingly powerful institutions of national culture and state power." Apart from formal curriculum-based education, children also learn about cultural norms and patterns of behavior deemed appropriate to their class, ethnicity, gender, religion, and socioeconomic background through seemingly mundane everyday interactions that take place in schools.

Among migrant Chinese communities around the world, Chinese schools have played a crucial role in the maintenance of culture, languages, communities, and networks. For Chinese migrant families under colonial rule, community-run Chinese schools were often the only places where their children could receive an education and learn traditional moral values deemed crucial for the maintenance of Chinese cultural purity. For instance, in Thailand in the late 1950s, G. William Skinner (1957, 381) suggests that "without a Chinese education, grandchildren of Chinese immigrants at the present time [would have] become Thai." Particularly in the early twentieth century, cultural protectionism through education allowed generations of the Chinese diaspora in places such as Singapore, Malaya, and the Dutch East Indies to maintain a sense of connectedness to a greater pan-Chinese identity and to Mainland China (see Wang 1981, 1993). In most of these schools, Chinese students were conditioned and encouraged to socialize exclusively with other Chinese, which created a protected social environment and increased separation from the non-Chinese population.

In Indonesia, the ethnic Chinese had established their own Chinese-medium schools since the Dutch colonial period. According to Leo Suryadinata's (1972, 51) important study of Chinese education in colonial Dutch East Indies, at first, mostly wealthy Chinese families hired tutors for their children, and the first small-scale Chinese school was not established in Batavia until 1729, but it was soon closed due to "mismanagement." Citing Mary Somers's (1965) research on *peranakan* in Java, Leo Suryadinata suggests that the number of Chinese schools began to increase in the last quarter of the nineteenth century, so that by 1899 "there were 217 schools in Java (and Madura) with 4,452 students, and 152 schools in the Outer Islands with 2,170 students" (Suryadinata 1972, 51; see also Vandenbosch 1930). Importantly, these early schools were part of a larger network of Chinese teachers (from China and various Chinese-speaking overseas Chinese communities) in the Nanyang (Chinese for "Southern Ocean") who traveled between the different Chinese communities in Southeast Asia to promote both the maintenance of Chinese culture and linkages between the various communities (see Murray 1964; Lohanda 2002; Sai 2010).

When Chinese schools in Indonesia started to become more established, they were largely run by ethnic Chinese organizations representing various regional, political, and linguistic affiliations. Suryadinata (1972) notes that, while their curriculum was based on Confucian classics, these Chinese schools were initially also known as Hokkien schools since the medium of instruction was Hokkien to cater to the Hokkien migrant population. This began to change in the early twentieth century when pro-Republican Chinese organizations, such as the Chinese Association (Tiong Hoa Hwee Koan, THHK), began to establish Mandarin-language schools, such as the first THHK school set up in 1901 in the Patekoan area of Batavia near what is now Glodok (see Govaars-Tjia 2005; Sai 2010). Chinese schools in the Dutch East Indies were heavily influenced by both local and Mainland Chinese politics, and they often became sites of ideological struggles that reflected the dominant political discourses concerning the Chinese of the time (Lombard-Salmon 1971; Sai 2016). Many of the THHK leaders were sympathetic to the Republican cause in Mainland China and actively promoted pan-Chinese nationalism among the Indies Chinese, including through these schools.

Suryadinata (1972, 53) also notes that as Batavian Chinese schools began to modernize their curriculum, they also started introducing the teaching of English (and not Dutch) as a second language as part of the curriculum (see also Sai 2016). According to Suryadinata, English was chosen because it was deemed to have had wider use compared to Dutch. Modeled on other overseas Chinese schools, especially those in Japan, more progressive teachers began to abandon Confucian classics and to incorporate modern Chinese textbooks imported from Tokyo, Shanghai, and Singapore. In addition, more and more THHK schools adopted the Anglo-Chinese education model that was popular in British Malaya and taught English rather than Dutch as the secondary language. The popularity and independence of these Chinese schools roused the suspicions of the Dutch colonial government and soon prompted them to establish their own Dutch-language schools for Chinese—Hollandsch-Chineesch School—in order to counter the perceived threat of Chinese nationalism among Indies Chinese intellectuals (see also Govaars-Tjia 2005; Kuipers and Yulaelawati 2009; Willmott 1961).

Chinese schools continued to flourish after Indonesia's independence, with an estimated 250,000 students enrolled in such schools by 1950 (Suryadinata 1972, 64). Suryadinata argues that Chinese schools remained popular even after independence because the initially limited number of state-run schools "would not cope with the large number of children born after the war." Furthermore, "there was a lack of confidence among the Chinese on the quality of the newly opened Indonesian schools" (64). While not all Chinese children went to Chinese schools, these schools continued to be pivotal to the maintenance of Chinese languages and cultures as well as the ethnic *habitus* and social milieu.

Beginning in the early 1950s, the Indonesian "government began to exercise some control over [Chinese] schools. All Chinese-medium schools had to be registered with the Ministry of Education and the Indonesian language had to be taught from the third year at the primary school level" (65). It was also during this period that many Chinese schools became embroiled in the political division between leaders and educators who were pro-PRC and those who were pro-Taiwan (Willmott 1961). At the same time, the political situation in Indonesia became more unstable, with various regional separatist movements throughout the archipelago, as well as rising antiforeign and anti-Chinese sentiments. In 1957, the government further tightened restrictions by banning Indonesian citizens from attending Chinese schools. Additionally, "teachers in Chinese-medium schools and the schools themselves were required to obtain new permits from the Ministry of Education" and "all textbooks used in Chinese-medium schools had to be approved by the Minister of Education" (Suryadinata 1972, 67–68). These new regulations resulted in a drastic decrease in the number of Chinese schools, and those that were shuttered were quickly converted to national schools where the language of instruction was Indonesian.

Chinese schools finally ceased to exist when the government ordered their closure in the aftermath of the G30S/PKI and the anti-Communist purges that followed. Buildings and properties owned by Chinese organizations were seized and nationalized as state schools. The impacts were severe. Based on official figures from Indonesia's Ministry of Education, Siew-Min Sai (2010, 151) estimates that "in the 1960s, the ban on Chinese language education affected 629 schools, 6,478 teachers and 272,782 students in eleven cities across Indonesia. In Jakarta alone, 82 schools were shut down, 47,432 students could not continue their studies and 957 teachers lost their jobs." Onghokham (2009, 69) notes that the closure of Chinese schools was "the most significant act aimed at integrating the minority into Indonesian society."

CHINESE SCHOOLS IN THE NEW ORDER AND THE POLITICS OF BOUNDARY MAINTENANCE

After the closure of Chinese schools, students were absorbed into both state and private schools, although most went to private Christian schools. There are several reasons for this tendency among Chinese parents to avoid sending their children to state schools. First, until the fall of the New Order, there was an unofficial quota in place at state schools and universities limiting the number Chinese students taken in each academic year. Although no official government regulation was ever established to adjust this quota, restrictions on the number of Chinese in state education institutions are well known among the general public (see also Tjhin 2005; Dawis 2008). These quotas were put in place just after the closure of Chinese schools and universities in order to ensure that disadvantaged but high-achieving non-Chinese youth had priority to enter cheap but high-quality state universities. The (false) assumption here was that Chinese families could better afford to send their children to private schools.[2] Because of these quotas, many Chinese families did not bother to enroll their children in state education institutions, which they saw as lower in quality and, as a result, entered their children in private schools despite the higher fees. In comparison, most non-Chinese families could not afford to send their children to private schools and thus state schools became dominated by non-Chinese students.

Religion also played a part because the majority of non-Chinese students are Muslim, so they could not enroll in many Christian schools that had a religious entry requirement.[3] In contrast, many Chinese families were either already Christian or did not mind their children embracing their school's religion, so long as they did not embrace Islam, which is seen as the religion of the non-Chinese.[4] In this regard, private Christian school entry requirements became an effective filtering mechanism that automatically separated the majority of Chinese children from non-Chinese children. In his study of private Christian schools in Indonesia, Chang-Yau Hoon (2008, 157) makes a similar observation: "The entry criteria of religion and class serve precisely the interests of ethnic segregation in a subtle but significant way. This ethnic separation in education since childhood serves as a virtually impassable ethnic boundary which seriously impedes any opportunity for

Chinese to interact with *pribumi* children." From the early 1970s onward, the segregation between Chinese students in private schools and non-Chinese students in state schools became not only apparent but also one of the defining characteristics that emphasized the ethnic, class, and religious boundaries.

Another reason why wealthier Chinese families sent their children to private Christian schools was to prepare them for higher education overseas. Starting in the 1980s, affluent Chinese families who could afford to do so sent their children to schools in countries such as Singapore and Australia from a young age to receive a high-quality international education. Families who could not afford an overseas education at the primary and secondary levels settled for the next best thing and sent their children to Chinese-dominated private Christian schools that were reputed for their global outlook and good English-language programs, with the idea of later sending their children to overseas universities. This popularity of overseas education among middle- and upper-class Chinese families was usually based on a combination of practical, symbolic (prestige), and security reasons.

During the New Order, many Chinese parents distrusted the national education system. For them, an overseas education was a significant step for their children to eventually be able to leave Indonesia for the sake of their future and security. Once their children had settled overseas, there was always the possibility that the whole family could join them and escape the uncertainties of life in Indonesia. Until that happened, having their children go to private Christian schools became a way not just to prepare them academically but also to remove them from the potential dangers of encounters with the non-Chinese. As Hoon (2011, 409) notes in his survey of Chinese-majority Christian schools in Jakarta, a side effect of the international focus and exclusiveness of these schools is that "they tend to contribute little to equip students to live in the multicultural society of Indonesia." However, for Chinese families who feel little sense of belonging and have a mobile and cosmopolitan outlook, participating in a multicultural citizenry is not a priority.

While during the Dutch colonial and early independence eras, Chinese schools were characterized by their language of instruction and by the teaching of Chinese cultural materials, during the New Order, schools were labeled "Chinese" because of the demographics of their student bodies. Typically, these Chinese schools were privately run, affluent, and located in Chinese areas such as the inner West Jakarta suburbs of Tomang and Kedoya Selatan, and the northeastern suburb of Kelapa Gading. This is ironic considering that one of the main justifications for the closure of Chinese schools in the late 1960s was to encourage greater assimilation and equality between Chinese and non-Chinese students. However, as was the case with the government's forced assimilation of the Chinese that began in earnest after 1967, this government policy that was supposed to improve fairness also paradoxically emphasized differences between Chinese and non-Chinese. At the everyday level, this type of ethnic segregation led to a set of social stereotypes and fears founded on nothing more than biased presumptions.

Among Chinese families, a high degree of defensiveness, caution, and—in many cases—feelings of superiority are evident. For instance, my research participants often told me that they regarded non-Chinese children who went to state schools as rowdy and unruly. Such perceptions were reaffirmed with every news report of mass brawling (*tawuran*) and gang violence between warring state schools. This stereotype in turn scared many Chinese parents, who feared that their children would either be drawn into thuggish behavior or be bullied by state school students on the streets. Moreover, many middle- and upper-class Chinese parents were hesitant about their children socializing with non-Chinese friends at school, fearing that their children would become Muslim and lower their class status if they married a non-Chinese. Such concern was expressed by Inge, a fifty-three-year-old mother of three university-aged children who had gone to Chinese private schools and universities:

> I don't consider myself to be a racist at all. In fact, I have some *pribumi* friends, and I know that a lot of them are fine. But in regards to my children's education and influences, I wanted them to have the best. . . . Sometimes I see *pribumi* kids on the streets just hanging around like thugs. Have you seen Chinese kids hanging around like that? No, right? I think that's because we Chinese, we have a strong work ethic and regard education very highly. I don't really mind my kids having *pribumi* friends from their school or church, because at least I know they're from good families.

As can be seen from Inge's comment, Chinese parents had a variety of justifications for limiting their children's potential contact with non-Chinese children, sometimes even resorting to primordialist arguments about Chinese moral virtues.

Because of these fears, many Chinese parents have strongly discouraged or disallowed their children from entering (state or private) schools and universities dominated by non-Chinese; these parents have also encouraged their children to stick together with other Chinese when going out, with some even forbidding them from socializing with non-Chinese altogether. This has resulted in Chinese children commonly being labeled as rich snobs. Christopher, a twenty-nine-year-old engineer, initially wanted to enroll in the University of Indonesia (Universitas Indonesia, UI), as it is the best state university in the country, but was dissuaded from doing so:

> As I was finishing high school at [Regina Pacis Upper High School], I was getting really good grades, especially in the natural sciences. I really thought that I had a good chance of doing well in the state university entrance exams and getting into a university like UI or Bandung Institute of Technology [Institut Teknologi Bandung]. I knew that they have good engineering programs. But my parents were strongly against the idea, because they thought that I would have a hard time in a university dominated by *pribumi*. . . . So, I enrolled in Tarumanagara University near our home, which is not a bad university, but it was not my first preference.

Even in the post-Suharto era, Christopher's experience is repeated often among Chinese youth who, due to personal choices and/or family pressures, found themselves in education institutions dominated by Chinese.

Many of these Chinese schools (particularly the more expensive ones) are protected by high gates, walls, and fences, along with round-the-clock security, similar to many of the safety measures discussed in chapter 2. For many non-Chinese, these features represent the socioeconomic disparity that separates the Chinese and the rest of Indonesian society. Fauzan, a twenty-two-year-old university student from a Central Javanese background, remembered the feeling of envy that he felt as he passed by an elite Chinese school every day on his way to the state school he attended:

> Every morning my [public] bus would pass by this private school mostly attended by Chinese kids. My bus was hot and crowded, and these Chinese kids arrived [at] their private schools in their private cars driven by their private drivers. I didn't know any of these kids, of course, so I don't know what they were really like. But I remembered feeling really envious of the things they had that I didn't have. . . . I don't mean to judge, but no wonder some people really hate the Chinese. Even I was envious, and I wasn't even that poor. I could still go to school.

By contrast, for Chinese youths, these security measures symbolize a sheltered and protected social environment in a country where they frequently feel vulnerable and discriminated against. Fearful of being caught out alone outside their comfort zones, many Chinese youths admit to feeling safe and even proud to belong within their school compound. For instance, Nelly, a nineteen-year-old university student, recalled her days at IPEKA Puri Indah Christian School, a private school in the Puri Indah area of West Jakarta: "We pretty much only had Chinese kids at the school although there were a few students who were *pribumi.* But even though they were *pribumi,* they were different, not like those state school kids. . . . I think their families were quite well-off and lived in the area too. . . . I'm glad that I went to school separately from *kampung* [village] kids, I am scared of them." Here Chinese schools became safe spaces that Chinese youth could claim for themselves within the complex social world of Jakarta schools.

The segregation between the Chinese and non-Chinese also occurs within schools that seem to defy stereotypes at first glance. One such example is Jakarta State Upper High School 2 (Sekolah Menengah Atas Negeri 2 Jakarta, SMAN 2 Jakarta), a state high school located in the Taman Sari area of West Jakarta. SMAN 2 Jakarta is one of the few state high schools in Indonesia with a large proportion of Chinese students. This unusual profile means that the school is often cited as an example of a public school where Chinese and non-Chinese students coexist harmoniously. However, upon closer examination, the dynamics of socialization between the Chinese and non-Chinese students are not as straightforward as they seem.

SMAN 2 Jakarta used to be known as the Kuo Min Tang High School, was associated with pro-Taiwan groups, and was nationalized in 1959.[5] However, SMAN 2 Jakarta's location on Jalan Gajah Mada, near the commercial districts of Glodok, Mangga Dua, and Petak Sembilan where many Chinese merchant families live, means that up to 85 percent of the school's students at any given time are Chinese even after nationalization. These students usually come from poorer Chinese families who cannot afford to send their children to more expensive private schools, such as the nearby Ricci Catholic Upper High School 1 (Sekolah Menengah Atas Katolik Ricci 1). Non-Chinese students who attend SMAN 2 Jakarta are also usually from families with similar socioeconomic backgrounds. This situation makes SMAN 2 Jakarta quite different from other state schools, which tend to be dominated by non-Chinese students, with the exceptions of Jakarta State Upper High School 17 (Sekolah Menengah Atas Negeri 17 Jakarta) in Mangga Besar, South Jakarta, and Jakarta State Upper High School 19 (Sekolah Menengah Atas Negeri 19 Jakarta) in Tambora, West Jakarta, that have similar histories and student profiles.

A school official from SMAN 2 Jakarta I spoke to insisted that although the majority of the school's students are Chinese, both Chinese and non-Chinese students are treated equally, coexist harmoniously, and do equally well academically. SMAN 2 Jakarta is indeed in the top bracket of high-achieving state schools in Jakarta. Nevertheless, actual student experiences seem to be different, with former students telling me that most Chinese and non-Chinese students usually moved in different social spheres, though they participated in classes and school-related activities together. Yendi, a twenty-four-year-old former student of SMAN 2 Jakarta, explained such separation: "Chinese and *pribumi* students had separate groups in the school. Sure, we were all friends, but we didn't really hang out together in or out of school. After school the Chinese kids go somewhere like Gajah Mada Plaza, and the *pribumi* kids go elsewhere. . . . Why didn't we hang out together? I'm not sure. . . . I think it was just because things had always been that way. We had different families, cultures, and friends." The reality of life for SMAN 2 Jakarta students is that ethnic boundaries between the Chinese and non-Chinese still exist, even though these students inhabit the same spaces and have similar socioeconomic backgrounds. Here, the culture of ethnic segregation that has been inculcated in them from a young age seems to be stronger than socioeconomic solidarity.

SIMILAR BUT DIFFERENT: CHINESE AND NON-CHINESE SPACES IN EDUCATION

Chinese and non-Chinese schools commonly coexist in Jakarta, not just within a single suburb or area, but also within very close proximity to one another. A well-known example of this is on Jalan Letnan Jenderal S. Parman, a busy arterial road in West Jakarta, where three major universities and several public and private schools are located. Of these three universities, Tarumanagara and Krida Wacana Christian University (Universitas Kristen Krida Wacana) are considered to be Chinese dominated, while Trisakti is regarded as dominated by non-Chinese. (As mentioned in previous chapters, Trisakti was the site of the student protests and shootings that precipitated the May 1998 riots.) Similarly, among the high schools in the vicinity, a number are regarded as Chinese dominated; these include Regina Pacis Upper High School (Sekolah Menengah Atas Regina Pacis), BPK Penabur Christian Upper High School 1 (Sekolah Menengah Atas Kristen 1 BPK Penabur), and Sang Timur Catholic Upper High School (Sekolah

Menengah Atas Katolik Sang Timur). Others nearby are *pribumi* dominated, such as Jakarta State Upper High School 23 (Sekolah Menengah Atas Negeri 23 Jakarta) and Jakarta State Upper High School 65 (Sekolah Menengah Atas Negeri 65 Jakarta). The same situation can be found in other areas of Jakarta, even in South Jakarta, an area characterized as more cosmopolitan and ethnically integrated (*membaur*) than other areas of Jakarta. Although ethnic segregation is not as clearly delineated as in West or North Jakarta, the same situation also occurs in South Jakarta. In the Blok M commercial district of Kebayoran Baru, several state and private schools with vastly different student demographic profiles exist in close proximity to each other. In this area, private Christian schools run by foundations such as the Tarakanita Foundation (Yayasan Tarakanita) and Ora et Labora Christian Education Foundation (Yayasan Pendidikan Kristen Ora et Labora) have large numbers of Chinese students (although they have a greater proportion of non-Chinese students compared to private Christian schools in other parts of Jakarta), while nearby state schools like Jakarta State Upper High School 70 (Sekolah Menengah Atas Negeri 70 Jakarta) and Jakarta State Upper High School 6 (Sekolah Menengah Atas Negeri 6 Jakarta) have hardly any Chinese students at all.

In many of these cases, there are often only a few (if any) physical characteristics that distinguish Chinese educational institutions from non-Chinese ones. Since most Chinese schools and universities are privately owned, they generally appear to be better equipped and well maintained in terms of facilities and school grounds. However, this is not always the case. For example, Tarumanagara and Trisakti are located right next to each other and are quite similar in terms of educational quality and the facilities provided (figure 3.1). Both universities are run by private educational foundations; both offer a range of undergraduate and postgraduate degrees in engineering, business, medicine, design, and social sciences; and both attract predominantly middle-class students.

Interestingly, both universities were initially established by Chinese organizations in the late 1950s. Trisakti was first established in 1958 as the left-leaning Baperki University (Universitas Baperki, renamed Res Publica University [Universitas Res Publica] in 1963), owned and operated by the Consultative Council for Indonesian Citizenship (Badan Permusjawaratan Kewarganegaraan Indonesia, Baperki), an integrationist ethnic Chinese sociopolitical organization that was disbanded in 1965 after being accused of being sympathetic to Communism. While Res Publica University was run by a Chinese organization, it had a diverse faculty and student body,

FIGURE 3.1 Trisakti University and Tarumanagara University located next to each other on Jalan Letjen S. Parman in West Jakarta, 2009.

Source: Shutterstock.

with one of Indonesia's best-known political and literary figures, Pramoedya Ananta Toer, teaching literature there in the late 1950s. It was during his time there that Toer researched Indonesian literature and began formulating his arguments for his 1960 book *Hoa Kiau di Indonesia* (The Chinese in Indonesia) that criticized the government's treatment of the Chinese, for which he was imprisoned by Suharto from 1969 to 1979 (he remained under house arrest in Jakarta until 1992 following his release from Pulau Buru).

Tarumanagara was established in 1959 by the Sin Ming Hui organization (later known as Yayasan Candra Naya), and like Res Publica University it too had a diverse faculty. Both universities were temporarily closed in 1965 following G30S/PKI, after which all Chinese-owned educational institutions were audited, through which for instance, as Abdul Wahid (2018) notes, university faculty and students were screened for their possible involvement in PKI and the alleged coup. The Res Publica campus was also burned and attacked shortly after G30S/PKI (*Tempo* 2014). My informants who were university students at this time told me that while Tarumanagara was allowed to reopen relatively unchanged in 1967, by contrast and due to its links with the banned Baperki, Res Publica University was repossessed and handed over to be comanaged by the Indonesian National Armed Forces, the Ministry of Education, and the Institute for the Cultivation of National Unity (Lembaga Pembinaan Kesatuan Bangsa, LPKB), a government-sponsored Chinese organization whose purpose was to promote and ensure the smooth assimilation of the Chinese. Res Publica University reopened in 1965 as the state-controlled Trisakti University, and it is still the largest private university in the country, owned by a foundation of the Armed Forces.

Today, there is a significant difference between Trisakti and Tarumanagara in terms of their student populations. Trisakti is known to be a *pribumi*-dominated university, while Tarumanagara has such a large Chinese student body that it is popularly known among Jakartan youth as "Little Shanghai." It is unclear exactly why and when this division happened, especially considering both universities started out as Chinese owned. After speaking to several former students of Res Publica University, my reading of the situation is that when the university was reopened as state-controlled Trisakti, many Chinese (and some non-Chinese) former students were barred from reenrolling because of their suspected Communist ties. Furthermore, knowing that Trisakti was under the direct control of the state (and especially the Armed Forces), Chinese families became reluctant to send their children there and opted instead to enroll them at Tarumanagara or the nearby Krida Wacana Christian University, with this pattern continuing to the present. The example here of Trisakti and Tarumanagara illustrates once again how ethnically segregated spaces and boundaries have their roots in history.

Now the younger generation of Trisakti and Tarumanagara students know very little (if anything at all) about their universities' respective histories except the prevalent opinion that Trisakti is considered a non-Chinese university and Tarumanagara is Chinese. Ade, a twenty-six-year-old male non-Chinese Trisakti student, commented on the differences between Trisakti and Tarumanagara students:

> I think it's so strange how Trisakti and Tarumanagara are next door to each other, yet they're so different. In Tarumanagara, you'll rarely see *pribumi* kids. In there, they all have fair skin and slanted eyes. There's even a joke among Trisakti kids that you need a tourist visa to enter Tarumanagara and I think it's hilarious! We [Trisakti students] don't hang out with Tarumanagara kids because we just don't have anything in common. We have some Chinese kids too here in Trisakti, but I think they're different to Tarumanagara Chinese. They're tougher in a way and more willing to socialize with the *pribumi*.

Similarly, Tarumanagara students also have their own stereotypes of Trisakti students, as expressed by Fifi, a twenty-two-year-old female Tarumanagara student: "I'm a bit scared of Trisakti students, because they are predominantly *pribumi* and they seem rough. Even the girls appear so, too. They have frequent brawls between their own [faculties] over things such as car parking spots, and I hear that their freshmen induction programs, hazing [*plonco*], are really rough. Their students also frequently go to the streets for various demonstrations, and my family don't want me to be a part of that. I'm afraid that I'd be bullied or ostracized if I went there." When I asked whether she had contemplated enrolling at Trisakti instead of Tarumanagara, Fifi replied that the thought had not crossed her mind. Sissy, Fifi's twenty-two-year-old friend who also went to Tarumanagara, added, "Most of my friends from Sang Timur Catholic Upper High School also ended up here in Tarumanagara, so it's nice to see familiar faces. . . . In my family, we all go to Tarumanagara because it's near home and it's a good university. . . . I didn't think to enroll [in] Trisakti because nobody I knew goes there so I don't really know what it's like there." Ade's, Fifi's, and Sissy's comments highlight the point that many of the perceived contrasts between Chinese and non-Chinese institutions like Tarumanagara and Trisakti are often not based on actual significant tangible differences, such as major disparities in campus infrastructure or course offerings. These stereotypes arise instead from assumptions passed down and reinforced among families and social circles within their class and ethnic *habitus*.

It is clear from examples like SMAN 2 Jakarta, Trisakti, and Tarumanagara that ethnic boundaries are more often based on sociohistorical and symbolic factors, rather than any defining physical or socioeconomic characteristics. By continuing to make safe choices and enroll in the same schools and universities frequented by those in their *habitus,* the younger generation maintains existing ethnic boundaries even when such boundaries do not formally or physically exist. Yet there are also interethnic collaborations and relationships that cannot be discounted in and across both universities. For one, the teaching and administrative staff in both universities are a mixture of Chinese and non-Chinese, with the majority of faculty in Tarumanagara being non-Chinese (including those in leadership positions, such as the rector and some deans of faculties). There are also non-Chinese students who attend Tarumanagara and Chinese students who attend Trisakti mostly because of pragmatic reasons; for example, Trisakti is better known for its engineering program, so Chinese students also choose to study there. Furthermore, while the everyday spaces and social milieus of the two universities are mostly separate, the protests of May 1998 showed that students from the two universities could also support each other in times of need. During these protests, Tarumanagara students also stood together in solidarity with their Trisakti peers. When the army started opening fire at Trisakti, many Trisakti students also took shelter in the Tarumanagara campus during the chaos that followed the violence.

It should be emphasized that, despite the different *habitus* of Trisakti and Tarumanagara students, interethnic and cross-university collaborations (for example, competitions and events), friendships, and romantic relations do occur relatively frequently. Henson, a Chinese Trisakti law alumnus, decided to attend that university because of the law school's good reputation, and during his time there he was very active in the student union and participated in the annual student protests to demand justice for the four Trisakti students killed in the May 1998 riots. Henson reminded me that one of the Trisakti students killed in the shootings was Chinese (economics student Hendriawan Sie), and that the main Trisakti Faculty of Economics and Business building was later renamed the Hendriawan Sie Building. Jerry, a non-Chinese (of Ambonese descent) Tarumanagara design alumnus, met his Chinese wife at Tarumanagara when they were both studying there. Jerry told me that while some of his non-Chinese friends made fun of him for choosing to study at "Little Shanghai," he never had any problems being accepted into social groups at Tarumanagara:

> Sure, I was the darkest-skinned person in Tarumanagara at the time [*laughs*], but I never felt like the ethnic Chinese students didn't want to be friends with me. I think it's just a perception that Tarumanagara [is] a Chinese university, but in reality, the *pribumi* students there were not treated any differently, at least in my experience. . . . I went to my ethnic Chinese friends' homes after classes and for group work, and I also met my wife from these friendship circles. At first, I think her family in particular was wary of me, but I was Protestant Christian too and started going to their family's church, so I was accepted.

The fact that Jerry is Christian undoubtedly eased his acceptance among his would-be wife's Chinese Christian family. The story may have been different if Jerry were a Muslim non-Chinese. Indeed, the case studies presented in the chapter so far are complex and show that ethnic prejudices and segregation do exist in educational institutions where Chinese students learn the boundaries of their *habitus*. However, the interethnic collaborations and relationships that take place in and across education institutions such as Trisakti and Tarumanagara reveal how the boundaries of both the Chinese and *pribumi habitus* are not straightforward, and that there are in-between spaces within which meaningful interactions, acceptance, and boundary negotiations can take place.

GOING FULL CIRCLE: PAHOA INTEGRATED SCHOOL AND THE (RE)ESTABLISHMENT OF CHINESE SCHOOLS

As noted earlier, the educational landscape has become more complex for the Chinese since the early 2000s with the (re)establishment of Chinese schools that teach in Mandarin. The combination of the rise of China as a global economic powerhouse and the liberalization of Chinese-language teaching in Indonesia has sparked an enthusiasm for learning Mandarin among Chinese families. Thousands of Mandarin-language tuition centers, both large and small, have opened in most major cities, catering to both Chinese and non-Chinese families who want their children to acquire Mandarin-language skills (Chong 2018, 72; see also Hoon and Kuntjara 2019). Across the country, many state and private schools now offer Mandarin as a stand-alone subject or as one of the main languages of instruction (as part of the National Plus curriculum), with some schools even advertising their Chineseness by incorporating Chinese characters into their school logo. Most of these schools obviously target Chinese students, as they are located in residential areas and ethnic enclaves with large Chinese populations. According to data from the Association of Chinese Language Studies Program in Indonesia (Asosiasi Program Studi Mandarin Indonesia) and the Association of Trilingual National Schools in Indonesia (Perkumpulan Sekolah Nasional Tiga Bahasa Se-Indonesia), it is estimated that in 2018 there were seventy trilingual schools offering Mandarin as one of the languages of instruction and twenty-six universities offering Chinese-language programs (Hoon and Kuntjara 2019, 574, 586).

Unsurprisingly, this new trend has excited the older Chinese generation who experienced Chinese-language education and who see it as an opportunity to revive Chinese education for the younger generation. By far the most interesting aspect of this re-Sinification is that a number of these new National Plus trilingual schools have been established and managed by alumni of Chinese schools (such as THHK schools) that were forcibly closed in the mid- to late 1960s. Taking advantage of post-Suharto freedoms and the growing public interest in Mandarin, members of these alumni organizations (many of whom are successful retired businessmen) have visions of resurrecting the glory days of Chinese education, and reintroducing traditional Chinese educational values to young people who are regarded as a lost generation. After the forced closure of Chinese schools and the assimilation of Chinese students in the New Order, the evolution of Chinese schools seems to have come full circle.

One such newly (re)established school is Pahoa Integrated School in the Summarecon Serpong residential development area located in Tangerang in the southwestern suburbs of Jakarta.[6] Opened in 2008, Pahoa is a reincarnation of the original THHK school in the former Patekoan area (now Jalan Perniagaan) of West Jakarta that was forcibly closed in 1966. The school has proved a success. According to the school's board of trustees, within three years of opening, Pahoa boasted 2,449 students from kindergarten to high school level. Following in Pahoa's footsteps, other alumni groups of Chinese schools that were closed under the New Order have also (re)established schools in areas with large Chinese populations. These include the reopening of Pah Tsung School in Cengkareng in 2012 by alumni of the former Pah Tsen Tsung Sio Chinese School; the Jakarta Nanyang School in Bumi Serpong Damai City (a self-contained urban development) that was opened in 2012 by the alumni of the Sin Hoa Chinese School; and the Ma Chung alumni group–established Ma Chung University (Universitas Ma Chung) in 2007 in the East Java city of Malang.

Pahoa is a place of many contradictions. Some of these can be seen at first glance, as the school's buildings stand tall and imposing compared to the flat and rather barren newly developed landscape of the outer suburbs that surround them (figure 3.2). Inside, the contrasts continue and seem to underlie even the school's vision and mission.[7] On one hand, like other National Plus schools, Pahoa's international focus is intended to produce cosmopolitan and global-ready graduates who speak both English and Mandarin. On the other hand, there is a visible effort to instill strong traditional Confucian values in the students. It needs to be emphasized here that while Pahoa teaches Confucian moral values, it is not a Confucian religious school. The version of Confucian religion that was institutionalized as one of the state's six official religions in the post-Suharto era is different from classical Confucian moral values and philosophy such as those taught at Pahoa. Around the school buildings and grounds, colorful banners and posters in Indonesian, English, and Mandarin display Confucian sayings, such as "Treat others as you would like to be treated" and "Respect for others is the essence of virtue." There are

FIGURE 3.2 Pahoa School main building, 2009.
Source: Photograph by the author.

also banners that clearly state the values expected from Pahoa graduates: virtue, discipline, lawfulness, citizenry, and filial piety.

Indeed, one thing that sets Pahoa apart is the fact that, while the school is officially secular, it incorporates the teaching of Confucian moral values in all its educational activities. The school's decision to teach Confucian moral values is reminiscent of the history of overseas Chinese education that placed a heavy emphasis on the teaching of Confucian classics as a marker of Chineseness. As well as compulsory religious instruction classes as mandated by the state, Pahoa students are also required to attend moral virtue classes and character-building camps where they are taught Confucian philosophy. Pahoa also hosts workshops for parents of students, with weekend seminar events covering topics such as virtuous parenthood. It is clear from such programs that Pahoa wants the school's community to develop certain Chinese qualities that echo the teachings of the old THHK schools. Yet members of Pahoa's board of trustees told me that their aim was not to recreate the Chinese values of the old THHK schools for a new generation and insisted that the new Pahoa is different because it is not an exclusively

Chinese school and because it is committed to promoting multiculturalism and intergroup acceptance in Indonesia through education.

The school board claims that Pahoa accepts students from all ethnicities, religions, and socioeconomic backgrounds, despite the fact that the vast majority of its current students are middle- and upper-class Chinese who live in the nearby residential estates. Most importantly, the school board also claims that Pahoa was intended to be secular and without any religious affiliation. They reason is that such neutrality would allow the school to focus on a multicultural approach to moral education through the supposedly universal teachings of Confucius, with Confucian moral values being focused on humanitarianism and peace. Here, Confucian moral values have been reconceptualized and reimagined in order to adapt to a new learning environment. If in the past Confucian moral values were utilized as an ideological platform to maintain China-centric identities in the Dutch East Indies, Pahoa has repackaged them as a neutral educational tool to promote the universality and applicability of Chinese values in a more plural and globalized Indonesia.

In an interview I conducted in 2009, Pak Oki, a successful retired entrepreneur who was a THHK school alumni and a Pahoa board member, explained the importance of this strategy to increase the appeal of Chinese moral values (such as Confucianism) through schools:

> Being Chinese in Indonesia has always been a problem because the *pribumi* think that we only know about making money and being greedy. They don't understand that we have so much more to give and that the values that we live by are good. In fact, the *pribumi* themselves can benefit from some of our Confucian values, such as hard work and modesty. Everyone can apply these values. This is why we need to promote Confucianism, because if more people understand and apply Chinese values, then the Chinese will be more accepted in Indonesia. Schools are one way of doing this, although it is a long-term process.

This desire to make Chineseness more widely accepted in Indonesia is paired with a heavy emphasis on multiculturalism. For instance, the school always celebrates religious, cultural, and national events, such as Christmas, Eid, Vesak, Imlek, Kartini Day, and Independence Day, on a grand scale with school-wide commemorations.

Despite the school's optimistic approach to multiculturalism, a definite sense of melancholy, nostalgia, and trauma can be felt in the school's physical environment. All around the grounds, high walls and fences keep out potential intruders, while security guards watch the school day and night, highlighting the concerns about the safety of the school and its students. Pak Oki commented that everyone involved in the administration and management of Pahoa is acutely aware of the negative stereotypes that exist of Pahoa as a Chinese school: "We realize that people might think of our school as an exclusive Chinese school. . . . Worse, some people might suspect that we are trying to spread Chinese political ideas among the children. . . . We do worry that there are those who might have ill intentions toward our school. . . . We have to take measures to ensure the safety of our pupils, such as by putting in place good security systems." Pak Oki and other school board members told me that they also closely monitor the latest political developments to keep watch (*jaga-jaga*) and make sure that Pahoa is always protected and prepared amid changing political tides. Given the trauma of witnessing their old THHK school being forcibly closed, it is understandable why security measures are deemed necessary by the school board. However, the reality is that it is difficult to dispel negative stereotypes about schools like Pahoa when their very physical presence and student profiles signify the Chinese–*pribumi* socioeconomic disparity that has for so long divided them.

The atmosphere of nostalgia also permeates other parts of the school. In the main entrance there is a large hall dedicated to the history of THHK schools with framed photographs of past principals, teachers, students, and buildings. Wall panels detail the chronology of THHK schools up to their closure in 1966, although there is no elaboration on the government's ban against Chinese languages and schools during the New Order. When asked about the significance of visible commemorations of Pahoa's past throughout the new school, Pak Oki explained that it was important to the school's founders that incoming generations of students do not forget what a privilege it is now to be able to openly learn Mandarin, in an environment in which they can also learn about Chinese moral virtues:

> I remember going to school at the old Pahoa School in Patekoan, and I also remember the sadness I felt when the government forcibly closed the school. . . . Not just our school but also all Chinese schools in Indonesia. It was a tragedy for the Chinese, because without the schools, we lost all sense of who we are and the values that set us apart as a people. My children, for example, can't speak Mandarin, although I did try to instill Chinese moral values as much as I could while they were growing up. . . . The younger

> generation now, they are lucky that they could have [a] Chinese education again. . . . Chinese schools like Pahoa need to be resurrected so that the younger generation, my grandchildren's generation, can relearn what was lost. I'm old now, and so are my friends in the alumni group, but Pahoa is our legacy.

The commemoration hall at Pahoa was designed to ensure that all its present-day students remember the collective history of the closure of Chinese schools and internalize the memory as part of their shared heritage (figure 3.3). Memories of the New Order's forced assimilation policies have been constructed as an important part of the culture at Pahoa, where reflecting upon the contradiction between past oppressions and current freedoms is encouraged.[8]

Alongside the narrative of nostalgia in Pahoa, its founders evidently see a crucial link between Chinese identity and the ability to speak Mandarin.

FIGURE 3.3 A display wall at Pahoa School dedicated to the memory of the founders of the original THHK school in Patekoan, 2009.

Source: Photograph by the author.

Pak Oki's remark about the centrality of Mandarin in the resurrection of Chinese identity in Indonesia echoes a conviction shared by many older Chinese eager to use post-Suharto reforms to reintroduce the language for the younger generation. Sai (2010) highlights the importance of alumni and teachers of formerly banned Chinese schools in promoting the viability of Chinese languages.[9] She also suggests,

> Most significantly, their efforts in promoting the language are accompanied by crucial gestures in memory work that serve to localize the language in Indonesia. By "localization" of the Chinese language, I refer to the attempt by Chinese-educated alumni to initiate and sustain Chinese-language use and instruction within a multilingual framework throughout Indonesia. It also describes their attempt to re-narrate the history of the language in a way that allows the Chinese language, as well as themselves, to be integrated legitimately within the Indonesian nation. Through confronting the once de-legitimized past of the Chinese language and re-narrating its placement within the Indonesian nation, these alumni are trying to localize the language in Indonesia. (151–152)

Sai is right about the importance of memory work in alumni attempts to (re)establish Chinese schools and boost the popularity of Mandarin among Chinese.

However, the degree to which new Chinese schools are a product of their founders' ambitions and views on what constitutes proper Chinese culture must be examined more closely. Indeed, members of alumni groups, who are mostly *totok,* appear to project a high degree of cultural primordialism toward younger Chinese. The case of Pahoa highlights some important issues regarding the representation of Chineseness in Indonesian schools. The dominating influence of alumni groups in determining the curriculum and cultural teaching materials at new schools like Pahoa puts into serious question whose and which version(s) of Chineseness are being taught. For schools like Pahoa, the teaching of cultural heritage and values, and the celebration of unique Chinese traditions, are tricky and require some skillful balancing in order to avoid reinforcing essentialized differences.

This situation makes for a prime example of how the meaning of Chineseness is partly being defined by an older generation who have the money, institutional power, and social capital to influence public discourse. There is a danger that Chinese identities are being portrayed as monolithic, homogenous, and centered on the PRC when the reality at the grassroots level is different.

Alumni groups' efforts to promote Mandarin as *the* language of Chinese Indonesians are also problematic, considering that most Chinese families in Indonesia originally spoke regional Chinese languages such as Hakka or Hokkien and not Mandarin. Sai suggests that this Mandarin bias is reflective of the tendency among both contemporary Chinese and scholars to treat Chinese mother tongue languages as subbranches or dialects of Mandarin rather than as languages in their own right. Furthermore, Sai (ibid., 155) argues that "the contemporary revival of the Chinese language in Indonesia after 1998 reflects this academic discrimination between 'standard' Mandarin and 'substandard' Chinese regional dialects." This tendency can certainly be observed among alumni groups (such as Pahoa's founders), resulting in it being the only language promoted and associated with Chineseness in these newly established schools.[10] This linguistic bias underscores the constructed nature of the language and identity nexus and essentialist notions of tradition.

From the students' point of view, life at Pahoa is nothing out of the ordinary, although understandably a number of students feel some pressure to portray Confucian values and be seen as "proper" Chinese youth in their school life. Diana, a sixteen-year-old Pahoa student, admitted that she found it hard to juggle expectations to learn Mandarin, do well at school, and fulfill the expectations of the older generations:

> Pahoa is a new school and the school that I went to previously was just a normal Christian [private] school. But when Pahoa opened up a few years ago, my parents put me here because they thought the school's concept is unique and the location is near our house. I was a bit sad to leave my old school but now it's fine. The only thing is I find learning Mandarin really hard. I've had private lessons in the past but using it intensively at school is more difficult. . . . At Pahoa, I just think there is more pressure to display a Chinese character than at my old school . . . but I guess it's good for me to learn all that because my parents plan on sending me to China for university.

Not all students feel this kind of pressure. Hendry, a sixteen-year-old student, noted that he could still "be himself" even though he goes to school in an environment that emphasizes his Chineseness: "The rules and moral education here don't really affect me much. I mean, my family is quite a *totok* family and I speak some Mandarin and all that. But I just feel normal. . . . I have *pribumi* friends, not in Pahoa, but I'm friends with a number of neighborhood kids outside of school. . . . I don't really pay attention to the Confucian stuff they tell us here [*laughs*] because I find them boring." Diana's and

Hendry's comments show how even within a single school, students experience Chinese schooling in different ways. Meanwhile, at the other end of the spectrum, a number of Chinese youths from other schools I interviewed spoke of schools like Pahoa with disdain, saying that they would never agree to attend such schools because they are "too Chinese." Students' varied reactions to these schools indicate just how unpredictable the reception can be to this ongoing phenomenon.

Although schools like Pahoa are enjoying a steady increase in popularity,[11] their numbers are relatively small, and many more Chinese families still choose to send their children to standard private schools. Indeed, some Chinese parents are afraid of how the non-Chinese might react to the opening of more and more Chinese schools like Pahoa. For instance, Theo, a fifty-year-old Chinese father of a teenage daughter studying at a Christian private school, remarked, "Our generation tried hard throughout the New Order to assimilate and blend in with the *pribumi*. . . . But now Chinese schools that were closed have started opening up again and this is really getting me worried. What will the *pribumi* think about this? They're going to think even more that once a foreigner, always a foreigner. I tell you, those Chinese schools will be one of the first targets to be attacked if riots break out again." Theo's fears were echoed by others who were afraid of a backlash over an increasingly visible Chinese presence in the ideologically contested educational landscape. Dita, a thirty-six-year-old Chinese mother of two young children, told me in 2017 that she and her husband opposed the idea of sending their children to a Chinese school (such as Pahoa) because they were wary of how such exclusivity would be perceived:

> My parents sent me to a private Christian school with quite a lot of *pribumi* kids, so I grew up with a lot of *pribumi* friends. My husband's upbringing was the same, and we agreed that we wanted our kids to also go to a good school where they'll also have *pribumi* friends. I wouldn't want my kids to only be friends with other Chinese, and if we sent them to a school like Pahoa, then they'll only have Chinese friends. . . . I think that would be so unhealthy for my kids, and it would also confirm stereotypes about the Chinese being exclusive! Being exclusive only makes the image of the Chinese worse, especially nowadays with a lot of Muslim *pribumi* being more suspicious of other religions and cultures.

Dita's comments, made just a few months after the mass anti-Ahok rally by Muslim protesters in Jakarta, highlight a salient point regarding how new trilingual Chinese schools may be perceived by the general (non-Chinese) public at a time of rising ethnonationalism and religious intolerance.

The history of Chinese education in Indonesia reflects this community's struggle to maintain their cultural heritage and to carve out social spaces for themselves throughout different periods. Even under the New Order, the boundaries between the Chinese and non-Chinese were maintained, despite the closure of Chinese schools and the government's official assimilation policies. Here, economic capital is certainly a major factor in middle- and upper-class Chinese families being able to afford to send their children to more expensive fee-paying private schools. However, examples such as the stark difference in the ethnic profiles of the Trisakti and Tarumanagara student bodies demonstrate how the establishment of racialized spaces is not always due to economic factors and has more to do with longer-term historical and structural factors. While there are other types of educational institutions and school cultures in Jakarta (including single-sex schools, technical schools, and private tuition providers) that have not been discussed in this chapter, the case studies presented showcase the dynamics of racial politics in educational institutions and highlight the important role that these spaces play as sites where Chineseness is learned from an early age.

In more recent years, the trend of Mandarin-language learning that has reoriented many Chinese families toward new Chinese schools such as Pahoa has raised critical questions about how this tendency may influence the public perception of Chineseness. On the one hand, the growing popularity of Mandarin may have a positive impact, generating interest in Chinese languages and culture among non-Chinese, which could translate into greater interethnic understanding. On the other hand, there are legitimate worries that this closer focus on Chinese culture may also have the negative effect of reinforcing perceptions of the essential foreignness of the Chinese.

Ultimately, the desire for security, exclusivity, and cultural preservation has greatly influenced many Chinese families' decisions to send their children to Chinese-dominated private schools. However, it is important to also note that there are contrasting viewpoints among Chinese families about segregated schooling. There are pathbreaking Chinese parents who refuse to send their children to exclusive Chinese schools and universities because they want their children to be exposed to other cultures and not to fear the non-Chinese. This shows how there are families that reject the notion of Chinese exclusivity, and they represent the different ways in which the boundaries and rules of the Chinese *habitus* are being challenged.

Even among Chinese families who do send their children to private schools, their motivations for doing so cannot be generalized. For example, many middle- and upper-class parents (both Chinese and non-Chinese) who send their children to programs at private and international schools do so to prepare their children for further studies overseas, believing that an overseas education will result in better career options for their children in an increasingly competitive global environment. As noted in the discussion on Pahoa and the (re)establishing of Chinese schools, many parents who enroll their children in Chinese schools also do so because of similar instrumental motivations to equip their children with the Mandarin-language skills they deem necessary in a world where China is a dominant actor. In their minds, Mandarin skills not only strengthen their children's career prospects but also contribute to Indonesia's ability to be competitive in the future. As such, any analysis of the educational landscape must also take into consideration the broader contexts of modernity and globalization.

Educational institutions are indeed important sites within which young Chinese learn the characteristics and boundaries of their *habitus* and the associated patterns and behaviors that have been passed down from previous generations. Within the walls of their schools and universities, they not only acquire academic knowledge, they also acquire and build upon the cultural, social, and economic capital that is central to their social life and position as minorities within the social order. Nevertheless, there is also room for relative autonomy within the *habitus* where individuals can exercise agency in crafting their own narratives in ways that are different from earlier generations. Taking advantage of the relative freedoms of the post-Suharto era, some Chinese are creating their own spaces in which they can engage in activism, creative production, and self-reflection, often telling stories that challenge and subvert common narratives of ethnic Chinese history and Chinese–*pribumi* relations.

4 Performing Trauma and Indonesian Chineseness

Chinese Indonesian films and performing arts are relatively underanalyzed subjects of study. While there has been a good deal of scholarly attention on the social, economic, and political positions of the Chinese over the decades, the arts have mostly been regarded as less important or too marginal to warrant much in-depth analysis. Yet the few studies that have been done on the production and consumption of the arts and media among the Chinese reveal their importance in the processes of identity construction, as well as in the construction and maintenance of the Chinese *habitus*. For example, Josh Stenberg's book *Minority Stages* (2019) on diverse performing arts traditions—including glove and shadow puppetry, Chinese-language theater, and dance—of various Chinese communities across the Indonesian archipelago shows that these performances have been central to how Chinese individuals and groups have represented themselves within the contexts of both local and national politics. Similarly, Hew Wai Weng (2018) demonstrates that contemporary Chinese Muslim preachers and performers are both astute and strategic in adapting both Chinese and Islamic clothing, singing, and dancing styles to create a hybridity that is important to how Indonesian Chinese Muslimness is defined. In the field of media consumption, Aimee Dawis's *The Chinese of Indonesia and Their Search for Identity* (2009) reveals how during the New Order the consumption of Chinese martial arts television shows provided Chinese viewers with a sense of connection to a lost Chineseness at a time when their languages and cultural materials were banned.

The performing arts and visual culture are clearly important mediums through which the Chinese express and define themselves. As Jeffrey C. Alexander (2006, 32) argues, "Cultural performance is the social process by which actors, individually or in concert, display for others the meaning of their social situation." For more than thirty years of the New Order, the

Chinese were virtually absent from Indonesian arts and popular culture and therefore did not get much opportunity to "display for others the meaning of their social situation." It came as no surprise, then, that once more opportunities for self-expression arose after 1998, the Chinese were quick to reclaim their space within Indonesia's arts scene through various mediums. These ranged from public performances of traditional dances, such as the lion dance (*barongsai*) usually presented during Imlek, and the resurfacing of other forms of traditional arts to television drama series and films that represent the Chinese and the issues that matter to them (Setijadi-Dunn 2009; Setijadi 2013; Stenberg 2019).

While these new public representations of Chineseness may be analyzed in a multitude of ways, of key interest and relevance here are the ways in which themes of collective memory and trauma are expressed in the visual arts. Taking advantage of the newfound creative freedoms over the past two decades, Chinese filmmakers and artists began exploring concepts of racial trauma, personal and collective memory, violence, fear, and injustice in their works. Drawing on both personal and collective memories about past anti-Chinese discrimination and violence, these artists remember and present alternative views of Chinese Indonesian history. In doing so, they create new narratives that challenge the beliefs and historical taboos of the previous generations.

CHINESE INDONESIAN IDENTITY, PERFORMANCE, AND THE DILEMMAS OF REPRESENTATION

The field of cultural production is an extremely complex and uneven space governed by contradictory forces, such as those of approach and avoidance, identification and disidentification, and collaboration and conflict. Since no single mode of representation can accurately cover everyone within a particular group, all representations are inherently somewhat biased or problematic and thus are a potential cause for contestation. This is certainly true for the Chinese, whose diversity and heterogeneity mean that representation is not an unproblematic matter. In the post-Suharto era, during which the Chinese have been finally free to express and represent themselves in public forums and in popular culture, the questions of how they should be represented and who should do the representing are constant points of disagreement between various groups with different sociopolitical experiences and agendas. Indeed, for a minority keen to rehabilitate their image after decades of negative stereotypes, the Chinese are especially sensitive about how their stories are depicted in the media. As such, the challenge of representing Chineseness in the post-Suharto era lies in trying to find a balance between acknowledging a group identity while also being true to individual voices.

In many ways, representations of the Chinese in the performing arts have reflected their sociopolitical positions throughout different periods of Indonesian history. In the colonial era, strong Chinese cultural influences could be seen in the creation of idiosyncratic local music and theater genres, such as *gambang kromong* orchestra from the outskirts of Jakarta performed by the *benteng* Chinese community; *komedi stamboel* (a colonial-era hybrid genre of folk theater influenced by Western and Chinese opera and Arabic music); and *kroncong* (a folk music genre influenced by Portuguese musical traditions) (see Kartomi 2000; Cohen 2006; Hanan and Koesasi 2011). Similarly, Chinese film producers such as the Wong brothers (Nelson, Joshua, and Othniel) and The Teng Chun (Tahjar Ederis) were pioneers of colonial Indonesia's film industry, whose popular stars included Chinese actors such as Fifi Young and Tan Tjeng Bok (Setijadi-Dunn and Barker 2010, 37; Hanan 2017, 56–61; Barker 2019, 29). In preindependence films, Indies *peranakan* culture was often featured and expressed in details such as the long-sleeved blouse worn with a sarong or batik-printed cloth (*kebaya encim*) used by actors and designers; story lines also adopted an integrationist approach in which Chinese and non-Chinese cultures were shown as coexisting in relative harmony (Sen 2006; Setijadi-Dunn and Barker 2010). However, the situation changed drastically after the Japanese occupation in 1942 that saw the closure of many Chinese-owned film studios, theaters, and musical groups. The prominence of the Chinese in the performing arts would never be the same again, particularly with the rise of ethnonationalist sentiments that gave preference to non-Chinese cultural producers and artists after independence.

The Chinese were practically absent from the media, popular culture, and visual and performance arts throughout the New Order (Sen 1994; Heryanto 1998; Setijadi-Dunn and Barker 2010). Although there were Chinese actors, filmmakers, and artists during this time, many chose not to disclose or display their Chineseness in order to avoid discrimination and secure work. For instance, Teguh Karya (born Liem Tjoan Hok and later baptized as Steve Lim), one of Indonesia's most celebrated and prolific New Order–era filmmakers, was Chinese, but throughout his career he never featured Chinese actors in his films, addressed Chinese issues, or discussed his Chinese heritage in interviews (Sen 2006, 177). Throughout the New

Order, in the rare instances when the Chinese were the subject of books, television shows, or films, they were almost always represented according to the official discourse of assimilation. One such example is *Putri Giok* (The Jade Princess), a 1980 film directed by non-Chinese director Maman Firmansyah that portrays forbidden love between young Chinese and non-Chinese individuals. The film tells the story of a Chinese brother and sister who are both dating non-Chinese. Their father, a corrupt and wealthy real estate developer, does everything in his power to break up the relationships because of his disdain for the non-Chinese. However, in the end interracial love prevails and the Chinese father repents of his greed, ethnic exclusivity, and prejudice against the non-Chinese, finally agreeing to change his ways.

As Karl G. Heider (2021, 12–13) argues, *Putri Giok*'s story line is essentially an argument in support of the New Order's narrative of interethnic harmony but only through Chinese assimilation (see also Heider 1991). The representations of Chinese characters in the film (especially that of the corrupt and prejudiced father) are typical of the New Order period, when, as a people considered as inherently guilty of greed, corruption, and disloyalty, they were usually portrayed negatively in films, television shows, and literature. Under the New Order's tight censorship, there was relatively little that writers, artists, or producers could do to challenge the dominant ideological discourses about race, class, and religion. Those who addressed controversial themes such as discrimination against the Chinese risked being accused of threatening interethnic harmony by addressing topics related to tribalism, religion, race, and interclass relations, all considered to be taboo under the New Order. The fate of activist artists such as the writer Pramoedya Ananta Toer (who was sent to prison at Pulau Buru by Suharto from 1969 to 1979, after which he was put under house arrest in Jakarta until 1992) was also enough to deter most from stepping out of line. Consequently, Chinese actors who remained in the creative industries were mainly stuck playing predictable and stereotypical roles, such as comical characters with a strong Chinese accent (*pelo*) that emphasized their foreignness, or as corrupt businesspeople who exploit the non-Chinese underclass. Similarly, there was virtually no way for Chinese artists working in any medium to express their thoughts on discrimination or tell their own stories through their art, at least not within Indonesia.

As with most other areas of public life, the political reforms of the post-Suharto era mean there is now an atmosphere of greater openness and relative liberalization in which the Chinese can finally talk about previously taboo topics. Soon after the fall of the New Order, the Chinese began to receive unprecedented attention in literature, media, popular culture, and performance arts. Television channels now regularly broadcast documentaries and special news reports about Chinese culture and history in Indonesia, particularly around the time of Imlek celebrations. These programs usually focus on the uniqueness and distinctiveness of Chinese culture, though some do mention the history of assimilation under the New Order. On a larger scale, made-for-television films and serials such as *Lo Fen Koei* (2001), *Jangan Panggil Aku Cina* (Don't Call Me Chinese, 2002), and *Wo Ai Ni Indonesia* (I Love You Indonesia, 2004) centered around Chinese characters and topics, for example, Chinese–*pribumi* acculturation and the hardships suffered by poorer Chinese in rural areas. In literature, female Chinese authors, such as Marga T (born Marga Tjoa Liang Tjoe), Maggie Tiojakin, Lan Fang, and Tiffany Tsao, have written short stories and novels about the dilemmas and lives of contemporary Chinese women from different walks of life. This same reappearance of Chinese stories and subject matter can also be seen in other areas of popular culture and performance arts, including theater, dance, photography, and fine arts.

The return of the Chinese to the domains of media and public culture has generally been received positively. Newspaper and magazine articles have praised the boldness of both Chinese and non-Chinese filmmakers and artists creating public discourse on Chinese issues, and the reappearance of Chinese characters and themes in the media is often cited as one of the indicators of greater interethnic tolerance and civil society presence (Heryanto 2008; Hoon 2008). However, critics have also pointed to fundamental problems in how Chinese identities are commonly represented in the media. For instance, Chinese culture is still often portrayed in an essentialized fashion, featuring images such as burning joss sticks and hanging red lanterns, emphasizing the foreignness of the Chinese. Internal diversity among the Chinese is largely glossed over, and there is little or no acknowledgment of the long history of interethnic and cross-cultural tensions in the country. Jacqueline Lo (2000, 152–153) calls this mode of cultural representation "happy hybridity," and warns that there is a danger that cultural difference could be blindly celebrated "to the extent where it can produce a sense of political in-difference to underlying issues of political and economic inequalities." Indeed, the concern from early in the post-Suharto era was that representations of Chineseness in mainstream media would continue along stereotyped tropes that do not problematize embedded xenophobia or racialized politics.

As Krishna Sen (2006, 171) argues, while the reappearance of the Chinese in post-Suharto films is exciting, "it does not ensure a radical shift in a politics of representation, deeply embedded in the textual practices of the film industry and more widely in cultural and political history of modern Indonesia." Ariel Heryanto (2006, 78) makes a similar point when he argues that very few post-Suharto filmmakers have been successful in interrogating what he calls "the dualism of the *pribumi*/non-*pribumi* divide." For instance, in films such as *Ca-bau-kan* (The Courtesan, 2002) and *Gie* (2005), the supposed essential differences between the Chinese and *pribumi* are not questioned. Heryanto argues that this is a serious problem, and because of this common lack of critical interrogation, most representations of Chineseness do not break away from primordial conceptions of Chinese ethnicity that have dominated Indonesia's race rhetoric for so long. Sen's and Heryanto's criticisms echo the frustration of others who feel that artists and public performers are not doing enough to challenge existing discourses about the essential foreignness of the Chinese (see Tickell 2009; Khoo 2010; Setijadi 2013).

PERFORMING CHINESE INDONESIAN TRAUMA

In the post-Suharto years, Chinese artists and filmmakers have begun to break old stereotypes and conventions about how Chineseness can and should be portrayed in the public domain. As part of a generation that has developed its creative talents in the relative openness of the reform era, younger artists are depicting contemporary Chinese lives in ways that are more critical and honest. At the same time, within the broader context of grassroots efforts to challenge state narratives on history, the Indonesian arts space has also become much more open for both Chinese and non-Chinese artists to explore narratives related to historical traumas.[1]

Nancy Wood (1999) suggests that the field of collective memory as a whole can be treated as performative since the act of remembering, especially at the group level, requires efforts to generate/recreate the past in ways that make it feel real and embodied in the present. Wood also argues that, through a variety of mediums and channels (she calls them "vectors"), such as historiography, books, and films, individuals and groups are able to perform their personal trauma and at the same time engage in broader public debates about the commemoration of collectively traumatic historical events. In this regard, public performances can become a form of testimony, which can be therapeutic for the performers, especially in situations where formal recognition or commemoration and justice for traumatic events have not been (or could not be) achieved. While Wood's text refers to the legacies of trauma in postwar Europe, it is possible to utilize this framework of the performative nature of collective memory to understand contemporary Chinese representation in the arts sphere.[2]

Soon after the May 1998 riots and the fall of Suharto that same month, a number of Chinese artists began producing works that centered on their individual and collective memories of being Chinese in Indonesia. One of the first to do so was FX Harsono (Franciscus Xaverius Harsono, born 1949), one of Indonesia's foremost contemporary artists, who was also a leading figure in the progressive New Art Movement (Gerakan Seni Rupa Baru, 1974–1989). In the post-Suharto period, Harsono started to explore more extensively the issues of memory and Chinese identity, although he had rarely engaged with these themes previously. In October 1998, Harsono had a solo exhibition at Cemeti Art House in Yogyakarta. As part of the exhibition, in a ten-minute performance installation piece titled "Korban" (Burned Victims), Harsono arranged nine human torsos made of wood that were attached on steel poles and planted in the ground. Harsono then torched the torsos, and each was then displayed horizontally within a steel frame, along with a pair of burned shoes. The installation referenced the harrowing stories of people trapped in their own homes as well as in shopping malls during the burning and looting that occurred during the May 1998 riots (see Dirgantoro 2021 for a comprehensive analysis of Harsono's works, including "Korban"; see also Strassler 2018).

Since "Korban," Harsono has continued to produce artworks that deal with the themes of Chinese collective trauma. For instance, he addressed the topic of the forced name change policy of 1966 in his work *Memori Tentang Nama/Yang Dihapus Kutulis Ulang #1* (Memory of a Name/Rewriting the Erased #1, 2009). In this piece Harsono sat on a simple wooden chair at a table in the middle of a dark gallery space, where he repeatedly wrote his Chinese name in Chinese characters using ink and a calligraphy brush on pieces of paper before placing them on the floor. This performance was intended to symbolize Harsono's process of relearning how to write his former Chinese name that he had lost during the New Order.[3]

As well as Harsono, other post-Suharto Chinese artists have also touched on the topics of memory and trauma, including Anna Zuchriana, Octora, Rani Pramesti, and Dadang Christanto, as well as Tintin Wulia and Edita Atmaja (both of whose work I discuss below).[4] Using different mediums and performance styles, these artists explore the issue of the collective trauma of the Chinese from different angles, ranging from the anti-Communist killings of 1965–1966 to the erasure of Chinese names to a general feeling of persecution and paranoia to gender violence as evidenced in the rapes of Chinese women during the May 1998 riots.[5] Apart from performance art, depictions of memory and trauma can also be seen in films and other visual arts.

However, representation and activation of trauma through visual language are not without risk. Within the field of trauma studies, there has been much discussion on the difficulties of representing trauma. Considering the personal, intimate, and subjective nature of trauma, it is difficult—perhaps even impossible—to represent trauma in a way that could be said to represent a collective in a meaningful way. For example, Cathy Caruth (1991) suggests that there is an inherent contradiction in the representation of trauma between the truth of an event and the truth as seen from victims' perspectives, creating a dilemma for historical understanding and the representation of trauma. While victims' testimonies are vital to fill in the gaps when the accuracy of historical facts is called into question, these testimonies may also comprise bits and pieces of recollections that can often be doubted and contested. From an ethical perspective, there is also the worry that secondary trauma may occur through the transmission of the testimonies of victims and survivors. Through acting, listening, talking, and even just observing, trauma may be passed on to an audience.

Given that representations of trauma can never provide a total understanding of the past, the question remains of how artists should represent trauma in a way that is relevant and meaningful to the present time and to a generation that has no firsthand experience of the events. This concern can be used as a starting point to broaden the perspective of reading trauma in visual representations beyond merely providing factual testimonies. Indeed, artists have been both praised and criticized when their work engages with memory and trauma. Some of these criticisms include the potential for a further loss of dignity for victims through reenactments of violence as well as the aestheticization of violence in visual language and art.

The challenges of representing trauma have not stopped a new generation of young Chinese artists and filmmakers from expressing their personal trauma, or exploring critical questions to do with Chinese identity through their art. In the discussion that follows, I examine the works of several young independent filmmakers and two visual artists who convey both personal and collective trauma narratives related to historical instances of anti-Chinese discrimination.

WHAT'S IN A NAME? *SUGIHARTI HALIM* AND CHINESENESS IN THE EYES OF INDEPENDENT FILMMAKERS

The most noticeable reappearance of the Chinese in post-Suharto media has by far been through films. If, as discussed earlier, during the thirty-two years of New Order rule, Chinese Indonesians were almost never the main subject of films (the 1980 film *Putri Giok* being the exception), in the first decade of the post-Suharto era, at least seventeen films were made that featured Chinese characters or featured issues concerning the Chinese as their main subject matter. From 2010 to 2021, I estimate that there have been at least ten more feature films produced that have Chinese as central characters, including three films directed by Ernest Prakasa, which are discussed later in this chapter. This may not seem like a significant number of films compared to the total number of films produced in Indonesia in the post-Suharto years—Thomas Barker (2019) estimates that over 1,300 films were made between 1998 and 2017 alone. However, considering the lack of representation during the New Order, the production of post-Suharto feature films that shed the spotlight on Chinese Indonesians has been very important in terms of public visibility and recognition.

Beginning with Nia Dinata's 2002 film *Ca-bau-kan* (The Courtesan), which tells the story of the relationship between a rich Chinese businessman and his *pribumi* mistress (*nyai*) at the dawn of the independence era, and Riri Riza's 2005 biographical film *Gie,* about the short life of the 1960s political activist Soe Hok Gie, Chinese characters and stories have made a comeback to mainstream cinema screens in Indonesia. Since then, many more films about the Chinese have been made. These include Ariani Darmawan's *gambang kromong* documentary *Anak Naga Beranak Naga* (Dragons Beget Dragons, 2006), Allan Lunardi's thriller *Karma* (2008), Viva Westi's *May* (2008) (which largely centers around the May 1998 rapes of Chinese women), and Edwin's internationally acclaimed film *Babi Buta Yang Ingin Terbang* (Blind Pig Who Wants to Fly, 2008). Likewise, within the film industry itself, the Chinese mainly stayed behind the scenes as financiers and producers during the New Order. In the post-Suharto years Chinese film directors, actors, and technical crew have stepped up and have enjoyed greater visibility and freedom over the past two decades, particularly in independent film communities in urban centers such as Jakarta, Bandung, and Yogyakarta (see Barker 2011).

On May 13, 2008, I attended an independent film anthology screening at Jakarta's Ismail Marzuki Park (Taman Ismail Marzuki) cinema complex.

Organized by the Jakarta-based interethnic Umbrella Project (Proyek Payung) film collective, the anthology was called *9808* and was intended to commemorate the tenth anniversary of the start of the *reformasi* movement. In fact, by 2008 the *reformasi* spirit had waned among the disillusioned younger generation, so the filmmakers of Umbrella Project wanted to remind them that the *reformasi* struggle was not yet over. This young filmmakers' collective worked together and supported each other's projects, despite a modest budget and the films being intended only for limited screenings. Though the screening was relatively small scale, it was well attended by filmmakers, academics, film students, and journalists. The anthology was based around the general theme of fighting forgetting (*melawan lupa*), so all ten films screened that night dealt with the notion of remembering Indonesia's dark history of oppression, corruption, and authoritarianism. While the projects and film screenings were not mainstream, the Umbrella Project collective represents interethnic solidarity among activists in the post-Suharto era. It also reflects how the filmmakers have created an in-between artistic *habitus* that has attempted to bridge interethnic differences through the commemoration of the New Order's assimilation policies and the May 1998 riots as collective traumas that continue to haunt both Chinese and non-Chinese.

Of the ten films, four discussed issues surrounding the legacy of racism against the Chinese: Ariani Darmawan's *Sugiharti Halim* (2008), Edwin's *Trip to the Wound* (2008), Lucky Kuswandi's *A Letter of Unprotected Memories* (2008), and Ifa Isfansyah's *Huan Chen Guang* (2008). Three of the filmmakers are Chinese (Ifa Isfansyah is non-Chinese and from Central Java), and each film represents a range of Chinese experiences (and the different problems experienced) as interpreted by each filmmaker. There is space here to examine only one of the films, and I choose Darmawan's short film *Sugiharti Halim* mostly because the film was very popular among the audience that night, a testament to its cleverness and relatability.[6] I was intrigued by the film's synopsis in the *9808* program booklet that simply stated, "What's in a name? For Sugiharti Halim, a name can lead to a never-ending question. Sugiharti Halim offers a perspective that is comical, provocative, contextual, and deserving to be re-examined today."

Sugiharti Halim is a ten-minute dark comedy about the fictional life of Sugiharti Halim (played by Maria Nadia), a young, feisty Chinese woman who constantly complains about her given name (figure 4.1). As a middle-class, urban Chinese woman, Sugiharti feels that her Indonesian-sounding name does not suit her, since she thinks that it sounds like the name of a

FIGURE 4.1 Promotional image for the 2008 film *Sugiharti Halim*.
Source: Still image courtesy of Ariani Darmawan. Reproduced with permission.

lower-class *pribumi*. She partly blames her parents for choosing an unsuitable name, but she mainly blames the New Order's assimilation policy that forced the Chinese to assume Indonesian-sounding names in the first place. Sick of having to explain her name all the time, Sugiharti becomes embittered and defensive. As such, she uses every opportunity—even romantic dates—to vent these frustrations about her name. It is made clear from the film's opening preface that *Sugiharti Halim*'s plot is inspired by the experiences of millions of Chinese (including Darmawan's family), who, from 1966, had to change their Chinese names to Indonesian-sounding ones in accordance with a cabinet decision. Told from the perspective of a young Chinese woman who suffered the consequences of this forced name change, the film is an honest, semiautobiographical account of Darmawan's own experiences of growing up with her artificial, Indonesian-sounding name.

The film opens with Sugiharti—positioned as though sitting across the table from the audience—looking straight into the camera and introducing herself. She begins by chastising her parents for giving her a name that she insists does not suit her. From there begins an honest and funny account of Sugiharti's life as told through a montage of passionate stories that she tells her potential suitors over a number of dinner dates. In a way, Sugiharti's rant about her name's backstory is a test to see whether these men (whose point of view is a proxy for the viewer) can empathize with her circumstances. The stories range from her experiences of being continually asked about what her real Chinese name was to her opinion about the irony of Indonesian-sounding names like hers that end up widely recognizable as obvious Chinese names. In one of her monologues, Sugiharti tells the story of her family's surname of Halim:

> My family name, Halim, also has its own story. My late father was born with the name Liem Oen Hok. . . . When in 1965 our government forced the Chinese here to choose a citizenship—People's Republic of China or Indonesia—those who chose to be Indonesians usually adjusted their names, so my father changed his name to Taruna Halim. The funny thing is, it didn't occur to him that everyone with the surname Liem would also choose the same name of Halim. So [the name] Halim became synonymous with Chinese Indonesians. Isn't it fair to say that my father actually failed to camouflage his Chinese identity, and mine now?

Sugiharti's reflections on the irony of the New Order's failed assimilation policies are repeated a few times in the film. For instance, she tells her dates about the SBKRI document that proved that the Chinese were Indonesian citizens while simultaneously differentiating them based on their race.[7] At a critical point in the film, Sugiharti tells the story of how she was publicly humiliated and yelled at by a government official who demanded that she reveal her real Chinese name when she could not find her late father's SBKRI document for a passport application:

> The first time I applied for a passport, it was a hell of an experience. . . . I was scolded in the immigration room. The official there repeatedly asked me, "What is your Tionghoa [Chinese] name?" . . . I told him, "I don't have a Chinese name, sir, I swear to God I don't.". . . Patronizingly, the fat bald man . . . then demanded, "Show me your father's SBKRI then! You know what that is, right?" . . . He must have thought that I was stupid if he thought I didn't know about that racist document. . . . In the end he wanted money, around 300,000 [Indonesian rupiahs, approximately US$32 in May 2008] or something.

Visibly embittered by the traumatic experience of having to bribe the immigration official, Sugiharti ponders her name's worth: "I thought to myself, if I could sell my name for that much, would I be happier? Would I?"

Toward the end of the film, Sugiharti congratulates her latest date (played by Hengky Hidayat) for being the first one to make it through her entire monologue without leaving. The man then asks her what name would she choose if she could change her name to anything? To this, Sugiharti answers Julianne—a Western name with no associated traumatic memories. Sugiharti's date then goes on to tell her his own story of being born with the Chinese name Tan Ging Le after his father refused to change the family's name in 1966. He then says that he could stand his Chinese name until he entered high school, when other kids made fun of his name by calling him "crazy" (*gile*) instead of his actual name Ging Le. Ultimately, they started calling him crazy Chinese (*cina gile*) which to him was "double the insult." However, Ging Le then reveals to Sugiharti that as he grew older he decided that he did not want to spend his life being angry, and quoting William Shakespeare, he says, "What's in a name? That which we call a rose by any other name would smell as sweet." Ging Le then tells Sugiharti that even if she changed her name to Julianne, she would still be herself. After a long pause, the film ends with Sugiharti nodding reflectively and saying to herself, "Sugiharti Halim."

Speaking about her film, Ariani Darmawan (born 1977) said that although she is Chinese, she had not initially planned on making a film that dealt strictly with Chinese issues. Darmawan herself is a video artist and bookshop owner from Bandung who makes films mainly as a hobby. Growing up in a *peranakan* family that had many non-Chinese friends, Darmawan was never really conscious of her Chinese identity or paid much attention to how she might be different from her non-Chinese friends. However, as she learned more at university about Chinese history and oppression, she became fascinated by the issue of name changing that had also affected her family. When I interviewed Darmawan in June 2007, she told me that she came to realize how the forced name changing policy was a gross violation of human rights that robbed a group of people of their cultural identities:

> The issue of name changing is a really complex and problematic one. It is also a painful issue for so many Chinese who felt that they lost a part of [their] identity when they changed their names and were still discriminated against afterward. . . . Can you imagine what it would be like if someone suddenly forced you to pick another name out of the blue? That experience would be so traumatic! . . . Yet for so long, people have just simply grown up thinking that this kind of discrimination is acceptable. (interview, June 15, 2007)

Darmawan began developing the script for *Sugiharti Halim* in the mid-2000s, and when Umbrella Project approached her about the *9808* film anthology, she felt that the time was right for her to make the film. Her choice of using dark comedy was intended to reflect the bitter irony of the paradoxical name changing policy. In the same interview, Darmawan remarked, "The whole name changing ordeal was a joke. . . . The Chinese were supposed to become more 'Indonesian' by changing their names, but their Indonesian names actually had the effect of making them seem like fake Indonesians." When I asked whether *Sugiharti Halim*'s story line was inspired by her own life, Darmawan noted that Sugiharti's character is a combination of her and her Chinese friends' collective experiences of discrimination because of their names and ethnic identities:

> I was lucky because my name at least still sounds nice and Indonesians can easily pronounce it. Some of my friends really did end up with bizarre names, simply because their parents wanted to give them Indonesian-sounding names. That's so sad. . . . Growing up, I also remembered thinking that being asked to pay more to obtain my driver's license or passport because I am Chinese was just normal. But things like these are not normal, and people should stop thinking that it's normal, because it's wrong. (interview, June 15, 2007)

With *Sugiharti Halim,* Darmawan hoped to remind people that the Chinese are still dealing with the consequences of this discrimination on a daily basis and that through independent films like hers, more forgotten narratives about the lives of the Chinese can be brought to the fore. This is one of many stories that do not get attention in popular representations of Chineseness in an Indonesia that is dominated by symbolic and essentialized representations of multicultural harmony.

As noted earlier, Ariani Darmawan is not the only Chinese filmmaker who has expressed and explored the complexity of their Chinese identity through some of the films they made in the post-Suharto era. Educated, worldly, outspoken, and mainly middle class, all these filmmakers emerged from the many independent film communities that sprung up around art schools, such as Jakarta Arts Institute (Institut Kesenian Jakarta) and Bandung Institute of Technology in the period after 1998. Partly encouraged by the reappearance of Chinese themes and characters in films as discussed earlier, independent Chinese filmmakers have made films inspired by their own experiences of growing up as Chinese in both the New Order and the *reformasi* era. However, because these films are all based on personal histories, their representations of the Chinese are different from other typical portrayals of Chineseness in mainstream films. This is not to say that these filmmakers have made films only about Chinese Indonesians (indeed, most have gone on to direct and produce many more films that raise a diverse variety of issues), but, like Darmawan, they used their talents and resources to create films that reflect their personal and collective memories as Chinese. In these films, there is little or no inclusion of essentialized representations of Chinese culture or superficial multiculturalism. Instead, as seen in *Sugiharti Halim,* the dominant narratives are raw stories about ambiguous identities, persecution, and feelings of unbelonging. In 2008, Lucky Kuswandi made *A Letter of Unprotected Memories* (screened as part of the *9808* film anthology along with *Sugiharti Halim*) about his personal struggle to come to terms with the open celebration of Chineseness in the post-Suharto era, and Steven Facius Winata made *CINtA* (2009), a film that centers around an impossible love between a young *totok* man and a Muslim non-Chinese girl.

One of the most prolific Chinese filmmakers in the post-Suharto years is Edwin (born 1978), an international award-winning film director originally from Surabaya who has made short and feature films that address modern social issues such as isolation, family dysfunction, and dislocation (see Khoo 2010; Setijadi 2013). In two of his films—*Trip to the Wound* and *Babi Buta Yang Ingin Terbang* (figure 4.2)—Edwin specifically focuses on Chinese issues because it is, as he told me, a way to "vent years of confusion and unanswered questions" about his own identity as Chinese (interview, June 3, 2008). Remembering the past is an important part of Edwin's work, and through his abstract style of filmmaking, he wants to remind his audience not to stop talking about difficult issues.

In *Trip to the Wound,* for example, Edwin focuses on the notion of scars as evidence of deep trauma in the story of a young Chinese woman (played by Ladya Cheryl) who is fascinated by scars. She strikes up a conversation with a young man (played by Carlo Genta) sitting across the aisle from her on an overnight bus, and the two talked candidly about the scar stories of their relatives and friends. However, during the course of the trip, the mood becomes sadder, and wordlessly the woman invites the man to find her scar by slipping his hand under her skirt. Unable to find the scar, the young man asked her where it is. She turns away toward the window in silence as a tear rolls down her cheek. The young woman's private, invisible scar is an allegory of the collective trauma caused by the May 1998 rapes of Chinese women. Edwin's

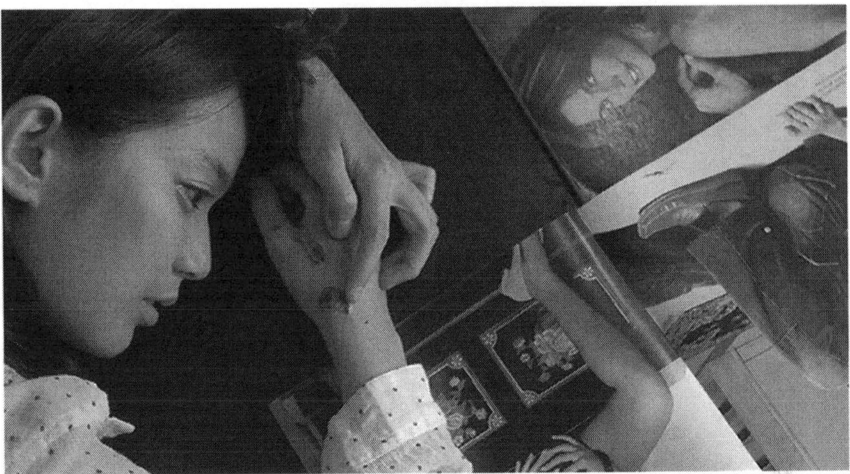

FIGURE 4.2 Still image from the 2008 film *Babi Buta Yang Ingin Terbang.*
Source: Image courtesy of Babibutafilm. Reproduced with permission.

subtle point is that the trauma of May 1998 left a permanent scar on the Chinese body that remains invisible yet forever felt.

In an interview we conducted just before the 2008 release of his first feature film, *Babi Buta Yang Ingin Terbang,*[8] Edwin noted that film is a medium through which he can explore his own ambiguous Chinese identity:

> Making films is like thinking aloud for me. . . . I don't make films like *Babi Buta* or *Trip to the Wound* because I want to make money. . . . I make them essentially for myself because the issues I raised in those films were issues that I experienced when I was growing up. . . . When I was little, my parents told me that I was lucky to have dark skin because then people wouldn't know that I was Chinese. Even then, I wondered why I had to be ashamed about being Chinese. . . . There are so many anxieties associated with being Chinese and I want to talk about them because there are not enough people talking about these hard topics. (interview, June 3, 2008)

More than a self-indulgent exercise, however, the creative space of filmmaking also allows Edwin to raise touchy questions and discuss sensitive subjects that challenge existing discourses: "Films give us [Chinese] the opportunity to explore questions that couldn't be explored throughout the New Order.

Indonesians have a bad habit of forgetting history and not questioning complex issues like racism, so I think through films like mine, people are at least reminded about historical ambiguities that still exist in our society" (interview, June 3, 2008). For filmmakers like Edwin and Ariani Darmawan, making films is a way they can speak out and present their versions of Indonesian Chineseness. The pictures they paint may not be rosy or idyllic, but they represent one end of the spectrum in Chinese identity politics in which the experience of being Chinese has often been confusing, unsettling, and at times traumatic.

In recent years, one of the most successful and popular young Chinese filmmakers is Ernest Prakasa (born 1982), who is also a comedian who often pokes fun at his own Chinese ethnicity (and stereotypes of Indonesian Chineseness) in his comedic performances and stand-up routines. Prakasa's popular film *Cek Toko Sebelah* (Check Out the Shop Next Door, 2016) tells the story of Erwin (played by Prakasa), a Chinese overseas graduate and corporate executive who struggles with his ill father's wish for him to take over the family's small neighborhood provision shop (figure 4.3). In this comedic tale of intergenerational differences, Prakasa includes a mixture of typical and atypical characters, such as Erwin's older brother (who is a reformed troublemaker), a Christian non-Chinese sister-in-law whom Erwin's father initially does not accept (ostensibly because she is not Chinese), the many non-Chinese characters who work at the provision shop (and who provide much of the comedic moments), and the non-Chinese owner of the shop next door with whom Erwin's dad is in direct competition.

The film makes obvious attempts to challenge some conventional narratives of the Chinese–*pribumi* divide by featuring interethnic relationships and friendships, as well as some stereotype-defying portrayals of class differences. For instance, the main Chinese family in the film and other Chinese in their milieu are depicted as lower class, while Erwin's boss and evil property developer are non-Chinese. Also, Erwin's father's shop extends credit to customers, while the shop next door owned by a non-Chinese does not. Memories of the May 1998 riots are subtly woven into the film's narrative, most notably through the story line that Erwin's father's first shop was destroyed during the riots, forcing him to relocate the business and his family. While in many ways the film is full of ethnic stereotypes (both about the Chinese and non-Chinese), a significant emphasis is also placed on interethnic solidarity and collaboration in overcoming crises.

Ernest Prakasa's success with this film, and in his career in general, in no small part comes from his ability to portray existing stereotypes of Indonesian

FIGURE 4.3 Promotional poster for the 2016 film *Cek Toko Sebelah.*
Source: Wikimedia Commons (Creative Commons License).

Chineseness and of Chinese–*pribumi* relations in a critical fashion through humor. Humor has enabled him to address serious matters—such as racism and class inequalities—in a digestible and relatable way, which also explains his film's popularity among both Chinese and non-Chinese citizens (*Cek Toko Sebelah* now has a spin-off television series). His is arguably the most popular film that centers around Chinese characters in the post-Suharto era, if compared to the more independent and art house films. It can of course be argued that poking fun at ethnic stereotypes only serves to confirm them in the eyes of the mainstream public. However, Prakasa's clever framing of these stereotypes as part of alternative narratives about Chinese–*pribumi* relations has allowed him to present new ways of viewing the heterogeneity of the lives of the Chinese. In interviews, Prakasa talks about how, having endured discrimination all his life for being Chinese, he now views himself as a "*cina* comedian who dares to speak up" (Samiadi 2012). Frequently referring to himself using the derogatory term *cina,* Prakasa also admits that openly joking about his ethnicity is his way of confronting and making peace with traumatic events that had happened to him in the past (Afrisia 2015).

Ernest Prakasa and the other Chinese filmmakers discussed in this chapter are examples of what Bourdieu (1977, 1990) calls "virtuosos" within the *habitus,* or social agents that have such a deep understanding of the conventions, objectives, and boundaries of their *habitus* that they know how to game the system or manipulate the rules in order to potentially challenge the social order and status quo. These filmmakers could challenge the inherited narratives and boundaries of Chineseness only because they have an intimate knowledge of the objective conditions and rules that have framed their memories and experiences. Similarly, in the realm of visual arts, a new generation of artists are also using their agency and social capital to speak up and create new spaces within which the collective memories of the Chinese may be remembered and reinterpreted.

MEET MY DEAD GRANDFATHER: THE ART OF TINTIN WULIA

Tintin Wulia (born Maria Clementine Wulia, 1972) is a Bali-born Chinese filmmaker and installation artist. In 1965, her paternal grandfather was taken away (and presumably killed) for being an alleged member of the PKI in Denpasar, Bali. Wulia's family never saw him again. Although they speculate that he was murdered on one of Bali's beaches, along with thousands of others, they have never found out exactly what happened to him. By the time Wulia was born seven years later, the family rarely spoke about what happened to her grandfather, out of both shame and fear for their own safety and welfare.[9] In an interview with me, Wulia mentioned that it was not until she was a teenager that her family started telling her about what happened, and even then the details were always limited. Despite this, Wulia told me that she grew up with a great sense of anxiety as well as an inherent feeling of victimization by the New Order:

> I always knew that my grandfather was missing [*hilang*], but for a long time, my family was very sketchy about the details of exactly what happened. To be honest, I think they probably don't know that much either. What I do know is that my grandfather was the vice president of the Denpasar branch of Baperki, and when the anti-Communist purges began in late 1965, he was quickly targeted for his alleged ties to the PKI. As far as we know, though, he never had any direct links with the PKI, but I guess none of that mattered at the time.... He [my grandfather] was taken away, along with other alleged Communists, and our family home was looted and burned down. My family never heard from him again, but they knew he was dead.... Because there was never any funeral or even proof that he was dead, my family lived with this constant sense of not knowing, but everyone did so in silence because they were afraid of speaking. . . . I grew up with this fear, this secret. But my family told me never to question what happened, and I grew up thinking that I deserved to be discriminated against because I am the granddaughter of a Chinese Communist. (interview, October 24, 2008)

As an artist, Wulia's memories of growing up under the dark shadow of her grandfather's disappearance and her family's subsequent shameful secret have profoundly affected her works and her writing.

For Wulia, dealing with the past through art is a form of therapy, providing a creative channel that allows her to ask unanswered questions, remember and commemorate her grandfather, and ponder how her own story relates to the experiences of so many others (both Chinese and *pribumi*) who suffered under the state-sponsored terror of the New Order. Often told in an abstract manner, Wulia's personal history and emotions permeate most of her art. In her 2000 short film *Violence against Fruits,* Wulia shot the seemingly mundane process of peeling, chopping, and then eating a Japanese persimmon—a fruit originally cultivated in China. This visual is accompanied by a dialogue between an unseen man and woman (one of whom is presumably the person chopping the fruit) about the reasons people do not eat dogs, going through such possibilities as dogs being man's best friend and also being capable of fighting back. Wulia said that she wanted to portray the general feeling of helplessness and victimization suffered by those who are at the mercy of humans. However, at a more personal level, the general theme of persecution evident in *Violence against Fruits* also represents Wulia's own experience of growing up with a feeling of perpetual victimization.

Wulia addressed the topic of her grandfather's disappearance more explicitly in a 2007 animated digital media piece titled *Have a Cup of Tea/ Meet My Dead Grandfather* (produced with multimedia artist Gyora Gal Glupczynski), in which an image of her grandfather is portrayed on board a train with many other individuals (many of whom are faceless), their place in the past signified by the sepia tone of the photographs (figure 4.4). The symbolism of the train in this piece may remind viewers of the trains used to transport millions of European Jews and other victims to their eventual deaths in Nazi concentration camps during the Holocaust. Another interpretation of this imagery is that Wulia's grandfather had shared the same horrible fate as so many others throughout history who have suffered due to discrimination and hate. Just where the metaphorical train is heading is less

FIGURE 4.4 *Train* (Tintin Wulia 2007). Detail from *Have a Cup of Tea/Meet My Dead Grandfather* (Gyora Gal Glupczynski and Tintin Wulia 2007, multimedia installation).

Source: Image courtesy of Tintin Wulia. Reproduced with permission.

relevant, as the point is that collective trauma and suffering are universal experiences that go beyond Chinese Indonesian history. In this regard, Wulia's experience of fear and loss are both rooted in her identity as the Chinese granddaughter of an alleged Communist who was murdered, yet also universal in their tragic commonality with others who have been persecuted throughout human existence.

One of Wulia's most personal works is arguably her 2008 *Great Wallpaper* mural series that focuses on the issue of bureaucratic racial discrimination. For this installation, Wulia painted a set of floor-to-ceiling watercolor murals of her family's SBKRI and name change documents issued in the late 1960s. Designed to function as a conversation starter for the audiences who view it, *Great Wallpaper* (figure 4.5) traces Wulia's family's efforts to fit in

FIGURE 4.5 Artist Tintin Wulia painting *Great Wallpaper No. 470/I/SBKRI/67* mural at Milani Gallery, Brisbane, Australia, 2021.

Source: Photo by Carl Warner.

with Indonesia's sociopolitical ideologies. For Wulia, these documents symbolize her family's bitter experience (and that of many other Chinese) of having no choice but to adhere to the New Order's discriminatory laws: "These [SBKRI and name change] documents implied that there was something inherently wrong with being Chinese. As a Chinese, you needed to be fixed and your existence in Indonesia needed to be justified by a few pieces of paper. . . . I grew up feeling guilty about being Chinese and I'm sure that many others did too" (interview, October 24, 2008). Wulia certainly succeeded in getting people to talk after seeing her murals. In an *Inside Indonesia* article, Wulia recounts her conversation with filmmaker Edwin (discussed in the previous section), who, upon seeing the *Great Wallpaper* installation, admitted that he had never seen his family's SBKRI documents because his parents hid them from him (perhaps out of shame) (Wulia 2008). Many others (both Chinese and *pribumi*) have since approached her with their own stories of dealing with systemic and racial discrimination. Creating art that gets people talking is important for Wulia, because in her opinion the only way to eliminate what she calls "irrational fear" is to talk about it.

Discussing her own art, Wulia said that because of her own experiences of being Chinese in Indonesia, she cannot help but be intrigued by the artificial nature of national belonging and geopolitical boundaries: "My grandfather was a staunch nationalist and very much felt that he and his family belonged in Indonesia. Yet he died as a man unwanted by the state, and although Indonesia is the only home we know, our family has had to continually prove our belonging [in Indonesia]. . . . I think this experience made me think about what it is that makes us belong to a place, and I have asked questions about this very issue in some of my work" (interview, October 24, 2008). Though not all of Wulia's artworks contain direct references to the question of Chinese belonging, most (if not all) of her work is inspired by an interest in how individual lives are entwined with larger political structures, such as the nation-state. For example, in her 2008 installation *(Re)collection of Togetherness,* Wulia displays a collection of handmade replica passports from various countries, based on samples from the Internet and the passports of her many international friends. This installation deconstructs the symbolic importance of the passport as a marker of an individual's belonging to a country and, as Wulia describes it, the "project is never-ending because as I see it, what I am doing is simply tracing the geopolitical movements of borders" (Cheng 2011). Wulia once again explores the notion of national belonging in her 2008 documentary *Pulang* (Homecoming), this time through a series of extensive conversations with the late Sobron Aidit (younger brother of the PKI leader D. N. Aidit), who was in exile in France. In this documentary, she looks at the common experiences of Chinese and non-Chinese victims of the 1965–1966 anti-Communist killings to examine themes of exile, unbelonging, and ostracization. In her interactive wall installation *Terra Incognita, et cetera* (2009), Wulia takes the theme of (un)belonging and place even further as she deconstructs modern national borders and reimagines the modern world as having undefined and impermanent geopolitical borders and therefore as being welcoming to those who would under normal circumstances be unwelcome. To create this interactive installation, Tintin Wulia painted a large wall mural of a blank Dymaxion world map. She then invited exhibition attendees to stake a territorial claim on whichever piece of land they liked on the map as a form of party game, with any remaining land at the end of the interactive performance being deemed unoccupied land (*terra nullius,* literally "land belonging to no one") (Wulia 2009).

Clearly, the theme of belonging is an important one for Wulia, stemming from her own experiences of feeling like she has never truly belonged in Indonesia because of her ethnicity and family history. Through both *(Re)collection of Togetherness* and *Terra Incognita, et cetera,* Wulia relates her own personal trauma to the themes of belonging, trauma, loss, and even statelessness at a more universal level. Yet the testimonies she has made through her art are also very much grounded in local Chinese Indonesian history. Tintin Wulia and her artwork represent an important voice not only in contemporary Indonesian art but also in the general public discourse on Chineseness, as the Chineseness that she portrays is one suffered by many Chinese: an identity laden with taboo and constructed in a persistent fear of persecution. Furthermore, the personal narratives that Wulia has presented in her works are a significant contribution to a country that is still struggling to come to terms with its dark history.

The work of Edita Atmaja (discussed in the next section) also speaks to the theme of trauma and was created in 2019, more than ten years after Wulia's and Harsono's artwork, which is testament to the reality that much of the collective trauma suffered by the Chinese remains unaddressed. As with Wulia, the theme of Atmaja's work involves a more abstract sense of fear and insecurity, rather than referring more specifically to a particular historical event. While Atmaja's work makes references to the May 1998 riots, she is more interested in how ordinary Chinese like herself try to protect themselves in the aftermath of anti-Chinese violence.

POWERFUL PROTECTION FOR LOCAL RESIDENTS: THE ART OF EDITA ATMAJA

In October 2019, an unusual and daring installation/performance art piece took place at the Kedai Kebun Forum art gallery in the southern city of Yogyakarta in Central Java. Titled *Tato Tolak Bala: Perlindungan Ampuh Warga Setempat* (Tattoos to Ward off Evil: Powerful Protection for Local Residents), the installation comprises a young female artist offering permanent tattoos to willing participants inside a temporary tattoo studio constructed in the gallery space (see figure 4.6). The tattoos on offer are no ordinary designs: they promise personal physical protection from danger for the bearer. There were a number of tattoo designs that the visitors (who were not charged a fee for the tattoos but could give donations) could choose from, with these designs promising either protection of their business premises or their homes, security while traveling, or protection of family members. It was obvious for visitors to see that every element of this performance art installation had the common themes of security and protection. From the

FIGURE 4.6 Temporary tattoo studio installation as part of Edita Atmaja's *Tato Tolak Bala: Perlindungan Ampuh Warga Setempat* exhibition, 2019.

Source: Image courtesy of Edita Atmaja. Reproduced with permission.

design of the welded metal frame (that made up the walls of the tattoo studio) that resembled a prison cell and/or a reinforced security gate, to the black-and-white photographs of gates and security checkpoints that were stuck to the outer surface of the metal frame, and of course the tattoo designs themselves, all the elements of the installation were meant to symbolize protection and security.

Indeed, the themes of security and protection were what inspired the artist, Edita Atmaja, to create this bold art installation. Edita Atmaja is a Jakarta-born Chinese (born 1986) who became fascinated with how middle- and upper-class Chinese families like her own reacted to traumatic events, such as the May 1998 riots, by erecting gates and private security checkpoints in order to ensure their own safety and safeguard their private property (much like the case study of the Kelapa Gading enclave discussed in chapter 2). Born into a middle-class Christian family, Atmaja grew up in an inner-city West Jakarta residential estate known to have a large concentration of Chinese residents. Similar to the residents of the Kelapa Gading estate, the Chinese who lived in the estate where Atmaja grew up mainly kept to themselves, and rarely ventured out from their immediate surroundings for daily activities such as schooling, shopping, and work. Atmaja herself went to local private Christian schools until she was sixteen years old, and in her second year of high school her parents sent her to join her older sibling in Auckland, New Zealand, in order to finish her schooling and go to university. Atmaja went on to complete a graphic design degree from a university in Auckland, and after six years in New Zealand she decided to return home to Jakarta to pursue a career as a graphic designer and illustrator. She later became a visual artist and briefly lived in Yogyakarta before moving back to Jakarta.

Atmaja told me that she initially never took much of an interest in exploring themes of security, personal and collective memory, or Chinese identity politics in her work as an artist. Prior to *Tato Tolak Bala,* Atmaja predominantly did botanical illustrations and work inspired by the natural world. However, after having more contact with other Chinese artists, such as FX Harsono, Atmaja came to realize that her art could be a platform through which she could explore issues of identity and belonging that she did not realize had actually been bothering her for many years. Atmaja also realized that she was interested in exploring why contemporary Chinese have the tendency to always seek safety or security (*cari aman*), especially after the May 1998 riots. In our interview, Atmaja reflected on her own personal memory of the riots:

> I was only twelve years old when the May [1998] riots happened, so I didn't really understand what was going on at the time. Back then, the riots happened not far from our residential complex and the rioters actually got very close to the street where our house was. Thankfully, the rioters didn't go further into the complex but the shops and houses on the main road were looted and ransacked. I remember that the supermarket I used to buy snacks from was looted, and they never reopened after that. . . . I didn't understand why the riots happened and my family never talked about the causes either, but I could feel that things dramatically changed after the riots. Suddenly people started erecting even bigger steel fences for their houses and even the backstreets had security posts and gates. Neighbors who used to be out and about stayed home a lot more, with some even leaving their houses, perhaps to migrate overseas. . . . I remember that suddenly everyone became obsessed with self-protection. (interview, April 12, 2020)

A few years after the riots, like many other middle- and upper-class Chinese families who could afford to, Atmaja's parents applied for and were granted permanent resident (PR) status in New Zealand. Atmaja and her sibling went to Auckland, with her parents taking turns to visit and stay with them for six months at a time in order to satisfy the minimum residential time required to maintain their PR status.

Looking back, Atmaja realized that her parents' decision to apply for a PR and move her and her sibling to New Zealand was motivated by the desire to secure a safer future for the family outside of Indonesia. When she decided to return permanently to Jakarta in her early twenties, her parents supported her decision, but Atmaja knew that her father would have preferred that she stay in New Zealand because it was a safer place to live. However, Jakarta—and Indonesia—in the mid-2000s were much safer places for the Chinese compared to in 1998, so Atmaja and her family did not feel any immediate threats at the time they returned. Yet Atmaja also realized that things never really went back to normal after the May 1998 riots:

> The tall steel gates were still there, and so were all the security checkpoints. . . . I didn't understand why all these safety measures were still in place, years after May [1998] and even when the situation was already much safer. . . . Residential roads were still cordoned off at night, and I had to wind down my car window and show my face to the security guard [*satpam*] who guarded my complex every night before I could get to my own house. I

remembered thinking to myself, "This isn't right, why do we live like this?" (interview, April 12, 2020)

These personal memories inspired Atmaja to create the *Tato Tolak Bala* installation, as well as drawing on the collective memories of many other Chinese who were affected by the May 1998 riots, either directly or indirectly. This source of inspiration was reflected in the following excerpt from the *Tato Tolak Bala* exhibition foreword written by the exhibition's curators, Dito Yuwono and Mira Asriningtyas (2020, text reproduced with permission):

> In one corner of Jakarta, a luxury residential area offers 24-hour security facilities, CCTV surveillance at every corner, identity card checks, and additional safety systems for critical moments: a guaranteed flood-free environment, direct access to the airport 15 minutes away, even a direct access to the sea if needed. High fences with a one gate system make this kind of housing closed to outsiders while hiding anything that is happening inside. There is full control and supervision over the flow of guests—in and out. For local residents, this tight security provides a sense of secure [*sic*] and comfort. But at the same time, this tight security is also an expression of deep-rooted fear and collective trauma for generations in the local community inside the fence. Suspicion easily arises from two directions: those who are inside the fence against outsiders, and those who are outside the fence against activities that they cannot see inside the fence.
>
> This extra security system did not just happen. Immediately after the May 1998 riots, residents in various residential areas began to build tall fences around the house and entrance with extra security system [*sic*]. The fear that was kept and used as a tool to maintain power for the New Order developed into a new business field for developers. The higher the price that is ready to be paid, the more sophisticated securities will be served for those with generational community trauma . . .
>
> However, memory is contestation. Collective memory will continue to change when each power change [*sic*]. 21 years later, the high fences at the entrance and around the locals' residence remained as monuments of fear that almost lost their roots. This memory space eventually forms the visual language of a place and makes it just a day-to-day view.

This inspiration for the artwork was also reflected in black-and-white photographs of the aftermath of the May 1998 riots that Atmaja had affixed to the outer frame of the tattoo studio installation. The photos depict a combination of ransacked and/or burning buildings, the heightened military presence, and the many reinforced security gates that had been installed in Chinese residential areas. During the performance itself, Atmaja sat inside the tattoo studio with a tattooing table and all her tattooing tools, ready for visitors. When a visitor walked into the gallery space to get tattooed, they were faced with the imposing metal frame of the tattoo studio and the photographs of the May 1998 riots. They were then invited into the safety of the tattoo studio. Once inside, Atmaja advised the visitor on what tattoo design they could consider getting before she then proceeded to tattoo them.

When I asked about how she came up with the concept of tattoos that could ward off evil, Atmaja explained that she was inspired by the widespread practice of wearing or displaying amulets and talismans for protection from physical and metaphysical harm. This is common practice among both Chinese and *pribumi,* and the amulets are known locally as *jimat.* Atmaja admitted that she did not know very much about Chinese, Buddhist, or Taoist amulet designs, so she decided to create her own designs that were inspired by what many Chinese regard as a symbol of safety: steel gates. Elaborating on this unique design concept, Atmaja explained, "My family is Christian, so I don't know anything about traditional Chinese amulet designs. . . . But I thought that a very common symbol of protection that most Chinese Indonesians could relate to is the common steel gate. This is why I decided to design tattoos that represent a symbol of safety" (interview, April 12, 2020). Why did Atmaja choose the medium of tattoo then? "There is a very definite permanence to tattoos. Once you get a tattoo done, the ink is indelible and it is a part of you, forever. . . . So, the idea is that the tattoos from *Tato Tolak Bala* will give the bearer a sense of protection and safety that is truly personal and lasting. Perhaps then this could help them get over their trauma and give them comfort" (interview, April 12, 2020). Atmaja told me that both Chinese and *pribumi* got tattoos from her and—like her—most of them were young, with only vague or secondhand memories of the May 1998 riots. Furthermore, because the exhibition was presented in Yogyakarta and not Jakarta, many of the visitors that got tattooed had not directly experienced or felt the impacts of the riots. However, Atmaja found that even the Chinese who were not in Jakarta at the time or were not directly impacted by the riots were still traumatized at a collective level. During the process of being tattooed, many of Atmaja's clients began telling her their own memories of May 1998, and hearing these stories proved to be therapeutic for her: "Most of the people I tattooed told me about what they remembered of May [1998], and how the incident made them feel insecure afterwards, both physically and at a more psychological level. . . . It reassured me that my own memories and feelings of insecurity are also shared by many others, and not just by fellow Chinese Indonesians" (interview, April 12, 2020). Tattooing oneself with a symbol of safety from evil forces may be regarded as extreme by some, but in Atmaja's interactive art installation, amulet tattoos became a medium in which collective memories of trauma were entwined in a very physical way with hopes for a safer future.

While the mediums of choice, narratives, and modes of representation vary, one commonality that exists among the new generation of Chinese Indonesian filmmakers and artists discussed here is that they are all addressing issues and experimenting with taboo and sensitive themes avoided by the previous generation. As Wulia argues, "Our generation demands explanation. However, as far as [our] parents are concerned, there is often a preference to remain silent" (interview, October 24, 2008). The filmmakers and artists discussed in this chapter are certainly not silent, passive, or unquestioning. Through their works, they are engaging in what Ien Ang (2000, xix) describes as "the destabilization and contestation of prevailing cultural purities, essentialisms and chauvinisms" (see also Werbner and Modood 1997).

By choosing to use the increased freedom of the post-Suharto era to ask pertinent questions about historical ambiguities and the persistent "Chinese problem," these artists are pushing the boundaries of acceptable behavior within their respective *habitus* as social agents. As Wulia stated, older generations of Chinese who have lived most of their lives under the New Order have been largely silent, repressing their trauma and not daring to dispute the prevalent state accounts of Chinese history. The broadening and deepening of the scope of civil society in the past two decades have emboldened these younger Chinese to challenge the status quo and claim a public space within which the Chinese can reflect upon and question their collective past. As public mediums, films, art, and visual culture are important platforms for the Chinese to gain greater recognition and to advocate for important causes for the wider community, such as righting the wrongs of past historical narratives. These are important developments for scholars to examine, especially given that the performing arts have been a somewhat neglected focus in most analyses on Chinese identity politics. As future generations continue to experiment with new modes of cultural production and representation, they will inevitably enrich the many complex ways in which contemporary Chinese identities may be understood and expressed.

5 Chinese Indonesian Organizations and Political Participation

Since 1998, Chinese participation in Indonesian politics has attracted considerable public attention. Indeed, one of the most visible forms of evidence of this return to the public domain has been the resurfacing of Chinese social and political organizations that were previously dormant throughout the New Order. In the media, Chinese organizations feature quite prominently, particularly during Imlek celebrations, which often feature government representatives standing alongside Chinese elders in public displays of unity and recognition. The media and public profiles of these organizations, combined with their relative success in advocating for Chinese rights, has created an image of a thriving—and triumphant—identity politics scene.

As of 2007, there were at least 176 known Chinese Indonesian organizations, ranging from political parties to alumni associations and sporting clubs, as well as clan associations, among others (Dawis 2010b, 61–62). It is difficult to estimate how many Chinese Indonesian organizations there are at present since many are unregistered and small in scale. However, considering the pace and enthusiasm with which the Chinese have been participating in social organizations in the post-Suharto era, as well as the ease with which groups can now establish and organize themselves on social media, it is safe to assume that the number is now even higher than 2007 estimates. Scholars and observers have generally been optimistic about the development of Chinese identity politics and political participation in the post-Suharto era, praising the success of this movement as proof of the continuing democratization process in Indonesia (see Suryadinata 2005; Dawis 2010a). Studies have also pointed out that the sheer number and variety of these organizations that have sprung up since 1998 highlight the heterogeneous nature of Chinese Indonesian identities (see Herlijanto 2005; Hoon 2009).

Another cause for celebration has been the active involvement of the Chinese, particularly from the younger generations, in the civil service and mainstream electoral politics. While Chinese involvement in both local and national politics was limited in the period immediately after 1998, the number of Chinese politicians started to increase in the early 2000s as Indonesia's national political scene stabilized. Since the 2004 national legislative election, more and more Chinese have been participating in local, regional, and national elections. Amid all these developments, the crowning glory of Chinese participation in politics was the phenomenal political rise of Ahok, the former regent of East Belitung regency in Bangka-Belitung province who eventually rose to become the governor of Jakarta from 2014 to 2017. For a Chinese politician to claim such a powerful elected government position was previously unthinkable during the New Order, when the Chinese were discouraged from entering politics, the military, and the civil service. Moreover, building on his image as a maverick anticorruption figure, Ahok's widespread popularity among both Chinese and non-Chinese was unprecedented. His political ascent inspired many young aspiring Chinese politicians to also break the stigma against active political engagement and to enter politics themselves.

The political engagement of the Chinese in the post-Suharto era has been largely driven by three main motivations that are interlinked: the first is the desire to ensure the safety of the Chinese community by having a greater influence in politics; the second is the need to represent Chinese interests in government policymaking; and the third is the desire to prove that the Chinese can also be good, loyal, and nationalist citizens of Indonesia. In other words, active political participation and representation over the past two decades can be seen as strategies to safeguard the interests of the Chinese as a national minority. These motivations are not so different from what drives other ethnic minorities to be involved in electoral politics and political lobbying. However, the historical context of being able to rejoin the political domain after more than three decades of absence, combined with the trauma of political disempowerment, make the case of the Chinese unique. Having said this, it does not mean that there are no genuinely reform-minded Chinese politicians who enter politics in order to serve the wider public (both Chinese and non-Chinese) and further Indonesia's reforms in different sectors. In particular, Ahok was, and still is, inspirational for reform-minded youth, since he has shown that a Chinese politician could also fight for better governance for all Indonesians.

Yet, two decades after the enthusiastic reestablishment of Chinese organizations, post-Suharto Chinese sociocultural organizations (for example, voluntary associations and clan/hometown associations) and grassroots political networks are facing pertinent challenges. Many of the organizations that were set up after 1998 have now become stagnant and/or dormant, with most facing issues of sustainability as they find it hard to recruit members from the younger generations. Furthermore, after the initial euphoria of the *reformasi* period died down and the Chinese largely got the public recognition they championed (such as Imlek being declared a national holiday and the abolition of the SBKRI document requirements), most of these organizations have lost steam and floundered without a specific direction or a common cause to fight for.

Amid the post-Suharto revival of Chinese politics, different groups are eager to put forward their interpretations of Indonesian Chineseness, as well as to represent various cultural, economic, and political interests. At times, this has led to disagreements and intergenerational conflict about how the Chinese should be portrayed and represented, and various factions within these organizations have been accused of utilizing the momentum of Chinese identity politics for their own personal gain.

In terms of participation in electoral politics, Chinese Indonesian politicians have been successful in rising to the ranks of MPs at both local and national levels, mayors, regents, governors, and ministers. However, they continue to face challenges that reflect the internal dynamics of both Chinese identity politics and racial politics in post-Suharto Indonesia. As seen in the case of Ahok's political rise and fall, anti-Chinese sentiments still linger beneath the surface and continue to be easy to stoke in times of political, economic, and social instability. The realization of this fact has reinforced the siege mentality of the Chinese who participate in organizational and electoral politics, where different individuals and groups plan their political moves carefully and strategically to maximize their chances of both individual and collective political safety and survival. Perhaps more than in any other domain, Chinese political participation reflects how the group's position in contemporary Indonesian society continues to be ambivalent and precarious.

THE TROUBLED HISTORY OF CHINESE POLITICS IN INDONESIA

Chinese Indonesian organizations have existed since the Dutch colonial period, with many initially starting out as Chinese clan associations organized along family name, lineage, hometown, or dialect lines. As scholars such as Wang Gungwu (2000) have pointed out, the formation of Chinese clan associations was the direct result of the major waves of migration of Chinese to Southeast Asia mostly from the southern coastal provinces of China in the nineteenth and early twentieth centuries. Due to the precarious status of the Chinese who lacked formal protection from the colonial authorities, the community took the initiative to form their own welfare and security organizations. Such associations and secret societies were common among the Chinese diaspora around the world, and they played key roles in local Chinese politics and the running of colonial societies more broadly (Wang 1988, 2000; see also Liu 1998). For instance, inspired by the pan-Chinese nationalist movement that was emanating from China in the early twentieth century, groups in overseas Chinese communities around the world formed organizations that promoted pan-Chinese nationalism and Confucian-based education for the Chinese. As discussed in chapter 3, in the Dutch East Indies, THHK was especially active in setting up Mandarin-language schools (Suryadinata 1972, 1976; Post 2019).

These early Chinese organizations were also very active in the establishment of Chinese-language presses. Leo Suryadinata (1976) argues that, in the beginning, the establishment of Chinese-language newspapers such as *Xin Bao* (first published in 1921 by the *peranakan* newspaper *Sin Po*) was directly related to the pan-Chinese nationalism that organizations such as THHK were trying to promote. Indeed, especially in the first half of the twentieth century, Chinese organizations in the East Indies were politically active, with a huge variety of political orientations and allegiances. This was especially so following the founding of the Chinese Communist Party in 1921 as Chinese organizations in the East Indies that were oriented toward China were split in their allegiance in support of either the Communists or Kuomintang Republicans (Suryadinata 1997). This is not to mention the Chinese who were divided about whether or not to support the cause of Indonesian independence that was beginning to coalesce in the early twentieth century. Those who were reluctant to support the independence movement were worried that the Chinese would be even more marginalized and persecuted as second-class citizens under an independent Indonesia led by the non-Chinese population (Suryadinata 1997).

After a period when most Chinese organizations were dormant during the Japanese occupation from 1942 to 1945, Chinese organizations resurfaced after Indonesia's independence in 1945. Things began to change in the 1950s after China became a Communist state, and the political loyalties of the Chinese in Indonesia were increasingly questioned, especially since many still had dual citizenship. In response to this growing political suspicion, in 1954 Baperki was formed with the aim of "protecting Chinese who were Indonesian citizens" (Hoon 2006c, 116; see also Tong 2010). Dominated by *peranakan* Chinese eager to achieve equality among all Indonesian citizens regardless of ethnicity, the organization championed an integrationist approach, through which the rights of the ethnic Chinese to openly practice their culture would be protected (Suryadinata 2001, 504).

During the Guided Democracy period (1957–1965), when PKI also grew stronger, Baperki became increasingly left-leaning and socialist, and came to be associated with PKI. Formed in 1963, Baperki's rival organization was LPKB (504–505). LPKB advocated for the complete assimilation of the Chinese, and while it was small, the organization drew support from those from the political right and the military (505). In 1977, LPKB transitioned into the Communication Body of Organizing National Unity (Badan Komunikasi Penhayatan Kesatuan Bangsa), an organization established under the Ministry of Internal Affairs "to assist the communication between the government and the Chinese community" (Aizawa 2011, 48).

With Sukarno's and PKI's downfall following the coup of G30S/PKI, Baperki was disbanded. Many Baperki leaders were also arrested and murdered in the subsequent anti-Communist purges of 1965–1966, such as the fate suffered by the grandfather of the artist Tintin Wulia (see chapter 4). Two of the main ways in which the New Order regime imposed the assimilation of the Chinese were by severely limiting their sociopolitical activities and prohibiting displays of Chinese culture. Chinese-language newspapers were disbanded, with the exception of *Harian Indonesia*, which was sanctioned by the government (Suryadinata 1997, 257). Many Chinese organizations were closed down, and those that wanted to stay operational had to convert to becoming either philanthropic or religious foundations (*yayasan*) that focused on community services, health, sports, or recreation instead (Coppel 1983). As Suryadinata (2001, 505) points out, there were no Chinese political organizations during the New Order, and for all intents and purposes the Chinese were erased from Indonesian politics.

POST-SUHARTO CHINESE POLITICS

Immediately after the fall of Suharto and the abolition of assimilationist laws, many Chinese organizations emerged from the shadows and reestablished themselves publicly (see Giblin 2003; Purdey 2003). Critically examining the reasons behind this, Ariel Heryanto (2008, 77) suggests that the desire to form or join ethnic-based political parties or social organizations was largely motivated by the Chinese's "long-repressed desire for public recognition and an emotional response to the 1998 racial violence." My interviews with several older generation Chinese confirm Heryanto's hypothesis. For instance, Darwin, a sixty-four-year-old respondent who is a member of several Chinese organizations, explained his reasons for joining them:

> During the Suharto era, the Tionghoa could not form any Chinese social or political organizations. This was a violation of our political rights as citizens of this country! During the colonial era, the Tionghoa had their own organizations, so during times of crisis they could help each other out. But during the New Order, the Tionghoa were defenseless and had no political power. Look at May 1998 for example. I am sure that we would not have been so defenseless if we had had organizations that unify the Tionghoa. . . . So now ethnic Chinese should join together in organizations. Not to do anything outlandish, but just so that we can look after our own interests. There is strength in numbers!

As reflected in Darwin's remarks, the central concerns among members of Chinese organizations are political representation and advocacy of citizen rights. Indeed, since their establishment following the events of 1998, these organizations have fought hard to gain public recognition of Chinese problems.

As mentioned in the earlier parts of the book, these organizations have been instrumental in lobbying for various Chinese causes, such as the repeal of Presidential Instruction No. 14/1967, which banned all public displays of Chinese cultural expressions, and the installment of Citizenship Law No. 12/2006, which recognizes all Indonesian-born Chinese as Indonesian citizens. Many of these organizations also have strong links with other nonethnic-based and pluralist NGOs such as the Humanitarian Volunteers Network (Jaringan Relawan Kemanusiaan), and many Chinese organization members are also members of other civil society organizations. Some of these organizations also maintain a close relationship with the government, and every Imlek, the president makes an appearance at the large-scale celebrations hosted by INTI, PSMTI, or MATAKIN.[1]

While Chinese organizations have different structures and purposes, they all share a similar collective goal of overcoming anti-Chinese stereotypes and proving their patriotism. Such goals can be seen in the organizations' mission statements; for instance, part of INTI's mission is "solving the Chinese problem" as well as playing "an active role in the nation's development" (INTI 2019). Likewise, PSMTI states that its commitment is to encourage all members of the Chinese tribe (*suku* Tionghoa) to actively engage in nation-building while preserving their own unique Chinese culture.[2] INTI was established in 1999, when, led by late pharmaceutical entrepreneur Eddie Lembong, a faction within PSMTI broke away because of ideological differences over whether Chinese identity politics should focus on emphasizing their Indonesianness or their Chineseness. Unhappy with the push by PSMTI elders to get the Indonesian government to recognize the Chinese as a separate *suku* and the organization's general emphasis on the uniqueness of Chinese culture, Lembong and other INTI leaders insisted that the Chinese should instead focus on proving themselves to be good, nationalist Indonesians.[3] In a way, this post-Suharto debate on how to be good Chinese citizens is reminiscent of the old New Order debate of assimilation versus integration. Here, it can be seen how there have been disagreements and rifts within the Chinese political *habitus* from very early on in the *reformasi* period with regard to how the Chinese as a collective should represent themselves within the new national political environment.

Apart from large organizations like INTI and PSMTI, smaller Chinese groups at both the national and regional levels have also faced confusion over whether they should emphasize their Chineseness or Indonesianness or even regional identities. The most common strategy has been to emphasize the state's ideology of Pancasila and the national slogan "Unity in diversity" (*Bhinneka tunggal ika*) as guiding principles while expressing their Chinese cultural uniqueness. In essence, the dilemma of Chinese organizations has been the constant struggle to fit their minority identity politics within the Indonesian state's framework of ethnonationalism. It may also be argued, however, that attempts by Chinese organizations to prove their patriotism *in spite of* their Chineseness have the paradoxical effect of confirming the outsider status of the Chinese that many within the community want to dispel.

In her study of Chinese Indonesian organizations and civil society groups, Susan Giblin (2003) points out the contradictions that exist in post-Suharto Chinese identity politics. On the one hand, mainstream Chinese groups lobby for the freedom to express Chinese culture and celebrate their ethnic differences. On the other hand, they also want to portray the Chinese as being just as Indonesian as the *pribumi*. These are two incompatible goals within the current ethnonationalist framework of national belonging, where, as Anthony Reid (1997) suggests, the boundaries of Indonesianness itself are maintained through constant comparison with Chineseness.

Here, Giblin (2003) uses Jean-François Lyotard's (1988) concept of the "*differend*" that "draws attention to the unbridgeable gap between each side of" the issue that "engenders a feeling of 'the sublime'" (Giblin 2003, 367–368). Gary Browning (2000, 78) explains this feeling of "the sublime" as the "painful realization of the unresolvable conflicts occasioned by imagination and reason in straining to imagine and compute at their absolute limits." Because the sublime refers more to a feeling than an action, what is left is the feeling of stagnation or what Lyotard suggests will be "restricted to a frustrating nihilism" (Williams 1998, 108). Although "frustrating nihilism" may sound pessimistic, the term resonates here as Chinese identity politics has thus far been unable to reconcile Chineseness with Indonesian nationalism. The result, according to Giblin (2003, 367), is that Chinese organizations are stuck in a conflicting situation in which the very thing that they desire (recognition of Chineseness as a unique culture) has the double-edged effect of maintaining the perception of the Chinese as outsiders. This means that unless a major paradigm shift takes place within Indonesia's nationalist discourse, the Chinese and their organizations will continue to face this problem of dislocation.

Such a paradigm shift seems unlikely, at least for now. As has been emphasized throughout this book, the reality is that despite changes in citizenship laws that abolished the formal distinction between the *pribumi* and non-*pribumi*, cultural primordialism is still prevalent at the everyday level. In Chinese identity politics, this kind of cultural primordialism is evident in organizational efforts to reorient Chinese Indonesians toward traditional Mainland Chinese culture as a way to remedy what are seen as the harmful effects of assimilation. This narrative is particularly prevalent among the older, pre-1965 generation who view themselves as elders and cultural gatekeepers of the Chinese community.

While Chinese Indonesians are a heterogeneous group and Chineseness can mean different things to different individuals, these elders wield a lot of influence over the public discourse on Chineseness because of their established financial and social capital. Consequently, only one or a few personas are displayed as representative of all within the group. Here, Chang-Yau Hoon (2006a, 157) observes that large umbrella organizations (such as INTI and PSMTI)—and particularly the groups' prominent elders—have a big say over how Chineseness is portrayed and presented to the public. One of these groups, PSMTI, is the same organization behind the Chinese Indonesian Cultural Park (see chapter 1). These organizations also often put on large-scale and highly publicized Chinese cultural events, which might easily be interpreted as representative of all Chinese. Through such events, dominant elders with the necessary economic and social capital can also project their visions of Chinese Indonesianness onto other Chinese, particularly the younger generation.

Examples of this kind of cultural control can be seen when organizations sponsor events designed to promote Chinese culture among the youth. For instance, PSMTI, in collaboration with the Jakarta provincial government and corporate sponsors (of mostly Chinese-owned businesses), hosts the annual Koko Cici Jakarta pageant ("*koko*" and "*cici*" meaning "older brother" and "older sister" in Hokkien, respectively), a beauty pageant and talent competition for Chinese youth living in Jakarta. In this event, entrants are encouraged to compete in the categories of Chinese traditional dress, language, and knowledge of Chinese arts and traditions to become Jakarta's Chinese cultural and tourism ambassadors for the year (see figure 5.1). As Hoon (2006a) suggests, the Koko Cici pageant is a prime example of efforts by organizations like PSMTI to instill their version of desirable Chinese qualities among the younger generation. Such expectations do not reflect the realities of life of contemporary young Chinese, especially bearing in mind that most neither speak Mandarin nor practice Chinese cultural traditions in their everyday lives. Nevertheless, these kinds of events form a key strategy in the efforts of mainstream Chinese organizations to educate the youth about Chinese culture.

During my fieldwork, many of the older Chinese I interviewed expressed "deep concerns" that young people are "disoriented" and "do not know their identity" anymore. Bima, a sixty-year-old man who is an elder in INTI, stated,

> The [Chinese] youth today, they do not now know who they are. During the Suharto era, our people were made to forget who we really are. Myself and the people of my generation, we never forgot [who we are] because we were taught to be proud of being Chinese even before Suharto. But the younger generation needs to be taught about who they are. We are the Chinese, people from a very sophisticated civilization, people who can survive anything. The younger generation should know this and not forget. It is the duty of elders like myself to remind the young people who they are.

FIGURE 5.1 Poster advertising the 2021 Koko Cici pageant in Jakarta.

Source: Image courtesy of PSMTI. Reproduced with permission.

On a similar note, Hari, a prominent seventy-five-year-old businessman and an active member of PSMTI, complained,

> Today's younger generation no longer cares about advocating Tionghoa rights in Indonesia. They grew up during the Suharto era where political passivism was encouraged. Back then, everything Chinese was considered to be negative. I have heard that now, young people are even embarrassed to be called Chinese and this is very sad. . . . Don't get me wrong, I was born in Indonesia, I made my fortune in Indonesia and I am now even creating livelihoods for Indonesians. I feel 100 percent Indonesian. However, if we don't have roots, we will die. This is why in this age, it is very important for the young to know more about Chinese traditions, so that they can keep them alive. If they don't start now, then who will defend the Tionghoa in the future?

Bima's and Hari's opinions reflect a common concern among older Chinese activists about cultural identity. However, also reflected in their remarks is a more serious concern about the lack of youth participation or interest in Chinese identity politics.

POLITICAL ACTIVISM AMONG CHINESE YOUTH

A significant problem faced by most mainstream Chinese organizations is sustainability and regeneration. In all these organizations, membership is dominated by the older generation, with the majority of leaders and members being over fifty years old. These older members have usually experienced some form of Chinese education or were members of Chinese organizations prior to the start of the New Order in 1965. Members under the age of thirty are rare. For instance, Aimee Dawis (2010b, 69) notes that in 2010 only forty-two of the Teochew Association's six hundred members were under forty. More than two decades after the beginning of post-Suharto Chinese identity politics, senior members are slowly retiring and there are not enough fresh members. If large organizations such as INTI and PSMTI do not start recruiting new members quickly, they could eventually die out. Such a generational crisis can even be seen in organizations founded by former student activists in and shortly after 1998: groups such as SNB have also struggled to attract younger members. This lack of fresh blood has made the formerly thriving Chinese identity politics movement seem out of date, stuffy, and predictable.

There are several reasons that may explain this lack of youth participation in Chinese identity politics. For one, there is a general feeling of apprehension about politics among today's Chinese youth. This was evident in interviews during which many young informants admitted to being afraid of political involvement. One respondent, Ina, a twenty-seven-year-old post-graduate economics student, explained to me that her reluctance to be involved in political activism was largely influenced by her parents, who told her that politics was dangerous for the Chinese: "My parents always forbade me from being involved in student politics when I was at university because they said that such activities are dangerous. I never participated in protests or anything like that because I was afraid that I would get hurt or jailed or something. . . . My parents told me that politics is not safe for Chinese people. . . . They said that in the past political activists would disappear and be killed." Comments such as Ina's were not uncommon among Chinese raised by parents who had been traumatized by the memories of the 1965–1966 anti-Communist purges, particularly the disappearances of Chinese Baperki activists. Trauma arising from what happened as a result of Baperki's integrationist politics has made many older Chinese wary of letting their children participate in post-Suharto politics. Furthermore, the retreat of the Chinese from the political stage during the New Order has also created a culture of political apathy among the younger generations.

Another major reason young Chinese do not participate in politics is that many of them are tired of politics as usual. Generally, politics and politicians do not have a good reputation among the younger generation, who automatically view anyone involved in politics as corrupt. In addition, many are critical of how the older generation conducts their politics. The generation that has grown up amid the promises of post-Suharto reforms expects changes in the way Chinese politics is conducted. Throughout the New Order, the younger generation was used to seeing performative politics in which members of the political and social elite gathered in lavish settings for photo opportunities and shows of harmony for the sake of the status quo. The fact that large Chinese organizations now hold the same kinds of public events has disenchanted many of the youth, who consider these activities as superficial. Furthermore, the organizations' clearly hierarchical and bureaucratic structures mean that younger recruits must submit to a strict seniority system in which older members still make most of the decisions about how the organizations are run.

From the younger generation's point of view, the lack of consultation between older and younger members in these organizations also means that most of their programs do not cater to their aspirations. Such lack of interest can be seen among young people like Franklin, a twenty-year-old university law student who had attended a few of INTI's events but then never went back:

> The elders seem to think that young people are interested in attending luxurious conventions where old people wear batik or suits to look important. They expect younger [members] to attend these boring things and then wonder why we don't. Why would the young people be interested in such superficial events? We would rather be doing something productive like sports or planning actual campaigns. If we want to help people or campaign for Chinese rights, then why sit around in a hotel ballroom? I would rather join an NGO or go to the streets to do something real.

For reasons very similar to Franklin's, only a small number of young people even consider joining these mainstream Chinese organizations. This lack of participation has led the older generation to brand the youth as lazy, apathetic, and spoiled.

However, realizing that they must accommodate youth's interests, more and more mainstream organizations are trying to create youth-specific channels and subgroups within their organizations. For instance, INTI and PSMTI often sponsor youth events in universities and schools. They are also serious in developing programs for their younger members; INTI, for example, recently formed its own youth subdepartment called Young Generation INTI (Generasi Muda INTI, GEMA INTI). GEMA INTI's task is to organize activities that cater to the interests of younger people, such as social gatherings, music nights, sporting events, and student symposiums on current sociopolitical issues.

Other similar youth subdivisions include the PSMTI Youth Association (Ikatan Pemuda PSMTI) and MATAKIN's Young Generation Confucians (Generasi Muda Konghucu, GEMAKU), among others. In each of these, Chinese youth are also encouraged to participate in the organizations' many social and charitable outreach events, where they are usually relied on to do hands-on tasks such as distributing aid to flood victims in Jakarta, victims in Aceh following the Indian Ocean tsunami of 2004, or victims of the 2006 Yogyakarta earthquake. A PSMTI member told me that these charitable activities not only serve humanitarian purposes but also appeal to the youth's sense of social responsibility and are a good training ground for youth participation in organizational efforts.

Ulung Rusman, who was INTI's vice secretary-general in charge of the development of its youth program at the time of my interview with him, remarked on the importance of young people like himself, not just for the long-term existence of INTI and other Chinese organizations but also for the continuation of Chinese identity politics in general. He suggested:

> Organizations like INTI need to expand and include the young people in the organization's strategies and plans. If INTI is going to strive to find an end to the "Chinese problem" as the organization's mission statement states, then it needs to invest in the younger generation who will become the leaders of the future. Especially if we look at how apolitical and apathetic the Tionghoa youth have become because of the Suharto legacy. As an organization, we are developing plans to educate young people more, through symposiums and training in how to develop a keen political awareness, especially about Chinese identity politics and putting forward Chinese issues, of which there are still many. If you look around now, [you see that] almost all organizations are investing in the young. For example, Islamic organizations are now very active in preparing young people to someday take over through suborganizations like Muhammadiyah Youth, Nahdlatul Ulama Youth [Gerakan Pemuda Ansor], and the likes. Tionghoa organizations like INTI must step up and do the same if we want to continue to have a political say. (interview, January 16, 2007)

However, Rusman also acknowledged that many of his peers disagree with this form of participation in Chinese identity politics, as they question its efficacy to bring about any real change, given INTI's highly hierarchical structure.

Jojo, a thirty-year-old respondent who has rejected offers to join mainstream Chinese organizations in the past, told me of the common view among younger members that they would always be regarded as inexperienced kids in organizations like INTI. He added that younger members would have to wait for years before they get the chance to have any say at all in how the organizations are run. Meanwhile, younger members with leadership aspirations must entertain and brownnose (*menjilat*) influential senior members in order to get close to the power holders in charge of decision making. I found that such perceptions were very common and were further amplified by the stereotype of members of mainstream organizations being rich tycoons who use their influence in the community to advance their business interests. As a consequence, many young people regarded

Chinese organizations as what Jojo called "old men's appreciation societies" in which young people's aspirations were largely neglected. My observation over the years is that this perception of Chinese organizations as the domain of the older generation has persisted until today, as informants told me that the only young Chinese who join the leadership of these organizations are those who want to climb the social ladder or to network for business purposes. Although organizations like INTI and PSMTI refute such accusations, it is hard to counter them when almost every public event and piece of media coverage (including in their own newsletters and magazines) features members who are prominent businessmen. On this point, Jojo added, "Every time organizations like INTI or PSMTI hold a luxurious Imlek celebration in a five-star hotel, extravagant trade exhibitions, or put on a big cultural show, it confirms existing public ideas of all ethnic Chinese being rich businessmen. We are not like that, and I personally certainly do not want to be associated with that image." This reluctance among many young Chinese to join mainstream Chinese organizations has led those interested in identity politics to start their own independent organizations that cater specifically to the needs and aspirations of youth.

In the last two decades, quite a number of these youth groups have emerged with varying interests, scope, forms, and size. A number of the young activists who founded them told me that they drew their inspiration from past Chinese organizations such as THHK mentioned earlier in the chapter. For instance, Wahyu Effendy, a former student activist who founded the now-defunct youth NGO GANDI, said that the youth have always been at the forefront of Chinese politics in Indonesia: "A few activist friends and I wanted to establish a young Chinese group that continued the spirit of reform in the early post-1998 years. . . . We wanted something different from the established Chinese organizations like INTI, so we thought why not make our own? Young Chinese have always been political and had their own organizations, so there is no reason the youth today shouldn't be the same" (interview, February 15, 2007). Like Wahyu, other young Chinese involved in youth organizations have (or at least had) the *reformasi* narrative as one of their main motivations. Central is the belief that, as demonstrated with historical events such as the *reformasi* movement that was kick-started by student protests, young people or the youth (*pemuda*) possess both the energy and the radical ideas to transform social movements such as Chinese identity politics.

This *pemuda* mythology is certainly a strong influence on young people who participate in Chinese politics. Many times during my interviews, these activists spoke of themselves as Chinese youth (*pemuda* Tionghoa) who could be relied upon to spearhead Chinese identity politics in the future. One such remark was made by Kenny, a twenty-eight-year-old lawyer involved in a number of these organizations: "If you look throughout Indonesia's history, it is always the young people who lead important events like Sumpah Pemuda [the 1928 Youth Pledge when youth from all over the Indonesian archipelago pledged their commitment to the would-be independent Indonesian nation], [the] independence movement and *reformasi*. . . . The Chinese are the same too, and now, as *pemuda* Tionghoa, we must also rise up and be willing to sacrifice our time for things that matter." In her analysis of the iconographies of Indonesian youth, Doreen Lee (2012) argues that this kind of *pemuda* self-image is quite common among post-Suharto activists, who imagine themselves as matching a romantic ideal of radical, nationalist youth. The term "*pemuda* Tionghoa" itself is a post-Suharto phenomenon because in the past *pemuda* usually only referred to *pribumi* youth. The use of the term "*pemuda* Tionghoa" can thus be seen as a strategy by post-Suharto Chinese youth to associate themselves more closely with the nationalist *pemuda* image. Here, the use of the more politically correct term "Tionghoa" rather than the derogatory *cina* also shows an attempt to move away from the negative connotations of *cina*.

During my fieldwork, almost all the Chinese youth organizations that I encountered had no conventional organizational structure (such as a chairperson, board members, and the like), though they did have leaders who were usually also the founders of the groups. Because of this lack of hierarchical structure, these groups more closely resemble social networks than associations. According to Alex, a founder of the Chinese Youth Network (Jaringan Tionghoa Muda, JTM), the younger generation prefer to call their groups "networks" rather than "organizations" because the former are considered to be more democratic: "The young people should have a space where we can get together once in a while to discuss things that matter to them. . . . The needs of young people are different from those of the older generation. We don't need pomp and formalities and are more interested in actual open [discussions] about current affairs. . . . We need open forums where people can express their opinions in a democratic way, whenever we want, without much hassle." The youth networks' horizontal structures mean that in theory all members are treated as equals and decisions are made through group consensus. Members of these networks claim that less bureaucracy allows for clearer communication and greater efficiency in organizing activities, and that their networks are more grassroots oriented, radical, and altogether different from mainstream organizations.

JTM was formed in 2003 by the founding members of an earlier Chinese youth group, Solidarity of Young Chinese Indonesians for Justice (Solidaritas Pemuda Pemudi Tionghoa Indonesia untuk Keadilan). After the initial excitement of *reformasi* had faded, the group became worried that people would forget about the fight to eradicate anti-Chinese discrimination at all levels. According to one of JTM's founding members, Denny, a main aim of the network is to educate their members about the importance of being politically aware and to discourage the apolitical behavior of many young Chinese caused by bad habits "systematically developed and encouraged by the New Order." At the time the network was established, its founding members felt the need to create a forum for young people who had a strong interest in Chinese identity politics and other matters relating to Chinese Indonesians.

As is the case for most Chinese youth organizations in the post-Suharto era, JTM has mainly been organized on the Internet, through a mailing list, social media channels, and informal chat platforms like WhatsApp where all members can post contributions to discussions and replies via email. The decision to run JTM online was made for a number of practical and ideological reasons to do with the lifestyles of contemporary young middle-class Chinese that comprise most of the network. Practically, it made sense for JTM to be Internet-based because it is free, there is no administrative overhead required compared to conventional organizations with a physical presence (for example, office space and staff), and all their target members have mobile Internet access through smartphones and other devices. From an ideological point of view, as mentioned before, many young Chinese activists, like JTM's founders, believe in being grounded at the grassroots level by minimizing hierarchy in order to ensure that all their members can have a say in a democratic environment. At the time of writing, JTM had around seventy core members, a Facebook group consisting of more than 2,300 members, and links with other young Chinese organizations and networks. As well as conducting discussions online, JTM members try to meet as a group every few months in restaurants and malls around Jakarta to socialize and engage in face-to-face dialogues.

As part of JTM's activities, the group's website administrators (or "moderators," as they are also known) informed the network about events and happenings in the Chinese identity politics circuit, as well as organized group trips to symposiums, seminars, cultural exhibitions, and other events arranged by organizations like INTI or PSMTI. JTM saw itself as a communication hub where politically minded Chinese youth could come together, exchange information, and get involved in various sociopolitical events. Alex from JTM noted,

> The whole point of having a network like JTM is so that Tionghoa youth from all backgrounds, walks of life, professions, and political, social, and cultural orientations can come together to talk online or in person. Talking is important because that's how ideas flow. . . . People say that there are a lot of improvements already in regard to the "Chinese problem" in Indonesia. I think that this is true to some extent, but there is still so much to do. If young Tionghoa have a channel through which they can talk about things that matter to us, then we can work out ways where we can put those ideas into action.

When they meet, the conversations mainly revolved around issues of politics, both those concerning the Chinese community and national politics in general.

A topic that seemed to be of particular interest among JTM members was the history of the Chinese in Indonesia, especially alternative histories that were largely buried during the New Order period. This interest in Chinese history could be seen in almost all aspects of JTM's activities. The discussions ranged from the exchange of information regarding the histories of prominent Chinese Indonesians, such as Baperki founder Siauw Giok Tjhan, to debates regarding significant historical events, such as the anti-Communist purges of 1965–1966 and the May 1998 riots.

I could not help but notice during my fieldwork that many JTM members were very anxious to prove their commitment and service to the Indonesian nation. This was evident in the group's online dialogues, where most topics usually boiled down to discussions on whether or not the Chinese could balance their Chineseness with Indonesian nationalism. For instance, during a conversation at a café, some JTM members talked about negative examples of Chinese that should be avoided (such as Eddy Tansil, a known fugitive and corrupt businessman), and positive, patriotic ones which all young Chinese should aspire to emulate (for example, former ministers Kwik Kian Gie and Mari Elka Pangestu). Conversations about whether overt displays of Chinese cultural expressions (such as extravagant Imlek celebrations) were beneficial or not to the Chinese community also often featured in mailing list discussions threads. Such conversations usually led to heated debates about whether an assimilationist or integrationist approach was the best way to ensure the safety of the Chinese in Indonesia in the long term.

As a network, JTM did not (and still does not) adhere to any particularly political or ideological view about the best approach to combating the notion of the "Chinese problem." However, Alex said that one of their main goals was to "encourage members to actively pursue righteousness and be good Chinese Indonesian citizens in all that they do." By proving that the Chinese youth can be upstanding, honest Indonesian citizens, JTM's leaders told me that they hoped that, over time, *pribumi* would change their minds and regard all Chinese as being equal citizens who belong in Indonesia. Here, Alex referred to Chinese historical figures such as Soe Hok Gie who were ardent Indonesian nationalists: "Throughout Indonesia's history, there have been many Tionghoa who have proved themselves to be good citizens who did great things for the country. Soe Hok Gie, for example, although he was Chinese, he was known for his activism and ideas about the betterment of Indonesia. We also have living figures who served this country their whole lives. We need to follow their examples and aspire to be like them." He added that young Chinese were apathetic and afraid to get involved in political activities. Because of this, Alex felt that it was JTM's duty to educate not just the younger generation but also all Chinese about what they need to do to become good citizens and active political participants in Indonesia.

It was this same motivation that inspired the publication of a book on behalf of JTM titled *Cokin? So What Gitu Loh? Pemikiran Tionghoa Muda* (Chinese? That's It, So What? Thoughts of Young Chinese), edited by Ivan Wibowo (2008), a Jakarta lawyer in his forties. The book is a compilation of editorial writings (previously published in various Indonesian newspapers) produced by several young Chinese researchers and social and political activists who are all JTM members. While the book's content does not contain anything particularly controversial, its title was considered bold by many Chinese because of the use of the term *cokin*, a Jakartan slang expression for Chinese that is considered both colloquial and derogatory. *Cokin*, combined with the defiant and confrontational question "So what?" created quite a stir among older Chinese, who considered the title too bold. Nevertheless, it seems that this reaction was exactly what Ivan had hoped for. According to him, the book's title was meant to be thought-provoking and draw the public's attention to Chinese youth's passion for the country:

> I intended for the book's title to be controversial and confronting. For many Chinese, especially the older generation, the term *cokin* is considered derogatory and insulting, but the younger generation are used to it and in Jakarta the term is now part of everyday language among the youth and

> considered to be "cool." By using this term, I want to show that the young Chinese whose articles I featured in the book can turn insult into empowerment. They are intelligent, influential young Chinese who contribute much to the country. So I wanted the title to reflect that. So people call you *cokin* or *cina*, so what? It's okay to be Chinese; these young authors in the book are proud of their Chineseness. (interview, August 28, 2010)

The strategy of using a controversial title to attract attention worked, as the first edition sold out within a few weeks of publication. In line with JTM's overall mission to educate Chinese youth about the importance of social and political activism, this book was intended to showcase the achievements of younger people, as Ivan said that he wanted the book to show people—particularly the older generation Chinese—what young Chinese can do. He hoped that by reading the book, Chinese readers could feel proud to be Chinese and Indonesian at the same time.

What is evident from JTM's various efforts in mobilizing Chinese youth is that political participation is regarded as an important step toward achieving the dual goals of securing the safety of the Chinese in Indonesia while at the same time showcasing their patriotism in the eyes of the non-Chinese. While their methods may differ, both older and younger Chinese seem to be motivated by the objective of strengthening the societal position of the Chinese by vowing to never again be in a situation of minimal political influence as they experienced during the New Order. This political trauma has been difficult for the Chinese to overcome, and in the post-Suharto era, when they are once again allowed to openly participate in the political domain, many are of the opinion that the only way to really advocate for Chinese rights and the safety of the community is to be elected to public office and thus have direct influence in policymaking.

CHINESE INDONESIANS IN NATIONAL POLITICS

Even in the years immediately following 1998, direct participation in national politics was largely rejected by the Chinese because political parties were viewed as being dominated by non-Chinese elites. However, as part of their bid to show commitment to pluralism, court Chinese votes, and—more importantly—secure Chinese campaign donations, major political parties such as the Democratic Party (Partai Demokrat), the Indonesian Democratic Party of Struggle (Partai Demokrasi Indonesia-Perjuangan,

PDI-P), and the National Awakening Party (Partai Kebangkitan Bangsa, PKB) started to recruit Chinese candidates for parliamentary elections.

Since the 2004 national legislative elections, more and more Chinese have been participating in local, regional, and national elections. As mentioned earlier, based on data from KPU (KPU 2004, 2014), I estimate that there were at least 100 ethnic Chinese candidates standing for legislative seats in the 2004 elections, 213 in the 2009 elections, and 315 candidates in the 2014 elections. Most of these candidates were backed by major political parties, with PDI-P, the NasDem Party (Partai NasDem), and PKB being the top three parties that put forward the most Chinese candidates. As center-left and more progressive parties, it is not surprising to see PDI-P and NasDem supporting Chinese candidates. However, for reasons that will be discussed below, as the political arm of the conservative Nahdlatul Ulama (NU), the largest independent Islamic organization in the world, PKB may seem like an unexpected political platform for aspiring Chinese politicians, yet it is a strategic choice.

In the 2014 elections, I estimate that sixteen Chinese candidates were elected to Indonesia's two national legislative chambers.[4] After the 2019 elections, the number went down slightly to fifteen, but this number is still high considering that the elections took place in the aftermath of the Ahok case. This is not to mention the number of Chinese who served as senators, regents, and district and village heads, and, in the case of Ahok, as governor of a province. Furthermore, as in the example of former ministers Mari Elka Pangestu and Kwik Kian Gie, there have been Chinese who have served as high-ranking officials.

The majority of the elected Chinese MPs that served from 2014 to 2019 represented urban electorates with sizeable Chinese populations, such as Medan, Surabaya, West Kalimantan, and the Special Capital Region of Jakarta III (Daerah Khusus Ibukota Jakarta III, DKI Jakarta III) constituency that covers the districts of North and West Jakarta. This hints at two trends: first, that ethnic Chinese candidates were deliberately vetted and placed by political parties in Chinese areas to win Chinese votes; and second, that Chinese voters tend to vote for Chinese candidates. However, these Chinese MPs themselves deny trying to exclusively win Chinese votes, explaining that Chinese votes alone would not be enough to secure electoral wins. Furthermore, they claim to represent all the residents in their constituencies, not just the Chinese.

When asked about his experiences of running as a Chinese candidate, Dr. Sofyan Tan, a PDI-P MP from Medan in North Sumatra (and a longtime community activist), said that his Chineseness was neither a significant asset nor a liability during his election campaigns: "The vast majority of the people who voted for me were non-Chinese. My voters were mostly Medan's [non-Chinese] urban poor who know me because of the [low-income] school I founded and also because of my charity [work] as a doctor.... Of course, I also received Chinese votes, but I still had to campaign hard and did not receive automatic votes" (interview, June 22, 2014). Tan also said that one of the biggest challenges he encountered during his campaign was actually from Medan's very diverse Chinese communities, where there were other Chinese politicians vying for regional and national political offices during the 2014 legislative elections: "There were other [Chinese] candidates that used their network and influence within the Chinese community to attack their political opponents. At some point there were even competing factions within the Chinese community over whom to support, and people were attacking each other.... But I didn't want to take part in that and concentrated on grassroots campaigning in the *kampung* [village] areas. . . . In the end I won by a big margin, and that shows that it's important to appeal to both Chinese and non-Chinese voters" (interview, June 22, 2014). Attacks from other Chinese politicians and community leaders are nothing new for Tan, and earlier experiences taught him to not rely only on Chinese votes. In the 2010 Medan mayoral race, Tan (who ran with non-Chinese Nelly Armayanti as his running mate) had been a first-round underdog, beating eight other pairs of candidates to reach the second round of voting after no pair managed to secure a clear majority. However, Tan's political rivals in the Medanese Chinese community started a campaign to convince Chinese voters not to vote for him because he was supposedly too much of a social activist who was closer to the local *pribumi* communities than to the Chinese (Chong 2015, 2018). Combined with the lack of support from Muslim communities that refused to vote for a non-Muslim (it was rumored that Tan's rival Chinese candidates joined forces with Muslim leaders to launch a scare campaign that focused on Tan's identity as a non-Muslim), Tan ultimately lost the mayoral race.[5]

Tan's experience shows how there is no such thing as a unified Chinese political voice, and that different factions within a Chinese community (even within a small locality) may have varying ideas about what constitutes the collective good of their *habitus* and what paths they should take to gain political power. What is most interesting about Tan's 2010 mayoral campaign is the fact that factions within the Chinese community in Medan opted to elect a non-Chinese candidate instead of electing someone from their own community who was deemed to be detrimental to their group's interests. To Tan's Chinese detractors, his closeness with Medan's lower-class non-Chinese communities posed a threat to their own standing within the local Chinese community.[6] These kind of rifts within the local Chinese political milieu reveal how the assumption that Chinese voters will always support Chinese candidates is wrong. At the same time, as a non-Muslim Chinese, Tan's popularity among the poorer non-Chinese was evidently also viewed as a threat by power holders within the local Muslim political *habitus*. We thus see how individuals like Tan who try to forge an alternative, in-between path can end up being viewed as rogue social operators who are then ostracized by those within their own *habitus*.

Other Chinese politicians who have been successfully elected to office agree with Tan's sentiments about the need to not appeal only to Chinese voters. Many also shared similar experiences, even those campaigning in areas where the Chinese are a majority. Daniel Johan, a PKB MP from West Kalimantan, noted,

> I had to appeal to West Kalimantan's extremely diverse ethnic communities. Yes, there is a large ethnic Chinese population in Singkawang and Pontianak, but there are also the local Malays, the indigenous Dayaks, the Javanese and Madurese migrants, not to mention the diverse religions. . . . I pride myself on [having visited] as many villages and local communities as possible during my campaign, and I had to show the people that even though I am Chinese, I care about West Kalimantan as a whole and that my race does not matter. . . . In a way, that was the hardest part of the campaigning: to convince the non-Chinese that I will also fight for them. (interview, July 5, 2014)

Indeed, after being absent for so long from electoral and party politics, Chinese candidates have to actively fight against the (mis)conception that Chinese politicians are interested only in fighting for Chinese interests.

Different politicians have tried to address this issue in different ways. Like Daniel Johan, the majority try to communicate an inclusive and impartial message. However, Johan is unique in his strategic decision to run with PKB, the largest Islamic party in Indonesia, especially considering that he is not Muslim himself. When asked why he decided to run with an Islamic party, Johan explained that he chose PKB because it was the party of the late former president Abdurrahman Wahid (Gus Dur), who championed the acceptance of the Chinese in Indonesian society:

> Gus Dur inspired me to go into politics. I was just a university student when he championed the recognition of ethnic Chinese as valuable members of the Indonesian nation. He [Gus Dur] even went as far declaring himself to be of Chinese descent! This made a really big impression on me, and I wanted to be part of a political party that he led.... Plus NU is Indonesia's largest Muslim organization, and I think it is important to have ethnic Chinese representation in this organization, even if I am not Muslim myself. I wanted to show the voters that I represent the same pluralism that Gus Dur championed. (interview, July 5, 2014)

More than two decades after the onset of post-Suharto reforms, Chinese politics has changed. With the majority of their initial reform demands having been met and the fact that they now enjoy greater mainstream political representation than ever before, it would be easy to assume that Chinese politicians no longer have specific collective goals to achieve, particularly with regard to securing equal rights for the Chinese. However, most active Chinese politicians disagree with this assumption, highlighting the fact that with such a turbulent history of anti-Chinese prejudice in Indonesia, fostering interethnic harmony requires continuous concerted efforts. Haripinto Tanuwidjaja, a senator representing Riau Islands province in the Regional Representative Council (Dewan Perwakilan Daerah), which is the upper house of the People's Consultative Assembly (Majelis Permusyawaratan Rakyat, MPR), said that it would be a mistake to be complacent about the position of the Chinese in Indonesia: "I got into politics because I was concerned over how politically weak we [Chinese] were in the aftermath of 1998. . . . The Chinese were always discouraged from entering politics, both by the New Order government and by our own families out of fear, and I wanted to change that.... Things are of course much better now, but the equality and harmony I want to achieve is essentially a utopia, so it is an ongoing task that needs to continue even after I'm gone. Anti-Chinese sentiments are still alive and well today" (interview, January 17, 2017). As Tanuwidjaja expressed, underlying anti-Chinese sentiments represent a constant and very real fear for the Chinese. However, these fears have arguably intensified from 2015 onward with what appears to be a more amplified anti-Chinese discourse in the media. Perhaps more than any other factor, this emergence of anti-Chinese narratives among some sections of Indonesian's non-Chinese population has been closely associated with the political rise and popularity of Ahok, the former governor of Jakarta.

THE AHOK EFFECT?

As mentioned at the beginning of the book, out of all the Chinese politicians in the post-Suharto era, the most controversial and widely popular is Ahok. Ahok was born on June 26, 1966, in the town of Manggar in East Belitung as the eldest son of a Hakka Chinese family. He began his political career in his home district of East Belitung in 2004, when he was elected to the Regional Legislative Council (Dewan Perwakilan Rakyat Daerah, DPRD).[7] Since the beginning of his political career, Ahok ran on an anticorruption platform, and from very early on, he conducted frequent surprise community visits that helped build his image as a hands-on and competent administrator among the voters (see Hatherell and Welsh 2017; Setijadi 2017). However, Ahok also exhibited his political ambition from early on, when he developed a reputation for quitting political offices in order to pursue a higher office after only a short time. For instance, Ahok left his seat in the local East Belitung DPRD after only one year in order to run successfully for the office of regent of East Belitung in 2005. Again, after just a little over a year as regent, Ahok resigned in December 2006 to (unsuccessfully) run as governor of Bangka-Belitung province (Setijadi et al. 2016). After he was successfully elected to the DPR to represent Bangka-Belitung province in 2009, he quit in 2011 after he secured a vice-governor nomination as Jokowi's running mate in the 2012 Jakarta gubernatorial election (Setijadi et al. 2016).

Ahok has also shown little loyalty to political parties. In his relatively short political career, he has joined and then left no fewer than four parties. In East Belitung, Ahok was supported by the New Indonesia Alliance Party (Partai Perhimpunan Indonesia Baru) in his bid to become regent; he then joined the Party of Functional Groups (Partai Golongan Karya, Golkar) in his bid to become a national MP for Bangka-Belitung province, before leaving in 2012 to join the Great Indonesia Movement Party (Partai Gerakan Indonesia Raya, Gerindra), who supported him as their candidate for vice-governor of Jakarta (Setijadi et al. 2016). He eventually became Jokowi's successor as governor of Jakarta in late 2014 after Jokowi was elected president. Ahok eventually left Gerindra in 2014 and at present he is affiliated with PDI-P since joining the party in early 2019 shortly after his release from prison.

I interviewed Ahok in 2008, not long after his failed bid to become governor of Bangka-Belitung province. Even then, he showed his characteristic ambition and self-belief:

> The idea to become a politician came from my father, who believed that the only way that we could fix this country's problems is by going into politics. He said to me, "Why not you, Hok?" While for a long time I never wanted to go into politics, but as I became more fed up with corruption and lack of good governance, I thought my father was right, why not me? . . . I don't think that just because I'm Chinese and a Christian, then I can't be elected by *pribumi* voters. . . . I think they can see for themselves the work that I do. . . . Even to become president one day, why not? (interview, August 15, 2008)

From that point, Ahok's political ascent was nothing short of phenomenal. His eventual elevation to the governorship of Jakarta made him the first Chinese elected to Jakarta's highest governmental office. Considering how influential the position is, Ahok's political rise symbolized just how far Chinese political participation had come since the end of the New Order.

Ahok is also very charismatic, and he has endeared himself to both the Chinese and non-Chinese in Jakarta and throughout the archipelago. Straight-talking and projecting an image of an effective bureaucrat, videos of Ahok conducting community visits or of him berating incompetent Jakarta city officials were uploaded to social media sites such as YouTube to the delight of many Indonesians, particularly the younger generation. To many voters previously disillusioned by corrupt and self-serving bureaucrats, Ahok—along with Jokowi—represented a welcome change and a fresh hope for good governance. In a city paralyzed by daily traffic jams and seasonal flooding, Ahok's implementation of programs (that were started during Jokowi's tenure as governor), such as the construction of Jakarta's long-awaited underground mass rapid transit train network and the swift evictions of slum areas along the city's riverbanks, popular among middle- and upper-class Jakartans, although some of his policies were also regarded to be hostile toward the city's poor and would later provide ammunition to the anti-Ahok protesters (see Wilson 2017; Padawangi 2018, 2019).

Among those with political aspirations, Ahok has become an inspiration with young Chinese people such as Roneld, a twenty-four-year-old from Bangka, who says that having Chinese politicians such as Ahok helps break stereotypes of the Chinese in the eyes of the non-Chinese: "I grew up with parents who told me that Chinese Indonesians should stay away from politics because it is dangerous business. But now you have someone like Ahok in a position of power, and even the *pribumi* like him! I think this is really encouraging for all Chinese Indonesians because there are no more limitations. . . . We [Chinese] need to prove that we are not all businessmen."

FIGURE 5.2 Official portrait of Basuki Tjahaja Purnama (Ahok) as governor of Jakarta Special Capital Region, 2014–2017.

Source: Wikimedia Commons (Creative Commons License).

However, not all Chinese are as enthusiastic about Ahok. Many, particularly from the older generation, have raised concerns about a potential backlash over Ahok's controversial popularity and character.

Indeed, the fears of those who were wary of Ahok's political career were realized when, on September 26, 2016, he told a small crowd in Jakarta's

Thousand Islands regency not to believe those who use verse 51 of the Al-Ma'idah chapter of the Qur'an to discourage Muslims from electing a non-Muslim leader like himself. Furthermore, Ahok told the crowd that they should not be influenced by religious provocation and to follow their instincts when voting (Setijadi 2016c, 2017). Soon after, edited video footage of Ahok's Al-Ma'idah remarks began circulating on social media, causing fury among Islamist groups that accused Ahok of blasphemy against Islam.

What came next were the biggest mass demonstrations in Indonesia's recent memory. Organized by the Islamic vigilante organization, the FPI, together with several other hard-line Islamist groups, after Friday midday prayers on November 4, 2016, approximately 150,000 Muslims took to the main streets of downtown Jakarta to demand Ahok's prosecution for blasphemy against Islam (Setijadi 2016c, 2017; Fealy 2016). What started as a relatively peaceful demonstration quickly turned violent when protesters refused to disperse, and neither Ahok's public apology, a message of calm from moderate Muslim leaders, nor Jokowi's assurance of due judicial process for the blasphemy investigation were enough to calm the situation. The protesters occupied the streets in front of the State Palace and Parliament House, causing Jakarta's central district to grind to a halt. As the violence spread, mobs looted shops and burned parked vehicles, and offshoot groups threatened to attack the Chinese-majority residential complex of Pantai Mutiara where Ahok and his family lived (Setijadi 2016c). For the Chinese, the acts of violence and racist rhetoric heard during the demonstrations invoked memories of the May 1998 riots, and many Jakarta Chinese were on guard, getting ready to defend their homes or leave the country if an anti-Chinese riot were to break out.

Over the next three months, two more mass demonstrations ensued, with the largest on December 2, 2016, attracting an estimated crowd of "500,000 to 750,000, making it probably the largest single religious gathering in Indonesian history" (Fealy 2016). Despite the demonstrations, Ahok managed to win the first round of the Jakarta gubernatorial election in February 2017 with 43 percent of the votes. But having failed to secure more than half the votes required for an outright first-round win, Ahok went head-to-head for a runoff battle against close runner-up Anies Baswedan, a former minister of education and culture under Jokowi who crossed over to Jokowi rival Prabowo Subianto's camp after he was removed from the post after just two years. Ahok lost this second-round fight, securing only 42 percent of the votes, while Anies won in a decisive victory with 58 percent of the votes. As I have discussed in more detail elsewhere (Setijadi 2017), perhaps

FIGURE 5.3 Anti-Ahok protesters descending on Central Jakarta on December 2, 2016.

Source: Shutterstock.

the most surprising aspect of Ahok's defeat was the large margin by which Anies was able to win. Analysts and reputable polling agencies had initially predicted a very tight race, so, as scholars have since pointed out (see Mietzner and Muhtadi 2018; Warburton and Gammon 2017), Anies's victory meant that religion and identity politics were more important determinants of contemporary Indonesian electoral behavior than initially thought.

Less than three weeks later, on May 9, 2017, the North Jakarta District Court found Ahok guilty of blasphemy against Islam and sentenced him to two years in jail. This sentence was harsher than the one-year suspended sentence that the prosecutors had demanded. Indonesia has a 100 percent conviction rate for blasphemy cases, so few had expected Ahok to be found innocent, but the severity of the sentence was surprising for most analysts and members of the public. After the verdict, Ahok served his sentence, joined PDI-P upon his release in 2019, and was appointed by Jokowi as the president commissioner of Pertamina, the state-owned oil and gas company.

While Ahok has since bounced back from his ordeal, the impacts of the resurfacing of anti-Chinese narratives could linger for much longer. While the politicization of the blasphemy case was primarily an issue of religion, Ahok's identity as a Chinese made it far easier for his opponents to rally angry mobs against him. Even before the blasphemy allegation, Ahok had been plagued by accusations of favoritism toward Chinese tycoons in business dealings throughout his tenure as vice-governor and governor. Ahok's Chineseness has always been a handicap, and the combination of Islamist rhetoric and anti-Chinese sentiments proved to be a potent formula in mobilizing the predominantly lower-class non-Chinese masses. Ahok was successfully painted as a tactless Chinese Christian capitalist who insulted Islam, the perfect embodiment of the enemy qualities that Indonesia's hardline extremists wage war against. Given his alleged ties to rich Chinese tycoons, his opponents framed a vote for Ahok as a vote for foreign influences, specifically China, in the Indonesian economy and politics. This was certainly a message that was exploited by presidential hopeful Prabowo, who urged Jakartans to vote for a pair of candidates who would return "the Indonesian nation's wealth back to the people of Indonesia" in his endorsement video for Anies (Baswedan 2017).

The implications of Ahok's notoriety and controversy for the Chinese community as a whole cannot be underestimated. Never before has a Chinese politician received such popularity, attention, and—at the same time—loathing on the national stage. The issues Ahok has become known for are contentious, and they strike at the very core of Indonesia's ethnonationalism, class inequality, Islamic politics, and the *pribumi*–Chinese divide. To have a brash, straight-talking, non-Muslim Chinese with alleged ties to big businesses in such a powerful position as the governor of Jakarta confirms the suspicions many non-Chinese have of the image of the arrogant, power-hungry, and self-serving Chinese. Hoaxes, fake news, memes, and rumors that circulate on social media platforms such as Facebook and messaging applications such as WhatsApp and Telegram allege various conspiracy theories (Kwok 2017). For example, one such theory is that the PRC government is involved in supporting Ahok's and Jokowi's political careers, and that they are actually agents of the PRC in its attempt to eventually colonize Indonesia.

While it is easy to dismiss such hoaxes and conspiracy theories as nonsense, their believability among some sections of society reveals the persistence of anti-Chinese narratives and that suspicions of Chinese Indonesians as China's fifth column still exist. Analysts have argued that religious and anti-Chinese attacks against Ahok were actually part of a larger concerted effort to destabilize Jokowi's administration (see Osman and Waikar 2018; Sulistiyanto 2018). Backed by Megawati's and Jokowi's PDI-P party, and widely perceived as Jokowi's close ally, an attack on Ahok was understood by most as an attack on Jokowi and the progressive, secular style of government both leaders represent (Fealy 2016; Setijadi 2017). Regardless of who the intended target of political attacks actually was, the very fact that anti-Chinese narratives could still be used as a powerful political tool (even against a popular politician like Ahok) twenty years after the beginning of the reforms demonstrates the enduring legacy of anti-Chinese sentiments. Judging from this trend, it is unlikely that the use of anti-Chinese rhetoric in national politics will stop, particularly in key junctures such as important elections.

Unsurprisingly, the Chinese are divided when it comes to Ahok. While the majority support him and insist that his tough policies and anticorruption stance have been positive for the image of the Chinese, others argue that Ahok's controversy has put the Chinese in harm's way.[8] Yohanes, a sixty-year-old North Jakartan small business owner, explained these concerns to me:

> Ahok has gone too far! At the beginning I was glad that a Chinese could be so successful in politics, and popular too. But then he became too arrogant! It looks bad for all of us [Chinese] when he yells at his *pribumi* underlings in public, or when he is being rude to other politicians. The blasphemy comment was the last straw for a lot of people, I think. . . . He [Ahok] has forgotten who he is, and who we are as Chinese. At the end of the day, we are still at the mercy of these people [the *pribumi*]. . . . Already they are now saying hateful stuff against the Chinese because of Ahok. . . . Look, during the November demonstration against Ahok, they almost attacked his [residential] complex! A lot of Chinese [live] there. If things get bad enough, I have no doubt the Chinese will get attacked.

Yohanes's fears are warranted given Indonesia's long history of anti-Chinese violence. Even at times when social unrest or a political catalyst were not caused by issues directly to do with them, the Chinese have often been targeted. For example, during the Malari incident in 1974, riots that actually began as anti-Japanese and antiforeign protests led to attacks on Chinese properties and businesses. As such, the fear of anti-Chinese reprisals for Ahok's actions was certainly real for many ethnic Chinese.

In many ways, Ahok is one of the virtuosos within a *habitus*, as discussed by Bourdieu. His ambition and boldness to run for some of the highest political offices despite the complicated sociopolitical history of the Chinese in the country challenged past conventions and taboos regarding how the Chinese should be seen and behave in public. Skillfully appealing to his fellow Chinese for votes and financial support when he needed to, Ahok also knew when to downplay his Chineseness in his political maneuvers. As with the case study of politicians such as Sofyan Tan discussed earlier, as a rogue social actor, Ahok also garnered mixed reactions from the Chinese community who feared that his highly visible presence would compromise their safety and the collective good of all Chinese. Nonetheless, Ahok also inspired many other Chinese politicians (particularly from the younger generation) who also want to challenge conventional rules about what constitutes proper political behavior. For them, the Ahok controversy only proved that the work of reforming ethnic politics is far from over, and that more Chinese need to be actively involved in politics in order to counter the resurgent wave of nativist and Islamist politics that has once again appeared on the national political stage, particularly since 2017.

POST-AHOK CHINESE INDONESIAN POLITICS

There are a few things that need to be considered when analyzing the state of Chinese politics in the wake of the Ahok case. First, it would certainly be too simplistic to say that the blasphemy controversy could cause anti-Chinese sentiments to be reignited and return to the level they were in during the New Order, as the case needs to be viewed within the context of the greater power play between Indonesia's political elites and various competing factions. Further, the controversy started as a religious issue, which reflects a trend of greater conservatism and religiopolitical polarization, not just in Indonesian society generally but also within Indonesian Islam more specifically. A full analysis of the complexity of the case and the 2017 Jakarta gubernatorial election is beyond the scope of the discussion here, but an important point to be made is that while the presence of anti-Chinese rhetoric was troubling, it was only one of many factors that contributed to the wider political commotion.

Second, the Jakarta gubernatorial election was only one of the 101 regional elections that took place simultaneously on February 15, 2017, across the archipelago. While Ahok's story in Jakarta dominated the election season, he was not the only Chinese candidate in contention, and elsewhere in Indonesia other Chinese politicians were successfully elected into office without problems or controversy, with some even being backed by the same Islamic parties that in Jakarta vehemently opposed Ahok. For instance, Tjhai Chui Mie became the first female mayor of the city of Singkawang in West Kalimantan after defeating another Chinese female candidate, Tjhai Nyit Khim. The victorious Tjhai Chui Mie was backed by PDI-P, NasDem, the Democratic Party, and People's Conscience Party (Partai Hati Nurani Rakyat, Hanura), while Golkar, the United Development Party (Partai Persatuan Pembangunan, PPP), and the Indonesian Justice and Unity Party (Partai Keadilan dan Persatuan) backed her opponent. While Singkawang is known for its large Chinese population, the town is also home to many Dayaks and Malays. In Banjarnegara regency in Central Java, which has a Javanese majority, the Chinese Muslim candidate Budhi Sarwono (Kho Wing Chin/Tjien) won the election for regent by a landslide against Hadi Supeno, who had previously served as vice-regent (as of May 2022, Budhi Sarwono has been under investigation for corruption, graft, and money laundering). Overall, as mentioned before, the number of elected Chinese members of both chambers of the national parliament also did not decrease significantly in the 2019 legislative elections.

However, the Ahok case has also amplified anxieties among the Chinese of their political position in Indonesia. Apart from the resurfacing anti-Chinese sentiments, there is also a very real worry about the return of nativist sentiments that has seen the increased use of the term *pribumi* in political rhetoric. Immediately after the conclusion to Ahok's trial, Islamic hard-liners kept up the political momentum by amplifying an antiforeign, anti-Chinese, and anticapitalist rhetoric. In an interview in May 2017, conservative Islamic scholar (*ulama*) and then chairman of the National Movement to Guard the Fatwa of the Indonesian Ulema Council (Gerakan Nasional Pengawal Fatwa Majelis Ulama Indonesia), the coalition behind mass anti-Ahok rallies, Bachtiar Nasir said about the Chinese, "It seems they [the Chinese] do not become more generous, more fair" (Allard and Da Costa 2017). In the same interview, Nasir also advocated for an affirmative action program for non-Chinese Indonesians, since he regarded the Chinese's wealth to be a problem (Allard and Da Costa 2017). Similarly, then vice-president Jusuf Kalla said to a Muhammadiyah crowd in 2017 that "in Indonesia, those who [are] rich and those who are poor are of different religions" (Warbuton and Gammon 2017). Meanwhile at a Golkar national meeting in May 2017, the commander of the National Armed Forces, general Gatot Nurmantyo, read a portion of a poem titled "But It Is Not Ours" (*Tapi Bukan Kami Punya*) while talking about economic inequality (Suryadinata 2017c), implying that Indonesia's wealth is not currently in the hands of the *pribumi*.

However, the return of pro-*pribumi* narratives in post-Suharto public discourse did not begin with the Ahok case.[9] In August 2015, a Gerindra-linked group established a new party called the Pribumi Party (Partai Priboemi), declaring its ambition of restricting the political and economic rights of those considered to be non-*pribumi* (Setijadi 2017; see also Chen 2022). While the party never claimed to be explicitly anti-Chinese, its existence as a political entity that publicly advocates a discriminatory stance against those considered to be "foreigners" indicates the growing appeal of xenophobic political mobilization. In the last few years, there have also been demands that previous governments' decisions to extend the political rights of non-*pribumi* be rescinded. For instance, in October 2016, the chairman of the Islamist PPP, Muhammad Romahurmuziy, proposed the restoration of the constitutional clause that the president must be an indigenous Indonesian (*orang Indonesia asli*) (Setijadi 2017). Romahurmuziy also asked that this criterion be applied to both presidential and vice-presidential candidates. The resurfacing of this kind of nativist political rhetoric is certainly alarming for all Chinese.

In terms of electoral politics, there was a concern that what had happened to Ahok would dissuade aspiring Chinese politicians from running for public office. However, this does not seem to have been the case. As mentioned earlier, in the 2019 general election, two years after Ahok's political downfall, the number of Chinese candidates was approximately the same as 2014, and an estimated fifteen were elected to the DPR and MPR, only one less compared to the previous election. As in previous elections, in 2019 Chinese politicians were also largely elected in areas with significant Chinese populations, such as in North Sumatra, North and West Jakarta, and West Kalimantan.

While the number of elected politicians decreased, many young Chinese politicians seemed to have become more vocal and bolder in the 2019 elections. In fact, as longtime observers of Chinese politics such as Suryadinata (2019) note, two new parties were established by politicians of Chinese descent. One is the Indonesian Unity Party (Partai Persatuan Indonesia), established in 2015 by Chinese media tycoon Hary Tanoesoedibjo. At one time, he was a close business associate of Suharto's children and was the running mate of former military commander Wiranto for the 2014 presidential election under the banner of Wiranto's Hanura. The other newly formed party is the Indonesian Solidarity Party (Partai Solidaritas Indonesia, PSI), founded in 2014 by a Christian former television presenter of Chinese, Malay, and Dutch descent, Grace Natalie Louisa. Both new parties each nominated over 550 candidates at both local and national levels in the 2019 elections, and by my calculations around 5 to 10 percent of each party's candidates were Chinese. Furthermore, the proportion of non-Muslim candidates from the two parties was very high, at least in comparison to other mainstream parties. Looking at the trends from the 2019 elections, it seems that, despite the political upheavals and resurfacing of anti-Chinese sentiments that surrounded Ahok's political rise and fall, a new generation of Chinese politicians has not been dissuaded from entering the turbulent waters of electoral politics.

PSI is of particular interest, because it was established by young people (many of whom are Chinese) who were inspired by the reforms that Jokowi and Ahok introduced when they came to power in Jakarta. In fact, a number of Ahok's former staff members during his time as governor joined PSI, such as Michael Victor Sianipar (Ahok's former personal aide, who became the head of the party's Jakarta branch) and Rian Ernest Tanudjaja (Ahok's former lawyer, who was PSI's legislative candidate for one of the Jakarta electorates in 2019 and is of mixed Chinese-German parentage). PSI claims to champion women's rights, a clean government, pluralism, and solidarity for Indonesia's multiethnic and multireligious society. Furthermore, it claims to be the party of young people (generally understood to be those under forty-five years of age), regardless of their religion and ethnicity. In fact, one of its selection criteria for electoral candidates was that they had to be under forty at the time of nomination. While PSI did not garner enough votes to secure seats in the DPR, many of the party's candidates got elected to smaller assemblies at the provincial and town levels. One such candidate is Chinese law graduate William Aditya Sarana, who, at twenty-three years of age became the youngest ever local parliamentarian for the province of Jakarta.

PSI is an example of a new political initiative by the younger generation who are trying to break the pattern of politics as usual in Indonesia. For young Chinese politicians such as Tanudjaja and Grace Natalie, the party has provided them with a platform to be involved in building a new political *habitus* where they can break free from the conventional political spaces and rules that have constrained Chinese political participation in the past, such as being the token Chinese candidate for traditional political parties such as PDI-P and Golkar. PSI's championing of pluralism in the face of rising political and religious polarization was certainly appealing to many Chinese voters during the 2019 legislative elections, and many of my Chinese informants said that they contemplated voting for the new party. However, some of them later told me that they did not end up voting for PSI because—paradoxically—they were worried that they would be throwing away their vote (*buang suara*) if PSI did not end up getting enough votes to pass the electoral threshold (currently 4 percent of total votes cast) for the DPR. To them, voting for Chinese, non-Muslim, or progressive candidates from more established parties was a safer way to ensure representation for the Chinese in national politics. However, PSI's image and political vision certainly appealed to many Chinese voters, and may gain the party more momentum in future elections.

Immediately after May 1998, the post-Suharto political landscape became a new and more open space where the Chinese from different backgrounds and affiliations could express themselves and lobby for representation in the political sphere. As a result, over the years, Chinese identity politics has become a heterogeneous and dynamic arena of contestation where different sections of the Chinese Indonesian community put forward their interpretation of what constitutes Chineseness and how to best represent it in the public domain. We also see contestations between the older and younger generations, as the younger generation wants a fresher, more active approach to Chinese sociopolitical activism. The perceived rigidity of older organizations has caused sustainability and regeneration problems because the younger generation either prefers to stay away from organizational activities altogether, or to start their own grassroots youth networks that are run almost exclusively online. As Piotr Sztompka (2004) argues, these sorts of contests over the public representation of collective identity are common among ethnic communities, particularly those seeking to reestablish a more significant presence in the aftermath of collective trauma, oppression, and major sociopolitical change.

Despite the structural and methodological differences between various groups, and between older and younger Chinese, I have shown how a major motivation in their political participation is the desire to ensure the safety of the Chinese and to represent their interests in government policymaking. In other words, in the post-Suharto era, active political participation can be seen as one of the strategies by which the Chinese try to safeguard their social, economic, political, and cultural capital and, by extension, the collective interests of their broader *habitus* as an ethnic minority at the national level. I have also established how another major motivation for their political participation is the desire to demonstrate that the Chinese can also be good nationalist citizens. This in itself reflects the continuation of the long-standing belief about how the Chinese need to continually prove their worth and belonging in Indonesia.

We also see how a new generation of Chinese are challenging old fears and stigma about political participation. In the realm of electoral politics, we have seen a gradual increase in Chinese participation in both national and local politics since the mid-2000s. Inspired by the rise of Chinese political players such as Ahok, aspiring young politicians have enthusiastically entered politics to challenge older narratives of victimization and break free from conventional rules of what constitutes acceptable Chinese behavior. Not content with just serving the interest of the Chinese as a group, this new generation of Chinese politicians wants to serve all Indonesians, regardless of their background, and to continue the spirit of reform in all areas of government and public service. In doing so, these younger Chinese forge a path for the creation of a new in-between *habitus* that has the potential of bridging the gap between the Chinese and non-Chinese in politics.

However, what happened to Ahok also shows that being in the political spotlight carries its own problems for Chinese politicians and for the Chinese more broadly. The speed with which anti-Chinese sentiments flared up during his blasphemy saga in 2017 highlights how, despite the reforms of the past two decades, anti-Chinese sentiments still linger just below the surface and are ready to be mobilized during times of political and economic instability. Placed within the broader context of Indonesian politics in the last decade, rising socioeconomic inequality and heightened Islamic conservatism have only heightened old notions of the essentialized differences between the Chinese and non-Chinese, making the Chinese once again the obvious targets of mob anger and frustration. Making matters worse is the return of xenophobic pro-*pribumi* narratives in public discourse.

In response, the Chinese community is divided on how to deal with the return of anti-Chinese rhetoric in the political domain. There are those in the minority who advocate for the formation of a Chinese political party in Indonesia (similar to the Chinese-dominated Democratic Action Party and the Malaysian Chinese Association in Malaysia) so that the Chinese vote could be focused on candidates committed to advancing the interests of Chinese Indonesians. Others vehemently oppose such an idea, arguing that forming an exclusively Chinese party would only serve to confirm existing perceptions that the Chinese care only about Chinese issues. In reality, despite the general motivation of ensuring the safety of the group, there is presently no unified Chinese vote or political movement. As this chapter has demonstrated, the interests, activities, and methods of involvement of the Chinese are extremely varied when it comes to politics, just as the Chinese as a group are heterogeneous.

Despite the anti-Chinese narratives that surrounded the Ahok saga, there have also been encouraging signs for Chinese political participation and representation. It must be reiterated that, while the return of anti-Chinese sentiments in the last few years is concerning, the Chinese are arguably much better placed politically now than at the beginning of the *reformasi* era, and certainly when compared to the New Order. Clearly, active political participation in the post-Suharto era is important for the empowerment of the Chinese as well as for their healing from the political trauma of the past.

6 Chinese Indonesians in the Time of China's Rise

The history and political position of the Chinese in Indonesia have in one way or another been shaped by China and by Sino-Indonesian relations. China's influence has been both direct—such as in the late 1950s, when Chinese Indonesians with dual Chinese-Indonesian nationality had to decide on which nationality to keep—as well as indirect—such as how the Chinese in modern Indonesian history have been viewed by some to be China's fifth column. As so-called essential outsiders in Indonesia (Reid 1997), the perceived loyalty of Chinese Indonesians toward the PRC was regarded with much suspicion throughout the New Order period. Indeed, one of the rationales behind the implementation of the New Order's assimilation policies was to supposedly give the Chinese an opportunity to prove their ideological loyalty to Indonesia. Yet, even in the post-Suharto era, China continues to exert a significant external influence on Chinese Indonesian identity politics.

Since the PRC instituted its reform and opening-up policy in the late 1970s under the leadership of Deng Xiaoping, the relationship between China and Indonesia has gradually recovered after a period of diplomatic freeze from the late 1960s to 1990 following allegations by the Suharto government of Chinese involvement in the abortive Communist coup of September 30, 1965 (Zhou 2019). Diplomatic ties resumed in 1990, and as China rose to become a regional and global powerhouse in the first two decades of the twenty-first century, its image among the Indonesian government and people has also changed. If the view of China for most of the last century was of a country plagued by political turmoil, ideological fundamentalism, and poverty, contemporary China has emerged as a wealthy and rapidly growing market, offering a range of new opportunities. While China is still regarded with suspicion by many countries around the world, the image of China in Indonesia has softened considerably over the last three decades, with the threat of Chinese Communism considered to be much diminished in light of China's increasing interest in capitalist expansion.

As China's economic and strategic interests in the Southeast Asian region continue to expand with ambitious programs such as the BRI (formerly One Belt One Road), maritime Southeast Asian countries such as Indonesia are earmarked to play important strategic roles in China's economic and infrastructural plans. As a result, as mentioned earlier in the book, the bilateral relationship between China and Indonesia has blossomed over the last fifteen years, evidenced by the establishment of agreements such as the Sino-Indonesian strategic partnership in 2005 and signing of an memorandum of understanding in 2013 between the two countries for further Chinese foreign direct investment in Indonesia as part of the BRI (Silaen and Sentana 2013; Xinhua 2015; *China Daily* 2017).

Over the last decade, Sino-Indonesian trade and Chinese foreign direct investment in Indonesia have increased substantially. According to data from the World Bank (2019), China has become Indonesia's number one trade partner since 2019. Likewise, China is already one of Indonesia's top sources of foreign investment, with the Indonesian Investment Coordinating Board (Badan Koordinasi Penanaman Modal, BKPM) reporting that China became Indonesia's second-largest foreign investor in 2020 after Singapore (Jibiki 2021). Considering that many Chinese state-owned enterprises and private companies channel their investments to Indonesia (and other Southeast Asian countries) through Singapore, it is entirely possible that the total amount of China's investments in Indonesia is much larger than what has been officially recorded. Chinese investment is very important for Indonesia, particularly for infrastructural projects, industrial parks, and maritime projects desperately needed to fulfill Joko Widodo's election promises (Grassi 2020; Tham and Negara 2020). This is partly why Jokowi's administration has arguably had the closest and most productive relationship with China under Xi Jinping compared to previous Indonesian governments. Within two years of his first term as president, Jokowi met Xi more than with any other head of state, and according to data from BKPM, the amount of Chinese investment in Indonesia increased by almost 300 percent from 2015 to 2016 alone (Susanty 2016; Setijadi 2016a). The potential overlap between Xi's BRI expansion plans and Jokowi's vision for Indonesia as a "global maritime hub" is not lost on the two countries (Tiola 2019), with Indonesia only too keen to receive Chinese investments to boost its economy. These trends are likely to intensify with the adoption of the Regional Comprehensive Economic Partnership, which came into force in January 2022, through which fifteen countries—with China and Indonesia to the fore—committed to "trade in goods, trade in services, investment, economic and technical cooperation, intellectual property, competition, dispute settlement, e-commerce, small and medium enterprises and other issues" (RCEP 2022).

These recent sociopolitical and economic developments have given Chinese Indonesians the opportunity to act as economic, social, and linguistic go-betweens in Sino-Indonesian relations. Indeed, prominent Chinese Indonesian businesspeople and community leaders are almost always included in official Indonesian trade and diplomatic missions to China. As I have discussed elsewhere (Setijadi 2016a, 2016b), a central assumption here is that a shared Chinese ethnicity gives Chinese persons an advantage in forging *guanxi*—kin and network-based preferential personal connections with business counterparts in Mainland China or other Chinese communities worldwide.[1] From the Indonesian government's point of view, Chinese Indonesian businesspeople and chambers of commerce, such as the Indonesia-China Business Council (ICBC) and the Indonesian Chinese Entrepreneur Association (Perkumpulan Pengusaha Indonesia Tionghoa, PERPIT), can utilize their business networks in order to promote Chinese capital investment into Indonesia (Setijadi 2016b). Similarly, these Chinese Indonesian businesspeople and organizations also often act as the first points of contact for PRC trade delegations or private entrepreneurs looking to do business in Indonesia.

This is not to say that Chinese Indonesians mediate all Sino-Indonesian interactions. Considering that data from BKPM (2018) indicate that over 65 percent of China's investments in Indonesia are driven by state-owned enterprises, it needs to be remembered that much of the mediation and dealmaking occurs at the government-to-government level. Additionally, PRC businesses also interact with non-Chinese businesspeople and enterprises. Especially among the PRC business elite, however, the assumption still stands that Chinese Indonesians possess an advantage due to their ability to engage in *guanxi* networking with their Mainland Chinese counterparts. This is certainly an advantage that many Chinese association members have capitalized on, particular in the last decade.

Within this new environment, being of Chinese ethnicity has become a more useful asset than ever before, with many Chinese taking advantage of this newfound social and cultural capital.[2] Because of this new strategic position, there has emerged a trend of Chinese Indonesians who are increasingly orienting themselves (or reorienting in the case of the older generation) culturally and linguistically toward the PRC over the last two decades. It is not difficult to understand why many Chinese Indonesians are attracted to the idea of assuming a more Sinified identity or persona. Especially among the older generation, who experienced Chinese education and felt like their cultural heritage was erased under the New Order's assimilation policies, the rise of China as a global superpower has roused a newfound sense of ethnic pride and legitimacy.

Younger Chinese Indonesians I encountered throughout my fieldwork have similarly expressed a desire to take advantage of China's rise as a major motivation for learning Mandarin, becoming acquainted with Chinese culture, and maintaining an active interest in social, economic, and political developments in the PRC (Setijadi 2015, 2016a). Not just in Indonesia, the same desire to ride the wave of China's rise has also resulted in the sharp increase in the uptake of Mandarin-language learning among Chinese populations around the world over the last two decades, and China is fast becoming one of the top global higher education destinations alongside traditional receiving countries such as the United States, Britain, and Australia (Xiang 2013; Ding 2016; Jiani 2017). For instance, the Indonesian embassy in Beijing reported that while in 1998 there were only around 1,000 Indonesian students studying at Chinese universities, by 2020, just before the COVID-19 pandemic, the same embassy suggested that there were 15,780 Indonesian students studying at various educational levels and institutions in China (*Buletin KBRI Beijing RICH* 2020, 30; see also Priyambodo 2012; Jegho 2021). While there are undoubtedly non-Chinese Indonesian students included in this figure, I was informed anecdotally by members of the Indonesian Student Association in the People's Republic of China (Perhimpunan Pelajar Indonesia di Tiongkok) that most Indonesian students in China are ethnic Chinese who hope to improve their future employment opportunities by not only having an overseas university degree from China but also possessing a greater knowledge of Chinese language and society.

Considering these trends, it is important to examine how post-Suharto Chinese make sense of and position themselves within the changing geopolitical landscape of China's global rise and the burgeoning bilateral relationship between China and Indonesia over the last twenty years. Some groups within different Chinese communities have reoriented themselves toward Chinese culture and languages in a process scholars have termed re-Sinification or re-Sinicization (Clammer 1975; Liu 2005; Hau 2014; Setijadi 2016b). The motivations for Chinese Indonesians to do so can be broken down into two major impulses: first, there is an emotional and sentimental desire to have a sense of belonging after decades of forced assimilation; and second, there is the more practical motivation to place themselves in a strategically advantageous position given China's visible economic and political ascent. Additionally, there is a perception among some Chinese that playing a greater and more strategic role in Sino-Indonesian relationships could increase the group's value in the eyes of both the Chinese and Indonesian governments. Many of these (mostly older) Chinese actors hope that this increased political capital could be leveraged for better protection for Chinese Indonesians (from both the Indonesian and Chinese governments) in times of economic or political instability.

However, there are also inherent problems that exist in the assumption that Chinese Indonesians could, would, and should play a mediating role in Sino-Indonesian relations at a time of China's rise. In the first place, there is an underlying essentialist assumption here that just because Chinese Indonesians are ethnically Chinese they are able to tap into some kind of primordial ability to reconnect with a form of "authentic" Chinese self after three decades of assimilation. Within the context of Indonesia's history of ethnonationalist prejudice against the Chinese, this kind of assumption is dangerous because it reinforces the long-standing suspicion held by many non-Chinese that the Chinese can never truly be Indonesian. Furthermore, considering the complex history of Sino-Indonesian relations and the fact that China has not come to the aid of Chinese Indonesians during past instances of anti-Chinese violence, there are also problems with the assumption that greater closeness with China will result in better protection for Chinese Indonesians in the future.

As the main case study in this chapter, I examine Chinese Indonesian individuals and organizations that have strategically placed themselves in trade, cultural, and diplomatic relations between Indonesia and China. These Chinese business elites are important to analyze because they are arguably the most influential and visible nongovernment players in Sino-Indonesian relations, particularly in the trade sector. They are mostly from *totok* backgrounds and are second- or third-generation Chinese who can speak Mandarin, mainly owing to their pre-1967 Mandarin-language education. They are now elderly (above sixty years old), and most own successful business enterprises. Some—such as Mochtar Riady (Lie Mon Tie, 李文正), Tahir (Ang Tjoen Ming), the late Eka Tjipta Widjaja (Oei Ek-Tjhong, 黃奕聰), and Murdaya Poo (Poo Tjie Goan)—are business magnates who head large conglomerates and often feature on the lists of the richest people in Indonesia. In their old age, they have become active (or even more active) in different Chinese Indonesian social and religious organizations, and have engaged in various philanthropic activities, particularly in the education sector, such as the building of educational institutions like the Mandarin-language Pahoa School and Ma Chung University (see chapter 3).

While they are few in number, these Chinese business elites possess a huge amount of social, economic, cultural, and political capital in their mediation of Sino-Indonesian business, and they receive considerable media and public attention for their wealth and various economic, philanthropic, and political activities. These tycoons are the embodiment of the stereotype of the Chinese as wealthy "economic animals," with ambiguous loyalty in the eyes of many non-Chinese (Chua 2004; Hoon 2006b, 344). Because of these negative perceptions, many Chinese Indonesians outside of this elite community worry that the appearance of their close involvement in trade dealings with China will only fuel suspicions of Chinese wealth and divided loyalties. It is precisely because of their visibility and high profile that it is important to understand how this small elite influences the discourse on Indonesian Chineseness in the time of China's rise.

RE-SINIFICATION: A "REORIENTATION" TOWARD CHINA?

In the current literature on overseas Chinese communities, re-Sinification (the term "re-Sinicization" is also used) is most commonly understood as the process by which Chinese who are regarded (both by themselves and others) as having lost their affinity with their Chinese heritage embark on a deliberate journey to rediscover their Chineseness and "voluntarily identify with their Chinese 'roots'" (Ang 2001a, 84; Katzenstein 2012). As I have pointed out elsewhere, the term has also been more broadly used to "describe the phenomenon of the increasing visibility, acceptability, and self-assertiveness of ethnic Chinese in Southeast Asia" and other parts of the world (Setijadi 2016b, 823). Nevertheless, as Caroline Hau (2014, 283) points out, the term is problematic as it implies "a unilinear, unidirectional, and foreordained process of 'becoming Chinese' that radiates (or is expected to increasingly radiate) outward from mainland China." For her part, Ien Ang (2001a, 84) argues that the process of re-Sinification is "driven by a passionate identification with and reification of 'Chineseness' as a globally relevant marker for identity and difference, and for which 'China' . . . culturally defined as much as geographically located, forms the centre."

There have been well-documented instances in the past when overseas Chinese communities experienced a resurgence of pride or at least interest toward Chinese culture and Mainland China as the perceived center of that culture. Re-Sinification among overseas Chinese communities was historically almost always a concerted political decision, particularly during times when these communities felt like their way of life and political rights were being threatened. As Claudine Salmon (2001) points out in her analysis of ancestral halls in nineteenth-century Java and Sulawesi, attempts at re-Sinification were often incited by resentment toward the repression of Chinese culture and identity imposed by state authorities. For instance, Salmon demonstrates that the founding of temples for new ancestor worship halls and social organizations among the *peranakan* in Java and Makassar was in large part a reaction to the Dutch colonial government's attempts to acculturate the *peranakan* by encouraging them to speak Dutch and enroll their children in Dutch-speaking schools. John R. Clammer's (1975, 13) study of re-Sinification among the Chinese in Malaya in the mid-twentieth century reveals a similar phenomenon, where "the pressures of Malay political and economic nationalism" from the late 1950s and early 1960s prompted sections within the Chinese community to engage in "the adoption once again of Chinese mores, the return to speaking Chinese as a language of regular communication, and political and social identification with the interests of the wider Chinese community." Clammer further notes that the phenomenon of re-Sinification could be observed among Chinese of different backgrounds, even among *peranakan* and those who had been acculturated to Malay society for generations.

In a way, re-Sinification can be seen as a form of resistance against what are perceived to be threats toward the right to *be* Chinese. The act of re-Sinifying can be empowering for Chinese individuals and groups who feel like they need to defend or reclaim what is theirs. For Chinese Indonesians, along with examples from the more distant past such as those in Salmon's study, the period of assimilation under the New Order was a very clear instance of an attack on and oppression of Chinese identity under the immediate direction of the state and indirectly by the majority non-Chinese society. As has been discussed extensively in the previous chapters, many Chinese Indonesians have attempted to re-Sinify in different ways in the post-Suharto era, and the push factor of wanting to reclaim a lost Chinese identity has been an obvious and persistent theme. What is less well known are the multiple pull factors that have drawn many Chinese Indonesians to reorient themselves toward China. While reorienting toward culture and language can be subtle and relatively harmless, a reorientation toward the PRC is a different thing altogether and potentially much more politically risky.

In addition to Chinese Indonesians, re-Sinification has also intensified in the last two decades among other Chinese communities around the world, with the PRC's dedicated efforts to re-Sinify the Chinese overseas and strengthen their cultural ties in the hope that they will serve (or at least sympathize with) China's national interests. Historically, overseas Chinese support (both in material and immaterial forms) had been important at pivotal moments in the development of the modern Chinese state (Godley 1989; Duara 1997; To 2014; Suryadinata 2017b; Strangio 2020; Repnikova 2022). After all, Sun Yat-sen himself traveled extensively in the late nineteenth and early twentieth centuries to Japan, Southeast Asia, Europe, and North America in order to garner direct support from the overseas Chinese for what would be the 1911–1912 Chinese Revolution (Xinhai Revolution). Referring to the huge financial contributions made by the overseas Chinese (specifically those living in Southeast Asia or Nanyang) to the revolutionary cause, Sun famously declared that the overseas Chinese were "the Mother of the Revolution" (Yen 1967 cited in Huang 2011, 206; Wang 1985; Kayloe 2017). This narrative of the usefulness of the overseas Chinese as patriotic revolutionaries, financiers, and a potential source of migrant manpower is one that has persisted over time and numerous regimes in China (Huang 2011, 223).

Furthermore, as Chak-yan Chang (1980, 281) argues, "during the first decade of the People's Republic of China from 1949, overseas Chinese affairs were considered important to the national interest of China," partly to create an image of international support toward Mao's brand of Communism, and so "a special department called the Overseas Chinese Affairs Commission was established under the Ministry of Foreign Affairs" (see also Peterson 2012). Many overseas Chinese were indeed inspired by the Communist revolution, and many (including some from Indonesia) moved to China to join the Communist nation-building efforts (Zhou 2019). While during the height of the Cultural Revolution from 1967 to 1969, the overseas Chinese (both those abroad and returnees to China) came under suspicion of being ideologically impure (Chang 1980, 281), under the leadership of Deng Xiaoping from 1978 onward, overseas Chinese affairs once again became an important focus for a China that was reopening itself to the world. Deng understood the importance of attracting overseas Chinese capital as one of the first steps in building global confidence in China's economic reforms following the political chaos of the Cultural Revolution. To reconnect with and attract investments from overseas Chinese, Deng began to establish more official linkages, such as through the establishment of the OCAO, which had previously operated under the direct purview of the PRC State Council (Cheung 2005).[3] Citing Chang's (2000) assessment of the OCAO, Gordon Cheung (2005, 64) argues that the office had five major functions:

1. helping the CCP to devise a sound and feasible overseas Chinese policy
2. supervising lower levels of government in implementing overseas Chinese policy
3. promoting and protecting the interests and welfare of overseas Chinese so that their patriotism could be fostered
4. encouraging and mobilizing overseas Chinese to work for China's reform and modernization
5. contributing to the four modernizations, and reunification with Hong Kong, Macau and Taiwan

It can be seen that the OCAO's functions are a clear reflection of China's developmentalist view of the role of the overseas Chinese, in which links with these communities are not just sentimental but are also very strategic.

Alongside the OCAO, since 1989, China has seen the establishment of other government entities, such as the Overseas Chinese Affairs Committee that reports straight to the National People's Congress (Liu 2005). China has also engaged in soft power efforts to attract overseas Chinese to reorient their gaze toward Chinese through initiatives such as investment and job recruitment programs, as well as education scholarships, Chinese heritage tourism, and root-seeking camps. According to Leo Suryadinata (2017b, 160), one significant development was the establishment of the Conference of the World Federation of Huaqiao Huaren Associations (CWFHHA) by the OCAO in 2001 that brings together Chinese community leaders from around the world to gather at the Great Hall of the People in Beijing once every two years. The symbolic message behind the establishment of this biennial conference is obvious: the focus of the activities of overseas Chinese is (or at least should be) centered on Beijing.

Scholars of overseas Chinese such as Hong Liu (2011, 829) argue that China's extensive soft power efforts indicate just how important Beijing regards the overseas Chinese to be a potential economic and political force that "could strengthen China's connections with the world." However, how these soft power efforts affect and are perceived by multiple generations of ethnic Chinese communities around the world who have been acculturated into their new nation-states (such as the case of Chinese Indonesians) is so far largely unknown.

What is clear is the narrative that Beijing continues to project of the role that it envisions for Chinese communities as it aggressively expands its global sphere of influence. At a speech given at the seventh CWFHHA in Beijing on June 7, 2014, Xi Jinping remarked,

> Common roots make us deeply rooted, a common soul makes us remember each other, a common dream makes us have one heart; we will be able to jointly write a new chapter in the development of the Chinese nation. . . . There are tens of millions of Chinese overseas compatriots (*haiwai qiaobao* 海外侨胞). . . . For a long time, overseas Chinese, generation after generation, inherited the excellent tradition of the Chinese nation: they did not forget their fatherland, they did not forget their ancestral province, they did not forget that in their body there is Chinese blood, [therefore] they have enthusiastically supported the Chinese revolution, China's construction and the reform of China. . . . The people of China will always remember the contribution of our Chinese compatriots overseas. (cited in Suryadinata 2017b, 19–20, italics and Chinese characters in original)

Furthermore, as I have discussed at length elsewhere (Setijadi 2016b), as reported by the PRC's Ministry of Foreign Affairs, in speeches given to various Chinese communities around the world over the last few years, Xi has repeatedly stressed the importance of the overseas Chinese as a bridge to "promote the friendly cooperation" between China and their host countries (MFA PRC 2013).

Observers have cautioned that the narrative that Beijing is sending to Chinese around the world is concerning and could even be potentially dangerous for Chinese communities that have had conflicts in their host societies, such as in Indonesia (Cheung 2005; Hearn 2012; To 2014; Suryadinata 2017b). In Indonesia, with its long history of public suspicion and distrust toward the Chinese as China's potential fifth column, the message that they could be mobilized to further China's interests abroad is one that has serious (and unwanted) political implications.

Scholars have also noticed an important change in the last two decades in the language that Beijing uses when referring to overseas Chinese, whereby, as Suryadinata (2017a, 104) notes, "during the Deng Xiaoping period, the distinction between *huaqiao* (華僑 Chinese citizens overseas) and *huaren* (華人 foreign citizens of Chinese descent) was quite clear." In the past, China's policies and appeals for mobilization applied only to the *huaqiao* as PRC citizens whose political loyalties lay with China. When referring to foreign citizens who are ethnically Chinese by descent, the term *huaren* was more commonly used instead. However, since the beginning of the twenty-first century, the distinction between *huaren* and *huaqiao* in Beijing's official narratives has become increasingly blurred (Suryadinata 2017a; see also Xi 2007; Setijadi 2016a). This can be seen in the fact that the CWFHHA has tended to combine *huaqiao* and *huaren* in its institutional focus. For instance, in a speech made at the CWFHHA in 2007, president Hu Jintao stated, "Although both *huaqiao* and *huaren* were overseas, their 'hearts are still linked to the Homeland'" (cited in Suryadinata 2017a, 104). As Suryadinata (2017b, 160–161) points out, Xi Jinping took this narrative further in his speech at the CWFHHA in 2014, when he referred to both *huaren* and *huaqiao* as *haiwai qiaobao* (海外僑胞, meaning "overseas compatriots" according to Suryadinata's translation), which has clear patriotic connotations.

As noted earlier, for many Chinese Indonesians, the rise of China has presented an unprecedented opportunity for advancement and strategic positioning. By gaining social, economic, and political capital through acting as mediators in Sino-Indonesian trade and diplomacy, they may also secure greater safety for the community. The logic here is that the more useful Chinese Indonesians are to both the Indonesian and Chinese governments, the more likely it will be that both governments will protect Chinese Indonesians in times of future unrest. In this way, the act of re-Sinifying—by reorienting oneself either culturally, economically, or politically—toward Mainland China can also be understood as motivated by the desire to achieve safety.

CHINESE INDONESIANS AS A "BEAUTIFUL BRIDGE"?

In the previous chapter, I discussed how Chinese sociocultural organizations such as INTI and PSMTI have played leading roles in lobbying the Indonesian government to advance the rights of the Chinese. Due to the wealth and political capital of many of the elders within these organizations, they have also been very influential in shaping the public image of Chinese Indonesians in the post-Suharto era, as seen in examples such as the Chinese Indonesian Cultural Park (chapter 2). Many of the older (over sixty years of age), mostly *totok*, Chinese-speaking business elites who dominate the leadership of organizations such as INTI and PSMTI are also prominent members of other Chinese Indonesian organizations and chambers of commerce that aim to bridge commercial exchanges between Indonesia and China. As such, they have become influential players in Sino-Indonesian trade and diplomatic relations in the past two decades.

Historically, influential Chinese Indonesians have been recruited into bridging roles in (re)establishing cordial relations between Indonesia and China, even during the New Order. In a memoir written for Nikkei Asia, Lippo Group founder and chairman Mochtar Riady recounted how Suharto sent him to China in 1986 as part of "a group of Indonesian business leaders" tasked with reestablishing business and diplomatic connections "in hopes of improving and eventually normalizing bilateral ties" (Riady 2018).[4] A banking and property tycoon, Riady said he traveled to Beijing in his capacity as the managing director of one of Indonesia's largest banks in order to establish banking agreements and to promote private sector exchanges with counterparts from the PRC. Riady, whose family hailed from Fujian, was chosen as part of Indonesia's delegation because of his Mandarin-speaking abilities as well as his *guanxi* networks in China. In the post-Suharto era, this type of mediation role played by Chinese Indonesians has become much more organized and formalized.

As discussed in previous chapters, after the initial euphoria and intense lobbying for greater recognition of Chinese Indonesian rights at the beginning of the post-Suharto era, many organizations and clan associations have since turned their attention to philanthropic, cultural, and commercial activities. In terms of commerce, more and more Chinese associations and prominent businesspeople have become actively involved in trade and cultural exchanges between Indonesia and China (Liu 1998; Setijadi 2016a, 2016b). Organizations such as INTI and PSMTI have in recent years hosted Chinese trade delegations (both official state and provincial government visits and those from private enterprises/associations) that visited Indonesia. These organizations have also led tours to ancestral village (*qiaoxiang*, 桥乡) regions in southern Chinese provinces such as Fujian and Guangdong from which the majority of Chinese in Indonesia originated. For example, in their May 2014 newsletter, PSMTI reported that a delegation from the association went on a visit to Beijing, Henan, and Guangdong at the invitation of the Chinese government-sponsored Chinese Overseas Exchange Association (COEA) (see Setijadi 2016b). While these tours are officially for the purposes of cultural heritage tracing and leisure, they also provide opportunities for members of the Chinese Indonesian associations to form potentially advantageous networks with businesspeople, regional governments, and local chambers of commerce in China.

In a 2014 interview with INTI's then chairman Rachman Hakim, he told me that commerce-related activities are not part of INTI's official agenda but the organization welcomes all parties who would like to engage in dialogue with its members, whether they are from China or elsewhere. However, Hakim did not deny that as an association with many entrepreneurs and businesspeople as members, there would be those who utilize INTI's vast internal and external networks to further their own business interests. He also noted that while these kinds of personal networking activities were outside of the organization's purview, as long as they did not interfere with INTI's mission then there was no harm in "hitting two birds with one stone" (interview, July 2014).

Apart from organizations like INTI and PSMTI, business associations such as PERPIT and ICBC help connect Chinese investors with Indonesian businesses and vice versa. Many of the executive members and elders of these associations are tycoons with strong business connections in both Indonesia and China, such as Mayapada Group chairman Dr. Tahir (Ang Tjoen Ming) and Harum Energy Group chairman Kiki Barki. Since it is common for these prominent businesspeople to serve as elders in multiple Chinese Indonesian organizations and chambers of commerce at the same time, they are important players in both domestic Chinese identity politics and in Sino-Indonesian business relations. For instance, as well as previously holding the chairmanship of INTI, Hakim—who is a successful businessman—was also vice president of PERPIT. Palm oil and property magnate Murdaya Poo holds advisory roles in PSMTI and the Chinese-dominated Indonesian Buddhist Council (Perwakilan Umat Buddha Indonesia), and the head of the automotive manufacturer New Armada Group, David Herman Jaya, was the chair of PSMTI as well as holding leadership roles in other Chinese associations. Importantly, many of these entrepreneurs/community leaders are members of influential national trade and business organizations, such as the Indonesian Chamber of Commerce and Industry (Kamar Dagang dan Industri Indonesia) and the Indonesian Employers' Association (Asosiasi Pengusaha Indonesia, APINDO). All these entrepreneurs are frequently listed as some of Indonesia's wealthiest individuals according to popular business publications such as *Forbes* magazine. These prominent business figures also hold numerous honorary positions in various clan associations and charitable/religious organizations, for example, the Taiwan-based Buddhist Tzu Chi Foundation that does extensive philanthropic work in Asia and around the world.

My informants told me that one must have wealth, strategic political connections, and esteem within the community in order to be elected as chairman or any of the other leadership positions in the major Chinese organizations. This is not surprising since, as scholars like Liu (1998, 590) note, it is commonplace for wealthy Chinese entrepreneurs to also serve as community leaders and as what Liu terms "neo-*kapitans*" in overseas Chinese organizations all over the world.[5] As neo-*kapitans*, wealthy businesspeople benefit from increased social status at three different levels: the local Chinese community, the transnational linkages of overseas Chinese associations and business networks, and among government officials and business communities in China. This increased social and symbolic capital explains why wealthy and prominent Chinese would want to volunteer time, effort, and financial resources to organizational activities.

Considering the social, economic, and political capital of their more prominent members, it is not a surprise that Chinese Indonesian organizations and their elders often became the first point of contact for businesses and trade delegations from the PRC. In an interview in late October 2016, Mochtar Riady told me that, as a prominent businessman and elder, he frequently received trade and business delegations from China who sought and valued his opinions on Indonesia's economic and political situations and investment potential. In fact, Riady was rushing through his interview with me on that day because there was a business delegation from one of the Chinese provinces that was waiting to meet him. Riady emphasized the importance of maintaining good relations with both public and private sector players in China, which was why he always tried to accommodate their requests for consultation. Realizing that their strength as mediators lies in the *guanxi* relationships they are able to forge with Chinese businesses and trade delegations, Chinese Indonesian elders and organizations strategically maintain good relations with the PRC embassy and consulates in Jakarta, Medan, Surabaya, and Bali, as well as with officials from the relevant state institutions in China. These *guanxi* connections are also the main reason why many Chinese Indonesian entrepreneurs join the associations.

In the last few years, in addition to establishing and maintaining relations with China, these Chinese Indonesian entrepreneur associations have also been connecting more with the global network of overseas Chinese entrepreneurs, so much so that in September 2015, PERPIT hosted the thirteenth World Chinese Entrepreneurs Convention (WCEC) in Bali (Setijadi 2016a, 8). Bringing the WCEC gathering to Indonesia was a triumph for PERPIT, not only because it promoted investments and trade in Indonesia but also because it demonstrated that Chinese Indonesian business leaders had the necessary prestige and clout in the global Chinese business scene. The WCEC gathering in Bali was officially opened by the former president, Megawati Sukarnoputri, while the then coordinating minister for political, legal, and security affairs, Luhut Binsar Pandjaitan, represented Jokowi at the event. While PERPIT's leaders' inability to get Jokowi to attend the event could be seen as somewhat of a failure, Megawati's and Pandjaitan's presence (along with that of several other government ministers and MPs) lent prestige to the gathering, and the event still attracted considerable media attention, particularly from Chinese-language newspapers in Indonesia and other Chinese-speaking countries.

Because of the informal nature of trade delegation visits and functions, it is difficult to gauge just how much trade and foreign direct investment are brought in through the *guanxi* activities of Chinese Indonesian entrepreneurs. While the vast majority of China–Indonesia trade is conducted at the government-to-government level, it is important to note the presence of prominent Chinese Indonesians at Sino-Indonesian trade events, as well as their position as one of the first points of contact for Chinese parties interested in conducting business in Indonesia. For instance, during Xi's state visit to Indonesia in October 2013, prominent Chinese Indonesian businesspeople such as Mochtar Riady, Tahir, and Sukanto Tanoto were invited to official state events and functions as part of Indonesia's delegation. Riady in particular had already known Xi from his time as part of an earlier Indonesian delegation, as noted above. In one of his memoirs, Riady (2018) claimed that he had "built close personal ties with Xi Jinping, who served as party leader in various parts of Fujian Province from the 1980s until 2002 before later becoming president of China."

The presence of prominent Chinese Indonesian businesspeople in Sino-Indonesian bilateral events does not just serve the purpose of forging commercial transactions and *guanxi* relationships; it also serves the political goal of reassuring the Chinese government and trade counterparts that Indonesia is now safe for people of Chinese descent (both overseas Chinese and those from the PRC). The Chinese Indonesian businesspeople themselves seem to understand the value and symbolism of their presence in these bilateral events, with some even seeing it as their patriotic duty to promote Indonesia as welcoming and safe for Chinese investments. In his capacity as PERPIT elder as well as then INTI chairman, Hakim contended that China's rise has provided Chinese Indonesians with an unprecedented strategic position to serve Indonesia: "Chinese Indonesians can be the mediator that connects China and Indonesia in economy and culture. We know both languages, we have business connections in both countries, and we are trusted by both governments. Even President Xi Jinping himself said that Chinese Indonesians are like a beautiful bridge for China and Indonesia. . . . We [Chinese Indonesians] should be proud of this, because this is a great opportunity to serve our country. If we can bring Chinese investors to Indonesia and introduce Indonesian businesses to China, is that not good service to the country?" (interview, July 2014). Hakim added that, as Chinese investment and infrastructure building in Indonesia intensify, Chinese Indonesians need to play an even bigger bridging role.

The oft-cited metaphor of Chinese Indonesians as a bridge is evidently important for the self-perception of Chinese elders (Setijadi 2016b). This can be seen in the interactions with Chinese government and trade delegations, as well as with business counterparts, where Chinese Indonesian elders display what Aihwa Ong and Donald M. Nonini (1997, 329) call "the homogenizing ideologies of Chinese racial and cultural essences," as perceived commonalities such as language, culture, and ancestral or hometown origins are strategically accentuated. As Liu (1998) points out, perhaps nowhere else is this self-essentializing discourse more evident than during large international gatherings of overseas Chinese clan, ancestral, and language-based associations, such as Teochew or Hakka international conventions, as well as business-based ones like the biennial WCECs. At the same time, however, they also accentuate their Indonesianness at these events through acts such as wearing clothes made from traditional Javanese batik, singing the national anthem, and speaking in Indonesian when dealing with Indonesian government officials and the media.

From China's perspective, having Chinese from Indonesia who are eager to engage in mutual commercial investments and connect with China culturally, sentimentally, and strategically is certainly advantageous. Over the last two decades, various Chinese state institutions have been known to honor a number of overseas Chinese who are deemed to have performed admirable service in fostering relations between China and their respective countries.[6] This does not just apply to prominent business tycoons, as such attention appears to be demonstrated for less prominent Chinese businesspeople and community leaders too. During my visit to the offices of Leo Chandra in 2014, a senior electronic goods entrepreneur from a *totok* background who was an elder in INTI, PERPIT, and other associations, I could see a large display of numerous medals and plaques that the Chinese state had awarded to Chandra for his long-standing service toward promoting good relations between China and Indonesia since the 1980s. Like other Chinese business elders that I have met, Chandra claimed to have links with Chinese state officials at both national and provincial levels, and that he was often invited by the OCAO to visit China and to attend annual global meetings of overseas Chinese in Beijing and other cities. Likewise, in the Medan office of local newspaper publisher Eddy Djuandi that I visited in 2014, a large framed photo of him with Xi Jinping and other members of an Indonesian delegation at a worldwide overseas Chinese associations convention in Beijing was displayed in a prominent position.

THE DANGERS OF RE-SINIFICATION

Of course, not all Chinese are happy with the recent push for re-Sinification. One point of major discontent, especially among those who do not speak Chinese, is the increasing use of Mandarin at public events hosted by Chinese Indonesian associations such as INTI and PERPIT. Indeed, in the last ten years in particular, I have observed that many events organized by Chinese Indonesian associations have been conducted bilingually in Indonesian and Mandarin. Even when events are not conducted in Mandarin, the associated promotional materials and stage backgrounds are often written both in Indonesian and simplified Chinese characters. This did not use to be the case in the early years of the post-Suharto era. Windu, a senior member of INTI who cannot speak Mandarin and is from a *peranakan* background, told me in 2014 that more and more non-Mandarin-speaking members felt isolated and excluded from association events:

> I think it is worrying that Chinese Indonesian associations now have a lot of their events conducted in Mandarin. More than anything else, we are an Indonesian organization, why conduct the events in Mandarin? We are not in China. . . . This [the use of Mandarin] alienates a lot of members like myself who do not speak Mandarin, and it also does not look good in the eyes of the *pribumi*. They [*pribumi*] are going to wonder what we are talking about, and they are going to think that now the Chinese are free, they are going to speak in their own language. . . . Now associations also race against each other to invite the Chinese ambassador and other officials to their events.

This kind of internal displeasure is typical among non-Mandarin-speaking members of Chinese organizations, particularly among those who worry about a potential backlash over Chinese Indonesians' closeness with China.

There is also a legitimate worry that Mandarin will eventually be the dominant language among Chinese speakers in Indonesia and that other Chinese languages will disappear from use. Eddy Djuandi, the Medanese newspaper publisher mentioned earlier, is a speaker of Hokkien (the dominant language among Chinese speakers in Medan), and he admitted that many in the Hokkien-speaking community expressed concern that the prominence of Mandarin will result in the decreased use of Hokkien, particularly among the younger generation. However, Djuandi also conceded that perhaps it was better to use Mandarin considering China's global rise. Here, Djuandi argued, "Putonghua [Standard Modern Chinese] is the language of China, and as Chinese, we have to be able to be able to speak it too" (interview, June 20, 2014). Thus, the challenge now for many Chinese speakers is to balance the increased use of Mandarin with the maintenance of mother tongue languages such as Hokkien.

While language use is a concern, the biggest point of contestation regarding re-Sinification thus far, predictably, is the public image of the Chinese Indonesian business elite and their perceived economic and political closeness with China. Considering the history of anti-Chinese sentiment in Indonesia as well as the history of fraught diplomatic relations with China, many are understandably worried about the potential dangers of re-Sinification and closer ties with China. As has been demonstrated throughout this book, despite improvements in *pribumi*–Chinese relations since 1998, there is a persistent presence of anti-Chinese rhetoric, either in the form of racist slurs or even racially motivated attacks. This is troubling for many Chinese Indonesians, who feel re-Sinification and an increasing closeness with China could potentially result in a backlash. Within the volatile environment of race relations and growing ethnonationalism in Indonesia, the implications of a more visible Chinese presence (both in terms of Chinese Indonesians and the PRC) are still unknown.

In a focus group discussion I conducted in June 2014 with seven senior members of Chinese Indonesian associations who expressed concerns about re-Sinification, I brought up the point argued by proponents of closer ties with China that playing the role of mediator in Sino-Indonesian relations may result in the greater protection of Chinese Indonesians in the future. This line of argument was almost unanimously rejected by the group. Timotius, a fifty-five-year-old medical doctor who was a member of INTI, spoke strongly against this argument, claiming instead that throughout history China had never stood up for Chinese Indonesians during times of need: "Anyone who thinks that China would rescue Chinese Indonesians in times of trouble in the future is kidding themselves. . . . When in the past has

China come to our [Chinese Indonesians'] aid when we were under attack? Were they there after 1965? No! Where they there in 1998? No! So, what makes people think that China is going to come to the aid of the ethnic Chinese here in the future?" Most of those in the focus group discussion agreed with Timotius, and their apprehension is not unfounded, considering China's belated response to the May 1998 riots. Despite the uproar among human rights groups in China as well as among overseas Chinese communities worldwide, it was only three months later, in August 1998, and after demonstrations at the Indonesian embassy in Beijing, that the then "Foreign Minister Tang Jiaxuan . . . called on the Indonesian government . . . to take measures to protect Chinese Indonesians" (Purdey 2006, 166).

I pushed Timotius further on his argument by pointing out that in recent years, China had come to the aid of overseas Chinese who found themselves in dire political situations. I cited the example of the 2006 anti-Chinese riots in the Solomon Islands, where China actively evacuated around four hundred Chinese (reportedly, these included Chinese citizens, Hong Kong citizens, and Taiwanese) who were deemed to be in danger (Suryadinata 2017b, 76), as well as the riots in Tonga the same year when China similarly intervened (80). I suggested that perhaps China's stance on protecting overseas Chinese has changed over the years since 1998. However, Timotius was not convinced: "Maybe now that China has more political power, they're more confident about throwing their weight around. . . . But I still think that China will only get involved if their own citizens are in danger. They won't care about ethnic Chinese who are already long-time citizens of other countries. . . . Besides, if something bad does happen, do you think that they [China] will jeopardize a lucrative relationship with Indonesia for the sake of the ethnic Chinese here [Indonesia]? No way!" Others in the focus group discussion agreed, saying that Chinese Indonesians are Indonesian citizens, and therefore the duty to protect them rests with the Indonesian government, not the PRC. I then asked whether the mediating role that Chinese Indonesians play in relations with China would make the community more valuable to the Indonesian government, who may in turn protect them better in times of need. To this, Sjarief, a sixty-year-old *peranakan* entrepreneur, responded:

> At the end of the day, governments always do what is politically popular. In this country [Indonesia], it has never been, and it will never be popular for the government to stand up for the Chinese in times of trouble. That is not going to change anytime soon. . . . Anyone who thinks that being

> economically useful to Indonesia is going to make the government defend the Chinese is kidding themselves! Were the Chinese not useful to the Indonesian economy and government throughout the New Order? What ended up happening was that we [Chinese Indonesians] were sacrificed as scapegoats. . . . What makes people think that this is not going to happen again?

Clearly, there is much skepticism among the Chinese community that Chinese Indonesians' usefulness in fostering Sino-Indonesian partnerships is going to lead to greater security and protection from either Indonesia or the PRC.

Considering the historical trauma of events such as the anti-Communist purges of 1965–1966 and the May 1998 riots, it is understandable why skepticism about governmental protection still exists among many Chinese. Furthermore, as discussed in previous chapters, recent political events in the 2010s have signaled the resurfacing of anti-Chinese and strong ethnonationalist sentiments, adding to the worry of a potential backlash. Even if the elite Chinese businesspeople who appear to be close to China are a small minority and do not represent all Chinese Indonesians, images of wealthy Chinese tycoons cavorting with both Chinese and Indonesian political elites only serve to reinforce old stereotypes of Chinese Indonesians as opportunistic "economic animals" with dubious political allegiances (Hoon 2006b, 344). Indeed, there have been instances when the alleged close relations between Chinese businesspeople and China have been portrayed in a negative light by the Indonesian media.

In August 2016, it came to light that in a 2011 interview (conducted in Mandarin) with China Central Television-2, Sukanto Tanoto, a Chinese Indonesian business tycoon and one of the country's richest men, said, "I was born and raised in Indonesia. And I studied, married, and started my business there [Indonesia]. As a result I always take Indonesia as my adoptive father. . . . But when I come back to China, I feel I have returned to the arms of my (mother) parents, to our motherland because all of us are Chinese. Blood is thicker than water. So I have always been considering China as my natural father" (PT. Sintola Solusindo Dinamika 2016, subtitles translated in original; Ardi 2019). These comments also led to further reports about the amount of money that Tanoto had personally donated to various projects and causes in China. It was revealed that in the lead-up to the 2008 Beijing Olympics, Tanoto was both the first private donor and the largest donor for the construction of the Beijing National Aquatics Center (Water Cube), donating US$5 million to the US$140-million project (Sukanto Tanoto Biography 2014a; Inside RGE 2014). He was even cited as saying, "Only when our motherland becomes strong, can we conduct our business with confidence. The Beijing Olympic Games provides an opportunity to gather Chinese people around the world to contribute to our motherland" (Sukanto Tanoto Biography 2014a). It was also revealed that during the SARS epidemic Tanoto had made huge donations to China amounting to millions of dollars. For his philanthropic work and infrastructure building in Beijing, Tanoto was awarded the "Jinghua Award by the Deputy Secretary of Municipal Party Committee and Mayor Wang Anshun at the Overseas Chinese Affairs meeting in Beijing, China in May 2014" (Sukanto Tanoto Biography 2014a). According to Tanoto's own biographical website, the Jinghua Award "recognizes overseas Chinese who have made significant contributions to developing the Beijing municipality" (Sukanto Tanoto Biography 2014b).

Tanoto's remarks and philanthropic work in China drew much criticism in the media, with politicians, academics, and fellow businesspeople speaking out and questioning Tanoto's loyalty. Then chairman of the conservative Islamist party PPP, Muhammad Romahurmuziy, publicly condemned Tanoto: "We are concerned about this statement made by someone who, all this time, has reaped the economic benefits of living in Indonesia" and "This clearly shows a lack of nationalism and we should take his [Sukanto's] citizenship" (*Lensa News* 2016). Parliamentarian Heri Gunawan of the Gerindra party, who serves on the banking and finance commission of the DPR, echoed Romahurmuziy's sentiments, further alleging that since Tanoto seemed to love China more than Indonesia, then the tycoon must keep most of his money in China, avoiding Indonesian taxation in the process (*Lensa News* 2016). It certainly did not help that prior to making the comments, Tanoto, his Royal Golden Eagle (RGE) group of companies, and their subsidiaries had already been accused of alleged tax evasion, bribery, and intimidation in addition to human rights abuses, particularly in regard to RGE's palm oil business (Alecci 2017). Speaking about Tanoto's comments in the context of the government's attempts to clamp down on tax evasion, prominent economist Mohamad Ikhsan Modjo argued that Tanoto should be the object of a tax investigation (JPNN 2016). He added, "Tanoto has received so many opportunities [in this country] that have made him filthy rich. But Tanoto has had so many cases that have resulted in a very bad image of himself as a business tycoon" (*Lensa News* 2016; JPNN 2016). Further reports about Tanoto's donations to infrastructure building and philanthropic work in China predictably drew criticism from many who questioned why

Tanoto chose to donate to causes in China when there are still so many who live below the poverty line in Indonesia.

These concerns about Tanoto's comments and activities in China also came about around the same time that the Ahok blasphemy allegations began to circulate. As discussed in chapter 5, even before these allegations, there had already been rumors and claims on social media that Ahok was using his powers as governor to further the interests of Chinese tycoons like Tanoto, who in turn served the interests of China. Negative press such as that covering Tanoto is exactly the kind of stereotype-affirming publicity that many concerned Chinese Indonesians worry will eventually induce a backlash from the non-Chinese general public.

Re-Sinification among some Chinese Indonesians can be understood as motivated by several interrelated factors. Domestically, the sentimental desire to reconnect with China and with Chinese heritage and culture stems from a deep sense of loss of cultural identity during the forced assimilation of the New Order. The resurfacing of Chinese identity politics in the early years of the post-Suharto era invigorated many who felt like they could finally learn to be Chinese again through such means as Chinese-language study and the reestablishment of ancestral ties. Externally, the rise of China as a regional and global power has led to the desire among many Chinese Indonesians to capitalize on their ethnicity as a form of social capital to strengthen *guanxi* networks both with China and with the transnational overseas Chinese networks. At the same time, the burgeoning Sino-Indonesian relationship in the last two decades has opened up the opportunity for Chinese Indonesians to strategically place themselves as cultural, linguistic, and commercial brokers.

However, as discussed in this chapter, senior members of the Chinese business elite have become the public face of re-Sinification in Indonesia. In their capacity as respected elders in Chinese Indonesian organizations and commercial associations, this wealthy and influential group has been at the forefront of efforts to forge closer ties with both the public and private sectors in China, as well as with overseas Chinese business networks. The focus of Chinese organizations such as INTI and PSMTI has shifted from lobbying for Chinese Indonesian rights during the early years of the post-Suharto era to playing a larger mediating role between Chinese and Indonesian business counterparts in more recent years. These developments have caused discontent among members of these organizations who have become wary of the organizations' new direction. Indeed, the trend of re-Sinification and closer ties with China has created disagreements among different groups of Chinese Indonesians, such as between the *totok* and *peranakan* groups, and between the older and younger generations. These internal divisions may widen even further in the future.

Considering the long history of Chinese political precarity in Indonesia, many Chinese Indonesians worry about the potential backlash that could occur if they appear to be too closely linked to China. This worry indicates that the negative ideological connotations and suspicions about the political loyalty of Chinese Indonesians are still alive and well. There have been regular attacks in the media from various right-wing, ethnonationalist, and Islamist groups accusing Chinese Indonesian businesspeople and politicians of being China's puppets in Indonesia, especially after the Ahok blasphemy case in 2017 (Chew and Barahamin 2019). While the China of today is indeed a very different country from the insular Communist country of the 1960s and 1970s, the image of China as an ideological and security threat has endured, and thus the perception of the Chinese as being China's fifth column is one that is still held by many non-Chinese.

By extension, to be publicly perceived as being too close to China is a political liability, and this is something that does not apply only to Chinese Indonesian politicians and businesspeople. During his presidential bid in 2014, one of the smear campaigns launched by political opponents against the Javanese Jokowi was the accusation that he was secretly of Chinese descent (Setijadi 2016a). While Jokowi is not Chinese, the smears successfully generated negative publicity due to his possible Chineseness and political loyalties vis-à-vis China. Throughout his presidency, Jokowi has also frequently been perceived as too agreeable and lenient toward China, especially in his attempts to secure Chinese investment and loans for Indonesian infrastructural projects. These accusations intensified after the tender for the Jakarta-Bandung high-speed rail project was given to China rather than Japan (Salim and Negara 2016). The opaque tender process and the sudden awarding of the project to China led to accusations that Jokowi and his ministers favored China and took backdoor routes and incentives to make the deal happen. Furthermore, the inflow of BRI-related Chinese investments and projects in Indonesia since Jokowi's election in 2014 has also been followed by rumors that thousands (and even millions) of low-skilled Chinese laborers will come into Indonesia under deals struck by the government. Even *Tempo* magazine, arguably Indonesia's most respected news and current affairs publication, ran a story in its August–September 2015 edition about how Chinese migrants will "flood" into the country. The magazine's

FIGURE 6.1 Front cover of the August–September 2015 edition of *Tempo* magazine, featuring a social realist illustration of President Jokowi as a Chinese laborer, with the tagline "Welcome Chinese Laborers."

Source: Tempo Media Group.

front cover featured an illustration of Jokowi as a Chinese laborer in the socialist realist style of Cold War–era propaganda posters with the tagline "Welcome Chinese Laborers" (*Selamat Datang Buruh Cina*) (figure 6.1).

A more optimistic perspective would be that the social and political situations in the post-Suharto era are indeed different from those of the past, and that today Indonesia could benefit from closer ties with China as an emerging global superpower. The Chinese business elites discussed in this chapter were certainly optimistic about their role as a bridge in Sino-Indonesian relations and saw no inherent contradiction between their close links to China and their loyalty to Indonesia. They also shared the common perception that the more valued Sino-Indonesian relations are, then the more secure their sociopolitical position in Indonesia will be. However, considering the recent resurfacing of both anti-China and anti-Chinese sentiments, there is a real danger that the negative public image of elite Chinese businesspeople could trigger further backlashes in the future.

The case studies presented here illustrate the difficulty Chinese Indonesians face when it comes to balancing between strategically capitalizing on their Chinese ethnicity by asserting themselves in Sino-Indonesian relations while avoiding the potential backlash from appearing too close to China. The rise of China clearly presents an unprecedented opportunity for some Chinese Indonesians to accumulate social, economic, and political capital that could boost their importance and standing in both Indonesia and China. Yet, what is also clear from recent reactions against the perceived closeness between Chinese Indonesian business elites and China is that old suspicions regarding the political and primordial loyalties of Chinese Indonesians are still very much alive. The trauma of past violence and state-sponsored oppression that resulted from this very suspicion of Chinese Indonesians as China's fifth column is making many Chinese worry about how they may once again be targets of mob anger should there be another backlash against a Chinese presence (here perceived as both the PRC and Chinese Indonesians) in Indonesia.

Conclusion

> There are people who belong to more than one world, speak more than one language (literally and metaphorically), inhabit more than one identity, have more than one home; who have learned to negotiate and translate *between* cultures, and who, because they are irrevocably the product of several interlocking histories and cultures, have learned to live with, and indeed to speak from, *difference*. They speak from the "in-between" of different cultures, always unsettling the assumptions of one culture from the perspective of another, and thus finding ways of being both *the same as* and at the same time *different from* the others amongst whom they live.
>
> —Stuart Hall (1995, 206, emphasis in original)

As the products of what Stuart Hall describes as "several interlocking histories and culture," the Chinese in Indonesia can be said to be living an "in-between" existence at a time of significant sociopolitical flux. As I have shown, the lives of the Chinese in the post-Suharto era are a complex combination of old fears and exciting new ways to define and perform Chineseness. While it is true that the atmosphere of openness after 1998 has resulted in greater acceptance of Chinese culture in the public domain, the fundamental ideological notion of the Chinese as essential outsiders in Indonesia remains prevalent. Social segregation between the Chinese and non-Chinese continues to be the norm because fear, trauma, and mutual prejudice still define Chinese–non-Chinese relations in many ways. As a result, the Chinese and non-Chinese still mostly occupy separate spaces in their day-to-day lives, and many young Chinese reach adulthood with little or no social contact with any non-Chinese, apart from those in their family's employ. In the long run, I argue that this trend points to the persistence of the "Chinese problem," in which they continue to be perceived as an irreconcilable other in Indonesian society.

In analyzing the revival of Chinese culture since 1998, I have been conscious of what Jacqueline Lo (2000, 153) terms "happy hybridity," that is, a situation in which essentialized cultural differences are celebrated and consumed without any critical reflection of the underlying political and social issues that are still present. In assuming this critical stance, I agree with other scholars who have expressed similar skepticism about whether celebrations of Chineseness at the macro level have resulted in any real changes in how the Chinese and non-Chinese view and treat each other at the micro level (see Hoon 2006a; Chua 2008; Tsai 2008; Hoon and Kuntjara 2019). I contend that much of the problem is due to the unchanging discourse of ethnonationalism that remains at the core of national belonging and dominates political rhetoric to this day. In the conclusion of her PhD thesis submitted in January 1998—a few months before the events of May 1998 and the reforms that followed—the anthropologist Thung Ju Lan (1998, 320) writes, "Obviously, as long as the Indonesian assimilationists insist upon the indispensable importance of absolute homogeneity for all Indonesian citizens, refuse to acknowledge the weaknesses of a policy of assimilation, and work toward a better solution, ethnic and racial problems will continue to retard the nation-building process in Indonesia." Thung's critical assessment proved to be prophetic. While assimilationist policies were officially abolished after May 1998, the prevalence of what she calls "the indispensable importance of absolute homogeneity" in the form of a narrative of nativeness has persisted. This means that, despite open and public displays of multiculturalism and recognition at the surface level, the Chinese have continued to be regarded as foreigners with a tenuous sense of belonging in Indonesia.

This is a narrative that has persisted not only among the non-Chinese but also among the Chinese themselves. Evidence of this can be seen in the continuing prevalence of the discourse of assimilation (*asimilasi*) versus integration (*integrasi*) in both the public and private domains. Today, more than two decades after the beginning of the reform period, different groups of Chinese are still debating whether the best approach for them is one of assimilation (by hiding, downplaying, or erasing elements of their Chineseness) or integration (by embracing and expressing Chinese cultural forms liberally). Now that they can publicly do so, is it wise for the Chinese to openly celebrate their Chineseness or would this just further accentuate the image of their foreignness? In the realm of Chinese identity politics, both the older and younger generations are inherently unsure of how to characterize, display, and perform their Chineseness in a time of greater openness, and this has caused much disagreement within the broader community.

Many Chinese still debate how they can better prove their sense of loyalty, patriotism, and belonging. This can be observed in the many examples provided throughout the book, where, for instance, Chinese politicians feel like they need to work harder than their non-Chinese counterparts in order to demonstrate their service and commitment to the nation. Now that the Chinese are much more active and better represented in electoral and institutional politics than ever before, this also means that they are under even greater public scrutiny. The infamous rise and fall of the former Jakarta governor Ahok serves as a harsh reminder that anti-Chinese sentiments are still alive and well, no matter how patriotic and loyal to the country the Chinese try to prove themselves to be. Unsurprisingly, for many Chinese, the precarity of their belonging has continued to be the source of much anxiety and insecurity. As Susan Giblin (2003, 353) points out, this has led to a situation where the Chinese are stuck in "two double binds"—they simultaneously strive to overcome negative stereotypes of their exclusivity while trying to protect their in-group safety and interests. Arguably, no other ethnic group in Indonesia has faced or continues to face the same conundrum or level of public scrutiny.

I have focused on how collective memory and intergenerational trauma have shaped Chinese identity politics over the past two decades and more. In my exploration of different domains of everyday life, such as the home, local neighborhoods, and educational institutions, I have found that, while some patterns of socialization and interactions between the Chinese and non-Chinese have changed, most have stayed broadly the same. For instance, while the majority of the Chinese I interviewed said they felt safer, they also revealed clear examples of ethnic boundary maintenance through strategies such as residential enclaving, educational and work choices, religious choices, and—perhaps more importantly—choices regarding social circles, friends, spouses, and partners. Many of the research participants I interviewed stated that, while they have non-Chinese friends and acquaintances, the strength and depth of Chinese–non-Chinese relationships are ultimately limited due to a lack of trust between the two groups.

This inherent distrust is a direct result of both Indonesia's long history of anti-Chinese discrimination as well as more recent traumatic events, particularly the May 1998 riots. Furthermore, the persistence of a culture of impunity, injustice, and historical denial means that many Chinese continue to feel great distrust toward the state. Considering that they still regularly experience bureaucratic and social discrimination and seeing that not much has changed in substantive terms, it is little wonder that the discourse of victimhood has persisted, with many believing it is not a matter of if but when the next anti-Chinese attacks will happen.

In this regard, Pierre Bourdieu's concept of the *habitus* has been useful in framing my analyses of how collective memory and trauma shape individual subjectivities. Defined as acquired dispositions that are manifested in feelings, thoughts, and tastes, the *habitus* is a model of social environments that explains how individual subjectivities are shaped by in-group collective histories (Bourdieu 1990). In the case of the Chinese in Indonesia, Bourdieu's *habitus* has helped me explain how memories, value systems, and capital are embedded within specific spaces and passed down from one generation to the next. The inheritance of narratives of victimization plays an important role in the maintenance of the boundaries of their *habitus* and collective social behavior.

Nevertheless, that is not the end of the story. I have also shown how a new generation of Chinese is challenging the rules and boundaries of their *habitus*. Discontented with living in fear and hiding behind victimhood narratives, some young Chinese are forging their own in-between *habitus* and utilizing the new spaces enabled by democratization to explore and articulate their trauma, while at the same time writing their own narratives on how to be Chinese in Indonesia. These young people, who refuse to live by the rules their parents have set for them, are forming new kinds of friendships, relationships, and alliances with progressive-minded non-Chinese who also want to challenge older narratives about nativism and what it means to belong. For the Chinese filmmakers discussed in chapter 4, film has become a medium through which they can discuss and present their anxieties of growing up as young people with an ambivalent sense of belonging. Likewise, for Chinese artists, art has become a vehicle for them to address the themes of belonging, historical amnesia, and trauma in an honest way. In the realm of politics, undeterred by what happened to Ahok, young Chinese are still entering the political fray and—in the case of PSI—even forming their own interethnic political party. Apart from securing their group's safety or access to capital, this new breed of Chinese politicians is also trying to represent a pluralist ideology in national politics in order to challenge long-standing corrupt political practices.

While Bourdieu's concept of the *habitus* has been useful in my analyses of in-group trauma and boundary-making practices, it is not fully adequate for the task of explaining individual agency and creativity in breaking free from the constraints of the social structures imposed by society and the state. Bourdieu's vision of individuals within the *habitus* as ultimately adhering to the rules and boundaries of the collective does not account for how the young Chinese are actively forging their own paths for activism, cultural production, and self-reflection. Bourdieu also argues that individuals always work toward the maintenance of the objective structures of their *habitus*. Yet many of the young Chinese I interviewed and discuss here engage in activities and life choices that openly challenge and subvert the previous generations' ideas of the collective good and Chinese–non-Chinese relations. In doing so, they try to dismantle rather than maintain the objective structures of the Chinese *habitus*. Returning to Stuart Hall's (1995, 206) quote at the beginning of this chapter, these young Chinese are those "who have learned to negotiate and translate *between* cultures, and who, because they are irrevocably the product of several interlocking histories and cultures, have learned to live with, and indeed to speak from, *difference*." Through their activism and efforts to challenge stereotypes, these young Chinese are "unsettling the assumptions of one culture from the perspective of another" (ibid.).

Throughout the book, I have tried to do justice to the agency displayed by those Chinese who try to expose the ambiguities and contradictions of their respective *habitus*. Indeed, while I have intermittently painted a rather gloomy picture of the state of Chinese identity politics in Indonesia, my case studies also offer much hope and cause for modest optimism. Amid the persistent narratives of victimhood, there is clear evidence that some younger Chinese are challenging existing definitions, norms, and boundaries of Chineseness through their social, cultural, and political activities.

I have concentrated my analyses mostly on middle- and upper-class Chinese in Jakarta. But since the Chinese population is heterogeneous, it is important to acknowledge once again that different kinds of *habitus* exist among Chinese communities from various backgrounds, orientations, and localities across the Indonesian archipelago. This means that there are variations in the specific ways in which Chinese Indonesian history is remembered and embodied in the everyday lives of different groups. I would have liked to go into much more detail about how gender, social class, and religion intersect in shaping contemporary Chinese identities, but exploring those themes would have required extensive investigation that is beyond the scope of this study. By concentrating on the broader themes of common history and group trauma, my aim has been to shed light on the core commonalities of Chinese experiences in a way that also respects their vast heterogeneity as a group. I hope that this approach will pave the way for more comprehensive studies of how collective memory and intergenerational trauma are experienced and expressed differently by Chinese from diverse backgrounds. Future research on these topics is important, especially given that the domestic, regional, and global geopolitical landscapes that frame Chinese Indonesian identities are changing so rapidly.

CHINESE INDONESIANS TODAY

Since the turn of the century, the (re)emergence of China as a truly significant actor in the global political economy has presented new opportunities and challenges for Chinese Indonesians. At a time when China's global push is fueled by an enormous amount of capital investment and political will manifested in soft power, many Chinese recognize their potential as cultural, linguistic, and economic brokers in furthering the relationship between Indonesia and China. This is particularly true among business elites who possess significant *guanxi* connections in China and with ethnic Chinese diasporas around the world. Indeed, the importance of Chinese Indonesians as a bridge in Sino-Indonesian relations has not gone unnoticed by the governments in both countries.

However, the cultural implications of the rise of China for Chinese Indonesians are far more complex than the simplistic assertion of a re-Sinification or a turn to Chinese culture and identity that is oriented toward Mainland China. Contrary to common belief, there is nothing primordial about the move to connect oneself to a sense of lost Chineseness. This is certainly reflected in the case studies discussed in this book. Considering how acculturated ethnic Chinese communities in Southeast Asia have historically been, Caroline Hau (2014, 314) even suggests that the phenomenon of Sinification in Southeast Asia might be "better understood not as a recovery or revival (implied by the prefix 're-') of long-occluded Chineseness, but as a process of 'becoming Chinese.'" Those who do feel a sense of affiliation toward PRC culture and/or society have a number of different motives, and the local manifestations of this cultural affiliation vary greatly among individuals, groups, and generations. This is not to mention the possibility that closer association with China may be dangerous for Chinese communities in countries with long histories of anti-Chinese sentiment such as Indonesia. One thing for sure is that the rise of China as an exogenous force will continue to influence local Chinese identity politics in Indonesia in the foreseeable future.

At the same time, Indonesian society itself is also undergoing rapid transformation. The same processes of democratization that have enabled the revival of Chinese culture and identity politics have also created new spaces for political and religious factions that were previously suppressed and confined to the margins of society. In recent years, scholars have documented and analyzed trends such as the rise of Islamic conservativism and an amplified ethnonationalist rhetoric that have resulted in greater political polarization (see Aspinall et al. 2011; Mietzner 2012; Mietzner and Muhtadi 2019). In the 2014 and 2019 presidential elections, the nation was largely divided into two camps, with more conservative voters backing the presidential candidacy of Prabowo Subianto, while those who regard themselves as more progressive and pluralist supported Joko Widodo (Jokowi). These were not just ordinary political divisions associated with election cycles in any country. The schisms seen in the 2014 and 2019 elections reflect broader political trends over the last decade that suggest that Indonesian society has become even more polarized along religious and class lines.

Disappointed by the persistence of issues such as economic inequality, corruption, and the concentration of power among the political elites, many Indonesians (especially those from lower socioeconomic backgrounds) found a voice in conservative political and religious rhetoric. In both elections, Prabowo's populist strongman persona attracted voters who desired a return to a more authoritarian style of government, one that is perceived to be able to deliver greater stability. Support for Prabowo's opposition coalition from Islamist factions and hard-line Muslim groups such as the FPI further consolidated political and religious conservatives. In response, Jokowi also pandered more toward the conservative Muslim faction, most obviously in the choice of Ma'ruf Amin, an influential conservative Muslim Islamic scholar (*ulama*) linked to hard-line groups, as his vice president in 2019. Jokowi's government has also tried to court conservative voters by clamping down on leftist activists as well as oppressing minorities such as the LGBTQIA+ communities. In light of these recent developments, some scholars have suggested that the strength and quality of Indonesia's civil society is declining, and its democracy is slowly undergoing deconsolidation (see Aspinall et al. 2020; Mietzner 2020; Setijadi 2021).

Amid these domestic polarizations, the Chinese have once again found themselves in a vulnerable position. Being (mostly) non-Muslim, nonindigenous, and perceived to be at an economic advantage, the Chinese are at risk of being convenient scapegoats during these times of heightened religious conservativism and xenophobia, as they have been many times before in Indonesia's history. The heightened anti-Chinese sentiments surrounding Ahok's blasphemy case in 2017 were a stark wake-up call and a reminder of how quickly the situation could turn against the Chinese in times of political instability. An important lesson from the Ahok case is that, despite policy changes and surface-level recognition of the Chinese at the beginning of the reform era, rousing anti-Chinese sentiment is still an effective tool wielded by some non-Chinese politicians to rally angry mass protests. There is a real danger that if a populist and reactionary government were to come to power in the future, it might not have the political will to protect the Chinese in times of crisis.

It is once again commonplace to publicly refer to Chinese with the derogatory term *cina,* even though it was officially abolished from public use in favor of the term "Tionghoa" in 2014. Apart from more frequent use in everyday speech, even major national print publications such as *Tempo* magazine have been using the term to refer to both Chinese nationals and Chinese Indonesians, and prominent politicians have also been using it, especially when referring to Chinese Indonesians in a derogatory manner. Despite these very obvious regressions, it remains to be seen whether this trend points to a more serious return to pre-1998 levels of anti-Chinese antagonism. Despite efforts by young Chinese to reclaim *cina* for themselves by using it as a term of empowerment, the normalization of a name that was earlier regarded as derogatory is a sure sign that antipathy toward the Chinese is becoming an increasingly accepted part of society once more.[1]

At the time of writing in 2020 and 2021, the world was reeling from the effects of the COVID-19 pandemic. In Indonesia, the virus caused great devastation, and official World Health Organization figures reveal that there have been over 155,000 reported deaths as of April 2022 (WHO 2022). The public's anger toward the Jokowi government for its perceived mishandling of the pandemic is palpable, and as elsewhere around the world, strong antiforeigner sentiment has been brewing, particularly toward China (where the virus originated) and people of Chinese or East Asian appearance (Setijadi 2021). Mimicking Donald Trump's rhetoric, many Indonesians have taken to using "Chinese virus" to refer to COVID-19 on social media, while some Muslim clerics called for a decree (*fatwa*) to ban Chinese nationals from entering Indonesia, and to expel Chinese Indonesians from the country (Rakhmat 2020; Sibarani et al. 2020). In April 2020, the Jakarta-based

Institute for Policy Analysis of Conflict released a report demonstrating how affiliates of the Islamic State in Indonesia have increased anti-Chinese rhetoric on social media during the pandemic in the hope of using COVID-19 as a pretext to target either Chinese expatriates living in the country or those of Chinese descent (IPAC 2020). Combined with the preexisting negative sentiments about issues such as China's economic and political influence in the country, anger over foreign Chinese workers taking local jobs, and the Chinese state's treatment of Uighur Muslims in Xinjiang, anti-Chinese sentiments during the pandemic have been easy to stoke and should be taken seriously. Considering these recent developments, it is not difficult to imagine why the Chinese are feeling increasingly insecure about their position and general safety in Indonesia.

LOOKING BACK, LOOKING FORWARD

***Catatan Sepi si Anak Babi* / The Piglet's Lonely Note**

by Awi Chin (2020)[2]

Matamu tidak mampu melihat sempurna, kata mereka.
Kelopakmu tak mampu membuka rupa dan warna.
Ujug-ujug tatapmu malah semakin membalam.
Oleh air mata dan purbasangka yang melesak mendalam.

Jangan panggil aku Cina, pintamu.
Tetap saja panggilan anak babi menyindir merdu.
Maka merunduklah kepalamu sedari pagi sampai senja beradu.
Mencari jati diri yang tercecer di jalan yang berdebu.

Pada umur tujuh kamu bertanya pada ibu.
Apakah aku jua berbangsa dan bertanah air satu?
Keadilan sosial bagi seluruh rakyat Indonesia, jawabnya sendu.
Tetap saja batu itu menoreh luka di pelipis dan sisa hidupmu.

Your eyes cannot see perfectly, they said.
Your lids cannot fathom form and color.
But your gaze only deepens.
By the tears and prejudice that are left unshed.

Don't call me *Cina,* you plead.
Yet they kept calling you a piglet.

Then you keep your head down from dusk till the sun bleeds.
Searching for shattered identity on dusty concrete.

At the age of seven you asked your mother.
Am I red and white just like the others?
Social justice for all Indonesians, she whispered.
Still, that rock scarred your temple, leaving your life in endless
wonder.

In this poem, the young Chinese writer Awi Chin recounts his own experiences of growing up with an ambivalent sense of belonging in Indonesia. Bullied for being Chinese from a very young age, Chin grew up asking questions about why his non-Chinese friends told him that he was different from other kids at school. He still has the scar above his eye from when bullies threw rocks at him and called him "Piglet." Chin was only seven years old when his father's business in East Jakarta was looted and burned to the ground during the May 1998 riots. Deeply traumatized by the attack, his family eventually decided to move back to the West Kalimantan region of Sintang (which has a large concentration of Hakka Chinese) where the family originated. As an adult, Chin has since moved back to Jakarta, but he continues to question what his Chinese ethnicity means for his identity and life as an Indonesian.

To Chin, while his experiences of being attacked for his Chineseness are deeply personal, and as he told me, he also believes that this is something that most Chinese can relate to: "I think that most ethnic Chinese would know what it is like to be told that they don't belong [in Indonesia]. . . . They would know what it's like to be stereotyped and be told to go back to where they came from, even though they were born and bred in Indonesia. This is why I wrote this poem, because while my experiences are personal, they are also universal in many ways" (interview, August 29, 2020). Now in his late twenties, Chin belongs to a new group called Voice of Peranakan (Suara Peranakan), an online-based collective of Chinese Indonesian writers, scholars, and activists who proclaim themselves to be against all forms of racism, discrimination, and oppression (Suara Peranakan 2020).[3] Within only a few months of its founding (as of March 2022), the group managed to attract over eight thousand followers on Twitter, as well as a growing online presence on other social media platforms. The group publishes essays and other literary works addressing themes that include experiences of anti-Chinese discrimination. Like Chin, the majority of the group's members are young

Chinese in their twenties and thirties who feel it is important to continue talking about Chinese issues and to promote Chinese–non-Chinese harmony. The very fact that more than two decades since the onset of the reform era young Chinese who never had direct experiences of the May 1998 riots or the New Order assimilation policies are still concerned with discrimination shows the persistence of the "Chinese problem."

In the more than ten years that I have spent researching and writing this book, I have spoken to hundreds of Chinese from different age groups and walks of life. While their circumstances and life trajectories vary greatly, one thing that unifies all of them is their experience of being othered in Indonesia because of their Chinese ethnicity. From the story of Alin, the young clothes store owner whose distrust toward her non-Chinese employees (and non-Chinese in general) was highlighted at the start of the book, to the many artists, filmmakers, politicians, and entrepreneurs who in their own ways struggle to negotiate their identity as Chinese, their stories reflect a sense of ambivalence and residual trauma still felt today. In this regard, perhaps what unites the Chinese as a group is not a primordial sense of common ancestry or culture but a solidarity that comes from shared experiences of victimization and suffering.

In her discussion of Chinese Indonesian collective trauma and the discourse of victimization, Ien Ang—who herself is an ethnic Chinese born in Indonesia—asks what good such a discourse can achieve, apart from providing "therapeutic comfort to desperate, hurting souls" (Ang 2001b, 27). She elaborates by noting that her main concern lies in the fact that the majority of the Chinese have no other future than in Indonesia itself. This means that there is a real and grim possibility that they may end up living trapped under a shadow of ambivalence and victimhood for the foreseeable future. To be trapped in such a state may result in an inability to move on or to coexist harmoniously with the non-Chinese.

With this in mind, I have found that the best way to understand the Chinese Indonesian predicament is to accept that, until a significant paradigm shift occurs in how Chinese subjects are imagined and incorporated within Indonesia's ethnonationalist mode of belonging, collective trauma and victimhood will continue to be central elements in how Chinese Indonesians define themselves. In order to make sense of this possibility of unresolvedness, Ang borrows from Zygmunt Bauman's "postmodern wisdom" in which Bauman argues that "there are problems in human and social life with no good solutions, twisted trajectories that cannot be straightened up . . . moral agonies which no reason-dictated recipes can soothe, let alone cure"

(Bauman 1993, 245, cited in Ang 2001b, 27). Far from being nihilistic, both Ang and Bauman advocate more productive ways of conceptualizing the ambivalence of identities that would allow scholars to move beyond lamentations about why certain discourses or historical baggage continue to exist. The focus should then shift toward attempts to understand how individuals and groups self-reflect and negotiate their identities amid memories of the past, their present-day realities, and their hopes for the future.

This book has painted a complex, rich, and often contradictory picture of the status of the Chinese in the post-Suharto era. By examining the interrelationships between collective memories, everyday spaces, and sites of identity construction, I have introduced what is a relatively novel approach to studying Chinese Indonesians that allows for a more holistic view of how macro sociohistorical factors influence day-to-day realities at the micro level. In many ways, the routines and *habitus* of their everyday lives are shaped by the narratives of trauma and victimization that have for so long defined the Chinese experience. However, even within this seemingly unchanging discursive structure, some Chinese assert impressive agency in negotiating autonomous spaces from which they can speak about their experiences and aspirations. Many of the younger generation have been deeply reflective of the trauma and anxieties they felt while growing up. Yet rather than being defeated by their fears, they have chosen to ask difficult questions about their past, find new ways to explore their identity, and make the most of their difficult sociopolitical situation. In this regard, they are actively looking back at their past—both as individuals and as part of the Chinese collective—in order to move forward.

Previously, scholars studying the Chinese were preoccupied with trying to fit them into rigid categories of ethnic and national identity. The old *peranakan–totok* distinction is one example of this, in which individuals are categorized (and categorize themselves) based on how Chinese or Indonesian they are perceived to be. Considering the complexity of Chinese lives, I argue that as scholars we need to change the way we analyze identities by treating ambiguity as the norm rather than as an anomaly. People juggle many different cultural and ideological influences at the same time, and, correspondingly, they are rooted in multiple spaces with diverging aspirations. Their identities are fluid, and they are also strategic in where they place their affiliations. With the increasing availability of transnational cultural materials, it is safe to say that in the future more and more young Chinese will explore multiple modes of identification that transcend the traditional pathways of national belonging in Indonesia. If the examples discussed in this book are anything to go by, then we can expect Chinese identities in the future to be even more complex, diverse, and connected to regional and global cultural trends. To keep up with these trends, scholars need to keep an open mind and be prepared to view the Chinese beyond the traditional models of ethnic and national belonging.

GLOSSARY OF NON-ENGLISH TERMS

abang	older brother
adat	traditional or customary law
agama	religion
aib	stain, shame
aman	safe, secure
amor fati	love of destiny
angpao	red money envelope
anjungan	exhibition space
antar-golongan	interclass relations
asli	native or indigenous (literally "real" or "original")
barongsai	Chinese lion dance, usually performed during Chinese New Year (Imlek) season
benteng	fortress
beruntung	lucky
Bhinneka tunggal Ika	Unity in diversity, Indonesian national slogan
buang suara	throw away a vote
budaya kuliner	culinary culture
cari aman	seek security or safety
Chindo	new colloquial Jakartan term to refer to Chinese Indonesians. Used more frequently among the younger generation Chinese
Chineezenmoord	Chinese massacre (of 1740)
cici	older sister (Hokkien), commonly used as a colloquial term for an ethnic Chinese woman
cina	official term for ethnic Chinese and Mainland China during the New Order; also colloquial term (considered derogatory) used to refer to ethnic Chinese
cina benteng	fortress Chinese

cina gile	crazy Chinese
cokin	Chinese (Jakartan slang, derogatory)
etnisitas	ethnicity
Europeanen	Europeans
fatwa	nonbinding legal edict on a point of Islamic law (*sharia*) or a topic declared by a jurist (*mufti*) or a recognized Islamic body
gambang kromong	traditional orchestra which blends gamelan, Western music, and Chinese pentatonic base tones
gardu	security post, guardhouse
gile, gila	crazy
guanxi	Chinese kin and network-based preferential personal connections
haiwai qiaobao	overseas Chinese compatriots
hilang	missing
hitam tapi cina, hi-ta-ci	dark but Chinese
huaqiao	Chinese citizens overseas, sojourners
huaren	people of Chinese descent outside China
huru-hara	riot
Imlek	Chinese New Year (Hokkien), adopted into everyday Indonesian
Inlander	natives or indigenous populations
integrasi	integration
itikad baik	goodwill
jaga-jaga	keep watch
jago	local gangs, gang leaders
jimat	amulet
kampung	village
kapitan	high-ranking official, literally "captain"
kapitan Cina	literally "Chinese captain"
kasar	rough
keamanan	safety
kebaya encim	long-sleeved blouse worn with a sarong or batik-printed cloth
kebudayaan	ethnic culture
keluarga baik-baik	proper families
koko	Hokkien term for older brother, commonly used as a colloquial term for an ethnic Chinese man

komedi stamboel	hybrid genre of folk theater influenced by Western and Chinese opera, and Arabic music
Konfrontasi	Indonesia-Malaysia confrontation
Konghucu	Confucianism
kota mandiri	self-sustaining city within a larger city
kroncong	folk musical genre influenced by Portuguese musical traditions
kulit putih bersih	clean fair skin
lieux de mémoire	sites of memory
lokasi aman	safe location
macam-macam	causing or making trouble
macet	jammed (of traffic)
manja	spoiled
masalah cina	"Chinese problem"
mata sipit	slanted eyes
mbak	older sister
melawan lupa	fighting forgetfulness or forgetting
membaur	ethnically integrated
menjilat	brownnose
milik pribumi	*pribumi*-owned
Nanyang	Southeast Asia, literally "Southern Ocean"
Non	Miss
nyai	mistress
orang Indonesia asli	indigenous Indonesian
Pancasila	five basic principles of Indonesia's state ideology
pasti melarang	absolutely object
Pecinan	Chinatown
pelit	stingy
pelo	strong Chinese accent
pembantu	domestic servant
pemuda	youth
pemuda Tionghoa	Chinese youth
peranakan	acculturated Chinese communities and individuals, usually understood to have mixed *pribumi* and Chinese heritage
plonco	hazing
preman	protection racket
pribumi	indigenous or native Indonesian

qiaoxiang	home villages of migrants
ras	race
reformasi	post-Suharto reform period, literally "reformation"
rukun tetangga	residents' consortium
rumah toko, ruko	shophouse
satpam	security guard
sekolah dasar	primary school
seperti Singapur	like Singapore
sok baik	altruistic
sombong	snobby
sudah didepan pintu	at their doorstep
suku	ethnic group, tribe, tribalism
suku Tionghoa	Chinese tribe
syukuran	thanksgiving
tawuran	mass brawling
teman dekat	close friend
terra nullius	unoccupied land, literally "land belonging to no one"
Tionghoa	Chinese (Hokkien), now preferred term for ethnic Chinese persons in the post-Suharto era
totok	Chinese who migrated to Indonesia more recently and are less acculturated to local cultures, generally considering themselves to be "purer" Chinese than *peranakan*
tulou	earthen-walled village
uang keamanan lingkungan	neighborhood security fee
ulama, ulema	educated Muslims trained in religious law and doctrine who usually hold an official post, literally the "learned ones" (Arabic)
vreemde Oosterlingen	foreign Orientals
yayasan	foundation

NOTES

INTRODUCTION

1. In contemporary Indonesia, "race" is generally considered a taboo term because of the New Order's restrictions against discussions to do with tribalism (*suku*), religion (*agama*), race (*ras*), and interclass relations (*antar-golongan*), commonly known by the acronym SARA. Because of this, the Chinese are usually considered as belonging to a different ethnicity (*etnisitas*). The term "race" is sometimes used in everyday speech, but not in official discourses or in polite conversations. My research participants would use the term "ethnicity" rather than "race." Because of this, while acknowledging that race and ethnicity are regarded as different in academic scholarship, I mostly use the term "ethnicity" rather than "race" in my discussions of Chinese Indonesians.
2. The term "Chinese problem" has been used in Indonesian public discourse since the 1950s, when the issue of the dual nationality of Chinese Indonesians became a heated diplomatic issue between Indonesia and the People's Republic of China (PRC). Particularly in the late 1950s, the term was used as part of the nativist discourse of economic development, which culminated in Presidential Regulation No. 10 in 1959 (Peraturan Presiden No. 10 tahun 1959, known as PP10) that banned trade with foreign nationals in rural areas, with the regulation mostly applying only to the Chinese, both those who were still Chinese citizens and those who were already Indonesian citizens. The term became even more widely used during and after the anti-Communist purges of 1965–1966 and the takeover of the New Order regime. The term "Chinese problem" continued to be used in government communication and narratives throughout the New Order (Thung 1998).
3. According to the official 2020 national census data (the census is done once every ten years), Indonesia's population is 270 million; however, the official government statistical agency does not provide up-to-date data for the population of different ethnic groups (Badan Pusat Statistik 2021). In 2010, approximately 1.2 percent (around 2.8 million people) of the population were of Chinese descent. When interpreting this census data, we must keep in mind the issue of the underreporting of Chinese ethnicity, which occurs for a number of reasons, the main one being the fear and stigma that was associated with being identified as Chinese during the New Order. Many Chinese have classified themselves as members of the dominant *pribumi* ethnic group in the

region in which they lived, such as Javanese, Betawi, or Sundanese, during census counts (Suryadinata et al. 2003). Jamie Mackie (2005) suggests that the proportion of Chinese in Indonesia is actually at least 2 to 3 percent. The reality is that not even official agencies know exactly how many ethnic Chinese there are.

4. The recognition of Confucianism as a religion has caused confusion among many ethnic Chinese who regard themselves as believers in Confucian philosophy and moral values but not as adherents of the new Confucian religion. For instance, Pahoa Integrated School (Sekolah Terpadu Pahoa, discussed in chapter 3) prides itself as being an educational institution that teaches Confucian moral values to its students, but it does not regard itself as Confucian in any religious sense. See Evi Sutrisno's (2017, 2018) work on this topic for a more comprehensive analysis on the history of the Confucian religion in Indonesia.
5. In many earlier scholarly studies on Chinese Indonesians, analyses of the "Chinese problem" have more often than not led to an attempt to "solve" this problem through one of the two traditional approaches. As Dede Oetomo (1989, 45) suggests, "Many studies have thus been action-oriented, undertaken to evaluate the success or failure of assimilation," while other studies take another approach in which scholars are "remarkably sympathetic to the Chinese and their culture" and thus adopt a more integrationist approach. Although this assimilation versus integration debate has largely been deemed outdated, Oetomo's remark highlights the popularity of the assimilation and integration approaches as ways to fix the "Chinese problem," especially during the New Order.
6. The Chinese are commonly regarded as possessing different physical characteristics than the *pribumi.* For instance, the Chinese are stereotypically perceived to have slanted eyes (*mata sipit*) and clean, fair skin (*kulit putih bersih*). This notion of Chinese whiteness/fairness has complex ties to the historical perception of the Chinese as a capitalist class who do not toil outdoors (hence their skin stays fair, away from the ravages of the sun), unlike the working-class *pribumi* (see Saraswati 2013 for an analysis of perceptions of Chinese whiteness in postcolonial Indonesia). Such a stereotype is so common that it is considered an oddity if a Chinese person has darker skin or large eyes. A Chinese person with darker skin is colloquially called "*hitam tapi cina*" (meaning "dark but Chinese") or *hi-ta-ci* for short; many darker-skinned Chinese take pride in such a dark color because that means they can pass as *pribumi* if they want to.
7. The May 1998 riots (which began on May 4, 1998, in Medan) and attacks on ethnic Chinese also happened in cities like Solo and Surabaya, as well as in smaller incidents in towns such as Padang and Palembang. This study focuses on the riots and attacks that took place in Jakarta because they were the largest in scale, and the commemorations and identity politics that followed have taken place mostly in Jakarta.

8. Citing Dutch historical records from 1842, Jacqueline Knörr (2014) argues that the *cina benteng* got their name because (predominantly Muslim) Chinese settled in the area around the eastern bank of the mouth of the Ciliwung River where the Dutch had constructed a fort (*benteng* being the local Betawi word for fort/fortress). The *benteng* Chinese are mostly of *peranakan* descent (the result of centuries of mixed marriages, mostly with the Betawi people). Throughout the centuries, the *benteng* Chinese have maintained some Chinese traditions, such as wedding costumes and customs, while also developing their own hybrid cultural forms, such as *gambang kromong* orchestral music (see Cohen 2006 for more on *gambang kromong*).

CHAPTER 1: THE POLITICS OF REMEMBERING

1. As scholars such as Laura Lochore (2000) and Elaine Tay (2006) reported, in the immediate aftermath of the May 1998 riots, Internet bulletin boards and mailing lists (especially those associated with overseas Chinese online groups) were rife with supposed victim and eyewitness accounts of the attacks. It is impossible to verify the authenticity of these posts as they were made anonymously, but in the absence of verifiable eyewitness accounts and official victim statements, these posts became important sources of information that fueled popular imagination of the May 1998 riots and the plight of Chinese Indonesians. For some examples of these online posts, see Huaren.org, "A Victim's Account of Rapes and Murders," December 6, 1998, https://web.archive.org/web/20010418163512/http://www.huaren.org/focus/id/061398-01.html (accessed March 13, 2023); and Huaren.org, "Dear All People in the World—A Plea from a Riot Victim," September 4, 1998, https://web.archive.org/web/20010516173504/http://www.huaren.org/focus/id/090498-08.html (accessed March 13, 2023). The World Huaren Federation's website can be found at huarenworldnet.org, formerly huaren.org.
2. Ang derives the notion of "trapped in ambivalence" from Zygmunt Bauman (1991).
3. A May 1998 victims' organization member told me that a common narrative about the non-Chinese who died during the riots is that they were looters themselves. While it is true that some of those who died were looters, many were also innocent bystanders or workers in the shopping centers. According to victims' rights groups, this portrayal of non-Chinese victims as criminals was promoted by the government to absolve the state from any wrongdoing and to avoid having to compensate victims' families. Many non-Chinese victims' families continue to allege that security and military officials deliberately trapped people they perceived to be looters inside burning shopping centers.

4. For her efforts in bridging interethnic divides and in advocating for the victims of the May 1998 riots, Jusuf was awarded the Yap Thiam Hien Award for human rights in 2001.
5. *Republika* reported in 2015 that the Cultural Park was initially only approved for a 2.5-hectare plot since it is in a part of the TMII that is close to private dwellings and agricultural land. However, after lobbying by PSMTI, the TMII added another two hectares after extra plots were bought from neighboring private landowners (Putri 2015).
6. It is interesting to note that the design agency chosen for the project was from Xiamen (previously Amoy) in Fujian province rather than other major Chinese cities such as Beijing, Shanghai, or Guangzhou. I suspect that this had something to do with the fact that many Chinese Indonesian families (especially those from Hokkien backgrounds) trace their ancestry to Fujian, especially the areas surrounding Xiamen as the historical sending port of Chinese migrants. As with other overseas Chinese communities, Chinese Indonesian elders have traditionally maintained close ties with clan associations, community leaders, and government bodies in China, so it would not be surprising if the hiring of the firm had to do with the PSMTI elders' personal connections with those in Xiamen.
7. My attempts to access Parahyangan Catholic University's original designs for the project were unsuccessful, and I found the park's planners to be guarded about the tendering and decision-making processes.
8. See Taman Mini Indonesia Indah, "Anjungan Daerah," 2016, https://www.tamanmini.com/pesona_indonesia/anjungan.php (accessed March 13, 2023).

CHAPTER 2: ENCLAVES AND NARRATIVES OF TRAUMA IN EVERYDAY LIFE

1. The violence and anti-Chinese attacks of 1740 did not just occur in Batavia. In the aftermath of the Batavia massacre, violence spread all over Java after the Dutch declared what Kemasang (1982, 68) describes as "an open season" for the killing of the Chinese in Java. Anti-Chinese attacks and killings happened in cities such as Semarang (in 1741), Gresik, and Surabaya. The Chinese who fled to Central Java fought back and joined forces with troops under the command of Mataram Sultan Pakubuwono II, although this rebellion was also eventually quashed in 1743. For more on the Chinese involvement in the Java War, see Willem Remmelink's (1994) analysis of the alliance between Chinese rebels and the Mataram court in Central Java.
2. The increase in violence and criminality during the Indonesian National Revolution of 1945–1949 meant that the Chinese banded together even more. Chinese self-defense militia groups, for example, Pao An Tui, were formed to

defend Chinese homes, businesses, and residents from the *pribumi* militia (Ambekar and Divekar 1964; Amyot 1972).

3. To view old Kelapa Gading advertisements from the 1980s and 1990s, see Setiap Gedung Punya Cerita, "Summarecon Mall Kelapa Gading," October 5, 2021, https://setiapgedung.web.id/2021/10/summarecon-mall-kelapa-gading.html (accessed March 21, 2023). The amateur history blog Setiap Gedung Punya Cerita also contains information about other historic buildings and areas across Indonesia.
4. *Mbak* is a Javanese term meaning "older sister" and is also a common address for female domestic servants, even if the servant in question is not older.
5. Some residents did leave earlier, with many going straight to the airport to flee the country to places such as Singapore. My research participants told me that most of those who left to go overseas returned to Kelapa Gading not long after, but some never returned, either selling their houses at a low price or abandoning them altogether.
6. In the early years of *reformasi,* widespread violence did not just occur in Jakarta. Almost immediately following the fall of the New Order, outbreaks of communal violence, terror attacks, and separatist conflicts took place all over the Indonesian archipelago. For instance, peaking in August and September 1998 in the district of Banyuwangi, East Java, over a hundred people who were accused of sorcery were lynched for their alleged involvement in the mysterious killings of local Islamic leaders by assassins dressed in black (the episode was popularly called "ninja killings" in local media) (Herriman 2016). Religiously motivated violence between Muslim and Christian groups broke out in places such as Poso in Central Sulawesi and in Ambon and Halmahera islands in the Maluku archipelago. In 2001, interethnic conflict between the native Dayak and migrant Madurese populations in Central Kalimantan caused more than five hundred deaths and tens of thousands to be displaced from their homes. Large-scale violence also intensified in traditional hotbeds of separatist movements, such as in East Timor (which eventually became independent in 2002), Aceh, and Papua. Furthermore, several terror bombings took place in Jakarta and other highly populated areas, the most notable being the 2002 Bali bombings that killed 202 people. While these acts of violence did not have anything to do with the Chinese or with Jakarta specifically, news of violence in other places in Indonesia added to the atmosphere of insecurity and fear.
7. At the time of my fieldwork in 2009, Jakarta was still on high alert from a series of bombings by Islamist terrorists (including those linked to terrorist groups Jemaah Islamiyah with ties to al-Qaeda) that occurred in the early 2000s, including the bombing of the Jakarta Stock Exchange in 2000, the JW Marriott Hotel bombing in 2003, and the bombing of the Australian embassy in 2004. My interviews with Handy and Yohannes took place just days after

another series of bombings, this time targeting the JW Marriott and Ritz-Carlton hotels in South Jakarta on July 17, 2009.

8. In *A New Criminal Type in Jakarta: Counter-Revolution Today* (1998b), James T. Siegel argues that the New Order was marked by myths of criminality designed to instill fear, paranoia, and dependence on state military protection. Instances of crime and violence were sensationalized by the populist media and through gossip, creating a sense of inherent danger and threat from the lower classes among middle- and upper-class citizens.
9. In recent years, Kelapa Gading has marketed itself as a plural and multicultural neighborhood. For instance, its food courts have been marketed as representing culinary cultures (*budaya kuliner*) from all over the archipelago, and the estate's administrators also make a big effort to decorate the area on religious holidays and festivals (for example, Eid, Christmas, and Imlek) according to relevant religion or culture.
10. Kelapa Gading residents are evidently not the only ones who draw parallels between their estate and Singapore. In both the East Java capital of Surabaya and the North Sumatra capital of Medan, the middle- and upper-class CitraLand residential estates (developed by the Ciputra Group) advertise themselves as "the Singapore of Surabaya" and "the Singapore of Medan." See CitraLand Surabaya, "CitraLand Surabaya," 2021, https://citralandsurabaya.com (accessed March 21, 2023); and CitraLand Gama City, "CitraLand Gama City," 2023, https://citralandgamacity.com (accessed March 21, 2023). Also dominated by ethnic Chinese residents, the CitraLand estates even have their own replica Merlion (Singapore's national symbol) statues.
11. Advertisements for houses and apartments for sale in estates like Kelapa Gading now boast that the properties are situated in a safe location (*lokasi aman*).

CHAPTER 3: (RE)LEARNING CHINESENESS

1. A National Plus school offers an advanced hybrid curriculum based on the requirements of the national education curriculum for primary to senior school students. Because National Plus schools already satisfy the Ministry of Education and Culture's minimum requirements, any extra materials or educational activities offered on top of the national curriculum are unregulated and open to interpretation. Most National Plus schools offer bilingual education (in Indonesian and English), with an increasing number of schools (such as Pahoa) that mostly cater to Chinese students offering trilingual education in Indonesian, English, and Mandarin. These National Plus schools often also offer extensive extracurricular activities, such as Chinese calligraphy and dance classes, as well as a wide range of sporting activities. National Plus schools are privately owned and are much more expensive than state and conventional

private schools, so that only well-off families can afford to send their children to this kind of school.

2. The Chinese and *pribumi* have generally perceived these unofficial quotas differently. For the latter, the quotas were a justified act of affirmative action that put the *pribumi* on a level playing field with the Chinese, who could afford a private school education. For the Chinese, the quotas were extremely discriminatory as they denied many young Chinese entry into prestigious state universities, such as the University of Indonesia and Bandung Institute of Technology. The quotas were also seen as another example of state-sponsored discrimination against the Chinese. Over the years, these quotas have become harder to maintain, especially as many Chinese assumed more Indonesian-sounding names that were harder to distinguish from non-Chinese names on application forms. Nowadays, it is widely assumed that the quotas no longer exist. Nevertheless, the quotas were instrumental in creating and maintaining the perception of Chinese youth as rich private school students who had no place in state education institutions. For more on this, see Christine Susanna Tjhin (2005) and Andreas Ambrosius Susanto (2008).
3. In his study of a Chinese-dominated private Christian school in East Java, Christopher Bjork (2002) made a similar observation regarding the economic and religious barriers that prevent non-Chinese students from enrolling in Christian Chinese schools.
4. Islamic private schools (such as Al-Azhar schools) also exist, but they mainly cater to non-Chinese students from middle- and upper-class Muslim families. Few Chinese youths attend these Islamic private schools due to religious reasons.
5. This transition from Kuo Min Tang High School to SMAN 2 Jakarta is briefly explained on the school's website: SMA Negeri 2 Jakarta, "Sejarah," 2021, http://sman2jkt.sch.id/web/sejarah (accessed March 21, 2023).
6. Summarecon Serpong is typical of new residential developments that have emerged in the past two decades (see chapter 2). These developments are usually interconnected and make up a big part of Jakarta's megapolitan areas of Bogor, Depok, Tangerang, South Tangerang, and Bekasi (popularly known as Jabodetabek). Homes in these outer areas are cheaper and more spacious than those in central areas of Jakarta and are therefore popular among young, middle- and upper-class Chinese families. Pahoa was built in Summarecon Serpong because the estate developer's founder, Soetjipto Nagaria, is an alumnus of the original THHK school in Patekoan.
7. See my earlier assessment of Pahoa's vision, mission, and programs (Setijadi-Dunn 2010).
8. Similar narratives of commemoration can also be seen in the publication materials of other recently (re)established Chinese schools. For instance, Pah Tsung School's website contains a history section about the former Pah Tsen Tsung

Sio School that was closed in 1966. See Pah Tsung School, "About Us," 2023, https://www.pahtsung.sch.id/about-us (accessed March 21, 2023). Likewise, Jakarta Nanyang School's website also features a brief history of the former Sin Hoa School. See Jakarta Nanyang School, "History of JNY," 2022, https://jny.sch.id/about-jny/welcome-2/ (accessed March 21, 2023).

9. In the same article, Sai argues for the importance of looking at the complex relationship between Mandarin-language learning and identities in post-Suharto Chinese Indonesian scholarship. Sai (2010, 154) suggests that "scholars who examine linguistic ideologies productive of these multiple linkages are disinclined to assume an inevitable connection between language and identity, and, instead, are able to demonstrate the historicity of these linkages, which show identity formation to be a 'work-in-progress.'" Complexities such as language hybridization and other localization strategies should be considered when attempting to understand particular language and identity phenomena, especially in the study of diasporas.
10. For more on this privileging of Mandarin as the language of modern Chineseness, especially among overseas Chinese communities, see Rey Chow (1998).
11. See Grace Tan-Johannes (2018) for a news report on Chinese families in Jakarta who are sending their children to trilingual schools so that they can learn both Mandarin and Chinese culture.

CHAPTER 4: PERFORMING TRAUMA AND INDONESIAN CHINESENESS

1. The most internationally renowned work of visual art to date that deals with modern Indonesian history in the post-Suharto era is undoubtedly American British filmmaker Joshua Oppenheimer's 2012 documentary *The Act of Killing* (released as *Jagal* in Indonesia). Produced in a surrealist style, the documentary focuses on a group of former Medan-based death squad members who had participated in the 1965–1966 anti-Communist killings and who were given free artistic license to reenact their killings in whatever cinematic genre they wished. Oppenheimer's filmmaking approach of giving the self-confessed killers agency to put forward their perspectives has been widely considered as both bold and controversial. The documentary did not focus on the Chinese, but it did portray killings and violent crimes that specifically targeted the Chinese. The documentary went on to win major international film awards, and it was nominated for the 2013 Academy Award for best documentary feature. See Robert Cribb's (2014) and Ariel Heryanto's (2014) critical reviews of the documentary for more on its impact in Indonesia and internationally. In 2014, Oppenheimer released a companion film to *The Act of Killing* titled *The Look*

of Silence that tells the story of the 1965–1966 killings from the perspective of the victims' families.

2. In more recent years, there has been a growing literature on how collective memory and trauma are expressed in the arts in various Asian contexts. For instance, scholarship on Cambodian visual arts after the Cambodian genocide by scholars such as Soko Phay (2015) and Boreth Ly (2020) shows the importance of the arts in the processing of grief and trauma for Cambodians both at home and in the diaspora. In other parts of Asia, such scholars have also shown how the arts play a pivotal role in the representation of both perpetrators and victims in the aftermath of historical events such as Japanese colonization and military aggression in the Second World War, the Korean War and subsequent partition of Korea, the partition of India, and the Israel-Palestinian conflict, among others. For examples of some of these works, see Nurith Gertz and George Khleifi (2008), Akiko Hashimoto (2015), Hyunji Kwon (2016), Debali Mookerjea-Leonard (2017), and Dong-Yeon Koh (2022). For examples of how trauma from historical events such as the 1965–1966 killings and May 1998 riots are expressed through the arts, see Edwin Jürriens (2013), Wulan Dirgantoro (2021), and Dyah Pitaloka and Mohan J. Dutta (2021).
3. See Philip Smith (2015) and Karen Strassler (2018, 2020) for more in-depth analyses of FX Harsono's works that deal with themes of state violence, collective memory, and Chinese identities.
4. Dadang Christanto has been particularly prolific in producing artwork that does not only concern Chinese issues but also questions the truth behind the anti-Communist killings of 1965–1966. For a comprehensive look at Christanto's work and how it relates to post-Suharto discourses of art activism and memory work, see Suvendrini Perera (2006), Caroline Turner and Glen St. John Barclay (2011), and Wulan Dirgantoro (2020).
5. See Monika S. Winarnita and Ken M. P. Setiawan (2020) for an analysis of how Chinese Indonesian diasporic female artists and writers who have resettled in Australia commemorate the May 1998 anti-Chinese violence and rapes through their art and writing.
6. *Sugiharti Halim* was screened at the 2009 Singapore Short Film Festival and the 2010 Seoul International Women's Film Festival, and won the Best Film and Audience Award at the 2008 Konfiden Short Film Festival (Festival Film Pendek Konfiden) in Jakarta.
7. During the New Order, the SBKRI system was a form of bureaucratic discrimination and an easy tool for corrupt government officials to extort money from the Chinese. Those with SBKRI documents were often unofficially charged higher fees than others when processing official documents such as passports. The SBKRI system was formally abolished in July 2006. However, the Chinese are still frequently discriminated against on the basis of the SBKRI system.

8. *Babi Buta Yang Ingin Terbang* also raises the issue of identity anxiety and highlights the lack of belonging felt by a number of Chinese characters whose lives are intertwined. There is not sufficient space here to discuss this important film, but I have discussed it at length in Charlotte Setijadi (2013).
9. It is common knowledge that families of alleged PKI members are stigmatized in almost all aspects of life. A Communist blemish in a family's official records or disgraced reputation could result in discrimination and reduced employment and educational opportunities. This is why family members of alleged Communists largely refrain from talking about their family's blacklisted past and go to great lengths to conceal their family history. For more on this topic, see Charles A. Coppel (2008), Vannessa Hearman (2010), and Jess Melvin (2013).

CHAPTER 5: CHINESE INDONESIAN ORGANIZATIONS AND POLITICAL PARTICIPATION

1. It is widely known among Chinese activists that which Imlek celebration the president chooses to attend is a focus of contestation and lobbying. Competing Chinese organizations try to draw public attention to their problems by getting the president to come to their celebrations. There has been a big division among Chinese organizations about who "owns" Imlek. MATAKIN, which represents Confucians, argues that Imlek is a Confucian holy day and claims that Imlek celebrates the first day in the Confucian calendar that starts in 551 BCE (the year of Confucius's birth). Other organizations insist that Imlek is not a religious holiday but a traditional Chinese folk festival celebrating the start of the lunar new year and the first day of spring. Most Chinese organizations argue that Imlek belongs to all Chinese, not just the Confucians. Although Imlek was eventually declared a Confucian holiday, many organizations still reject this definition.
2. One of PSMTI's efforts to eradicate anti-Chinese sentiments is to argue that Chinese Indonesians are a unique tribe (*suku*), just like the Javanese, Batak, and Menadonese. As a *suku*, PSMTI contends that the Chinese should be regarded by default as part of the *pribumi* who can lay claim to belonging to the Indonesian nation. Although PSMTI leaders are optimistic about this strategy of indigenizing ethnic Chinese as a means for greater acceptance from the *pribumi*, most of the public at present still do not generally regard the Chinese as a *suku*. The Chinese Indonesian Cultural Park at the TMII is part of these efforts to indigenize the Chinese (see chapter 1).
3. Lembong ended up breaking away further from INTI in the early 2000s when he became disappointed that INTI was following the same narrative path as PSMTI in emphasizing Chinese cultural differences. In 2006, Lembong established Yayasan Nation Building, known as Yayasan NABIL (NABIL Foundation), an NGO dedicated to supporting nation-building in Indonesia. The

foundation sponsors various nation-building projects by individuals regardless of their ethnicity or religion, and it gives out an annual award to those regarded as having made valuable contributions to Indonesia's development.

4. Ethnic Chinese politicians are quite difficult to identify from electoral lists because the vast majority have Indonesian names and are thus hard to distinguish from non-Chinese politicians. Furthermore, not all Chinese politicians openly identify themselves as ethnic Chinese in their public profiles. Further background research on each of the candidates is required to establish whether or not they are ethnic Chinese. Because of this, various sources often have different estimates on the number of elected Chinese public officials throughout different time periods. For instance, Taufiq Tanasaldy (2013) estimates fourteen Chinese elected to both houses of national parliament in 2014, while others (such as Cui Yi Sheng 2014) estimate fifteen. Similarly, citing newspaper sources, Suryadinata (2019) estimates that only eleven Chinese politicians succeeded in national legislative elections in 2019, while I estimate fifteen. See also Jonathan Chen (2022).
5. For a more in-depth analysis of the religious dimensions of the 2010 Medan mayoral race, see Aspinall et al. (2011).
6. See also Chong Wu-Ling's (2018) comprehensive analysis of the 2010 Medan mayoral elections in which she utilizes Anthony Giddens's concept of structure and agency to explain why and how individual politicians such as Sofyan Tan defy the expectations of their *habitus*, pushing the boundaries of their communities in the process. Chapter 6 in Chong's book provides a particularly useful examination of the dynamics of local electoral politics involving Chinese politicians.
7. For a more comprehensive analysis of Ahok's biographical background, see Setijadi et al. (2016).
8. In various surveys, the vast majority of Chinese in Jakarta have been shown to vote for Ahok. For instance, a preelection survey for the first round of the 2017 Jakarta gubernatorial election by the polling organization Indikator Politik showed that 86 percent of the Chinese surveyed said they would vote for Ahok.
9. For a more recent assessment of the return of nativist discourses in Indonesian politics and how they affect representations of the Chinese in electoral politics after Ahok's reelection bid, see Chen (2022).

CHAPTER 6: CHINESE INDONESIANS IN THE TIME OF CHINA'S RISE

1. In the literature on overseas Chinese, these *guanxi* networks are often termed the "bamboo network" or "dragon network." For more on this topic, see Murray Weidenbaum and Samuel Hughes (1996) and A. B. Susanto and A. Patricia Susanto (2013).

2. During the New Order, there were prominent and wealthy Chinese Indonesians, such as Suharto ally Liem Sioe Liong and Mochtar Riady, who were tasked with establishing and maintaining ties with the Chinese government and businesses, especially during negotiations prior to the resumption of Sino-Indonesian diplomatic ties in 1990 (see Riady 2018). However, because of the sensitive nature of Sino-Indonesian relations (and of the economic and political roles of Chinese Indonesians) at the time, these activities were not made public; the scale of the interactions was also limited and nowhere near the scale seen now.
3. The OCAO was absorbed into the United Front Work Department of the Chinese Communist Party in 2018 in a reshuffling of government agencies.
4. Riady has also written about his experiences of representing Indonesia in reconnecting with China in his 2016 memoir (see Riady 2016).
5. The idea of neo-*kapitan*s references the colonial-era positions of *kapitan Cina* in the Dutch East Indies and other colonial settlements with large ethnic Chinese populations (they were called "Chinese captains" in British colonies). During the colonial period, a *kapitan Cina* was a high-ranking government position and was one of the key offices in the colonial management of multiethnic societies. *Kapitan*s were usually wealthy businesspeople who wielded much economic power (and were therefore highly revered) within local Chinese communities (Lohanda 1996). Prominent Chinese businesspeople in modern-day Southeast Asia (some of whom are descended from captains themselves) often view themselves as modern *kapitan*s who perform a gatekeeping and mediating role for their respective Chinese communities, particularly in dealings with the state. Liu's (1998) characterization of prominent elders within the Chinese community as neo-*kapitan*s points to the persistence of colonial race-based governance to this day, and that modern nation-states are now making use of ethnic Chinese in a similar manner as economic middlemen.
6. For more on the Chinese state's efforts to nurture support among the overseas Chinese, see Liu Hong (2011), Leo Suryadinata (2017b), Sebastian Strangio (2020), and Maria Repnikova (2022).

CONCLUSION

1. In more recent years, the term "Chindo" (a playful amalgamation of the English words Chinese and Indonesian) has become a popular colloquial term among young Chinese Indonesians in Jakarta to refer to themselves. My Chinese respondents tell me that "Chindo" is fast becoming a preferred neutral term among the youth since it is not considered to be racist like the terms *cina* or *cokin*, or as serious-sounding as the term "Tionghoa." The

creation and popularity of the term "Chindo" is yet another example of the continuous evolution of Chinese Indonesian forms of identification and terms of reference.

2. Collaboratively translated into English by Chin and the author. Reproduced with permission.
3. It is noteworthy that the group opted to use the term *peranakan* in their name. This term refers to mixed-race and acculturated Chinese communities and individuals who usually cannot speak Chinese languages. They have been described as having a set of hybrid cultural traits that are neither wholly Chinese nor wholly Indonesian. The term *peranakan* (and its opposite *totok*) has been regarded as outdated, but—as the Suara Peranakan group name suggests—it seems to have experienced a revival in recent times, particularly among those who want to emphasize their acculturation to Indonesian society, regardless of whether they are from traditionally *peranakan* families or not. For instance, Awi Chin is not from a *peranakan* family, but he joined Suara Peranakan because he felt affinity toward the group's goals of emphasizing pluralism.

REFERENCES

Abeyasekere, Susan. 1987. *Jakarta: A History*. Singapore: Oxford University Press.

Afrisia, Rizky Sekar. 2015. "Ernest Prakasa Menertawakan Tionghoa, Melupakan Trauma" [Ernest Prakasa Laughs at Being Chinese, Forgets Trauma]. *CNN Indonesia*. February 16. https://www.cnnindonesia.com/hiburan/20150216145504-234-32500/ernest-prakasa-menertawakan-tionghoa-melupakan-trauma (accessed August 8, 2015).

Aizawa, Nobuhiro. 2011. "Assimilation, Differentiation, and Depoliticization: Chinese Indonesians and the Ministry of Home Affairs in Suharto's Indonesia." In *Chinese Indonesians and Regime Change*, edited by Marlene Dieleman, Juliette Koning, and Peter Post, pp. 47–64. Leiden: Brill.

Alecci, Scilla. 2017. "Paradise Papers: Leaked Records Reveal Offshore Companies' Role in Forest Destruction." *Irish Times*, November 8. https://www.irishtimes.com/business/paradise-papers-leaked-records-reveal-offshore-companies-role-in-forest-destruction-1.3284502 (accessed April 25, 2022).

Alexander, Jeffrey C. 2004. "Toward a Theory of Cultural Trauma." In *Cultural Trauma and Collective Identity*, edited by Jeffrey C. Alexander, Ron Eyerman, Bernhard Giesen, Neil J. Smelser, and Piotr Sztompka, pp. 1–30. Berkeley: University of California Press.

———. 2006. "Cultural Pragmatics: Social Performance between Ritual and Strategy." In *Social Performance: Symbolic Action, Cultural Pragmatics, and Ritual*, edited by Jeffrey C. Alexander, Bernhard Giesen, and Jason L. Mast, pp. 29–90. Cambridge: Cambridge University Press.

Allard, Tom, and Agustinus Beo Da Costa. 2017. "Exclusive—Indonesian Islamist Leader Says Ethnic Chinese Wealth Is Next Target." Reuters, May 13. https://www.reuters.com/article/uk-indonesia-politics-cleric-exclusive-idUSKBN18817N (accessed April 16, 2022).

Ambekar, G. V., and V. D. Divekar, eds. 1964. *Documents on China's Relations with South and Southeast Asia, 1949–1962*. Bombay: Allied Publishers.

Amin, Khoirul. 2015. "Indonesia Eyeing More Investment from China." *Jakarta Post*, November 20. https://www.thejakartapost.com/news/2015/11/20/indonesia-eyeing-more-investment-china.html (accessed February 29, 2016).

Amyot, Jacques. 1972. *The Chinese and the National Integration in Southeast Asia*. Bangkok: Institute of Asian Studies, Faculty of Political Science, Chulalongkorn University, Monograph Series, No. 2.

Ananta, Aris, Evi Nurvidya Arifin, M. Sairi Hasbullah, Nur Budi Handayani, and Agus Pramono. 2015. *Demography of Indonesia's Ethnicity*. Singapore: Institute of Southeast Asian Studies.

Anderson, Benedict. 1983. *Imagined Communities: Reflections on the Origin and Spread of Nationalism*. London: Verso.

Ang, Ien. 2000. "Introduction: Alter/Asian Cultural Interventions for 21st Century Australia." In *Alter/Asians: Asian-Australian Identities in Art, Media and Popular Culture*, edited by Ien Ang, Sharon Chalmers, Lisa Law, and Mandy Thomas, pp. xiii–xxx. Sydney: Pluto Press.

———. 2001a. *On Not Speaking Chinese: Living between Asia and the West*. London: Routledge.

———. 2001b. "Trapped in Ambivalence: Chinese Indonesians, Victimhood, and the Debris of History." In *"Race" Panic and the Memory of Migration*, edited by Meaghan Morris and Brett de Bary, pp. 21–47. Hong Kong: Hong Kong University Press.

Ardi. 2019. "Sukanto Tanoto: Indonesia Ayah Angkat, Cina Ayah Kandung" [Sukanto Tanoto: Indonesia Is My Adoptive Father, China Is My Biological Father]. *Indonesiana*, April 27. https://www.indonesiana.id/read/86631/sukanto-tanoto-indonesia-ayah-angkat-cina-ayah-kandung (accessed July 10, 2021).

Arlini, Gloria. 2010. "Stories, Silence and Strategies: Collective Memory in a Chinese Indonesian Family." MSocSc diss., National University of Singapore.

Armitage, Andrew. 1995. *Comparing the Policy of Aboriginal Assimilation: Australia, Canada, and New Zealand*. Vancouver: UBC Press.

Aspinall, Edward, Sebastian Dettman, and Eve Warburton. 2011. "When Religion Trumps Ethnicity: A Regional Election Case Study from Indonesia." *South East Asia Research* 19 (1): 27–58.

Aspinall, Edward, Diego Fossati, Burhanuddin Muhtadi, and Eve Warburton. 2020. "Elites, Masses, and Democratic Decline in Indonesia." *Democratization* 27 (4): 505–526.

Badan Koordinasi Penanaman Modal [BKPM]. 2018. "Mengejar Investasi Negara Tirai Bambu" [Chasing Investments in the Bamboo Curtain Country]. BKPM, n.d. https://www5.bkpm.go.id/id/publikasi/detail/berita/mengejar-investasi-negeri-tirai-bambu (accessed July 5, 2021).

Badan Pusat Statistik. 2021. *Statistik Indonesia 2022* [Statistical Yearbook of Indonesia 2022]. Jakarta: Badan Statistik Indonesia.

Badan Pusat Statistik Kota Jakarta Utara. 2021. "Jumlah Penduduk (Jiwa), 2018–2020" [Total Population (Lives), 2018–2020]. March 3. https://jakutkota.bps.go.id/indicator/12/29/1/jumlah-penduduk.html (accessed November 21, 2021).

Bagaeen, Samer, and Ola Uduku, eds. 2015. *Beyond Gated Communities*. London: Routledge.

Barker, Thomas. 2011. "A Cultural Economy of the Contemporary Indonesian Film Industry." PhD diss., National University of Singapore.

———. 2019. *Indonesian Cinema after the New Order: Going Mainstream*. Hong Kong: Hong Kong University Press.

Baswedan, Anies. 2017. "Dukungan Prabowo Subianto" [Prabowo Subianto's Support]. YouTube, February 10. https://www.youtube.com/watch?v=UobDp32v30Q (accessed February 22, 2017).

Bauman, Zygmunt. 1991. *Modernity and Ambivalence*. Cambridge: Polity Press.

———. 1993. *Postmodern Ethics*. Oxford: Blackwell.

Bell, Duncan S. A. 2003. "Mythscapes: Memory, Mythology, and National Identity." *British Journal of Sociology* 54 (1): 63–81.

Bjork, Christopher. 2002. "Reconstructing Rituals: Expressions of Autonomy and Resistance in a Sino-Indonesian School." *Anthropology & Education Quarterly* 33 (4): 465–491.

Blakely, Edward J., and Mary Gail Snyder. 1999. *Fortress America: Gated Communities in the United States*. Washington, DC: Brookings Institute.

Blussé, Leonard. 1981. "Batavia, 1619–1740: The Rise and Fall of a Chinese Colonial Town." *Journal of Southeast Asian Studies* 12 (1): 159–178.

Bourdieu, Pierre. 1971. "Systems of Education and Systems of Thought." In *Knowledge and Control: New Directions in the Sociology of Education*, edited by Michael F. D. Young, pp. 189–209. London: Collier-Macmillan.

———. 1974. "The School as a Conservative Force: Scholastic and Cultural Inequalities." In *Contemporary Research in the Sociology of Education: A Selection of Contemporary Research Papers Together with Some of the Formative Writings of the Recent Past*, edited by John Eggleston, pp. 32–46. London: Routledge.

———. 1977. *Outline of a Theory of Practice*. Translated by Richard Nice. Cambridge: Cambridge University Press.

———. 1984. *Distinction: A Social Critique of the Judgement of Taste*. Translated by Richard Nice. Cambridge, MA: Harvard University Press.

———. 1986. "The Forms of Capital." In *Handbook of Theory and Research for the Sociology of Education*, edited by John G. Richardson, pp. 241–258. New York: Greenwood Press.

———. 1989. "Social Space and Symbolic Power." *Sociological Theory* 7 (1): 14–25.

———. 1990. *The Logic of Practice*. Translated by Richard Nice. Stanford, CA: Stanford University Press.

———. 1993. "How Can 'Free-Floating Intellectuals' Be Set Free?" In *Sociology in Question*. Translated by Richard Nice, pp. 41–48. London: SAGE Publications.

———. 1998. *The State Nobility: Elite Schools in the Field of Power*. Translated by Lauretta C. Clough. Stanford, CA: Stanford University Press.

———. 1999. "The Contradictions of Inheritance." In *The Weight of the World: Social Suffering in Contemporary Society*, by Pierre Bourdieu, Alain Accardo, Gabrielle Balazs, Stéphane Beaud, François Bonvin, Emmanuel Bourdieu, Philippe Bourgois, Sylvain Broccolichi, Patrick Champagne, Rosine

Christin, Jean-Pierre Faguer, Sandrine Garcia, Remi Lenoir, Françoise Œuvrard, Michel Pialoux, Louis Pinto, Denis Podalydès, Abdelmalek Sayad, Charles Soulié, and Loïc J. D. Wacquant; translated by Priscilla Parkhurst Ferguson, Susan Emanuel, Joe Johnson, and Shoggy T. Waryn, pp. 507–513. Stanford, CA: Stanford University Press.

Bourdieu, Pierre, and Jean-Claude Passeron. 1990. *Reproduction in Education, Society, and Culture*. London: SAGE Publications.

Browning, Gary. 2000. *Lyotard and the End of Grand Narratives*. Cardiff: University of Wales Press.

Brubaker, Rogers. 1985. "Rethinking Classical Sociology: The Sociological Vision of Pierre Bourdieu." *Theory and Society* 14 (6): 745–775.

Budiman, Arief. 2005. "Portrait of the Chinese in Post-Soeharto Indonesia." In *Chinese Indonesians: Remembering, Distorting, Forgetting*, edited by Tim Lindsey and Helen Pausacker, pp. 95–104. Singapore: Institute of Southeast Asian Studies.

Buletin KBRI Beijing RICH. 2020. "3000 Beasiswa Tiongkok untuk Mahasiswa Indonesia" [3000 Chinese Scholarships for Indonesian Students]. *Buletin KBRI Beijing RICH* 1:30.

Bunnell, Tim, and Michelle Ann Miller. 2011. "Jakarta in Post-Suharto Indonesia: Decentralisation, Neo-liberalism and Global City Aspiration." *Space and Polity* 15 (1): 35–48.

Bustami. 2014. "Inilah 560 Anggota DPR RI Yang Telah Ditetapkan KPU" [These Are the 560 Members of the Indonesian People's Representative Council Who Have Been Appointed by the General Electoral Commission]. *Sayangi*, May 14. http://www.sayangi.com/politik1/read/23129/inilah-560-anggota-dpr-ri-yang-telah-ditetapkan-kpu (accessed April 5, 2016).

Cagaptay, Soner. 2004. "Race, Assimilation and Kemalism: Turkish Nationalism and the Minorities in the 1930s." *Middle Eastern Studies* 40 (3): 86–101.

Caldeira, Teresa P. R. 2000. *City of Walls: Crime, Segregation, and Citizenship in São Paulo*. Berkeley: University of California Press.

Caruth, Cathy. 1991. "Unclaimed Experience: Trauma and the Possibility of History." *Yale French Studies* 79:181–192.

Chang, Chak-yan. 1980. "Overseas Chinese in China's Policy." *China Quarterly* 82:281–303.

———. 2000. "The Overseas Chinese." In *Fujian: A Coastal Province in Transition and Transformation*, edited by Y. M. Yeung and David K. Y. Chu, pp. 57–82. Hong Kong: The Chinese University Press.

Chang, Vincent K. L. 2020. *Forgotten Diplomacy: The Modern Remaking of Dutch-Chinese Relations, 1927–1950*. Leiden: Brill.

Chen, Jonathan. 2022. "Representing Chinese Indonesians: Pribumi Discourse and Regional Elections in Post-reform Indonesia." *Journal of Current Southeast Asian Affairs* 41 (1): 59–87.

Chen, Yi-Ling, and Hyun Bang Shin, eds. 2019. *Neoliberal Urbanism, Contested Cities, and Housing in Asia*. London: Palgrave Macmillan.

Cheng, Enoch. 2011. "Interview with Tintin Wulia." Asia Art Archive, July 1. https://aaa.org.hk/en/ideas/ideas/interview-with-tintin-wulia (accessed January 13, 2021).

Cheung, Gordon C. K. 2005. "Involuntary Migrants, Political Revolutionaries and Economic Energisers: A History of the Image of Overseas Chinese in Southeast Asia." *Journal of Contemporary China* 14 (42): 55–66.

Chew, Amy, and Andre Barahamin. 2019. "Chinese Indonesians in Jakarta Fear Attacks on the Community, as Anti-China Hoaxes Spread on Social Media." *South China Morning Post*, May 22. https://www.scmp.com/week-asia/politics/article/3011392/chinese-indonesians-jakarta-fear-attacks-community-anti-china (accessed July 31, 2021).

Chin, Awi. 2020. "Catatan Sepi si Anak Babi" [The Piglet's Lonely Note]. Suara Peranakan, August 26. https://web.archive.org/web/20210317130710/https://suaraperanakan.wordpress.com/2020/08/26/catatan-sepi-si-anak-babi/ (accessed August 11, 2021).

China Daily. 2017. "President Xi's Statements on the Belt and Road Initiative." State Council Information Office, People's Republic of China, April 17. http://www.scio.gov.cn/31773/35507/35520/Document/1548585/1548585.htm (accessed July 1, 2021).

Chong, Wu-Ling. 2015. "Local Politics and Chinese Indonesian Business in Post-Suharto Era." *Southeast Asian Studies* 4 (3): 487–532.

———. 2018. *Chinese Indonesians in Post-Suharto Indonesia: Democratisation and Ethnic Minorities*. Hong Kong: Hong Kong University Press.

Chow, Rey. 1998. "Introduction: On Chineseness as a Theoretical Problem." *boundary 2* 25 (3): 1–24.

Chua Beng Huat, and Koichi Iwabuchi. 2008. "East Asian TV Dramas: Identifications, Sentiments and Effects." In *East Asian Pop Culture: Analysing the Korean Wave*, edited by Chua Beng Huat and Koichi Iwabuchi, pp. 1–12. Hong Kong: Hong Kong University Press.

Chua, Amy. 2004. *World on Fire: How Exporting Free Market Democracy Breeds Ethnic Hatred and Global Instability*. London: Heinemann.

Chua, Christian. 2008. *Chinese Big Business in Indonesia: The State of Capital*. London: Routledge.

Clammer, John R. 1975. "Overseas Chinese Assimilation and Resinification: A Malaysian Case Study." *Southeast Asian Journal of Social Science* 3 (2): 9–23.

Cohen, Matthew Isaac. 2006. *The Komedie Stamboel: Popular Theater in Colonial Indonesia, 1891–1903*. Athens: Ohio University Press.

Colen, Shellee, and Roger Sanjek. 1990. "At Work in Homes I: Orientations." In *At Work in Homes: Household Workers in World Perspective*, edited by Roger Sanjek and Shellee Colen, pp. 1–13. Washington, DC: American

Anthropological Association, American Ethnological Society Monograph Series, No. 3.

Coppel, Charles A. 1983. *Indonesian Chinese in Crisis*. Kuala Lumpur: Oxford University Press.

———. 2008. "Anti-Chinese Violence in Indonesia after Soeharto." In *Ethnic Chinese in Contemporary Indonesia*, edited by Leo Suryadinata, pp. 117–136. Singapore: Institute of Southeast Asian Studies.

Cornell, Stephen, and Douglas Hartmann. 2006. *Ethnicity and Race: Making Identities in a Changing World*. 2nd ed. New York: SAGE Publications.

Cowherd, Robert. 2021. "Batavian Apartheid: Mapping Bodies, Constructing Identity." *Southeast of Now: Directions in Contemporary and Modern Art in Asia* 5 (1/2): 15–46.

Cribb, Robert, ed. 1990. *The Indonesian Killings of 1965–1966: Studies from Java and Bali*. Clayton, Vic.: Centre of Southeast Asian Studies, Monash University.

———. 2009. *Gangsters and Revolutionaries: The Jakarta People's Militia and the Indonesian Revolution, 1945–1949*. Singapore: Equinox Publishing.

———. 2014. "The Act of Killing." *Critical Asian Studies* 46 (1): 147–149.

Cribb, Robert, and Charles A. Coppel. 2009. "A Genocide That Never Was: Explaining the Myth of Anti-Chinese Massacres in Indonesia, 1965–66." *Journal of Genocide Research* 11 (4): 447–465.

Cribb, Robert, and Audrey Kahin. 2004. *Historical Dictionary of Indonesia*. 2nd ed. Latham, MD: Scarecrow Press.

Croce, Mariano. 2015. "The *Habitus* and the Critique of the Present: A Wittgensteinian Reading of Bourdieu's Social Theory." *Sociological Theory* 33 (4): 327–346.

Cui Yi Sheng. 2014. "Zhishao You Shiwu Wei Huayi Dangxuan 2014–2019 Nianjie Guohui Yiyuan" [At Least 15 Ethnic Chinese Elected as National Parliamentarians]. *Guoji Ribao*, May 17.

Davidson, Andrew P., and Kuah-Pearce Khun Eng. 2008. "Introduction: Diasporic Memories and Identities." In *At Home in the Chinese Diaspora: Memories, Identities and Belongings*, edited by Kuah-Pearce Khun Eng and Andrew P. Davidson, pp. 1–11. London: Palgrave Macmillan.

Dawis, Aimee. 2008. "Chinese Education in Indonesia: Developments in the Post-1998 Era." In *Ethnic Chinese in Contemporary Indonesia*, edited by Leo Suryadinata, pp. 75–96. Singapore: Institute of Southeast Asian Studies.

———. 2009. *The Chinese of Indonesia and Their Search for Identity: The Relationship between Collective Memory and the Media*. Amherst, NY: Cambria Press.

———. 2010a. "China and the Cultural Identity of the Chinese in Indonesia." In *Connecting and Distancing: Southeast Asia and China*, edited by Ho Khai Leong, pp. 153–180. Singapore: Institute of Southeast Asian Studies.

———. 2010b. "Orang Tionghoa Berorganisasi: Yang Kini Lanjutan Dari Masa Lalu?" [Chinese People Organize: The Present as a Continuation of the Past?]. In *Setelah Air Mata Kering: Masyarakat Tionghoa Pasca-Peristiwa Mei 1998* [After the Tears Have Dried: Chinese Society Post-May 1998], edited by I. Wibowo and Thung Ju Lan, pp. 49–74. Jakarta: Kompas.

Dewan Perwakilan Rakyat Republik Indonesia [DPR-RI]. 2010. "Dewan Perwakilan Rakyat Republik Indonesia: Anggota per Daerah Pemilihan" [People's Representative Council of the Republic of Indonesia: Members per Electoral District]. November 22. https://dpr.go.id/id/anggota/per-daerah-pemilihan (accessed April 5, 2016).

DiMaggio, Paul. 1979. "Review Essay: On Pierre Bourdieu." *American Journal of Sociology* 84 (6): 1460–1474.

Ding, Xiaojiong. 2016. "Exploring the Experiences of International Students in China." *Journal of Studies in International Education* 20 (4): 319–338.

Dirgantoro, Wulan. 2020. "From Silence to Speech: Witnessing and Trauma of the Anti-Communist Mass Killings in Indonesian Contemporary Art." *World Art* 10 (2–3): 301–322.

———. 2021. "From Purgation to Remembrance: Memorialising the May 1998 Violence in Post-authoritarian Indonesian Visual Art." *Australian and New Zealand Journal of Art* 21 (1): 115–132.

Duara, Prasenjit. 1997. "Nationalists among Transnationals: Overseas Chinese and the Idea of China, 1900–1911." In *Ungrounded Empires: The Cultural Politics of Modern Chinese Transnationalism*, edited by Aihwa Ong and Donald Nonini, pp. 49–60. New York: Routledge.

Duyvendak, Jan Willem. 2011. *The Politics of Home: Belonging and Nostalgia in Western Europe and the United States*. London: Palgrave Macmillan.

Effendi, Wahyu, and Prasetyadji. 2008. *Tionghoa Dalam Cengkeraman SBKRI: Mengapa Surat Bukti Kewarganegaraan Republik Indonesia Masih Saja Menjadi Masalah? Bagaimana Solusinya? Bagaimana Etnis Tionghoa Mengantisipasi dan Menghadapinya?* [Chinese in the Grip of SBKRI: Why Is the Proof of Citizenship of the Republic of Indonesia Still a Problem? What's the Solution? How Do Ethnic Chinese Anticipate and Deal with It?]. Edited by Proyus Tanuhandaru. Jakarta: Visimedia.

Elmhirst, Rebecca. 1999. "'Learning the Ways of the *Priyayi*': Domestic Servants and the Mediation of Modernity in Jakarta, Indonesia." In *Gender, Migration, and Domestic Service*, edited by Janet Henshall Momsen, pp. 237–257. London: Routledge.

Farnell, Brenda. 2000. "Getting Out of the *Habitus:* An Alternative Model of Dynamically Embodied Social Action." *Journal of the Royal Anthropological Institute* 6 (3): 397–418.

Fealy, Greg. 2016. "Bigger than Ahok: Explaining the 2 December Mass Rally." Indonesia at Melbourne, December 7. http://indonesiaatmelbourne.unimelb

.edu.au/bigger-than-ahok-explaining-jakartas-2-december-mass-rally/ (accessed February 1, 2017).

Gertz, Nurith, and George Khleifi. 2008. *Palestinian Cinema: Landscape, Trauma, and Memory*. Edinburgh: Edinburgh University Press.

Giblin, Susan. 2003. "Civil Society Groups: Overcoming Stereotypes? Chinese Indonesian Civil Society Groups in Post-Suharto Indonesia." *Asian Ethnicity* 4 (3): 353–368.

Godley, Michael R. 1989. "The Sojourners: Returned Overseas Chinese in the People's Republic of China." *Pacific Affairs* 62 (3): 330–352.

Govaars-Tjia, Ming Tien Nio. 2005. *Dutch Colonial Education: The Chinese Experience in Indonesia, 1900–1942*. Translated by Lorre Lynn Trytten. Singapore: Chinese Heritage Centre.

Grassi, Sergio. 2020. "Indonesia's Global Maritime Fulcrum and China's Belt Road Initiative: A Match Made at Sea?" Friedrich-Ebert-Stiftung, April 4. https://www.fes-asia.org/news/indonesias-global-maritime-fulcrum-chinas-belt-road-initiative-a-match-made-at-sea/ (accessed July 3, 2021).

Halbwachs, Maurice. 1985. *Das Gedächtnis und seine sozialen Bedingungen* [Memory and Its Social Conditions]. Frankfurt: Suhrkamp.

———. 1992. *On Collective Memory*. Edited and translated by Lewis A. Coser. Chicago: University of Chicago Press.

Hall, Stuart. 1995. "New Cultures for Old." In *A Place in the World? Places, Cultures, and Globalization*, edited by John Allen and Doreen B. Massey, pp. 175–214. Oxford: Oxford University Press.

Han, Christine, and Yaobin Tong. 2021. "Students at the Nexus between the Chinese Diaspora and Internationalisation of Higher Education: The Role of Overseas Students in China's Strategy of Soft Power." *British Journal of Educational Studies* 69 (5): 579–598.

Hanan, David. 2017. *Cultural Specificity in Indonesian Film: Diversity in Unity*. London: Palgrave Macmillan.

Hanan, David, and Basoeki Koesasi. 2011. "*Betawi Moderen:* Songs and Films of Benyamin S from Jakarta in the 1970s—Further Dimensions of Indonesian Popular Culture." *Indonesia* 91:35–76.

Harff, Barbara, and Ted Robert Gurr. 1988. "Toward Empirical Theory of Genocides and Politicides: Identification and Measurement of Cases since 1945." *International Studies Quarterly* 32 (3): 359–371.

Harun, Refly, Waskito Wardoyo, Andi Irman, Israwati Amir, Ahmad Maulana, and Teguh Setiono. 2004. *Profil dan Program Anggota DPR-RI 2004–2009* [Indonesian People's Representative Council 2004–2009 Member Profiles and Programs]. Jakarta: Media Center.

Hashimoto, Akiko. 2015. *The Long Defeat: Cultural Trauma, Memory, and Identity in Japan*. Oxford: Oxford University Press.

Hatherell, Michael, and Alistair Welsh. 2017. "Rebel with a Cause: Ahok and Charismatic Leadership in Indonesia." *Asian Studies Review* 41 (2): 174–190.

Hau, Caroline S. 2014. *The Chinese Question: Ethnicity, Nation, and Region in and beyond the Philippines*. Singapore: NUS Press.

Hearman, Vannessa. 2010. "Guerrillas, Guns, and Knives? Debating Insurgency in South Blitar, East Java, 1967–68." *Indonesia* 89:61–92.

Hearn, Adrian H. 2012. "Harnessing the Dragon: Overseas Chinese Entrepreneurs in Mexico and Cuba." *China Quarterly* 209:111–133.

Heider, Karl G. 1991. *Indonesian Cinema: National Culture on Screen*. Honolulu: University of Hawai'i Press.

———. 2021. *Visual Research and Indonesian Ethnography: Beyond Description*. London: Routledge.

Hellman, Jörgen, Marie Thynell, and Roanne van Voorst, eds. 2018. *Jakarta: Claiming Spaces and Rights in the City*. London: Routledge.

Herlijanto, Johanes. 2005. "The May 1998 Riots and the Emergence of Chinese Indonesians: Social Movements in the Post-Soeharto Era." 亞太研究論壇 (*Asia-Pacific Research Forum*) 27:64–80.

Herriman, Nicholas. 2016. *Witch-Hunt and Conspiracy: The "Ninja Case" in East Java*. Singapore: NUS Press.

Heryanto, Ariel. 1998. "Ethnic Identities and Erasure: Chinese Indonesians in Public Culture." In *Southeast Asian Identities: Culture and the Politics of Representation in Indonesia, Malaysia, Singapore, and Thailand*, edited by Joel S. Kahn, pp. 95–114. Singapore: Institute of Southeast Asian Studies.

———. 1999. "Rape, Race and Reporting." In *Reformasi: Crisis and Change in Indonesia*, edited by Arief Budiman, Barbara Hatley, and Damien Kingsbury, pp. 299–334. Melbourne: Monash Asia Institute, Monash University.

———. 2006. *State Terrorism and Political Identity in Indonesia: Fatally Belonging*. New York: Routledge.

———. 2008. "Citizenship and Indonesian Ethnic Chinese in Post-1998 Films." In *Popular Culture in Indonesia: Fluid Identities in Post-authoritarian Politics*, edited by Ariel Heryanto, pp. 70–92. London: Routledge.

———. 2014. "Great and Misplaced Expectations." *Critical Asian Studies* 46 (1): 162–166.

Hew, Wai Weng. 2018. *Chinese Ways of Being Muslim: Negotiating Ethnicity and Religiosity in Indonesia*. Copenhagen: NIAS Press.

Himawan, Eunike Mutiara, Annie Pohlman, and Winnifred Louis. 2022. "Revisiting the May 1998 Riots in Indonesia: Civilians and Their Untold Memories." *Journal of Current Southeast Asian Affairs*. 41 (2): 240–257.

Hirsch, Marianne. 1997. *Family Frames: Photography, Narrative, and Postmemory*. Cambridge, MA: Harvard University Press.

———. 2008. "The Generation of Postmemory." *Poetics Today* 29 (1): 103–128.

Hitchcock, Michael. 1998. "Tourism, *Taman Mini*, and National Identity." *Indonesia and the Malay World* 26 (75): 124–135.

Hobsbawm, Eric. 1983. "Introduction: Inventing Traditions." In *The Invention of Tradition*, edited by Eric Hobsbawm and Terence Ranger, pp. 1–14. Cambridge: Cambridge University Press.

Hoëvell, Wolter Robert van. 1840. "Batavia in 1740." *Tijdschrift voor Nederlandsch-Indië* 3 (1): 447–557.

Hoon, Chang-Yau. 2006a. "Assimilation, Multiculturalism, Hybridity: The Dilemmas of the Ethnic Chinese in Post-Suharto Indonesia." *Asian Ethnicity* 7 (2): 149–166.

———. 2006b. "Reconceptualising Ethnic Chinese Identity in Post-Suharto Indonesia." PhD diss., University of Western Australia.

———. 2006c. "A Hundred Flowers Bloom: The Re-emergence of the Chinese Press in Post-Suharto Indonesia." In *Media and the Chinese Diaspora: Community, Communications and Commerce*, edited by Sun Wanning, pp. 91–118. London: Routledge.

———. 2008. *Chinese Identity in Post-Suharto Indonesia: Culture, Politics, and Media*. Eastbourne: Sussex Academic Press.

———. 2009. "More than a Cultural Celebration: The Politics of Chinese New Year in Post-Suharto Indonesia." *Chinese Southern Diaspora Studies* 3:90–105.

———. 2011. "Mapping 'Chinese' Christian Schools in Indonesia: Ethnicity, Class and Religion." *Asia Pacific Education Review* 12 (3): 403–411.

———. 2013. "Multicultural Citizenship Education in Indonesia: The Case of a Chinese Christian School." *Journal of Southeast Asian Studies* 44 (3): 490–510.

———. 2016. "Mapping Chineseness on the Landscape of Christian Churches in Indonesia." *Asian Ethnicity* 17 (2): 228–247.

Hoon, Chang-Yau, and Esther Kuntjara. 2019. "The Politics of Mandarin Fever in Contemporary Indonesia: Resinicization, Economic Impetus, and China's Soft Power." *Asian Survey* 59 (3): 573–594.

Howell, David L. 2004. "Making 'Useful Citizens' of Ainu Subjects in Early Twentieth-Century Japan." *Journal of Asian Studies* 63 (1): 5–29.

Huang, Jianli. 2011. "Umbilical Ties: The Framing of the Overseas Chinese as the Mother of the Revolution." *Frontiers of History in China* 6 (2): 183–228.

Hui, Yew-Foong. 2011. *Strangers at Home: History and Subjectivity among the Chinese Communities of West Kalimantan, Indonesia*. Leiden: Brill.

iGADING. 2009. "Kecamatan Kelapa Gading" [Kelapa Gading District]. https://web.archive.org/web/20090810050934/http://www.igading.com/?link=kecamatan (accessed December 19, 2021).

Inside RGE. 2014. "RGE Chairman Sukanto Tanoto Receives Award in Beijing." September 12. https://www.inside-rge.com/corporate/sukanto-tanoto-receives-award-beijing/ (accessed July 20, 2021).

Institute for Policy Analysis of Conflict [IPAC]. *IPAC Short Briefing No. 1: COVID-19 and ISIS in Indonesia*. Jakarta: IPAC.

Jaringan Pemberitaan Nusantara Negeriku [JPNN]. 2016. "Pemerintah Disarankan Ubah Pendekatan Tax Amnesty, Mulai Sasar Taipan" [Government Urged to Change Tax Amnesty Approach, Beginning with Targeting Tycoons]. JPNN, September 13. https://www.jpnn.com/news/pemerintah-disarankan-ubah-pendekatan-tax-amnesty-mulai-sasar-taipan (accessed July 10, 2021).

Jegho, Leonardus. 2021. "Reputation of China's Universities Draws Thousands of Indonesian Students." *China Daily*, May 6. https://www.chinadaily.com.cn/a/202105/06/WS60934f20a31024ad0babc299.html (accessed May 20, 2021).

Jenkins, Richard. 1982. "Pierre Bourdieu and the Reproduction of Determinism." *Sociology* 16 (2): 270–281.

Jiani, M. A. 2017. "Why and How International Students Choose Mainland China as a Higher Education Study Abroad Destination." *Higher Education* 74 (4): 563–579.

Jibiki, Koya. 2021. "Indonesia's Investment Race Shaken Up by China as Japan Fades." Nikkei Asia, February 16. https://asia.nikkei.com/Economy/Indonesia-s-investment-race-shaken-up-by-China-as-Japan-fades (accessed July 10, 2021).

Jurriëns, Edwin. 2013. "Social Participation in Indonesian Media and Art: Echoes from the Past, Visions for the Future." *Bijdragen tot de Taal-, Land- en Volkenkunde* 169 (1): 7–36.

Jusuf, Ester Indahyani, Hotma Timbul, Olisias Gultom, and Sonjang Frishka. 2007. *Kerusuhan Mei 1998: Fakta, Data, dan Analisa: Mengungkap Kerusuhan Mei 1998 Sebagai Kejahatan Terhadap Kemanusiaan* [May 1998 Riots: Facts, Data and Analysis: Exposing the May 1998 Riots as Crimes against Humanity]. Edited by Raymond R. Simanjorang. Jakarta: Solidaritas Nusa Bangsa and Asosiasi Penasehat Hukum dan Hak Asasi Manusia Indonesia.

Kaboel, Assa R., and Nita Madona Sulanti. 2010. "Bahasa Mandarin Dimana-Mana: Studi Kasus di Wilayah DKI Jakarta" [Mandarin Everywhere: A Case Study in the Special Capital Region of Jakarta]. In *Setelah Air Mata Kering: Masyarakat Tionghoa Pasca-Peristiwa Mei 1998* [After the Tears Have Dried: Chinese Society Post–May 1998], edited by I. Wibowo and Thung Ju Lan, pp. 208–231. Jakarta: Kompas.

Kartomi, Margaret J. 2000. "Indonesian-Chinese Oppression and the Musical Outcomes in the Netherlands East Indies." In *Music and the Racial Imagination*, edited by Ronald Radano and Philip V. Bohlman, pp. 271–317. Chicago: University of Chicago Press.

Katzenstein, Peter J., ed. 2012. *Sinicization and the Rise of China: Civilizational Processes beyond East and West*. London: Routledge.

Kayloe, Tjio. 2017. *The Unfinished Revolution: Sun Yat-sen and the Struggle for Modern China*. Singapore: Marshall Cavendish.

Kemasang, A. R. T. 1982. "The 1740 Massacre of Chinese in Java: Curtain Raiser for the Dutch Plantation Economy." *Bulletin of Concerned Asian Scholars* 14 (1): 61–71.

Khoo, Gaik Cheng. 2010. "Spotlight on the Films of Indonesian Filmmaker Edwin." *Asian Cinema* 21 (2): 135–149.

King, Anthony. 2000. "Thinking with Bourdieu against Bourdieu: A 'Practical' Critique of the Habitus." *Sociological Theory* 18 (3): 417–433.

Kitamura, Yumi. 2007. "Museum as the Representation of Ethnicity: The Construction of Chinese Indonesian Ethnic Identity in Post-Suharto Indonesia." *Kyoto Review of Southeast Asia* 8–9. http://kyotoreview.org/issue-8-9/museum-as-the-representation-of-ethnicity-the-construction-of-chinese-indonesian-ethnic-identity-in-post-suharto-indonesia/ (accessed March 1, 2022).

Kleinman, Arthur, Veena Das, and Margaret Lock, eds. 1997. *Social Suffering.* Berkeley: University of California Press.

Klinken, Gerry van. 2005. "The Battle for History after Suharto." In *Beginning to Remember: The Past in the Indonesian Present*, edited by Mary S. Zurbuchen, pp. 233–258. Singapore: Singapore University Press.

Knörr, Jacqueline. 2014. *Creole Identity in Postcolonial Indonesia*. New York: Berghahn Books.

Koh, Dong-Yeon. 2022. *The Korean War and Postmemory Generation: Contemporary Korean Arts and Films*. London: Routledge.

Komisi Pemilihan Umum [KPU]. 2004. *Daftar Nama Calon Legislatif* [List of Legislative Candidates]. Jakarta: Komisi Pemilihan Umum.

———. 2014. "Open Data Caleg 2014" [2014 Legislative Candidates Open Data]. https://caleg.kpu.go.id (accessed April 5, 2016).

Kompas. 2010. "Taman Budaya Tionghoa, Pluralisme Indonesia di TMII" [Chinese Cultural Park, Indonesian Pluralism at TMII]. February 28. http://megapolitan.kompas.com/read/2010/02/28/12530792/Taman.Budaya.Tionghoa.%20.Pluralisme.Indonesia.di.TMII (accessed March 1, 2016).

Koning, Juliette, and Heidi Dahles. 2009. "Spiritual Power: Ethnic Chinese Managers and the Rise of Charismatic Christianity." *Copenhagen Journal of Asian Studies* 27 (1): 5–37.

Kuipers, Joel C., and Ella Yulaelawati. 2009. "Religion, Ethnicity, and Identity in Indonesian Education." In *The Routledge International Companion to Multicultural Education*, edited by James A. Banks, pp. 449–460. London: Routledge.

Kusno, Abidin. 2003. "Remembering/Forgetting the May Riots: Architecture, Violence, and the Making of 'Chinese Cultures' in Post-1998 Jakarta." *Public Culture* 15 (1): 149–177.

———. 2006. "Guardian of Memories: *Gardu* in Urban Java." *Indonesia* 81:95–149.

———. 2010. *The Appearances of Memory: Mnemonic Practices of Architecture and Urban Form in Indonesia*. Durham, NC: Duke University Press.

———. 2012. "Master Q, Kung Fu Heroes and the Peranakan Chinese: Asian Pop Cultures in New Order Indonesia." In *Popular Culture Co-productions and Collaborations in East and Southeast Asia*, edited by Nissim Otmazgin and Eyal Ben-Ari, pp. 185–202. Singapore: NUS Press.

———. 2016. *Visual Cultures of the Ethnic Chinese in Indonesia*. Lanham, MD: Rowman & Littlefield.

Kwok, Yenni. 2017. "Where Memes Could Kill: Indonesia's Worsening Problem of Fake News." *Time*, January 5. http://time.com/4620419/indonesia-fake-news-ahok-chinese-christian-islam/ (accessed February 22, 2017).

Kwon, Hyunji. 2016. "Writing Witnessing, Witnessing Writing: Working through Trauma Using Performative Autoethnography." *Visual Culture & Gender* 11:8–17.

Lamb, Kate. 2016. "Waiting for Glodok: The Ghost Street Haunted by Indonesia's Riots." *Guardian*, November 22. https://www.theguardian.com/cities/2016/nov/22/glodok-jakarta-recover-indonesia-1998-riots-chinatown (accessed December 1, 2016).

Lee, Doreen. 2012. "Images of Youth: On the Iconography of History and Protest in Indonesia." *History and Anthropology* 22 (3): 307–336.

Leeuwen, Lizzy van. 2011. *Lost in Mall: An Ethnography of Middle-Class Jakarta in the 1990s*. Leiden: Brill.

Leisch, Harald. 2002. "Gated Communities in Indonesia." *Cities* 19 (5): 341–350.

Lensa News. 2016. "Tidak Nasonalis, Kewarganegaraan Taipan Sukanto Tanoto Bisa Dicabut" [Not Nationalist, Tycoon Sukanto Tanoto's Citizenship Can Be Revoked]. September 15. http://lensa-nws.blogspot.com/2016/09/tidak-nasonalis-kewarganegaraan-taipan.html (accessed July 10, 2021).

Lestari, Sri. 2018. "Kerusuhan Mei 1998: 'Apa Salah Kami Sampai (Diancam) Mau Dibakar dan Dibunuh?'" [May 1998 Riots: "What Did We Do Wrong (to Be Threatened) to Be Burned and Killed?]. *BBC Indonesia*, May 16. https://www.bbc.com/indonesia/indonesia-43940188 (accessed August 1, 2018).

Levinson, Bradley A., and Dorothy C. Holland. 1996. "The Cultural Production of the Educated Person: An Introduction." In *The Cultural Production of the Educated Person: Critical Ethnographies of Schooling and Local Practice*, edited by Bradley A. Levinson, Douglas E. Foley, and Dorothy C. Holland, pp. 1–54. Albany: SUNY Press.

Lindsey, Tim. 2001. "The Criminal State: Premanisme and the New Indonesia." In *Indonesia Today: Challenges of History*, edited by Grayson Lloyd and Shannon Smith, pp. 283–297. Lanham, MD: Rowman & Littlefield.

Liu, Hong. 1998. "Old Linkages, New Networks: The Globalization of Overseas Chinese Voluntary Associations and Its Implications." *China Quarterly* 155:582–609.

———. 2005. "New Migrants and the Revival of Overseas Chinese Nationalism." *Journal of Contemporary China* 14 (43): 291–316.

———. 2011. "An Emerging China and Diasporic Chinese: Historicity, State, and International Relations." *Journal of Contemporary China* 20 (72): 813–832.

Lo, Jacqueline. 2000. "Beyond Happy Hybridity: Performing Asian-Australian Identities." In *Alter/Asians: Asian-Australian Identities in Art, Media, and Popular Culture*, edited by Ien Ang, Sharon Chalmers, Lisa Law, and Mandy Thomas, pp. 152–168. Sydney: Pluto Press.

Lochore, Laura. 2000. "Virtual Rape: Vivian's Story." *Intersections: Gender, History and Culture in the Asian Context* 3. http://intersections.anu.edu.au/issue3/laura3.html (accessed August 1, 2018).

Lohanda, Mona. 1996. *The Kapitan Cina of Batavia, 1837–1942: A History of Chinese Establishment in Colonial Society*. Jakarta: Djambatan.

———. 2002. *Growing Pains: The Chinese and the Dutch in Colonial Java, 1890–1942*. Jakarta: Yayasan Cipta Loka Caraka.

Lombard-Salmon, Claudine. 1971. "Le sjair de 'L'Association Chinoise' de Batavia (1905)" [The Poem of "The Chinese Association" of Batavia (1905)]. *Archipel* 2:55–101.

Long, Nicholas J. 2019. " 'Straightening What's Crooked'? Recognition as Moral Disruption in Indonesia's Confucianist Revival." *Anthropological Forum* 29 (4): 335–355.

Low, Kelvin E. Y. 2015. *Remembering the Samsui Women: Migration and Social Memory in Singapore and China*. Singapore: NUS Press.

Ly, Boreth. 2020. *Traces of Trauma: Cambodian Visual Culture and National Identity in the Aftermath of Genocide*. Honolulu: University of Hawai'i Press.

Lyons, Lenore, and Michele Ford. 2013. "The Chinese of Karimun: Citizenship and Belonging at Indonesia's Margins." In *Chinese Indonesians Reassessed: History, Religion, and Belonging*, edited by Siew-Min Sai and Chang-Yau Hoon, pp. 121–137. London: Routledge.

Lyotard, Jean-François. 1988. *The Differend: Phrases in Dispute*. Translated by Georges Van Den Abbeele. Minneapolis: University of Minnesota Press.

Mackie, Jamie. 2005. "How Many Chinese Indonesians?" *Bulletin of Indonesian Economic Studies* 41 (1): 97–101.

Mageo, Jeannette Marie. 2001. "Introduction." In *Cultural Memory: Reconfiguring History and Identity in the Postcolonial Pacific*, edited by Jeannette Marie Mageo, pp. 1–10. Honolulu: University of Hawai'i Press.

McVey, Ruth Thomas. 1992. "The Materialization of the Southeast Asian Entrepreneur." In *Southeast Asian Capitalists*, edited by Ruth Thomas McVey, pp. 7–34. Ithaca, NY: Southeast Asia Program, Cornell University.

Melvin, Jess. 2013. "Why Not Genocide? Anti-Chinese Violence in Aceh, 1965–1966." *Journal of Current Southeast Asian Affairs* 32 (3): 63–91.

Merry, Sally Engle. 2001. "Spatial Governmentality and the New Urban Social Order: Controlling Gender Violence through Law." *American Anthropologist* 103 (1): 16–29.

Mietzner, Marcus. 2012. "Indonesia's Democratic Stagnation: Anti-reformist Elites and Resilient Civil Society." *Democratization* 19 (2): 209–229.

———. 2020. "Sources of Resistance to Democratic Decline: Indonesian Civil Society and Its Trials." *Democratization* 28 (1): 161–178.

Mietzner, Marcus, and Burhanuddin Muhtadi. 2018. "Explaining the 2016 Islamist Mobilisation in Indonesia: Religious Intolerance, Militant Groups and the Politics of Accommodation." *Asian Studies Review* 42 (3): 479–497.

———. 2019. "The Mobilisation of Intolerance and Its Trajectories: Indonesian Muslims' Views of Religious Minorities and Ethnic Chinese." In *Contentious Belonging: The Place of Minorities in Indonesia*, edited by Greg Fealy and Ronit Ricci, pp. 155–174. Singapore: ISEAS-Yusof Ishak Institute.

Ministry of Foreign Affairs, People's Republic of China [MFA PRC]. 2013. "Xi Jinping Attends Welcome Luncheon Hosted by Overseas Chinese in Malaysia, Hoping That Overseas Chinese Will Make New Contributions to Friendly Cooperation between China and Malaysia." October 4. https://www.mfa.gov.cn/ce/cegy//eng/zgyw/t1085195.htm (accessed March 1, 2016).

Mookerjea-Leonard, Debali. 2017. *Literature, Gender, and the Trauma of Partition: The Paradox of Independence*. London: Routledge.

Murray, Douglas P. 1964. "Chinese Education in South-East Asia." *China Quarterly* 20:67–95.

Nagel, Joane. 1994. "Constructing Ethnicity: Creating and Recreating Ethnic Identity and Culture." *Social Problems* 41 (1): 152–176.

Nash, Roy. 1990. "Bourdieu on Education and Social and Cultural Reproduction." *British Journal of Sociology of Education* 11 (4): 431–447.

Nora, Pierre. 1989. "Between Memory and History: *Les lieux de mémoire*." *Representations* 26:7–24.

Oetomo, Dede. 1989. "The Ethnic Chinese in Indonesia." In *The Ethnic Chinese in the ASEAN States: Bibliographical Essays*, edited by Leo Suryadinata, pp. 43–96. Singapore: Institute of Southeast Asian Studies.

Olick, Jeffrey K., and Joyce Robbins. 1998. "Social Memory Studies: From 'Collective Memory' to the Historical Sociology of Mnemonic Practices." *Annual Review of Sociology* 24:105–140.

Ong, Aihwa, and Donald Nonini. 1997. "Afterword: Toward a Cultural Politics of Diaspora and Transnationalism." In *Underground Empires: The Cultural Politics of Modern Chinese Transnationalism*, edited by Aihwa Ong and Donald Nonini, pp. 323–332. London: Routledge.

Onghokham. 2009. *Riwayat Tionghoa Peranakan di Jawa* [History of the Peranakan Chinese in Java]. Depok, Indonesia: Komunitas Bambu.

Osman, Mohamed Nawab Mohamed, and Prashant Waikar. 2018. "Fear and Loathing: Uncivil Islamism and Indonesia's Anti-Ahok Movement." *Indonesia* 106:89–109.

Padawangi, Rita. 2018. "In Search of Alternative Development in Post-*reformasi* Jakarta." In *Jakarta: Claiming Spaces and Rights in the City*, edited by Jörgen

Hellman, Marie Thynell, and Roanne van Voorst, pp. 173–194. London: Routledge.

———. 2019. "Forced Evictions, Spatial (Un)certainties and the Making of Exemplary Centres in Indonesia." *Asia Pacific Viewpoint* 60 (1): 65–79.

Parker, Lyn. 2003. *From Subject to Citizens: Balinese Villagers in the Indonesian Nation State*. Copenhagen: NIAS Press.

Pemberton, John. 1994. "Recollections from 'Beautiful Indonesia' (Somewhere beyond the Postmodern)." *Public Culture* 6 (2): 241–262.

Perera, Suvendrini. 2006. "'They Give Evidence': Bodies, Borders and the Disappeared." *Social Identities* 12 (6): 637–656.

Perhimpunan Indonesia Tionghoa [INTI]. 2019. "Visi dan Misi" [Vision and Mission]. https://web.archive.org/web/20210413082946/https://inti.or.id/visi-dan-misi/ (accessed July 14, 2021).

Peters, Robbie. 2013. *Surabaya, 1945–2010: Neighbourhood, State, and Economy in Indonesia's City of Struggle*. Honolulu: University of Hawai'i Press.

Peterson, Glen. 2012. *Overseas Chinese in the People's Republic of China*. London: Routledge.

Phay, Soko. 2015. "Missing Images of Genocide and Creation in Cambodia." *Journal of Literature and Trauma Studies* 4 (1/2): 87–98.

Pitaloka, Dyah, and Mohan J. Dutta. 2021. "Performing Songs as Healing the Trauma of the 1965 Anti-Communist Killings in Indonesia." In *Traumatic Pasts in Asia: History, Psychiatry, and Trauma from the 1930s to the Present*, edited by Mark S. Micale and Hans Pols, pp. 226–244. New York: Berghahn Books.

Post, Peter. 2019. "Bringing China to Java: The Oei Tiong Ham Concern and Chen Kung-po during the Nanjing Decade." *Journal of Chinese Overseas* 15 (1): 33–61.

Prasetyo, Stanley Adi. 2010. "Adakah Media Untuk Keturunan Tionghoa?" [Is There a Media for Those of Chinese Descent?]. In *Setelah Air Mata Kering: Masyarakat Tionghoa Pasca-Peristiwa Mei 1998* [After the Tears Have Dried: Chinese Society Post-May 1998], edited by I. Wibowo and Thung Ju Lan, pp. 166–183. Jakarta: Kompas.

Priyambodo R. H. 2012. "Indonesian Students in China Set Up Association." *ANTARA News*, October 29. http://www.antaranews.com/en/news/85291/indonesian-students-in-china-set-up-association (accessed March 1, 2016).

PT. Sintola Solusindo Dinamika. 2016. "Sebut Indonesia 'Bapak Angkat,' Sukanto Tanoto Dinilai Lukai" [Calling Indonesia His "Adoptive Father," Sukanto Tanoto's Comments Seen as Hurtful]. Facebook, September 5. https://ms-my.facebook.com/SintolaSolusindoDinamika/videos/sebut-indonesia-bapak-angkat-sukanto-tanoto-dinilai-lukai/1184223261629700/ (accessed April 27, 2022).

Purdey, Jemma. 2002. "Problematizing the Place of Victims in *Reformasi* Indonesia: A Contested Truth about the May 1998 Violence." *Asian Survey* 42 (4): 605–622.

———. 2003. "Policial Change: Reopening the *Asimilasi* vs *Integrasi* Debate: Ethnic Chinese Identity in Post-Suharto Indonesia." *Asian Ethnicity* 4 (3): 421–437.

———. 2004. "Describing Kekerasan: Some Observations on Writing about Violence in Indonesia after the New Order." *Bijdragen tot de Taal-, Land- en Volkenkunde* 160 (2/3): 189–225.

———. 2006. *Anti-Chinese Violence in Indonesia, 1996–1999*. Honolulu: University of Hawai'i Press.

Purwanto, Edi, Daniel D. Kameo, John Joi Ihalauw, and Sony Heru Priyanto. 2017. "The Complexity of Poverty among Benteng Chinese in Tangerang District, Indonesia." *Journal of Applied Economic Sciences* 12 (49): 820–831.

Putri, Winda Destiana. 2015. "Desain Taman Budaya Tionghoa TMII, Langsung dari Cina" [TMII Chinese Cultural Park Design, Direct from China]. *Republika*, September 28. https://www.republika.co.id/berita/gaya-hidup/travelling/15/09/28/nvcmol359-desain-taman-budaya-tionghoa-tmii-langsung-dari-cina (accessed March 1, 2016).

Rakhmat, Muhammad Zulfikar. 2020. "Indonesia Must Tackle Corona-Driven Growth in Anti-Chinese Xenophobia." Nikkei Asia, August 4. https://asia.nikkei.com/Opinion/Indonesia-must-tackle-corona-driven-growth-in-anti-Chinese-xenophobia (accessed August 10, 2021).

———. 2021. "Despite COVID-19, Indonesia-China Relations Continue to Develop." *Diplomat*, August 10. https://thediplomat.com/2021/08/despite-covid-19-indonesia-china-relations-continue-to-develop/ (accessed August 20, 2021).

Reed-Danahay, Deborah. 2005. *Locating Bourdieu*. Bloomington: Indiana University Press.

Regional Comprehensive Economic Partnership [RCEP]. 2022. "About." https://rcepsec.org/about/ (accessed May 3, 2022).

Reid, Anthony. 1980. "The Structure of Cities in Southeast Asia, Fifteenth to Seventeenth Centuries." *Journal of Southeast Asian Studies* 11 (2): 235–250.

———. 1997. "Entrepreneurial Minorities, Nationalism, and the State." In *Essential Outsiders: Chinese and Jews in the Modern Transformation of Southeast Asia and Central Europe*, edited by Daniel Chirot and Anthony Reid, pp. 33–71. Seattle: University of Washington Press.

Remmelink, Willem G. J. 1994. *The Chinese War and the Collapse of the Javanese State, 1725–43*. Leiden: KITLV Press.

Repnikova, Maria. 2022. *Chinese Soft Power*. Cambridge: Cambridge University Press.

Riady, Mochtar. 2016. *Mochtar Riady: My Life Story*. Singapore: John Wiley and Sons.

———. 2018. "Expanding into China at the Dawn of Economic Reform: Mochtar Riady's Story." Nikkei Asia, September 29. https://asia.nikkei.com/Spotlight/My-Personal-History/Expanding-into-China-at-the-dawn-of-economic-reform-Mochtar-Riady-s-story-20 (accessed July 15, 2019).

Robinson, Geoffrey. 1995. *The Dark Side of Paradise: Political Violence in Bali*. Ithaca, NY: Cornell University Press.

Romadoni, Ahmad. 2014. "Ahok: Tanpa Tragedi Mei 98, Tak Ada Ahok Jadi Wagub DKI" [Ahok: Without the Tragedy of May 98, There Is No Me Becoming Deputy Governor of DKI]. *Liputan6*, May 18. https://www.liputan6.com/news/read/2051239/ahok-tanpa-peristiwa-mei-1998-tak-ada-ahok-jadi-wagub-dki (accessed May 9, 2022).

Roth, Michael S., and Charles G. Salas. 2001. *Disturbing Remains: Memory, History, and Crisis in the Twentieth Century*. Los Angeles: Getty Research Institute.

Sai, Siew-Min. 2006. "'Eventing' the May 1998 Affair: Problematic Representations of Violence in Contemporary Indonesia." In *Violent Conflicts in Indonesia: Analysis, Representation, Resolution*, edited by Charles A. Coppel, pp. 39–57. London: Routledge.

———. 2010. "Pugilists from the Mountains: History, Memory, and the Making of the Chinese-Educated Generation in Post-1998 Indonesia." *Indonesia* 89:149–178.

———. 2016. "Mandarin Lessons: Modernity, Colonialism and Chinese Cultural Nationalism in the Dutch East Indies, c.1900s." *Inter-Asia Cultural Studies* 17 (3): 375–394.

Salim, Wilmar, and Siwage Dharma Negara. 2016. "Why Is the High-Speed Rail Project So Important to Indonesia?" *ISEAS Perspective* 16:1–10.

Salmon, Claudine. 2001. "Ancestral Halls, Funeral Associations, and Attempts at Resinicization in Nineteenth-Century Netherlands India." In *Sojourners and Settlers: Histories of Southeast Asia and the Chinese*, edited by Anthony Reid with Kristin Alilunas Rodgers, pp. 183–204. Honolulu: University of Hawai'i Press.

Salmon, Claudine, and Myra Sidharta. 2018. "Sino-Insulindian Private History Museums, Cultural Heritage Places, and the (Re)construction of the Past." *Asian Culture* 42:1–29.

Samiadi, Lika Aprilia. 2012. "Ernest Prakasa: 'Gua Komedian Cina yang Berani Speak Up'" [Ernest Prakasa: "I Am a Chinese Comedian Who Dares to Speak Up"] Yahoo! Indonesia, March 28. https://web.archive.org/web/20120331124218/http://id.omg.yahoo.com/blogs/blog-editor/ernest-prakasa—komedian-cina-yang-berani-speak-up.html (accessed August 8, 2012).

Saraswati, L. Ayu. 2013. *Seeing Beauty, Sensing Race in Transnational Indonesia*. Honolulu: University of Hawai'i Press.

Savage, Mike. 2008. "Histories, Belongings, Communities." *International Journal of Social Research Methodology* 11 (2): 151–162.

Schlehe, Judith. 2011. "Cultural Politics of Representation in Contemporary Indonesia." *European Journal of East Asian Studies* 10 (2): 149–167.

Schreiner, Klaus H. 2005. *"Lubang Buaya:* Histories of Trauma and Sites of Memory." In *Beginning to Remember: The Past in the Indonesian Present,* edited by Mary S. Zurbuchen, pp. 261–277. Singapore: Singapore University Press.

Schwartz, Barry. 2015. "Rethinking the Concept of Collective Memory." In *Routledge International Handbook of Memory Studies,* edited by Anna Lisa Tota and Trever Hagen, pp. 9–21. London: Routledge.

Sen, Krishna. 1994. *Indonesian Cinema: Framing the New Order.* London: Zed Books.

———. 2006. "'Chinese' Indonesians in National Cinema." *Inter-Asia Cultural Studies* 7 (1): 171–184.

Setijadi, Charlotte. 2013. "Chineseness, Belonging and Cosmopolitan Subjectivities in Post-Suharto Independent Films." In *Chinese Indonesians Reassessed: History, Religion, and Belonging,* edited by Siew-Min Sai and Chang-Yau Hoon, pp. 65–82. London: Routledge.

———. 2015. "Being Chinese Again: Learning Mandarin in Post-Suharto Indonesia." In *Multilingualism in the Chinese Diaspora Worldwide: Transnational Connections and Local Social Realities,* edited by Li Wei, pp. 141–158. London: Routledge.

———. 2016a. "Ethnic Chinese in Contemporary Indonesia: Changing Identity Politics and the Paradox of Sinification." *ISEAS Perspective* 12:1–11.

———. 2016b. "'A Beautiful Bridge': Chinese Indonesian Associations, Social Capital and Strategic Identification in a New Era of China-Indonesia Relations." *Journal of Contemporary China* 25 (102): 822–835.

———. 2016c. "Divisive Politics and Discontent of Urban Poor Factors behind Jakarta Unrest." *Straits Times,* November 8. https://www.straitstimes.com/opinion/divisive-politics-and-discontent-of-urban-poor-factors-behind-jakarta-unrest (accessed August 4, 2021).

———. 2017. "Ahok's Downfall and the Rise of Islamist Populism in Indonesia." *ISEAS Perspective* 38:1–9.

———. 2019. "Anti-Chinese Sentiment and the 'Return' of the *Pribumi* Discourse." In *Contentious Belonging: The Place of Minorities in Indonesia,* edited by Greg Fealy and Ronit Ricci, pp. 194–213. Singapore: ISEAS-Yusof Ishak Institute.

———. 2021. "The Pandemic as Political Opportunity: Jokowi's Indonesia in the Time of Covid-19." *Bulletin of Indonesian Economic Studies* 57 (3): 297–320.

———. 2023. "'We Are People of the Islands': Translocal Belonging among the Ethnic Chinese of the Riau Islands." *Asian Ethnicity* 24 (1): 132–150.

Setijadi-Dunn, Charlotte. 2009. "Filming Ambiguity." *Inside Indonesia,* January 11. https://www.insideindonesia.org/filming-ambiguity (accessed April 10, 2022).

———. 2010. "Cautiously Promoting Humanism." *Inside Indonesia*, October 4. https://www.insideindonesia.org/cautiously-promoting-humanism (accessed October 5, 2010).

Setijadi, Charlotte, Deasy Simandjuntak, and Dirk Tomsa. 2016. "Candidates, Coalitions and Prospects for the 2017 Jakarta Gubernatorial Election." *ISEAS Perspective* 57:1–7.

Setijadi-Dunn, Charlotte, and Thomas Barker. 2010. "Imagining 'Indonesia': Ethnic Chinese Film Producers in Pre-independence Cinema." *Asian Cinema* 21 (2): 25–47.

Setiono, Benny G. 2008. *Tionghoa dalam Pusaran Politik* [Chinese in the Vortex of Politics]. Jakarta: TransMedia Pustaka.

Sibarani, Rifka, Birut Zemits, and Stephen Miller. 2020. "How to Communicate COVID-19 Risk without Fuelling Anti-Chinese Sentiment in Indonesia." *Jakarta Post*, March 10. https://www.thejakartapost.com/academia/2020/03/10/how-to-communicate-covid-19-risk-without-fuelling-anti-chinese-sentiment-in-indonesia.html (accessed August 4, 2021).

Siegel, James T. 1998a. "Early Thoughts on the Violence of May 13 and 14, 1998, in Jakarta." *Indonesia* 66:75–108.

———. 1998b. *A New Criminal Type in Jakarta: Counter-Revolution Today*. Durham, NC: Duke University Press.

Silaen, Linda, and I Made Sentana. 2013. "Chinese, Indonesian Companies Sign $28 Billion in Deals." *Wall Street Journal*, October 3. https://www.wsj.com/articles/SB10001424052702303722604579112940343117368 (accessed February 29, 2016).

Skinner, G. William. 1957. *Chinese Society in Thailand: An Analytical History*. Ithaca, NY: Cornell University Press.

Smelser, Neil J. 2004. "Psychological Trauma and Cultural Trauma." In *Cultural Trauma and Collective Identity*, edited by Jeffrey C. Alexander, Ron Eyerman, Bernhard Giesen, Neil J. Smelser, and Piotr Sztompka, pp. 31–59. Berkeley: University of California Press.

Smith, Philip. 2015. "Writing in the Rain: Erasure, Trauma, and Chinese Indonesian Identity in the Recent Work of FX Harsono." *Journal of Southeast Asian Studies* 46 (1): 119–133.

Somers, Mary F. 1965. "Peranakan Chinese Politics in Indonesia." PhD diss., Cornell University.

Somers Heidhues, Mary. 2003. *Golddiggers, Farmers, and Traders in the "Chinese Districts" of West Kalimantan, Indonesia*. Ithaca, NY: Cornell University Press.

———. 2009. "1740 and the Chinese Massacre in Batavia: Some German Eyewitness Accounts." *Archipel* 77:117–147.

Stenberg, Josh. 2019. *Minority Stages: Sino-Indonesian Performance and Public Display*. Honolulu: University of Hawai'i Press.

Stoler, Ann Laura. 2002. *Carnal Knowledge and Imperial Power: Race and the Intimate in Colonial Rule*. Berkeley: University of California Press.

Strangio, Sebastian. 2020. *In the Dragon's Shadow: Southeast Asia in the Chinese Century*. New Haven, CT: Yale University Press.

Strassler, Karen. 2004. "Gendered Visibilities and the Dream of Transparency: The Chinese-Indonesian Rape Debate in Post-Suharto Indonesia." *Gender & History* 16 (3): 689–725.

———. 2018. "Zones of Refuge: Fugitive Memories of Violence in the Work of FX Harsono." *History of the Present* 8 (2): 177–208.

———. 2020. *Demanding Images: Democracy, Mediation, and the Image-Event in Indonesia*. Durham, NC: Duke University Press.

Suara Peranakan. 2020. "Suara Peranakan: About." June 12. https://suaraperanakan.wordpress.com/about/ (accessed August 20, 2021).

Sukanto Tanoto Biography. 2014a. "The Reason Why Sukanto Tanoto Donated to the Beijing Olympic Games 2008." July 18. https://www.sukantotanotobiography.com/reason-sukanto-tanoto-donated-beijing-olympic-games-2008/ (accessed April 25, 2022).

———. 2014b. "Sukanto Tanoto Receives the Jinghua Award." September 10. https://www.sukantotanotobiography.com/sukanto-tanoto-receives-jinghua-award/ (accessed April 25, 2022).

Sulistiyanto, Priyambudi. 2018. "Indonesia in 2017: Jokowi's Supremacy and His Next Political Battles." In *Southeast Asian Affairs 2018*, edited by Malcolm Cook and Daljit Singh, pp. 153–166. Singapore: ISEAS-Yusof Ishak Institute.

Sully, Nicole. 2004. "An Everyday Nostalgia: Memory and the Fictions of Belonging." Paper presented at the Cultural Studies Association of Australasia (CSAA) Annual Conference, Perth, Australia, December 6–9.

Suprajitno, Setefanus. 2020. "Reconstructing Chineseness: Chinese Media and Chinese Identity in Post-reform Indonesia." *KEMANUSIAAN: The Asian Journal of Humanities* 27 (1): 1–23.

Suryadinata, Leo. 1972. "Indonesian Chinese Education: Past and Present." *Indonesia* 14:49–71.

———. 1976. *Peranakan Chinese Politics in Java, 1917–42*. Singapore: Institute of Southeast Asian Studies.

———. 1978. *Pribumi Indonesians, the Chinese Minority, and China: A Study of Perceptions and Policies*. Singapore: Heinemann Educational Books (Asia).

———, ed. 1997. *Political Thinking of the Indonesian Chinese, 1900–1995: A Sourcebook*. Singapore: Singapore University Press.

———. 2001. "Chinese Politics in Post-Suharto's Indonesia: Beyond the Ethnic Approach?" *Asian Survey* 41 (3): 502–524.

———. 2004. *Chinese Indonesians: State Policy, Monoculture, and Multiculture*. Singapore: Eastern Universities Press.

———. 2005. "Buddhism and Confucianism in Contemporary Indonesia: Recent Developments." In *Chinese Indonesians: Remembering, Distorting, Forgetting,* edited by Tim Lindsey and Helen Pausacker, pp. 77–94. Singapore: Institute of Southeast Asian Studies.

———. 2010. "Akhirnya Diakui: Agama Konghucu dan Agama Buddha Pasca-Soeharto" [Finally Recognized: Post-Suharto Confucianism and Buddhism]. In *Setelah Air Mata Kering: Masyarakat Tionghoa Pasca-Peristiwa Mei 1998* [After the Tears Have Dried: Chinese Society Post-May 1998], edited by I. Wibowo and Thung Ju Lan, pp. 75–104. Jakarta: Kompas.

———. 2015. "Why Have Two World Chinese Entrepreneur Conferences?" *Straits Times*, September 2. https://www.straitstimes.com/opinion/why-have-two-world-chinese-entrepreneur-conferences (accessed March 1, 2016).

———. 2017a. "Blurring the Distinction between *Huaqiao* and *Huaren:* China's Changing Policy towards the Chinese Overseas." In *Southeast Asian Affairs 2017*, edited by Daljit Singh and Hoang Thi Ha, pp. 101–114. Singapore: ISEAS-Yusof Ishak Institute.

———. 2017b. *The Rise of China and the Chinese Overseas: A Study of Beijing's Changing Policy in Southeast Asia and Beyond.* Singapore: ISEAS-Yusof Ishak Centre.

———. 2017c. "General Gatot and the Re-emergence of Pribumi-ism in Indonesia." *ISEAS Perspective* 49:1–7.

———. 2019. "Chinese Participation in the 2019 Indonesian Elections." *ISEAS Perspective* 58:1–8.

Suryadinata, Leo, Evi Nurvidya Arifin, and Aris Ananta. 2003. *Indonesia's Population: Ethnicity and Religion in a Changing Political Landscape.* Singapore: Institute of Southeast Asian Studies.

Susanto, Andreas Ambrosius. 2008. "Under the Umbrella of the Sultan: Accommodation of the Chinese in Yogyakarta During Indonesia's New Order." PhD diss., Radboud Universiteit Nijmegen.

Susanto, A. B., and Patricia Susanto. 2013. *The Dragon Network: Inside Stories of the Most Successful Chinese Family Businesses.* New York: John Wiley and Sons.

Susanty, Farida. 2016. "China Strengthens Grip on Indonesia." *Jakarta Post*, November 24. http://www.thejakartapost.com/news/2016/11/24/china-strengthens-grip-on-indonesia.html (accessed July 15, 2021).

Sutrisno, Evi Lina. 2002. "The May 1998 Riot in Surabaya: Through the Local People's Narratives." MSocSc diss., University of Amsterdam.

———. 2017. "Confucius Is Our Prophet: The Discourse of Prophecy and Religious Agency in Indonesian Confucianism." *Sojourn: Journal of Social Issues in Southeast Asia* 32 (3): 669–718.

———. 2018. "Negotiating the Confucian Religion in Indonesia: Invention, Resilience and Revival (1900–2010)." PhD diss., University of Washington.

Sztompka, Piotr. 2000. "Cultural Trauma: The Other Face of Social Change." *European Journal of Social Theory* 3 (4): 449–466.

———. 2004. "The Trauma of Social Change: A Case of Postcommunist Societies." In *Cultural Trauma and Collective Identity*, edited by Jeffrey C. Alexander, Ron Eyerman, Bernhard Giesen, Neil J. Smelser, and Piotr Sztompka, pp. 155–195. Berkeley: University of California Press.

Tan, Mely G. 2004. "Unity in Diversity: Ethnic Chinese and Nation-Building in Indonesia." In *Ethnic Relations and Nation-Building in Southeast Asia: The Case of the Ethnic Chinese*, edited by Leo Suryadinata, pp. 20–44. Singapore: Institute of Southeast Asian Studies.

———. 2008. *Etnis Tionghoa di Indonesia: Kumpulan Tulisan* [Ethnic Chinese in Indonesia: A Collection of Writings]. Jakarta: Yayasan Obor Indonesia.

Tanasaldy, Taufiq. 2013. "Opportunities and Challenges: Social and Political Activism of the Indonesian Chinese in Post-reform Indonesia." *RIMA: Review of Indonesian and Malaysian Affairs* 47 (2): 91–116.

Tan-Johannes, Grace. 2018. "Why More Chinese Indonesians Are Learning Mandarin, and Nurturing Their Children's Sense of Belonging to Chinese Culture." *South China Morning Post*, August 23. https://www.scmp.com/lifestyle/families/article/2160779/three-reasons-more-chinese-indonesians-are-learning-mandarin-and (accessed September 1, 2018).

Tay, Elaine. 2006. "Discursive Violence on the Internet and the May 1998 Riots." In *Violent Conflicts in Indonesia: Analysis: Representation, Resolution*, edited by Charles A. Coppel, pp. 58–71. London: Routledge.

Taylor, Jean Gelman. 1983. *The Social World of Batavia: European and Eurasian in Dutch Asia*. Milwaukee: University of Wisconsin Press.

Tempo. 2014. "Siapa Membakar Kampus Res Publica?" [Who Burned the Res Publica Campus?]. March 31. https://majalah.tempo.co/read/intermezzo/145038/siapa-membakar-kampus-res-publica (accessed September 1, 2018).

Tham Siew Yean, and Siwage Dharma Negara. 2020. *Chinese Investments in Industrial Parks: Indonesia and Malaysia Compared*. Singapore: ISEAS-Yusof Ishak Institute, Economics Working Paper No. 2020–08.

Thomson, Alistair. 1999. "Moving Stories: Oral History and Migration Studies." *Oral History* 27 (1): 24–37.

Thung Ju Lan. 1998. "Identities in Flux: Young Chinese in Jakarta." PhD diss., La Trobe University.

———. 2012. "Contesting the Post-colonial Legal Construction of Chinese Indonesians as 'Foreign Subjects.'" *Asian Ethnicity* 13 (4): 373–387.

Tickell, Paul. 2009. "Indonesian Identity after the Dictatorship: Imagining Chineseness in Recent Literature and Film." In *The Politics of the Periphery in Indonesia: Social and Geographical Perspectives*, edited by Minako Sakai, Glenn Banks, and J. H. Walker, pp. 274–295. Singapore: NUS Press.

Tiezzi, Shannon. 2015. "Indonesia, China Seal 'Maritime Partnership.'" *Diplomat*, March 27. http://thediplomat.com/2015/03/indonesia-china-seal-maritime-partnership/ (accessed February 29, 2016).

Tiola. 2019. "Jokowi's Global Maritime Fulcrum: 5 More Years?" *Diplomat*, June 11. https://thediplomat.com/2019/06/jokowis-global-maritime-fulcrum-5-more-years/ (accessed April 25, 2022).

Tjhin, Christine Susanna. 2005. "Reflections on the Identity of the Chinese Indonesians." MA diss., Australian National University.

To, James Jiann Hua. 2014. *Qiaowu: Extra-Territorial Policies for the Overseas Chinese*. Leiden: Brill.

Toer, Pramoedya Ananta. 1960. *Hoa Kiau di Indonesia* [The Chinese in Indonesia]. Jakarta: Bintang Press.

Tong, Chee Kiong. 2010. *Identity and Ethnic Relations in Southeast Asia: Racializing Chineseness*. London: Springer.

Tsai, Yen-ling. 2008. "Strangers Who Are Not Foreign: Intimate Exclusion and Racialized Boundary in Urban Indonesia." PhD diss., University of California Santa Cruz.

———. 2013. "Materializing Racial Formation: The Social Lives of Confiscated Chinese Properties in North Sumatra." In *Chinese Indonesians Reassessed: History, Religion, and Belonging*, edited by Siew-Min Sai and Chang-Yau Hoon, pp. 83–102. London: Routledge.

Turner, Caroline, and Glen St. John Barclay. 2011. "Recovering Lives through Art: Hidden Histories and Commemoration in the Works of Katsushige Nakahashi and Dadang Christanto." *Life Writing* 8 (1): 67–85.

Turner, Sarah. 2003. "Setting the Scene: Speaking Out: Chinese Indonesians after Suharto." *Asian Ethnicity* 4 (3): 337–352.

Unidjaja, Fabiola Desy, and Leony Aurora. 2004. "Memorial to Commemorate 1998 Riots." *Jakarta Post*, May 14.

Vandenbosch, Amry. 1930. "A Problem in Java: The Chinese in the Dutch East Indies." *Pacific Affairs* 3 (11): 1001–1017.

Vermeulen, J. Th. 1938. *De Chineezen te Batavia en de troebelen van 1740* [The Chinese in Batavia and the Troubles of 1740]. Leiden: Eduard Ijdo.

Vickers, Adrian. 2010. "Where Are the Bodies: The Haunting of Indonesia." *Public Historian* 32 (1): 45–58.

Wahid, Abdul. 2018. "Campus on Fire: Indonesian Universities during the Political Turmoil of 1950s–1960s." *Archipel* 95:31–52.

Wandita, Galuh. 1998. "The Tears Have Not Stopped, the Violence Has Not Ended: Political Upheaval, Ethnicity, and Violence against Women in Indonesia." *Gender and Development* 6 (3): 34–41.

Wang Gungwu. 1981. "Southeast Asian *Hua-Ch'iao* in Chinese History-Writing." *Journal of Southeast Asian Studies* 12 (1): 1–14.

———. 1985. "South China Perspectives on Overseas Chinese." *Australian Journal of Chinese Affairs* 13:69–84.

———. 1988. "The Study of Chinese Identities in Southeast Asia." In *Changing Identities of the Southeast Asian Chinese Since World War II*, edited by

Jennifer W. Cushman and Wang Gungwu, pp. 1–21. Hong Kong: Hong Kong University Press.

———. 1993. "Greater China and the Chinese Overseas." *China Quarterly* 136: 926–948.

———. 2000. *The Chinese Overseas: From Earthbound China to the Quest for Autonomy*. Cambridge, MA: Harvard University Press.

Warburton, Eve, and Liam Gammon. 2017. "Class Dismissed? Economic Fairness and Identity Politics in Indonesia." *New Mandala*, May 5. https://www.new-mandala.org/economic-injustice-identity-politics-indonesia/ (accessed April 16, 2022).

Wargadiredja, Arzia Tivany. 2018. "Reflections of May '98 Looters, Victims of the New Order's 'Organized Riots.'" *Vice*, May 21. https://www.vice.com/en/article/a3av7e/reflections-of-may-98-looters-victims-of-the-new-orders-organized-riots (accessed March 1, 2016).

Weidenbaum, Murray, and Samuel Hughes. 1996. *The Bamboo Network: How Expatriate Chinese Entrepreneurs Are Creating a New Economic Superpower in Asia*. New York: Simon and Schuster.

Weix, G. G. 2000. "Inside the Home and Outside the Family: The Domestic Estrangement of Javanese Servants." In *Home and Hegemony: Domestic Service and Identity Politics in South and Southeast Asia*, edited by Kathleen M. Adams and Sara Dickey, pp. 137–156. Ann Arbor: University of Michigan Press.

Werbner, Pnina, and Tariq Modood. 1997. *Debating Cultural Hybridity: Multicultural Identities and the Politics of Anti-racism*. London: Zed Books.

Wibowo, Ivan, ed. 2008. *Cokin? So What Gitu Loh? Pemikiran Tionghoa Muda* [Chinese? That's It, So What? Thoughts of Young Chinese]. Jakarta: Komunitas Bambu.

Widodo, Johannes. 2004. *The Boat and the City: Chinese Diaspora and the Architecture of Southeast Asian Coastal Cities*. Singapore: Marshall Cavendish Academic.

Williams, James. 1998. *Lyotard: Towards a Postmodern Philosophy*. Cambridge: Polity Press.

Willmott, Donald E. 1961. *The National Status of the Chinese in Indonesia, 1900–1958*. Ithaca, NY: Modern Indonesia Project, Southeast Asia Program, Department of Far Eastern Studies, Cornell University.

Wilson, Ian Douglas. 2015. *The Politics of Protection Rackets in Post-New Order Indonesia: Coercive Capital, Authority and Street Politics*. London: Routledge.

———. 2017. "Jakarta: Inequality and the Poverty of Elite Pluralism." *New Mandala*, April 19. https://www.newmandala.org/jakarta-inequality-poverty-elite-pluralism/ (accessed May 18, 2017).

Winarnita, Monika Swasti. 2012. "The Politics of Commemorating the May 1998 Mass Rapes." *RIMA: Review of Indonesian and Malaysian Affairs* 45 (1/2): 133–164.

Winarnita, Monika Swasti, and Ken M. P. Setiawan. 2020. "Commemorating Gendered Violence Two Decades On: Chinese Indonesian Women's Voices in the Diaspora." In *Gender, Violence, and Power in Indonesia: Across Time and Space*, edited by Katharine McGregor, Ana Dragojlovic, and Hannah Loney, pp. 119–142. London: Routledge.

Wood, Nancy. 1999. *Vectors of Memory: Legacies of Trauma in Postwar Europe*. London: Bloomsbury.

World Bank. 2019. "Indonesia Trade Summary 2019 Data." World Integrated Trade Solution, n.d. https://wits.worldbank.org/CountryProfile/en/Country/IDN/Year/LTST/Summary (accessed July 3, 2021).

World Health Organization [WHO]. 2022. WHO Health Emergency Dashboard: Indonesia. https://covid19.who.int/region/searo/country/id (accessed April 12, 2022).

Wulia, Tintin. 2008. "The Name Game." *Inside Indonesia*, October 12. https://www.insideindonesia.org/the-name-game (accessed January 13, 2022).

———. 2009. "Terra Incognita et cetera." April 5. https://tintinwulia.com/blog/?p=370 (accessed January 13, 2022).

Xi, Cheng. 2007. "The 'Distinctiveness' of the Overseas Chinese as Perceived in the People's Republic of China." In *Beyond Chinatown: New Chinese Migration and the Global Expansion of China*, edited by Mette Thunø, pp. 49–66. Copenhagen: NIAS Press.

Xiang Biao. 2013. "A Ritual Economy of 'Talent': China and Overseas Chinese Professionals." In *The Cultural Politics of Talent Migration in East Asia*, edited by Brenda S. A. Yeoh and Shirlena Huang, pp. 154–171. New York: Routledge.

Xinhua. 2015. "Chronology of China's Belt and Road Initiative." State Council, People's Republic of China, March 28. http://english.www.gov.cn/news/top_news/2015/04/20/content_281475092566326.htm (accessed July 1, 2021).

Yelvington, Kevin A. 2002. "History, Memory and Identity: A Programmatic Prolegomenon." *Critique of Anthropology* 22 (3): 227–256.

Yen Ching Hwang. 1976. *The Overseas Chinese and the 1911 Revolution: With Special Reference to Singapore and Malaya*. Kuala Lumpur: Oxford University Press.

Young, Allan. 1997. *The Harmony of Illusions: Inventing Post-traumatic Stress Disorder*. Princeton, NJ: Princeton University Press.

Yuwono, Dito, and Mira Asriningtyas. 2020. "Tato Tolak Bala: Perlindungan Ampuh Warga Setempat" [Tattoos to Ward off Evil: Powerful Protection of Local People]. Mira Asriningtyas, September. http://www.miraasriningtyas.com/2020/09/tato-tolak-bala-perlindungan-ampuh.html (accessed January 14, 2022).

Zhou, Taomo. 2019. *Migration in the Time of Revolution: China, Indonesia, and the Cold War*. Ithaca, NY: Cornell University Press.

Zurbuchen, Mary S. 2002. "History, Memory, and the '1965 Incident' in Indonesia." *Asian Survey* 42 (4): 564–581.

———, ed. 2005a. *Beginning to Remember: The Past in the Indonesian Present.* Singapore: Singapore University Press.

———. 2005b. "Historical Memory in Contemporary Indonesia." In *Beginning to Remember: The Past in the Indonesian Present*, edited by Mary S. Zurbuchen, pp. 3–32. Singapore: Singapore University Press.

INDEX

Page numbers in boldface refer to illustrations

Aceh, 166; anti-Chinese violence in, 45; separatist movement in, 239n6; terrorism in, 25

Act of Killing, The (Oppenheimer), 242n1

activism, 36, 123, 172, 221; political, 34, 165, 173; sociopolitical, 31, 38, 189

affirmative action, 55, 186, 241n2

Ahok (Basuki Tjahaja Purnama), 56, 155–156, 177–180, **180**, 181–185, 190, 220, 245nn7–9; blasphemy case, 5, 14, 174, 181–182, 185–186, 213–214, 224; and China, 183; and Chineseness, 183–184; downfall, 5, 32, 38, 182, 187–188, 219; and Jokowi, 4, 178–179, 182–183, 188; and *pribumi,* 179, 184, 186

Aidit, D. N., 147

Aidit, Sobron, 147

Alexander, Jeffrey C., 6, 24, 124

Amin, Ma'ruf, 223

Ampera Cabinet Presidium Circular 6 (1967), 10, 13

Anak Naga Beranak Naga (Dragons Beget Dragons) (Darmawan), 132

Ang, Ien, 44, 66, 153, 197, 227–228, 237n2

anti-Chinese: attacks, 3, 16, 40, 43–44, 48, 52, 87–88, 183, 220, 238n1; discrimination, 1–3, 6, 8, 10–11, 19–20, 23, 26, 37, 45–46, 60, 66, 68, 97, 125–127, 131, 136–137, 142, 144, 170, 219, 226, 241n2; events, 33, 92; media, 177; narratives, 5, 177, 182–184, 190; opposition, 91; prejudice, 177; racism, 38; riots, 41, 44, 47, 88, 181, 210; sentiments, 32, 38, 101, 156, 177, 183–186, 188, 190, 209, 211, 216, 219, 222, 224–225, 244n2; violence, 8, 20, 23, 26, 37, 40–41, 44–46, 49, 51–52, 62, 65–66, 68, 83, 89, 92, 147, 184, 196, 243n5

anti-Communist: discourses, 18; purges, 16, 20, 23, 25, 41, 45, 55, 66, 101, 131, 143, 147, 158, 165, 171, 211, 235n2, 242n1, 243n4

Anti-Discrimination Movement (Gerakan Perjuangan Anti-Diskriminasi, GANDI), 13, 168

anticolonial struggle, 7

Arlini, Gloria, 43

Armayanti, Nelly, 175

artist(s), 32, 125–131, 133, 136, 142–144, 148–149, 153, 158; Balinese, 54; and censorship, 127; and Chineseness, 129; and collective memory, 38, 125, 130, 151, 243n3; and identity, 227; and identity politics, 149; and May 1998 riots, 130–131, 147, 150–152, 243n5; and trauma, 130–131, 220

artistic *habitus*, 133

arts: and identity, 131, 149; under New Order, 126

Asriningtyas, Mira, 151

assimilation, 10, 16, 27, 41, 65, 104, 110, 158, 160–161, 195–196, 198, 213, 236n5; abolition of, 158; and Chineseness, 11; discourse, 60, 127, 218; history of, 128; laws, 12, 64, 158; and May 1998 riots, 218; policies of New Order, 2, 4, 9–11, 15, 26, 35, 118, 122, 133–135, 160, 192, 195, 198, 213, 218, 227; of students, 114

association(s), 205, 208–209; business, 204; clan, 13, 38, 154, 156–157, 203–204, 207, 238n6; commercial, 213; social, 13; victims', 55; voluntary, 13, 38, 156
Association of Chinese Language Studies Program in Indonesia (Asosiasi Program Studi Mandarin Indonesia), 113
Association of Trilingual National Schools in Indonesia (Perkumpulan Sekolah Nasional Tiga Bahasa Se-Indonesia), 113
Atma Jaya Catholic University of Indonesia (Universitas Katolik Indonesia Atma Jaya), 79
Atmaja, Edita, 38, 130, 147–148, **148**, 149–153

Babi Buta Yang Ingin Terbang (Blind Pig Who Wants to Fly) (Edwin), 132, 138–139, **139**, 244n8
Bali, 7, 54, 142, 205–206; anti-Communist purges in, 25; bombings, 239n6
Balinese, 7, 26; artist, 54
Bandung, 3, 32, 132, 136, 214
Bandung Institute of Technology (Institut Teknologi Bandung), 105, 137, 241n2
Bangka-Belitung, 11, 155, 178
Baperki University (Universitas Baperki), 108. *See also* Res Publica University
Barki, Kiki, 204
Baswedan, Anies, 181
Batavia, 72–73, 99–100; Chinese massacre (*Chineezenmoord*), 23, 73, 238n1; Chinese population, 73. *See also* Jakarta
Bauman, Zygmunt, 227–228
Beautiful Indonesia Miniature Park (Taman Mini Indonesia Indah, TMII), 13, 37, 40, 58–60, **61**, 62, 65, 238n5, 244n2
Beijing, 18, 58, 61–63, 200–202, 208, 212, 238n6; Indonesian embassy in, 17, 195, 210
Beijing Olympics, 211–212
belonging, 16, 20–21, 59, 61, 65, 97, 103, 146–147, 149, 189, 195, 219–220, 226; ethnic, 64; and ethnicity, 31, 64; ethnonationalist, 58, 227; and identity, 149; narratives of, 31; national, 4, 64, 146, 161, 218, 228–229; structures of, 6; and trauma, 147
Belt and Road Initiative (BRI), 18, 193, 214
bombing(s): Australian embassy, 239n7; Bali, 239n6; Jakarta Stock Exchange, 239n7; JW Marriott Hotel, 239n7; MacDonald House, 50; Ritz-Carlton Hotel, 240n7
boundary: of Chineseness, 142, 161, 221; class, 97, 103; ethnic, 102; of *habitus,* 63, 69, 95, 112, 122–123, 142, 153, 220; maintenance, 95, 102, 219; negotiations, 113; religious, 97, 103
boundary-making practices, 27–28, 30, 35, 95, 220
Bourdieu, Pierre, 6, 28–32, 95, 98, 142, 184, 220–221. See also *habitus*
Brotherhood Monument (Monumen Persaudaraan), 54
Buddhist: amulet design, 152; organizations, 204
Bumi Serpong Damai, 92, 114
business elite(s), 38, 196–197, 209, 213, 216, 222; Chinese (PRC), 194; *totok,* 19, 196, 202
"But It Is Not Ours" (*Tapi Bukan Kami Punya*), 186

Ca-bau-kan (The Courtesan) (Dinata), 129, 132
Cabinet Presidium Decision No. 127 (1966), 9
Cambodian(s): diaspora, 243n2; genocide, 24, 243n2; visual arts, 243n2
capital, 31, 64, 92, 220, 222; cultural, 22, 29, 123, 189, 194, 197; economic, 22, 29, 35, 63, 89, 122–123, 162, 189, 197, 202, 205, 216; overseas Chinese, 199; political, 35, 63, 65, 189, 196–197, 202, 205, 216; social, 22, 29, 34, 63, 65, 119, 123, 142, 161–162, 189, 194, 197, 202, 205, 213, 216

"Catatan Sepi si Anak Babi" (The Piglet's Lonely Note) (Chin), 225–226
Catholic, 84; church, 78, 90
Cek Toko Sebelah (Check Out the Shop Next Door) (Prakasa), 140–141, **141**
censorship: and artists, 127; under New Order, 127
Central Jakarta, 1, 5, 71, 74, **182**
Central Java, 58, 78, 133, 148, 186, 238n1
Central Kalimantan, 239n6
Central Sulawesi, 239
Chandra, Leo, 207–208
Charismatic Christianity, 36
chauvinism, 153
Chin, Awi, 225–226, 247nn2–3
China, People's Republic of (PRC), 10–11, 17, 19, 23, 38–39, 61–65, 116, 143, 157, 198–200, 202, 204, 211–213, 224, 238n6, 246n4; and Ahok, 183; and Chineseness, 197, 214; citizenship of, 135; Confucianism in, 14; foreign policy, 18; as global power, 16–17, 113, 123, 192, 195, 213, 216, 222; human rights groups in, 210; and Indonesian Communist Party (PKI), 11; and Jokowi, 193, 206, 214; and May 1998 riots, 210; and New Order, 203, 246n2; and overseas Chinese, 18, 38, 43, 99–100, 199–202, 205, 210, 213, 222; and pan-Chinese nationalist movement, 157; politics, 100; relations with Indonesia, 11, 17–19, 38, 66, 192–197, 203–211, 214, 216, 222, 235n2; soft power, 200, 222; students in, 17, 195; and *totok,* 8, 19
China Ethnic Museum, 58
Chinatown (Pecinan), 34, 27, 40, 51, 61. *See also* Glodok
Chinese (language), 8–9, 11–13, 15, 17, 35, 101, 113, 117, 119–120, 122, 157–158, 195, 206, 209, 213, 247n3
Chinese (PRC): business elites, 194; Communism, 108; films, 16; foreign direct investment, 18, 193, 206; government, 18, 183, 196, 200, 202–204, 206–207, 222, 246nn2–3; private companies, 193; state, 199, 203, 207–208; state-owned enterprises, 193; universities, 17, 195
Chinese Association (Tiong Hoa Hwee Koan, THHK), 100, 113, 157, 168; schools, 114–117, **118**, 157, 241n6
Chinese Communist Party (CCP), 157, 246n3
Chinese of Indonesia and Their Search for Identity, The (Dawis), 124
Chinese Indonesian Association (Perhimpunan Indonesia Tionghoa, INTI), 13, 18–19, 57, 63, 159–162, 164, 166–168, 170, 202–204, 206–209, 213, 244n3
Chinese Indonesian Cultural Park (Taman Budaya Tionghoa Indonesia), 13, 37, 40, 58, 60–61, **61**, 62–65, 162, 202, 238n5, 244n2
Chinese Indonesian Reform Party (Partai Reformasi Tionghoa Indonesia, PARTI), 13, 54
Chinese–Malay race riots, 55
Chinese massacre (*Chineezenmoord*), 23, 73, 238n1
Chinese Muslim(s), 11, 36, 124, 186
Chinese Overseas Exchange Association (COEA), 203
"Chinese problem" (*masalah cina*), 3–5, 10, 39, 153, 160, 167, 171–172, 218, 227, 235n2, 236n5; and the state, 4
Chinese Revolution (Xinhai Revolution), 199
Chinese Youth Network (Jaringan Tionghoa Muda, JTM), 169–173
Chineseness, 9, 16, 19–20, 37, 63–65, 98, 113, 116, 122, 124, 156, 161, 171, 173, 175, 189, 217–219, 222, 226; and Ahok, 183–184; and artists, 129; and assimilation, 11; boundaries of, 142, 161, 221; celebrations of, 3, 138, 218; and China, 197, 214; and Confucianism, 115; and culture, 161; discourse on, 34, 39, 147, 161, 197; in films, 138, 140; global, 63; and identity politics, 160; images of, 16–17; and Mandarin, 16, 242n10;

narratives of, 142; norms of, 221; representations of, 125–126, 128–129, 137; and schools, 119–120; stereotypes of, 140–141; symbol(s) of, 63
Christanto, Dadang, 130, 243n4
Christian(s), 4, 84, 102, 112, 140, 149, 152, 179, 183, 187, 239n6; churches, 30; schools, 36, 97, 102–103, 106, 108, 120–121, 149, 241n3
cina benteng (fortress Chinese), 35, 126, 237n8
CINtA (Winata), 138
Ciputra (Tjie Tjin Hoan), 10
citizenship, 10, 212; of China, 135; dual, 158; laws, 161; status, 15
Citizenship Law No. 12/2006, 12–13, 159
civil rights, 5
civil society, 12, 15, 27, 34, 54, 94, 128, 153, 159–160, 223
Clammer, John R., 198
clan associations, 13, 38, 154, 156–157, 203–204, 207, 238n6
class, 4–5, 8, 22, 28, 30, 34–36, 58, 70, 82, 84, 89, 91, 98–99, 102, 104, 221, 223; avoidance, 71; barriers, 81; boundaries, 97, 103; differences, 35, 80, 140; discourses of, 127; *habitus,* 35, 111; inequality, 141, 183; marginalization, 96; privilege, 92; socioeconomic, 34–35, 58, 80, 84, 89, 91
Cokin? So What Gitu Loh? Pemikiran Tionghoa Muda (Chinese? That's It, So What? Thoughts of Young Chinese) (Wibowo), 172
collaboration, 30, 125; interethnic, 83, 111–112, 140
collective identity, 24, 88, 189
collective memory, 6, 21–22, 46, 49, 64, 129, 220, 243nn2–3; and artists, 38, 125, 130, 151, 243n3; Chinese, 3, 6, 19–20, 23, 26–27, 32–33, 37, 39, 65, 83, 125, 149, 219, 222; of May 1998 riots, 16, 26, 151
collective trauma, 24, 27, 44, 66, 89, 130, 133, 138, 145, 147, 151, 189, 227; narratives, 131
colonialism: Dutch, 88
commemoration, 42–43, 49–50, 53, 66, 116, 130, 133; of May 1998 riots, 36, 53, 57, 66, 243n5; narratives of, 241n8; politics of, 36, 64, 236n7; public, 22–23, 40, 52, 55–57, 60, 64, 129; sites of, 46, 49
communal violence, 239n6
Communication Body of Organizing National Unity (Badan Komunikasi Penhayatan Kesatuan Bangsa, BAKOM PKB), 158
Communism, 108; Chinese, 193, 199
Conference of the World Federation of Huaqiao Huaren Associations (CWFHHA), 200–202
Confucian(s), 13, 36, 244n1; beliefs, 14; classics, 100–115; education, 157; philosophy, 115, 236n4; school, 114; values, 114–116, 120, 236n4
Confucianism (Konghucu), 12, 15, 36, 116; in China, 14; and Chineseness, 115; history of, 236n4
conservatism, 52, 57, 185; Islamic, 190, 223
Consultative Council for Indonesian Citizenship (Badan Permusjawaratan Kewarganegaraan Indonesia, Baperki), 108–109, 143, 158, 165, 171
Coppel, Charles A., 45
corruption, 24, 127, 133, 179, 186, 223
COVID-19 pandemic, 195, 224–225
Cribb, Robert, 45, 242n1
criminality, 52, 76, 87–88, 93, 238n2, 240n8
cultural: affiliation, 66, 222; capital, 22, 29, 123, 189, 194, 197; center(s), 57; difference(s), 128, 218, 244n3; diversity, 58; education, 38; events, 19, 116; exchanges, 18, 203; expression, 3, 16, 64, 159, 171; gatekeepers, 65, 161; groups, 30; heritage, 64, 119, 122, 195, 203; history, 129; identity, 33, 136, 164, 213; ideology, 38, 58; influences, 228; intermediaries, 18; norms, 36, 59, 99; policy, 58, 60; practices, 14, 20, 27; preservation, 97, 122; primordialism, 119, 161; production, 31, 125, 153, 221;

protectionism, 99; representation, 128; rights, 14; traditions, 8, 11, 33, 35, 162; trauma, 24, 26, 43
Cultural Revolution, 199
culture, 9, 12–14, 17, 19, 21, 27, 37, 40, 58, 62, 65, 100, 107, 119, 121–122, 128, 138, 158, 160, 195, 198, 207, 217–218, 221, 227, 236n5, 240n9, 242n11; and Chineseness, 161; ethnic, 59; and ethnicity, 59, 65; and *habitus,* 30, 101; and heritage, 58, 213; and identity, 9, 11, 35, 222–223; local, 8; national, 11, 99; New Order, 165; pan-Chinese, 16; *peranakan,* 62–63, 126; popular, 125–126, 128; public, 25, 128; and schools, 99, 122; visual, 124, 153; and youth, 162
customary law (*adat*), 59

dance, 59, 124–125, 128
Darmawan, Ariani, 132–134, **134**, 136–138, 140
Dayak(s), 176, 186, 239n6
democracy, 12, 15, 223
Democratic Action Party, 190
Democratic Party (Partai Demokrat), 173, 186
democratization, 154, 220, 223
Deng Xiaoping, 192, 199, 201
diaspora, 242n9; Cambodian, 243n2; Chinese, 14, 18, 99, 157, 222. *See also* overseas Chinese
differences: class, 35, 80, 140; cultural, 128, 218, 244n3
Dinata, Nia, 132
disappearance(s), 25, 41, 44, 55, 143–144, 165
discourse(s): anti-Communist, 18; assimilation, 60, 127, 218; on Chineseness, 34, 39, 147, 161, 197; of class, 127; ideological, 127; of *pribumi,* 20; of security, 74; of victimhood, 41, 44, 67, 220
discrimination, 24, 226–227, 244n9; anti-Chinese, 1–3, 6, 8, 10–11, 19–20, 23, 26, 37, 45–46, 60, 66, 68, 97, 125–127, 131, 136–137, 142, 144, 170, 219, 226, 241n2; bureaucratic, 243n7; ethnic, 26; language, 120; racial, 145–146; social, 220; state, 8
diversity: Chinese, 8, 11, 14, 35, 125, 128; cultural, 58; ethnic, 58; religious, 58
Djuandi, Eddy, 208–209
domestic workers (staff), 37, 69, 71, 80–84, 87–88, 90, 239n4
Dutch, 7, 72–73, 187, 237n8, 238n1; colonial government, 100, 198; colonial period, 70, 82, 99, 103, 156, 246n5; colonialism, 88; language, 100, 198
Dutch East Indies, 82, 99–100, 116, 157, 246n5

East Belitung, 4, 155, 178
East Java, **57**, 114, 239n6, 240n10, 241n3
East Timor (Timor-Leste), 25, 239n6,
economic: capital, 22, 29, 35, 63, 89, 122–123, 162, 189, 197, 202, 205, 216; inequality, 186, 190, 223; power, 246n5; rights, 186
education: Confucian, 157; cultural, 38; history of, 122; institutions, 37, 102, 105, 108–109, 112–113, 122–123, 197, 219, 241n2; multicultural, 30, 53, 116; system, 103, 240n1
Edwin, 132–133, 138–140, 146
election(s): Jakarta gubernatorial, 4, 178, 181, 185, 245n8; local, 14, 155, 187; national, 14, 155, 174–175, 184, 186–188, 245n4; presidential, 187, 223; regional, 155
electoral politics, 35, 38, 155–156, 176, 187–189, 219, 245n6, 245n9
elite(s), 70, 73, 173; business, 38, 196–197, 202, 216, 222; political, 55, 185, 211; power, 223
English (language), 16, 23, 98, 100, 103, 114
ethnic: belonging, 64; boundary, 102; culture, 59; discrimination, 26; enclave, 90–91; *habitus,* 101, 111; identity, 6, 19, 27, 63, 228; identity politics, 19, 27, 63; marginalization, 96; minority, 3, 6, 10, 16, 27, 36, 87, 155, 189; politics, 6, 185; taxonomy, 64

ethnicity, 1, 17, 19, 36, 42, 60, 89, 99, 129, 140, 142, 147, 158, 188, 194, 216, 226–227, 235n1, 235n3, 245n3; and belonging, 31, 64; and culture, 59, 65; narratives of, 31; and national identity, 64; as social capital, 213
ethnonationalism, 8, 122, 160, 183, 209, 218
ethnonationalist: belonging, 58, 227; politics, 26
Europe, 24, 199; legacies of trauma, 130
European(s), 7, 74, 80; Jews, 144
exclusion, 65, 71; racial, 37, 69, 82, 95
extrajudicial killings, 41

fact-finding team: May 1998 riots, 42
Fang, Lan, 128
fifth column, 62, 183, 192, 201, 214, 216
film(s), 32, 127–129, 131–133, 153, 242n1; Chinese (PRC), 16; Chinese-Indonesian, 38, 124–126, 132–143, 220, 244n8; Chineseness in, 138, 140; and identity, 137–139; industry, 126, 129, 132; and May 1998 riots, 132–133, 139–140; during New Order, 127, 132, 139; preindependence, 126
filmmaker(s), 38, 125–126, 129, 131, 133, 137–138, 140, 142, 146, 153, 220, 227, 242n1; non-Chinese, 128
fine arts, 128
Firmansyah, Maman, 127
Forbidden City, 61–63, 65
forced removals, 41
foreign direct investment: Chinese, 18, 193, 206
foreign policy: China (PRC), 18
forgetting, 21, 49–50, 54; fighting, 41, 133; history, 140; politics of, 22
Fujian, 61–62, 203, 206, 238n6; government, 62

Garuda Wisnu Kencana statue, 54
gated community, 29, 68–72, 74–75, 77, 79, 84, 92, 94–95
gatekeepers: cultural, 65, 161
gender, 34, 36, 83, 99, 221; violence, 41, 131
General Electoral Commission (Komisi Pemilihan Umum, KPU), 14, 174
genocide, 50; Cambodian, 24, 243n2; Rwandan, 24
Giblin, Susan, 160–161, 219
Giddens, Anthony, 31, 245n6
Gie (Riza), 129, 132,
global Chineseness, 63
global maritime hub, 193
global power: China as, 16–17, 113, 123, 192, 195, 213, 216, 222
globalization, 123
Glodok, 37, 40, 47–48, **49**, 50–51, 54, 68, 73–75, 79, 87, 91–92, 100, 106. *See also* Chinatown
Glupczynski, Gyora Gal, 144, **144**
Golkar (Partai Golongan Karya, Party of Functional Groups), 178, 186, 188
government, 8, 11–12, 18, 25, 34, 41–42, 50–51, 53–54, 57, 60, 158–160, 187–188, 192–193, 202, 207, 210–212, 214, 222–224 235nn1–2, 237n3; Chinese (PRC), 18, 183, 196, 200, 202–204, 206–207, 222, 246nn2–3; Dutch colonial, 100, 198; Fujian, 62; Jakarta provincial, 51, 56, 75, 162, 179; local, 2, 15; national, 51; New Order, 4, 9–10, 177; officials, 24, 135, 205, 243n7; policy, 104, 122, 155, 189; populist, 224; reform, 190; and schools, 101–102, 117
governmentality: spatial, 71
governor: Jakarta, 155, 177, 179–180, 183, 219
Great Indonesia Movement Party (Partai Gerakan Indonesia Raya, Gerindra), 178, 212
Great Wallpaper (Wulia), 145, **145**, 146,
group(s): consciousness, 20, 24; cultural, 30; identity, 21, 126; identity politics, 11; Muslim, 223
guanxi (personal networks), 17, 38, 194, 203, 205–206, 213, 222, 245n1
gubernatorial election (2012): Jakarta, 4, 178
gubernatorial election (2017): Jakarta, 5, 181, 185, 245n8

Guided Democracy, 158
Guidelines for the Appreciation and the Practice of Pancasila (Pedoman Penghayatan dan Pengamalan Pancasila, P4), 99
Gunawan, Heri, 212
Gus Dur. *See* Wahid, Abdurrahman

Habibie, Bacharuddin Jusuf (B. J.), 12, 25, 42, 50, 54
habitus, 6, 28–31, 33, 38, 52, 69, 83, 91–92, 94–95, 98, 123–124, 175, 184, 189, 220–221, 228, 245n6; artistic, 133; boundaries of, 63, 69, 95, 112, 122–123, 142, 153, 220; class, 35, 111; and culture, 30, 101; ethnic, 101, 111; and history, 28; Muslim, 176; political, 63, 160, 176, 188, 190; *pribumi,* 113; of students, 112; and victimhood, 44, 96. *See also* Bourdieu, Pierre
Hakim, Rachman, 204, 206–207
Hakka, 4, 61, 64, 90, 178, 226; language, 8, 120, 207
Halbwachs, Maurice, 6, 21
Hall, Stuart, 217, 221
"happy hybridity," 128, 218
Harian Indonesia, 158
Harsono, FX (Franciscus Xaverius), 130, 149
Hasan, Bob, 10
Have a Cup of Tea/Meet My Dead Grandfather (Wulia), 144, **144**
heritage, 9, 17, 118, 126, 197, 200; cultural, 64, 119, 122, 195, 203; and culture, 58, 213
Heryanto, Ariel, 129, 159
Hew Wai Weng, 11, 36, 124
Hidayat, Hengky, 136
historical: memory, 6; narratives, 46, 123, 153; trauma, 89, 129, 211
history, 23–24, 28, 32, 37–38, 40–41, 56, 58–59, 62, 65–67, 69, 89, 110, 118, 123, 125–126, 133, 136, 144–145, 147, 153, 169, 171–172, 177, 184, 192, 214, 219, 221, 224; of assimilation, 128; colonial, 15; complexity of, 44; of Confucianism, 236n4; cultural, 129; depoliticization, 51; of education, 122; and *habitus,* 28; local, 88, 92; and memory, 41, 46; oral, 46; political, 129; of Sino-Indonesian relations, 196, 209; sociopolitical, 184; state, 129; and visual art, 242n1
Hoa Kiau di Indonesia (The Chinese in Indonesia) (Toer), 109
Hokkien, 10, 90, 100, 238n6; language, 8, 80, 100, 120, 162, 209; schools, 100
Hollandsch-Chineesch School (HCS), 100
Holocaust, 24, 144
Hong Kong, 17, 200, 210
Hoon, Chang-Yau, 30, 36, 102–103, 161–162
Hu Jintao, 202
Huan Chen Guang (Isfansyah), 133
human rights, 9, 12, 238n4; groups in China, 210; violations, 24–25, 53, 136, 212
Humanitarian Volunteers Network (Jaringan Relawan Kemanusiaan, JRK), 159

identity, 15, 19, 21, 24, 30, 63, 98, 119, 130–131, 135–136, 145, 147, 182, 195, 197–198, 217, 226–227; and art, 131, 149; and artists, 227; collective, 24, 88, 189; construction, 26–27, 124, 228; cultural, 33, 136, 164, 213; and culture, 9, 11, 35, 222–223; erasure of, 16; ethnic, 6, 19, 27, 63, 228; and film, 137–139; formation, 6, 21, 242n9; group, 21, 126; and language, 120, 242n9; local, 7; and Mandarin, 118; national, 7, 64, 228; pan-Chinese, 99; representation of, 64; and youth, 162
identity politics, 5–6, 12, 14–16, 26–27, 30, 32, 34, 36–41, 43–44, 52, 140, 149, 153–154, 156, 160–161, 164–165, 167–170, 189, 192, 204, 213, 218–219, 221, 223, 236n7; and artists, 149; and Chineseness, 160; ethnic, 19, 27, 63; group, 11; minority, 26, 160; and religion, 182
ideological discourse(s), 127

ideology: cultural, 38, 58; New Order, 58; political, 220; sociopolitical, 146; state, 98, 160
Imlek (Chinese New Year), 2, 4, 12–13, 19, 33, 36, 116, 125, 128, 154, 156, 159, 168, 171, 240n9, 244n1
inclusion, 71; politics of, 69; racial, 37, 69, 82, 95
Indian(s), 7–8, 59
Indonesia-China Business Council (ICBC), 194, 204
Indonesian (language), 16, 51, 56, 101, 114, 207–208, 240n1, 246n1
Indonesian archipelago, **xxiii**, 7–8, 58–59, 90, 124, 169, 221, 239n6
Indonesian Buddhist Council (Perwakilan Umat Buddha Indonesia), 204
Indonesian Chamber of Commerce and Industry (Kamar Dagang dan Industri Indonesia, KADIN), 204
Indonesian Chinese Clan Social Association (Paguyuban Sosial Marga Tionghoa Indonesia, PSMTI), 13, 19, 57–65, 159–162, 164, 166, 168, 170, 202–204, 213, 238nn5–6, 244nn2–3
Indonesian Chinese Entrepreneur Association (Perkumpulan Pengusaha Indonesia Tionghoa, PERPIT), 194, 204–208
Indonesian Communist Party (Partai Komunis Indonesia, PKI), 45, 109, 142–143, 147, 158, 244n9; and China, 11
Indonesian Democratic Party of Struggle (Partai Demokrasi Indonesia-Perjuangan, PDI-P), 173–174, 178, 182–183, 185, 188
Indonesian Employers' Association (Asosiasi Pengusaha Indonesia, APINDO), 204
Indonesian Hakka Museum, 64
Indonesian Investment Coordinating Board (Badan Koordinasi Penanaman Modal, BKPM), 193–194,
Indonesian National Armed Forces, 60, 87, 110, 186
Indonesian Solidarity Party (Partai Solidaritas Indonesia, PSI), 187–189, 220
Indonesian Student Association in the People's Republic of China (Perhimpunan Pelajar Indonesia di Tiongkok, PPI Tiongkok), 195
Indonesian Unity Party (Partai Persatuan Indonesia, Perindo), 187
Indonesianness, 160–162, 207
inequality: class, 141, 183; economic, 186, 223; socioeconomic, 190
Institute for the Cultivation of National Unity (Lembaga Pembinaan Kesatuan Bangsa, LPKB), 110, 158
Institute for Policy Analysis of Conflict, 225
integration, 15, 160, 218, 236n5
interethnic collaboration, 83, 111–112, 140
intergenerational trauma, 6, 16, 27, 32, 69, 219, 222
Isfansyah, Ifa, 133
Islam, 102, 185; blasphemy against, 5, 181–183; conversion to, 11
Islamic, 124, 186; conservatism, 190, 223; leaders, 239n6; organizations, 167, 174, 181; party, 176, 185; politics, 183; practices, 11; schools, 97, 241n4
Islamic Defenders' Front (Front Pembela Islam, FPI), 4–5, 181, 223
Islamic State, 225
Islamist: groups, 4, 19, 181, 214; politics, 185

Jakarta, **xxiv**, 1, 13, 19, 33–35, 37, 48, **49**, 50–51, 61, 68–69, 71–72, 74, 77, 85, 90–91, 114, 126–127, 132, 149–152, 170, 172, 179, 188, 205, 221, 226, 239nn6–7, 241n6, 246n1; anti-Chinese violence in, 92; anti-Communist purges in, 101; everyday life in, 88; fieldwork in, 3, 32; flood victims in, 166; gated communities, 92; governor, 155, 177, 179–180, 183, 219; gubernatorial election (2012), 4, 178; gubernatorial election (2017), 5, 181, 185, 245n8; inner-city, 75; May 1998 riots in, 3, 12,

33, 236n7; Muslim protest in, 121, 181; population, 76; provincial government, 51, 56, 75, 162, 179; school(s), 103, 106–108, 114, 122. *See also* Batavia
Jakarta Arts Institute (Institut Kesenian Jakarta), 137
Jakarta Stock Exchange, 239n7
Jangan Panggil Aku Cina (Don't Call Me Chinese), 128
Japanese, 74; colonization, 243n2; military administration, 88; occupation, 74, 126, 157
Java, 35; anti-Chinese attacks in, 238n1; assimilation policies, 11; *peranakan* in, 99, 198; school(s), 99
Java War, 238n1
Javanese, 1, 9, 78, 82, 176, 186, 207, 214, 236n3, 244n2; language, 239n4
Jaya, David Herman, 204
Jemaah Islamiyah, 239n7
Jews, 144
Jinghua Award, 212
Johan, Daniel, 176
Jokowi (Joko Widodo), 181, 214, **215**, 216, 223–224; and Ahok, 4, 178–179, 182–183, 188; and China, 193, 206, 214
Justice and Unity Party (Partai Keadilan dan Persatuan, PKP), 186
Jusuf, Ester Indahyani, 53
Jusuf, Teddy (Deyi Xiong), 60

Kalla, Jusuf, 186
kapitan cina, 246n5
Karma (Lunardi), 132
Karya, Teguh (Liem Tjoan Hok, Steve Lim), 126
Kelapa Gading, **xxv**, 37, 48, 68–69, 71–72, 74–77, **77**, 78–80, 82–83, **85**, 85–95, 103, 149, 239n3, 239n5, 240n9–11; and May 1998 riots, 68, 76, 83, 86–88, 91–92; *pribumi* in, 79–80, 94
Kerusuhan Mei 1998: Fakta, Data, dan Analisa (Jusuf), 53
Khaerun, Haji Akhmad, 74
Khmer Rouge, 24
Khouw Kim An, 54
Kitamura, Yumi, 60, 62–63
Koko Cici pageant, 162, **163**
"Korban" (Burned Victims) (Harsono), 130
Korean War, 243n2
Kota Dua, **xxiv**, 34, 40
Krida Wacana Christian University (Universitas Kristen Krida Wacana), 107, 110
Kuomintang Republicans, 157
Kusno, Abidin, 49–50, 74, 88
Kuswandi, Lucky, 133, 138
Kwik Kian Gie, 171, 174

language(s): Chinese, 8–9, 11–13, 15, 17, 35, 101, 113, 117, 119–120, 122, 157–158, 195, 206, 209, 213, 247n3; discrimination, 120; Dutch, 100, 198; English, 16, 23, 98, 100, 103, 114; Hakka, 8, 120; Hokkien, 8, 80, 100, 120, 162, 209; and identity, 120, 242n9; Indonesian, 16, 51, 56, 101, 114, 207–208, 240n1, 246n1; Javanese, 239n4; Mandarin, 1, 13, 15–17, 19, 37, 98, 100, 113–114, 117–120, 122–123, 157, 162, 195–1967, 203, 208–209, 211, 240n1, 242nn9–11; Teochew, 1, 8, 207
law(s): assimilation, 12, 64, 158; customary, 59; citizenship, 161; discriminatory, 146
leaders, 101, 164–167; community, 32, 175, 194, 200, 204–205, 207, 238n6; Islamic, 239n6; Muslim, 175, 181; regional, 7
Lembong, Eddie, 160, 244n3
Letter of Unprotected Memories, A (Kuswandi), 133, 138
LGBTQIA+ communities, 223
Liem Sioe Liong (Sudono Salim), 10, 246n2
Liu, Hong, 200, 205, 207, 246n5
Lo Fen Koei, 128
Lo, Jacqueline, 128, 218
lobbying, 13, 65, 159, 202–203, 213, 238n5, 244n1; political, 155
local: culture, 8; elections, 14, 155, 187; government, 2, 15; history, 88, 92; identity, 7; politics, 124, 157, 189

Look of Silence, The (Oppenheimer), 242n1
Louisa, Grace Natalie, 187
Lunardi, Allan, 132
Lyotard, Jean-François, 161

Ma Chung University (Universitas Ma Chung), 114, 197
Madurese, 176, 239n6
Makassar: *peranakan* in 198
Malari riots, 55, 184
Malay(s), 55, 91, 176, 186–187; society, 198
Malaya, 99–100, 198
Malaysia, 55, 91, 190
Malaysian Chinese Association, 190
Mandarin, 1, 13, 15, 17, 19, 113–114, 117–120, 122–123, 162, 195–196, 203, 208–209, 211, 242nn9–11; and Chineseness, 16, 242n10; and identity, 118; pop music, 17; schools, 16, 37, 98, 100, 113, 122, 157, 197, 240n1; and universities, 113
Mangga Dua, 46–48, 51, 87, 91, 106
Mao Zedong, 199
Marga T (Marga Tjoa Liang Tjoe), 128
marginalization, 67; class, 96; ethnic, 96; political, 21; socioeconomic, 21
masalah cina. *See* "Chinese problem"
massacres, 74; Batavia, 23, 73; Tanjung Priok, 25, 55
May (Westi), 132
May 1998 Monument (Monumen Mei 1998), 55, 56, **57**
May 1998 riots, **xxiv**, 2, 5, 20, 23, 25, 35–36, 40–48, 50–56, 66, 92–94, 107, 152–153, 159, 171, 181, 189, 211, 219, 226–227, 236n7, 237n1; and artists, 130–131, 147, 150–152, 243n5; and assimilationist policies, 218; and China (PRC), 210; collective memory of, 16, 26, 151; commemoration of, 36, 53, 57, 66, 243n5; fact-finding team, 42; and film(s), 132–133, 139–140; in Jakarta, 3, 12, 33, 236n7; and Kelapa Gading, 68, 76, 83, 86–88, 91–92, 94; legacy of, 12; and media, 44; and *pribumi*, 44, 48, 53, 88; and private security, 89, 149; rapes during, 12, 23, 36, 42–43, 51–52, 83, 91, 131–132, 138, 243n5; and the state, 55–57, 237n3; and student protests, 112; and trauma, 23, 41, 44, 91, 139, 243n2; victims, 12, 40, 43, 45, 53–56, 92, 237n3, 238n4; violence, 23, 41, 43, 45, 54, 60
Medan, 3, 32, 205, 208–209, 240n10, 242n1, 245n6; Chinese in, 11, 31, 69, 92, 174–176, 209; May 1998 riots, 236n7
media, 9, 11, 13, 15, 17, 28, 126, 128, 132, 154, 168, 197, 206–207, 211–212, 214; anti-Chinese, 177; consumption, 124; control of, 41; international, 43; and May 1998 riots, 44; under New Order, 126; populist, 240n8; production, 124; reports, 32; social, 5, 154, 170, 179, 181, 183, 213, 224–226; tycoon, 187
Memori Tentang Nama/Yang Dihapus Kutulis Ulang #1 (Memory of a Name/Rewriting the Erased #1) (Harsono), 130
memorialization, 23, 56
memory, 21, 52, 92, 118–119, 181, 243n4; collective, 3, 6, 19–23, 26–27, 32–33, 37–39, 46, 49, 64–65, 83, 125, 129–130, 149, 151, 219–220, 222, 243nn2–3; historical, 6; and history, 41, 46; narratives of, 21; public, 88; representations of, 20; sites of, 22, 40, 46; and society, 21–22; and trauma, 24, 125, 130–131; of violence, 93
memory making, 19, 21, 26, 45–46
migration of Chinese, 8, 157
military, 8–10, 41–42, 48, 50, 53, 55, 87, 89, 92, 152, 155, 158, 237n3, 240n8; New Order, 25, 41, 74; power, 9, 74
militia(s), 74; *pribumi,* 239n2
Ministry of Education, 101, 110, 240n1
Ministry of Foreign Affairs (China), 199, 201
minority, 21, 27, 102, 123, 190, 223; Chinese as, 6, 8, 10, 75, 125, 155, 189, 211; ethnic, 3, 6, 10, 16, 27, 36, 87, 89, 155, 189; identity politics, 26, 160; religious, 36
Minority Stages (Stenberg), 124

modernity, 123; East Asian, 17
Modjo, Mohamad Ikhsan, 212
Muhammadiyah, 186
Muhammadiyah Youth, 167
multicultural: citizenry, 103; education, 30, 53, 116; harmony, 37, 40, 137; society, 103
multiculturalism, 116, 138, 218
multiethnic society, 188
museum(s), 41, 57–58, 60, 64
music, 32, 59, 126; Arabic, 126; Korean, 17; pop, 17; transnational Chinese, 16
Muslim(s), 5, 79, 121, 138, 175–176, 181, 237n8, 239n6, 241n4; Chinese, 11, 36, 124, 186; clerics, 224; groups, 223; *habitus,* 176; leaders, 175, 181; organization(s), 177; students, 102, 104
Muslimness, 124

NABIL Foundation (Yayasan NABIL), 244n3
Nadia, Maria, 133
Nagaria, Soetjipto, 74, 241n6
Nahdlatul Ulama (NU), 174, 177
Nahdlatul Ulama Youth (Gerakan Pemuda Ansor), 167
Nanyang, 100, 199. *See also* Southeast Asia
narrative(s), 6, 12, 22, 33, 45–46, 53, 92, 94, 125, 137–138, 147, 201, 235n1, 241n8; anti-Chinese, 5, 177, 182–184, 190; of belonging, 31; Chinese–*pribumi* relations, 142; of Chineseness, 142; of collective trauma, 131; of commemoration, 241n8; of ethnicity, 31; historical, 46, 123, 153; and memory, 21; national, 58; of nativeness, 218; oral, 32; *pribumi,* 186, 190; *reformasi,* 168; state, 55, 129; trauma, 6, 31, 41–44, 52, 68–69, 129, 131, 228; of victimization, 37, 42, 66, 96, 190, 220–221, 228
NasDem Party (Partai NasDem), 174, 185
Nasir, Bachtiar, 186
nation-building, 4, 7–8, 98, 160, 199, 218, 244n3
national: belonging, 4, 64, 146, 161, 218, 228–229; cultural policy, 60; culture, 11, 99; education system, 103, 240n1; elections, 14, 155, 174–175, 184, 186–188, 245n4; government, 51; identity, 7, 64, 228; narrative, 58; politics, 4, 35, 124, 155, 171, 173, 184, 189, 220; schools, 101; symbols, 41, 54
National Awakening Party (Partai Kebangkitan Bangsa, PKB), 174, 176
National Commission on Violence Against Women (Komisi Nasional Anti Kekerasan Terhadap Perempuan, Komnas Perempuan), 55
National Movement to Guard the Fatwa of the Indonesian Ulema Council (Gerakan Nasional Pengawal Fatwa Majelis Ulama Indonesia, GNPF-MUI), 186
National People's Congress (China), 200
National Plus: curriculum, 98, 113; schools, 16, 113–114, 240n1
National Revolution, 238n2
nationalism, 161, 212; economic, 198; identity, 64, 228; Indonesian, 171; pan-Chinese, 100, 157. *See also* ethnonationalism
nativeness, 61; narratives of, 218; and *pribumi,* 7
nativism, 220; and New Order, 61, 65
nativist: discourse, 235n2, 245n9; political rhetoric, 187; politics, 185; sentiments, 186
Netherlands East Indies Constitution (Regeringsreglement voor Nederlands Indië), 6–7
New Art Movement (Gerakan Seni Rupa Baru), 130
New Criminal Type in Jakarta, A (Siegel), 240n8
New Economic Policy (Malaysia), 55
New Indonesia Alliance Party (Partai Perhimpunan Indonesia Baru, PPIB), 178
New Order, 3, 13–14, 16, 59–60, 121, 124, 130, 137, 151, 153, 155, 159, 164–165,

170–171, 173, 191, 211, 235nn1–3, 240n8; anti-Chinese discrimination under, 23, 97, 146, 185; arts under, 126; assimilation policies, 2, 4, 9–11, 15, 26, 35, 118, 122, 133–135, 160, 192, 195, 198, 213, 218, 227; censorship under, 127; and China (PRC), 203, 246n2; and criminal gangs, 89; cultural policy, 58; culture, 165; disappearances under, 55; end of, 8, 12, 33, 41, 53, 87, 128, 179, 239n6; film(s) during, 127, 132, 139; government, 4, 9–10, 177; ideology, 58; legacies of, 12; media under, 126; military, 25, 41, 74; and nativism, 61, 65; political organizations under, 154, 158; popular culture under, 126; racial classification under, 60; schools under, 99, 102–103, 114, 117, 122; society under, 58, 60; state, 58; state-sponsored terror, 143; and students, 98, 114; universities under, 102; violations of human rights, 25
newspapers, 43, 128, 157–158, 172, 206, 208–209
9808 anthology, 133, 137–138
nongovernmental organization(s), 50, 53, 56, 94, 159, 166, 168, 244n3
Nora, Pierre, 22, 46
norms: of Chineseness, 221; cultural, 36, 59, 99; social, 31
North Jakarta, 5, 40, 51–52, 54, 75, 108, 184
North Sumatra, 11, 174, 187, 240n10
Nuarta, Nyoman, 54
Nurmantyo, Gatot, 186
Nusantara, 58

Octora, 130
officials: government, 24, 135, 205, 243n7
One Belt One Road (OBOR). *See* BRI
Onghokham (Ong Hok Ham), 9, 101
Oppenheimer, Joshua, 242n1
opposition: anti-Chinese, 91
Ora et Labora Christian Education Foundation (Yayasan Pendidikan Kristen Ora et Labora), 108
oral: history, 46; narratives, 32
organization(s): Islamic, 167, 174, 181; Muslim, 177; political, 9, 154, 158–159; representations, 43–44, 65; Republican Chinese, 100; security, 157; sociocultural, 38, 155, 202; sociopolitical, 54, 108
Our Hope Foundation (Yayasan Harapan Kita), 60
overseas Chinese, 18, 100, 197–201, 206–208, 210, 212–213, 237n1, 238n6, 242n10, 245n1, 246n6; capital, 199; and China, 18, 38, 39, 43, 99–100, 199–202, 205, 210, 213, 222; education, 115; organizations, 157, 205; schools, 100. *See also* diaspora
Overseas Chinese Affairs Commission (China), 199
Overseas Chinese Affairs Committee (China), 200
Overseas Chinese Affairs Office (China) (OCAO, Qiaoban), 18, 199–200, 208, 246n3

Pahoa Integrated School (Sekolah Terpadu Pahoa), 37, 114–115, **115**, 116–118, **118**, 119–123, 197, 236n4, 240n1, 241nn6–7
pan-Chinese, 65; culture, 16; identity, 99; nationalism, 100, 157; nationalist movement, 157
Pancasila, 63, 99, 160
Pancasila Youth (Pemuda Pancasila), 89
Pandjaitan, Luhut Binsar, 206
Pangestu, Mari Elka, 171, 174
Pantai Indah Kapuk, 48, 92
Pantai Mutiara, 5, 181
Pao An Tui, 238n2
Papua, 25, 239n6
Parahyangan Catholic University (Universitas Katolik Parahyangan), 62, 238n7
participation: political, 6, 35–36, 38, 154–156, 164–165, 167, 173, 179, 188–191
party: Islamic, 176, 185; politics, 176
Patekoan, 100, 114, 117–118, 241n6
Pentecostal Christianity, 36

People's Conscience Party (Partai Hati Nurani Rakyat, Hanura), 186–187
People's Consultative Assembly (Majelis Permusyawaratan Rakyat, MPR), 177, 187
People's Representative Council of Indonesia (Dewan Perwakilan Rakyat Republik Indonesia, DPR), 4, 178, 187–188, 212
peranakan, 8, 15, 63, 99, 136, 157–158, 198, 208, 210, 214, 228, 237n8, 247n3; architecture, 51, 63; culture, 62–63, 126; in Java, 99, 198; organizations, 198; and *totok,* 8, 15, 214, 228
performative politics, 165
performing arts, 124, 146, 153
Petak Sembilan, 73, 106
photography, 128
Pluit, 51–52, 68, 79, 87, 93
pluralism, 51, 173, 177, 188, 247n3
Poey Wie Tiong (Poerwito), 10
policies: assimilation, 2, 4, 9–11, 15, 26, 35, 118, 122, 133–135, 160, 192, 195, 198, 213, 218, 227; China (PRC), 202; cultural, 58, 60; government, 104, 122, 155, 189; schools, 11
political: activism, 34, 165, 173; capital, 35, 63, 65, 189, 196–197, 202, 205, 216; elites, 55, 185, 211, 223; *habitus,* 63, 160, 176, 188, 190; history, 129; ideology, 220; imprisonments, 41; lobbying, 155; marginalization, 21; organizations, 9, 154, 158–159; participation, 6, 35–36, 38, 154–156, 164–165, 167, 173, 179, 188–191; power, 11, 44, 159, 175, 210; rights, 159, 186–187, 198
politician(s), 4, 19, 31–33, 38, 56, 155–156, 165, 174–179, 183–185, 187–188, 190, 214, 219–220, 224, 227, 245n4, 245n6
politics, 4–6, 10, 14, 24, 28, 31–32, 34, 154–156, 158, 165, 168, 171, 173, 177, 179, 183–185, 187–190, 220; China (PRC), 100; of commemoration, 36, 64, 236n7; electoral, 35, 38, 155–156, 176, 187–189, 219, 245n6, 245n9; ethnic, 6, 185; ethnonationalist, 26; of forgetting, 22; identity, 5–6, 11–12, 14–16, 26–27, 30, 32, 34, 36–41, 43–44, 52, 140, 149, 153–154, 156, 160–161, 164–165, 167–170, 189, 192, 204, 213, 218–219, 221, 223, 236n7; Islamic, 183; Islamist, 185; local, 124, 157, 189; national, 4, 35, 124, 155, 171, 173, 184, 189, 220; party, 176; *peranakan–totok,* 15; performative, 165; race, 66; racial, 27, 38–39, 69–70, 88, 98, 122, 128, 156; of remembering, 22; of representation, 44, 64, 129; and social activism, 34; student, 165; and youth, 165
Pontianak, 1, 3, 11, 32, 176
Poo, Murdaya (Poo Tjie Goan), 196, 204
popular culture, 125, 128; under New Order, 126
populist, 223; government, 224; media, 240n8
postmemory, 26
power, 28, 151; economic, 246n5; elite, 223; holders, 63, 167, 176; institutional, 119; military, 9, 74; political, 11, 44, 159, 175, 210; relations, 22; soft, 200, 222; state, 99
Prakasa, Ernest, 132, 140, 142
Pramesti, Rani, 130
prejudice, 28, 217, 225; anti-Chinese, 4, 5, 177, 196; against non-Chinese, 3; race, 28; racial, 39; religious, 39
preservation: cultural, 97, 122
Presidential Decision No. 52 (1977), 10
presidential elections, 187, 223
Presidential Instruction No. 14 (1967), 4, 12, 159
Presidential Instruction No. 26 (1998), 12
pribumi, 1–3, 7–8, 12, 27, 33, 39, 70, 84, 88, 91, 93–94, 103–104, 116–117, 120–121, 123, 128–129, 134, 140–143, 146, 152, 160–161, 172, 183, 208–209, 235n3, 236n6, 241n2, 244n2; and Ahok, 179, 184, 186; communities, 175; discourse of, 20; domestic servants, 82, 90; *habitus,* 113; in Kelapa Gading, 79–80, 94; and May 1998 riots, 44, 48, 53, 88;

militia, 239n2; narratives, 186, 190; and nativeness, 7; population, 7; racist attitudes toward, 23; society, 10; students, 105–108, 110–112, 121; trade, 7; as victims, 44; voters, 179; youth, 169
Pribumi Party (Partai Priboemi), 186
primordialism: cultural, 119, 161
private security, 88–89, 92, 95, 149
privilege, 94, 117; class, 92
production: arts, 124; cultural, 31, 125, 153, 221; media, 124
Prosperous Indonesia Hakka Association (Perhimpunan Hakka Indonesia Sejahtera), 64
protection: rackets (*preman, jago*), 89; state, 95–96, 240n8; symbol(s) of, 152
protectionism: cultural, 99
PSMTI Youth Association (Ikatan Pemuda PSMTI, IP-PSMTI), 166
PT Summarecon Agung Tbk, 74–75
public: commemoration, 22–23, 40, 52, 55–57, 60, 64, 129; culture, 25, 128; memory, 88; representations, 43–44, 65
Pulang (Homecoming) (Wulia), 146
Pulo Gadung, 87
puppetry, 124
purges: anti-Communist, 16, 20, 23, 25, 41, 45, 55, 66, 101, 131, 143, 147, 158, 165, 171, 211, 235n2, 242n1, 243n4
Purnama, Basuki Tjahaja. *See* Ahok
Putri Giok (The Jade Princess) (Firmansyah), 127, 132

Qiu Yuanping, 18
quotas: education, 102, 241n2

race, 4–5, 7, 19, 20, 73, 129, 135, 176, 235n1, 246n5; discourses on, 127; politics, 66; prejudice, 28; relations, 3, 209; riots, 55
racial, 218; barriers, 81; categorization, 20; discrimination, 145–146; exclusion, 37, 69, 82, 95; inclusion, 37, 69, 82, 95; politics, 27, 38–39, 69–70, 88, 98, 122, 128, 156; prejudice, 39; taxonomy, 64, trauma, 125; violence, 159
racism, 1, 17, 140, 141, 226; anti-Chinese, 38, 133
rape(s): May 1998 riots, 12, 23, 36, 42–43, 51–52, 83, 91, 131–132, 138, 243n5
(Re)collection of Togetherness (Wulia), 146–147
re-Sinification, 39, 113, 195, 197–199, 208–209, 213, 222
reform(s): government, 190; post-Suharto, 3, 5, 32, 119, 165, 177. See also *reformasi*
reformasi, 2, 4, 32, 56, 138, 156, 160, 168–170, 191; and Chinese culture, 13; and democratic practices, 41; and identity politics, 15; narrative, 168; and Umbrella Project, 133; and violence, 239n6. *See also* reform
regional: elections, 155; leaders, 7
Regional Comprehensive Economic Partnership, 193
Regional Legislative Council (Dewan Perwakilan Rakyat Daerah, DPRD), 178
Regional Representative Council (Dewan Perwakilan Daerah, DPD), 177
Reid, Anthony, 7, 73, 161
religion(s), 4, 14–15, 24, 36, 84, 99, 102, 114, 127, 182, 188, 221, 235n1, 236n4, 240n9; and identity politics, 182
religious: boundaries, 97, 103; conservatives, 223–224; diversity, 58; expression, 3; intolerance, 122; organizations, 19, 196, 204; polarization, 188, 223; practices, 11, 27; prejudice, 39; rights, 14
remembering, 20–21, 45, 50, 129, 133, 138; politics of, 22, 40
representation(s), 28, 43, 66; of Chineseness, 125–129, 137–138; cultural, 128; of identity, 64; of memory, 20; and politics, 44, 64, 129; public, 43–44, 65; sociopolitical, 13; of trauma, 131
Republic of Indonesia Certificate of Citizenship (Surat Bukti Kewarganegaraan Republik Indonesia, SBKRI), 10, 15, 135, 145, **145**, 146, 156, 243n7

Republican Chinese organizations, 100
Res Publica University (Universitas Res Publica), 108–110. *See also* Baperki University
Riady, Mochtar (Lie Mon Tie), 92, 196, 203, 205, 206, 246n2, 246n4
Riau Islands, 11, 32, 177
rights, 2, 12–13, 154, 158, 164, 166, 173, 202–203, 213; civil, 5; cultural, 14; economic, 186; human, 9, 12, 24–25, 53, 136, 210, 212, 238n4; political, 159, 186–187, 198; religious, 14; victims', 237n3; women's, 188
riots: anti-Chinese, 41, 44, 47, 88, 181, 210; race, 55
Riza, Riri, 132
Romahurmuziy, Muhammad, 187, 212
Rusman, Ulung, 167
Rwandan genocide, 24

Sacred Pancasila (Pancasila Sakti), 55
Sai, Siew-Min, 43, 101, 119, 120, 242n9
Salmon, Claudine, 64, 198
Sarana, William Aditya, 188
Sarwono, Budhi (Kho Wing Chin/Tjien), 186
school(s): Al-Azhar, 241n4; Chinese Association, 114–117, **118**, 157, 241n6; and Chineseness, 119–120; Christian, 36, 97, 102–103, 106, 108, 120–121, 149, 241n3; Confucian, 114; and culture, 99, 122; and government, 101–102, 117; Hokkien, 100; Islamic, 97, 241n4; Jakarta, 103, 106–108, 114, 122; in Java, 99; Mandarin, 16, 37, 98, 100, 113, 122, 157, 197, 240n11; national, 101; National Plus, 16, 113–114, 240n1; under New Order, 99, 102–103, 114, 117, 122; policies, 11; security, 105, 117; state, 101–108, 113
Schwartz, Barry, 22, 64
Second World War, 243n2
security, 3, 21, 23, 68, 76–77, 87–88, 90, 97, 103, 122, 148–152, 211, 237n3; discourse of, 74; guard(s), 37, 47, 69, 71, 77–78, 85–87, 89–90, 93, 117, 150; and May 1998 riots, 89, 149; measures, 70, 74, 86–88, 91, 105, 117; money, 29, 48; organizations, 157; private, 88–89, 92, 95, 149; school, 105, 117; state, 48, 87, 89; threat, 78, 214. *See also* surveillance
segregation, 71, 97, 106; class, 70; ethnic, 102, 104, 107–108, 112; racial, 37; social, 73, 217; of students, 103
Semarang, 3, 32; anti-Chinese attacks, 238n1
separatist movement(s): in Aceh, 239n6; in East Timor, 239n6; in Papua, 239n6; regional, 101
September 30 Movement/Indonesian Communist Party (Gerakan 30 September/Partai Komunis Indonesia, G30S/PKI), 11, 55, 101, 109, 158
sexual violence, 56, 83
shantytowns, 70, 76
Sianipar, Michael Victor, 188
Siauw Giok Tjhan, 171
Sie, Hendriawan, 53, 112
Siegel, James T., 23, 240n8
Simatupang, Awan, 55
Sin Ming Hui (Yayasan Candra Naya), 109
Sin Po, 157
Singapore, 50, 79, 90, 99–100, 239n5, 240n10; investments, 193; schools, 103; state, 91
Singkawang, 11, 176, 185–186
Sino-Indonesian relations, 18, 192, 194, 196, 197, 204, 209, 211, 213, 216, 222; diplomatic, 38, 202, 203, 246n2; history of, 196, 209; trade, 193, 202, 203, 206
sites of commemoration, 46, 49
"sites of memory," 22, 40, 46
social: activism, 34; associations, 13; capital, 22, 29, 34, 63, 65, 119, 123, 142, 161–162, 189, 194, 197, 202, 205, 213, 216; discrimination, 220; media, 5, 154, 170, 179, 181, 183, 213, 224–226; relations, 28–29
society, 17, 28, 30, 41, 50, 55, 58–59, 66, 91, 102, 105, 140, 156, 176, 183, 185, 195,

218, 221, 223–224, 247n3; civil, 12, 15, 27, 34, 54, 94, 128, 153, 159–160, 223; Malay, 198; and memory, 21–22; multicultural, 103; multiethnic, 188; under New Order, 58, 60; *pribumi,* 10
sociocultural organizations, 38, 155, 202
socioeconomic: change, 72; class, 34–35, 58, 80, 84, 89, 91; inequality, 190; marginalization, 21
sociology of labor, 82
sociopolitical: activism, 31, 38, 189; change, 189; environment, 2; flux, 217; history, 184; ideology, 146; movements, 21; organization(s), 54, 108; process, 19; representation, 13; situation, 228
Soe Hok Gie, 9, 132, 172
Soeharto, Ibu Tien (Siti Hartinah), 58, 60
soft power: China, 200, 222
Solidarity for the Motherland and Nation (Solidaritas Nusa Bangsa, SNB), 53, 164
Solidarity of Young Chinese Indonesians for Justice (Solidaritas Pemuda Pemudi Tionghoa Indonesia untuk Keadilan), 170
Solo, 12, 236n7
South Jakarta, 106, 108, 240n7
South Sulawesi, 59
Southeast Asia, 50; Chinese in, 100, 157, 197, 199, 222. *See also* Nanyang
spatial governmentality, 71
Special Capital Region of Jakarta III (Daerah Khusus Ibukota Jakarta III, DKI Jakarta III), 174
state, 24, 26–27, 30, 53, 65, 198, 220–221, 246n5; apparatuses, 42; Chinese (PRC), 199, 203, 207–208; and "Chinese problem," 4; discrimination, 8; history, 129; ideology, 98, 160; and May 1998 riots, 55–57, 237n3; narratives, 55, 129; New Order, 58; power, 99; protection, 95–96, 240n8; schools, 101–108, 113; security, 48, 87, 89; terrorism, 25, 54, 143; universities, 102, 105, 110, 241n2; violence, 24, 243n3
State Council (China), 200
state-owned enterprises: Chinese, 193, 194
Stenberg, Josh, 124,
stereotypes, 3, 5, 7, 20, 23, 65, 68–69, 84, 94, 96–97, 106, 111, 117, 121, 125, 159, 167, 179, 197, 211, 213, 219, 221, 236n6; of Chineseness, 19, 129, 140–141; class, 140; ethnic, 140, 142; social, 104
structures of belonging, 6
student(s): assimilation of, 114; in China, 17, 195; *habitus,* 112; Muslim, 102, 104; and New Order, 98, 114; politics, 165; *pribumi,* 105–108, 110–112, 121; protests, 112; segregation of, 103
Subianto, Prabowo, 181, 223
Sugiharti Halim (Darmawan), 133–134, **134**, 135–138, 243n6
Suharto, 9, 12, 40–41, 60–61, 89, 109, 127, 130, 158–159, 162, 164, 167, 192, 203, 246n2
Sukarnoputri, Megawati, 12, 54, 206
Sumardi, Sandyawan, 42
Sumpah Pemuda (Youth Pledge), 169
Sun Yat-sen, 199
Sundanese, 7, 84, 93, 236n3
Sunter, 75, 78, 83, 87
Supeno, Hadi, 186
Supreme Council for the Confucian Religion in Indonesia (Majelis Tinggi Agama Khonghucu Indonesia, MATAKIN), 13, 159, 244n1
Surabaya, 3, 31, 32, 69, 92, 138, 174, 205, 236n7, 238n1, 240n10
surveillance, 71, 151. *See also* security
Suryadinata, Leo, 99–101, 157, 158, 187, 200, 202, 245n4
symbol(s): of Chineseness, 63; in Islamic religious practices, 11; national, 41, 54; of protection, 152; status, 88

Tahir (Ang Tjoen Ming), 196, 204, 206
Taiwan, 17, 98, 101, 106, 200, 204
Tan, Sofyan, 174–176, 185, 245n6
Tan Tjeng Bok, 126
Tanah Abang, 1, 74–75, 79,
Tanasaldy, Taufiq, 245n4

Tang Jiaxuan, 210
Tanjung Priok massacres, 25, 55
Tanoesoedibjo, Hary, 187
Tanoto, Sukanto, 206, 211–213
Tansil, Eddy, 171
Tanudjaja, Rian Ernest, 188
Tanuwidjaja, Haripinto, 177
Taoist: amulet design, 152
Tarakanita Foundation (Yayasan Tarakanita), 108
Tarumanagara University (Universitas Tarumanagara), 105, 107–109, **109**, 110–113, 122
Tato Tolak Bala: Perlindungan Ampuh Warga Setempat (Tattoos to Ward off Evil: Powerful Protection for Local Residents) (Atmaja), 148, **148**, 149, 151, 152
taxonomy: ethnic, 64; racial, 64
Tay, Elaine, 237n1
Taylor, Jean Gelman, 73
television, 16–17, 50, 80, 124–125, 127–128, 141, 187
Tempo (magazine), 214, **215**, 224
Teochew, 90; language, 1, 8, 207
Teochew Association, 164
Terra Incognita, et cetera (Wulia), 147
terrorism: in Aceh, 25; in East Timor, 25; in Papua, 25; state, 25, 54, 143
terrorist attacks, 88
The Teng Chun (Tahjar Ederis), 126
theater, 59, 124, 126, 128
Thousand Islands, 181
Thung Ju Lan, 15, 218
Tiananmen Square protests, 55
Tiojakin, Maggie, 128
Tionghoa, 10, 13, 135, 159, 160, 164, 167–169, 171–172, 224, 246n1
Tjhai Chui Mie, 185
Tjhai Nyit Khim, 185
Toer, Pramoedya Ananta, 9, 109, 127
totok, 8, 16, 37, 68, 79, 119–120, 138, 196, 207, 247n3; business elite, 19, 196, 202; and China, 8, 19; and *peranakan*, 8, 15, 214, 228
trade: Sino-Indonesian, 193, 202, 203, 206
tradition(s), 4, 27, 37, 40, 59, 64, 79, 119–120, 162, 164; cultural, 8, 11, 33, 35, 162; patronage, 90
Tragedy of 12 May Monument (Monumen Tragedi 12 Mei), 53
Train (Wulia), **144**
trauma: and artists, 130–131, 220; and belonging, 147; collective, 24, 27, 44, 66, 89, 130, 133, 138, 145, 147, 151, 189, 227; cultural, 24, 26, 43; historical, 89, 129, 211; intergenerational, 6, 16, 27, 32, 69, 219, 222; and May 1998 riots, 23, 41, 44, 91, 139, 243n2; and memory, 24, 125, 130–131; narratives, 6, 31, 41–44, 52, 68–69, 129, 131, 228; racial, 125; representations of, 131
traumatic events, 24, 26, 45, 51, 130, 142, 149, 219
Trip to the Wound (Edwin), 133, 138–139
Trisakti University (Universitas Trisakti), 47, 53, 107–108, 109, **109**, 110–113, 122; protests, 107
Trump, Donald, 224
Tsai, Yen-ling, 70, 82
Tsao, Tiffany, 128
Twenty-first Century Maritime Silk Road Economic Belt (New Maritime Silk Road), 18
tycoon(s), 167, 183, 197, 203–204, 207, 211–213; media, 187
Tzu Chi Foundation, 204

Uighur Muslims, 225
Umbrella Project (Proyek Payung), 133, 137; and *reformasi*, 133
United Development Party (Partai Persatuan Pembangunan, PPP), 186–187, 212
United States, 17, 195
"Unity in Diversity" (*Bhinneka Tunggal Ika*), 58, 160
universities, 33, 37, 97, 102, 104, 107–112, 122–123, 166, 241n2; Chinese (PRC), 17, 195; closure, 109; and Mandarin, 113; under New Order, 102; overseas, 103; state, 102, 105, 110, 241n2

University of Indonesia (Universitas Indonesia, UI), 105, 241n2

values: Confucian, 114–116, 120, 236n4; educational, 114; moral, 99, 114–117, 236n4
victim(s), 50, 66–67, 131; anti-Communist purges, 45, 55, 147; associations, 55; groups, 41, 53, 55–56, 60, 237n3; Holocaust, 144; of May 1998 riots, 12, 40, 43, 45, 53–56, 92, 237n3, 238n4; *pribumi,* 44; rights, 237n3; of violence, 23–24, 54, 65
victimhood, 43, 227; discourse(s) of, 41, 44, 67, 220; and *habitus,* 44, 96; narratives of, 44, 220–221
victimization, 43–44, 66, 143–144; discourse(s) of, 24, 227; narratives of, 37, 42, 66, 96, 190, 220–221, 228
violence: aestheticization of, 131; anti-Chinese, 8, 20, 23, 26, 37, 40–41, 44–46, 49, 51–52, 62, 65–66, 68, 83, 89, 92, 147, 184, 196, 243n5; communal, 239n6; gender, 41, 131; and May 1998 riots, 23, 41, 43, 45, 54, 60; and memory, 93; racial, 159; sexual, 56, 83; state, 24, 243n3
Violence against Fruits (Wulia), 143–144
visual art(s), 142; Cambodian, 243n2; and trauma, 125, 131
visual culture, 124, 153
Voice of Peranakan (Suara Peranakan), 226
voluntary associations, 13, 38, 156

Wahid, Abdurrahman (Gus Dur), 12, 54, 176
Weix, G. G., 82
West Jakarta, 34, 47, 53, 94, 103, 106–107, **109**, 114, 149, 174, 187
West Java, 7
West Kalimantan, 1, 11, 174, 176, 185, 187, 226
West Nusa Tenggara, 59
Westi, Viva, 132
Wibowo, Ivan, 172
Widjaja, Eka Tjipta (Oei Ek-Tjhong), 196
Widodo, Joko. *See* Jokowi
Wilson, Ian, 89
Winata, Steven Facius, 138
Wiranto, 187
Wo Ai Ni Indonesia (I Love You Indonesia), 128
women, 34, 80, 128; assault on, 12, 36 42, 51, 91; rape of, 23, 36, 43, 51, 83, 91, 131–132, 138; rights, 188
Wood, Nancy, 129–130
World Chinese Entrepreneurs Convention (WCEC), 205–207
World Huaren Federation, 43, 237n1
Wulia, Tintin (Maria Clementine Wulia), 38, 130, 142–144, **144**, 145, **145**, 146–147, 153, 158

xenophobia, 128, 224
Xi Jinping, 18, 193, 201–202, 206–208
Xiamen City Planning Group, 62
Xin Bao, 157
Xinjiang, 225

Yap Thiam Hien, 9
Yogyakarta, 130, 132, 148–149, 152; earthquake 166
Young, Fifi, 126
Young Generation Confucians (Generasi Muda Konghucu, GEMAKU), 166
Young Generation INTI (Generasi Muda INTI, GEMA INTI), 166
youth: and culture, 162; and identity, 162; and politics, 165; *pribumi,* 169
Yudhoyono, Susilo Bambang, 13
Yuwono, Dito, 151

Zheng He, 61–62, 65
Zuchriana, Anna, 130

ABOUT THE AUTHOR

Charlotte Setijadi is assistant professor of humanities (Education) in the School of Social Sciences, Singapore Management University. She obtained her PhD in anthropology from La Trobe University, and she has held post-doctoral and research fellowships at Nanyang Technological University and ISEAS-Yusof Ishak Institute. Her research on Chinese Indonesian identity politics, Indonesian political culture, and China's soft power efforts in Southeast Asia has been published in academic journals such as the *Journal of Contemporary China, Asian Survey, Asian Ethnicity,* and *Bulletin of Indonesian Economic Studies.*